DOMESDAY BOOK

Cambridgeshire

History from the Sources

DOMESDAY BOOK

A Survey of the Counties of England

LIBER DE WINTONIA

Compiled by direction of

KING WILLIAM I

Winchester
1086

DOMESDAY BOOK

general editor

JOHN MORRIS

18

Cambridgeshire

edited by

Alexander Rumble

from a draft translation prepared by

Jennifer Fellows and Simon Keynes

PHILLIMORE
Chichester
1981

1981
Published by
PHILLIMORE & CO. LTD.
London and Chichester
Head Office: Shopwyke Hall,
Chichester, Sussex, England

ISBN 0 85033 387 3 (case)
ISBN 0 85033 388 1 (limp)

Printed in Great Britain by
Titus Wilson & Son Ltd.,
Kendal

CAMBRIDGESHIRE

Introduction
ICC Sample
The Cambridgeshire Inquiry
IE Sample
The Ely Inquiry

The Domesday Survey of Cambridgeshire

Notes
Appendix
Index of Persons
Index of Places
Map
Systems of Reference
Technical Terms

History from the Sources
General Editor: John Morris

The series aims to publish history
written directly from the sources
for all interested readers, both
specialists and others. The first
priority is to publish important
texts which should be widely
available, but are not.

DOMESDAY BOOK

The contents, with the folio on which each county begins, are:

Supplementary volume (35) BOLDON BOOK

Domesday Book is termed *Liber de Wintonia* (The Book of Winchester) in column 332c

INTRODUCTION

The Domesday Survey

In 1066 Duke William of Normandy conquered England. He was crowned King, and most of the lands of the English nobility were soon granted to his followers. Domesday Book was compiled 20 years later. The Saxon Chronicle records that in 1085

> at Gloucester at midwinter ... the King had deep speech with his counsellors ... and sent men all over England to each shire ... to find out ... what or how much each landholder held ... in land and livestock, and what it was worth ... The returns were brought to him.[1]

William was thorough. One of his Counsellors reports that he also sent a second set of Commissioners 'to shires they did not know, where they were themselves unknown, to check their predecessors' survey, and report culprits to the King.'[2]

The information was collected at Winchester, corrected, abridged, chiefly by omission of livestock and the 1066 population, and fair-copied by one writer into a single volume. Norfolk, Suffolk and Essex were copied, by several writers, into a second volume, unabridged, which states that 'the Survey was made in 1086'. The surveys of Durham and Northumberland, and of several towns, including London, were not transcribed, and most of Cumberland and Westmorland, not yet in England, was not surveyed. The whole undertaking was completed at speed, in less than 12 months, though the fair-copying of the main volume may have taken a little longer. Both volumes are now preserved at the Public Record Office. Some versions of regional returns also survive. One of them, from Ely Abbey,[3] copies out the Commissioners' brief. They were to ask

> The name of the place. Who held it, before 1066, and now?
> How many *hides*?[4] How many ploughs, both those in lordship and the men's?
> How many villagers, cottagers and slaves, how many free men and Freemen?[5]
> How much woodland, meadow and pasture? How many mills and fishponds?
> How much has been added or taken away? What the total value was and is?
> How much each free man or Freeman had or has? All threefold, before 1066,
>   when King William gave it, and now; and if more can be had than at present?

The Ely volume also describes the procedure. The Commissioners took evidence on oath 'from the Sheriff; from all the barons and their Frenchmen; and from the whole Hundred, the priests, the reeves and six villagers from each village'. It also names four Frenchmen and four Englishmen from each Hundred, who were sworn to verify the detail.

The King wanted to know what he had, and who held it. The Commissioners therefore listed lands in dispute, for Domesday Book was not only a tax-assessment. To the King's grandson, Bishop Henry of Winchester, its purpose was that every 'man should know his right and not usurp another's'; and because it was the final authoritative register of rightful possession 'the natives called it Domesday Book, by analogy

---

[1] Before he left England for the last time, late in 1086. [2] Robert Losinga, Bishop of Hereford 1079-1095 (see *E.H.R.* 22, 1907, 74). [3] *Inquisitio Eliensis*, first paragraph. [4] A land unit, reckoned as 120 acres. [5] *Quot Sochemani.*

from the Day of Judgement'; that was why it was carefully arranged by Counties, and by landholders within Counties, 'numbered consecutively ... for easy reference'.[6]

Domesday Book describes Old English society under new management, in minuté statistical detail. Foreign lords had taken over, but little else had yet changed. The chief landholders and those who held from them are named, and the rest of the population was counted. Most of them lived in villages, whose houses might be clustered together, or dispersed among their fields. Villages were grouped in administrative districts called Hundreds, which formed regions within Shires, or Counties, which survive today with minor boundary changes; the recent deformation of some ancient county identities is here disregarded, as are various short-lived modern changes. The local assemblies, though overshadowed by lords great and small, gave men a voice, which the Commissioners heeded. Very many holdings were described by the Norman term *manerium* (manor), greatly varied in size and structure, from tiny farmsteads to vast holdings; and many lords exercised their own jurisdiction and other rights, termed *soca*, whose meaning still eludes exact definition.

The Survey was unmatched in Europe for many centuries, the product of a sophisticated and experienced English administration, fully exploited by the Conqueror's commanding energy. But its unique assemblage of facts and figures has been hard to study, because the text has not been easily available, and abounds in technicalities. Investigation has therefore been chiefly confined to specialists; many questions cannot be tackled adequately without a cheap text and uniform translation available to a wider range of students, including local historians.

Previous Editions

The text has been printed once, in 1783, in an edition by Abraham Farley, probably of 1250 copies, at Government expense, said to have been £38,000; its preparation took 16 years. It was set in a specially designed type, here reproduced photographically, which was destroyed by fire in 1808. In 1811 and 1816 the Records Commissioners added an introduction, indices, and associated texts, edited by Sir Henry Ellis; and in 1861-1863 the Ordnance Survey issued zincograph facsimiles of the whole. Texts of individual counties have appeared since 1673, separate translations in the Victoria County Histories and elsewhere.

This Edition

Farley's text is used, because of its excellence, and because any worthy alternative would prove astronomically expensive. His text has been checked against the facsimile, and discrepancies observed have been verified against the manuscript, by the kindness of Miss Daphne Gifford of the Public Record Office. Farley's few errors are indicated in the notes.

[6] *Dialogus de Scaccario* 1,16.

The editor is responsible for the translation and lay-out. It aims at what the compiler would have written if his language had been modern English; though no translation can be exact, for even a simple word like 'free' nowadays means freedom from different restrictions. Bishop Henry emphasized that his grandfather preferred 'ordinary words'; the nearest ordinary modern English is therefore chosen whenever possible. Words that are now obsolete, or have changed their meaning, are avoided, but measurements have to be transliterated, since their extent is often unknown or arguable, and varied regionally. The terse inventory form of the original has been retained, as have the ambiguities of the Latin.

Modern English commands two main devices unknown to 11th century Latin, standardised punctuation and paragraphs; in the Latin, *ibi* ('there are') often does duty for a modern full stop, *et* ('and') for a comma or semi-colon. The entries normally answer the Commissioners' questions, arranged in five main groups, (i) the place and its holder, its hides, ploughs and lordship; (ii) people; (iii) resources; (iv) value; and (v) additional notes. The groups are usually given as separate paragraphs.

King William numbered chapters 'for easy reference', and sections within chapters are commonly marked, usually by initial capitals, often edged in red. They are here numbered. Maps, indices and an explanation of technical terms are also given. Later, it is hoped to publish analytical and explanatory volumes, and associated texts.

The editor is deeply indebted to the advice of many scholars, too numerous to name, and especially to the Public Record Office, and to the publisher's patience. The draft translations are the work of a team; they have been co-ordinated and corrected by the editor, and each has been checked by several people. It is therefore hoped that mistakes may be fewer than in versions published by single fallible individuals. But it would be Utopian to hope that the translation is altogether free from error; the editor would like to be informed of mistakes observed.

The maps are the work of Alison Hawkins and Jim Hardy.

The preparation of this volume has been greatly assisted by a generous grant from the Leverhulme Trust Fund.

This support, originally given to the late Dr. J. R. Morris, has been kindly extended to his successors. At the time of Dr. Morris's death in June 1977, he had completed volumes 2, 3, 11, 12, 19, 23, 24. He had more or less finished the preparation of volumes 13, 14, 20, 28. These and subsequent volumes in the series were brought out under the supervision of John Dodgson and Alison Hawkins, who have endeavoured to follow, as far as possible, the editorial principles established by John Morris.

Conventions

★   refers to a note of discrepancy between the MS and the Farley text.

[ ]   enclose words omitted in the MS.   ( )   enclose editorial explanations.

AN EXTRACT TO SHOW THE NATURE OF ENTRIES IN THE *INQUISITIO COMITATUS CANTABRIGIENSIS* (ICC)

In hundr de tripeláue iurauerunt homines . scił . Rad . p̄positus de hundr . Wilłs de caillei . Ranulf⁹ de Barentona . Tedbald⁹ hō hardeuuini . stanhard⁹ de hauekestona . Godric⁹ de fulemere . Aluric⁹ de tripeláue . Sigar⁹ dapifer . Et oñis alii frāci 7 angli.

In hoc hundr tⁱppeláue p .VIII. ħ . se defend . t. r. e. 7 mᵒ . Et de his .VIII. ħ . tenet abb de elẏ .v. ħ . 7 dimid .VIII. č . est t̂ra .III. č . 7 .IIII. ħ . in dominio .v. car̃ . uillanis .XII. uillani .v. bor .v. serui . Prat̂ .I. carruce . Pastura ad peč . uille .c. o .XXX. por . Pastura de .II. soccis .I⁹. runci. Int̂ totū ual .XI. li . t. r. e. XII. ł . Hec t̂ra iacet 7 iacuit ī eccłia de elẏ . In hac uilla tⁱppeł . tenet hardeuuin⁹ .I. ħ . de uictu monachoʒ . p q̃ndā respectū sub rege . donec alloquat̂ inde ⸫ Regi . In hac hida ē t̂ra .I. car-

ruce . 7 ē car̃ .LX. oues .XVII. por . Semper ualuit 7 ual .XX. soł . Hec iacet 7 iacuit in eccłia de elẏ . t. r. e. Et de his .VIII. ħ . tenebat hardeuuin⁹ .II. ač . de t̂ra abbis . de quibʒ ñ ħt aliquē aduocatum . nec libatorē . sʒ sup abbem occupauit⸫ ut homines de hund testāt̂ . Et de his .VIII. ħ . tenet sigar⁹ de gaufrido de magnauilla .I. ħ . 7 dimid .II. carrucis ē t̂ra .I̊ᵗ. č . in dominio . 7 .I. uil-

lanis . 7 .IIII. uillani .I⁹. ser . Pasta ad peč . uille .v. animał . ocio .CC. oues .XX. min⁹ . un⁹ runč . Int̂ totū ualet 7 ualuit .XL. soł . Hanc

t̂rā tenuit istemet sigar⁹ . potuit dare 7 uende cui uoluit . S; socam ei⁹ retinuit dñs ei⁹.

In THRIPLOW Hundred these men swore ... *

In this Hundred, THRIPLOW answered for 8 hides before 1066; now (for the same). Of these 8 hides, the Abbot of Ely holds 5½ hides. [DB ref. 5,20]. Land for 8 ploughs. 3 ploughs and 3 hides in lordship; 5 ploughs with the villagers. 12 villagers; 5 smallholders; 5 slaves. Meadow for 1 plough; pasture for the village livestock; 100 sheep; 30 pigs; pasture at 2 ploughshares; 1 cob. In total, value £11; before 1066 £12. This land lies and lay in (the lands of) the Church of Ely.

In this village of THRIPLOW, Hardwin holds [DB ref. 5,21. 26,56] under the King 1 hide of the supplies of the monks, through a postponement until he speaks to the King about it. In this hide is land for 1 plough; the plough is there. 60 sheep; 17 pigs. Value always was and is 20s. This lies and lay before 1066 in (the lands of) the Church of Ely.

Of these 8 hides also, Hardwin held 2 acres of the Abbot's land [DB ref. 5,22. 26,57], for which he does not have any patron nor deliverer but he appropriated it in the Abbot's despite, as the men of the Hundred testify.

Of these hides, also Sigar holds 1½ hides [DB ref. 22,3] from Geoffrey de Mandeville. Land for 2 ploughs. 1 plough in lordship; 1 with the villagers, 4 villagers; 1 slave. Pasture for the village livestock; 5 cattle; 180 sheep; 1 cob. In total, value is and was 40s. Sigar held this land himself; he could grant and sell to whom he would, but his lord retained his jurisdiction.

---

* Here follow the names of the jurors in this Hundred, see below Appendix H.

THE CAMBRIDGESHIRE INQUIRY, *Inquisitio Comitatus Cantabrigiensis* (ICC)

In the Cambridgeshire Inquiry, usually referred to by the abbreviation ICC, students of DB have a most important record of the proceedings in the shire court of Cambridgeshire when the representatives of its various Hundreds appeared in turn to ratify or give evidence upon the findings of the DB Commissioners; the order in which the Hundreds were called being apparently a topographical sequence of, firstly, the southern Hundreds from NE to NW and, secondly, the Two Hundreds of Ely. No similar record has survived for other counties, although references throughout DB to the testimony of 'the men of the Hundred' imply that similar proceedings occurred in other shire courts.

Since ICC duplicates much of the information found in the DB text, but Hundred by Hundred rather than Landholder by Landholder, it provides an opportunity to check the accuracy of the DB text against the record of one of the intermediate stages of the Survey. In addition, ICC also contains many items of information omitted from DB, including the names of the jurors of most of the Hundreds, the names of minor pre-Conquest landholders, the names of some places which are anonymous in DB, and statistics of livestock in each holding. On two occasions it provides us with a whole entry omitted from DB (see below, B note and 31,3 note). In the present volume, all divergent and extra information in ICC which falls within the terms of DB has been given in the notes to the relevant DB entry, while the jurors are included in the Appendix; the livestock statistics (mostly of cattle, sheep, pigs, and horses) have not been given, but are readily available in the translation of ICC in *The Victoria History of Cambridgeshire*, i (1938), 400–427.

The record of ICC survives in only one manuscript (British Library, Cotton Tiberius A. vi, folios 76–113, with one folio lost between 111–112), written in the second half of the twelfth century. This MS is a copy of what seems to have been a damaged record (now lost) of the proceedings of the shire court in 1086. Due to the damage to its exemplar, the text of ICC for part of the county is lacking to us, mostly concerning the Hundreds of Longstow, Papworth, Northstow, Chesterton, and the Two Hundreds of Ely; some of this lost information can be made good by reference to the Ely Inquiry, however (see below). ICC was edited, with parallel DB text, by N.E.S.A. Hamilton in 1876 and was later translated in the *Victoria History* (see above). For further comments on its significance, see J.H. Round, *Feudal England* (1895), 17–35 and V.H. Galbraith, *Domesday Book: its place in administrative history* (Oxford, 1974), 39–46.

A specimen entry from ICC, with translation and references to the corresponding entries in DB, is given opposite. For some of the same information in IE, see below, IE sample.

AN EXTRACT TO SHOW THE NATURE OF ENTRIES
IN THE *INQUISITIO ELIENSIS* (IE)

In treppeſlaue hund'. In treppeſlaue hunď. iṗe abbas

ely tenet in treppeſlaue. v. ħ. & dim. vIII. c. ibi ĕ. t.

III. c. &. III. ħ. in dominio. v. c. hoɱ. .xII. v. v. pra-

tum. I. c. paſtura ad pecora uille. o. c; p. xxIx. unũ

runč. de paſtura duos ſochos. In totis ualentiis ualet.

xI. li. qñ reč. xI. liƀ. t. ʀ. e. xII. liƀ. H̃ tra iacet &

iacuit ĭ ecctia. S̃. Ædelď. in dominio.

In eadem uilla hŧ harduuin⁹ ſub aƀbe. I. ħ. p q̊ddam

reſpectũ iṗi⁹ abbatis de dñico uictu monachorɛ donec

cũ rege inde loquat. I. c. ibi eſt tra. & ibi ĕ. car. o.

lxxvII. In totũ ualet & ſemp ualuit uiginti. s. ħ. tra

iacuit in ecctia sc̃e Æᴅᴇʟᴅe. in dominio in morte Reg̃

Æduuardi. In eaď uilla tenebat iṗe Harduuin⁹. II. ac.

de tra p. aƀbis. de quibʒ iṗe harduuin⁹ non hŧ aduoca-

tum aliquĕ. uł liƀatorem. ut homines de. h. teſtantur.

In THRIPLOW Hundred
In Thriplow Hundred, the Abbot of Ely himself holds 5½ hides [DB ref. 5,20] in THRIPLOW. Land for 8 ploughs. 3 ploughs and 3 hides in lordship. 5 ploughs with the men. 12 villagers; 5 smallholders; 5 slaves. Meadow for 1 plough; pasture for the village livestock; 100 sheep; 29 pigs; 1 cob; from the pasture, 2 ploughshares. Total value £11; when acquired £11; before 1066 £12. This land lies and lay in lordship in the (lands of the) Church of St. Etheldreda.
    In the same village, Hardwin has under the Abbot 1 hide of the lordship supplies [DB ref. 5,21. 26,56] of the monks, through a postponement of the Abbot himself, until he speaks with the King. Land for 1 plough; the plough is there. 77† sheep. In total, value is and always was 20s. This land lay in lordship in the (lands of the) Church of St. Etheldreda in 1066. In the same village, Hardwin [DB ref. 5,22. 26,57] himself held 2 acres of the aforesaid Abbot's land for which Hardwin himself does not have any patron or deliverer, as the men of the Hundred testify.

†In error for *oues. lx; .xvii. porci* (60 sheep; 17 pigs), compare ICC.

THE ELY INQUIRY, *Inquisitio Eliensis* (IE)

The Ely Inquiry, usually referred to as IE, is a collection of material relating to holdings of Ely Abbey in Cambridgeshire, Essex, Hertfordshire, Huntingdonshire, Norfolk and Suffolk whose source appears to have been drafts (now lost) of the returns for three different circuits of the DB Survey. It was put together, for the benefit of Ely Abbey, very soon after 1086, but survives only in three manuscripts written in the second half of the twelfth century—British Library, Cotton Tiberius A. vi, folios 38–70 (MS A; which also contains ICC, see above); Trinity College Cambridge 0.2.41, pages 161–274 (MS B) and 0.2.1, folios 177v–213 (MS C)—of these, B and C are derived from a common source, while A is a copy of B. Although B is now thought to be the most reliable of the three manuscripts, IE was reproduced in record type in 1816 by Sir Henry Ellis from C (see DB 4, 495–528). N.E.S.A. Hamilton also used C as the base text for his edition of IE in 1876 (*Inquisitio Comitatus Cantabrigiensis*, 97–168), but also gave variant readings from B and A in footnotes. Footnotes to the Victoria County History translation of DB Cambridgeshire (see above, ICC) also supply items of extra information from IE, translated from Hamilton's edition.

For Cambridgeshire, IE (Hamilton 97–124) supplies details of the Ely Abbey holdings in the county in a sequence of Hundreds similar, but not identical, to that in ICC (see above), followed by summaries of the holdings of Picot the Sheriff, Hardwin of Scales, and Guy of Raimbeaucourt, three laymen who had seized several of the Abbey's holdings. Much of the information given in IE also occurs in DB, but some does not, the extra information being similar in type, and often identical in content, to that described above as additional in ICC. Hamilton also edited some other documents, subsidiary to IE, which are dependent upon, or relevant to, the DB Survey. The *Inquisitio Eliensis* Breviate (IEBrev; Hamilton 168–173) gives summaries of the numbers of ploughs and people in each of the Abbey's holdings, and the *Nomina Villarum* (IENV; Hamilton 174–175) lists the number of ploughs held by the villagers therein. These are followed (Hamilton 175–195) by lists of holdings taken from the Abbey and an account of an inquiry into the Abbey's losses held between 1071 and 1075. In the present volume, reference to IE and its related documents has only been made, in the notes to the relevant DB entry, where information occurs which is divergent or extra to that in both DB and ICC. The lists of Cambridgeshire Hundred jurors are included in the Appendix below; for the jurors of three Hertfordshire Hundreds, also in IE, see the Appendix to the Hertfordshire volume.

For further comments on IE, see R. Welldon Finn, 'The Inquisitio Eliensis reconsidered', *English Historical Review* lxxv (1960), 385–409. For the Ely Abbey claims, see E. Miller, 'The Ely land pleas in the reign of William I', *English Historical Review* lxii (1947), 438–456 and *Liber Eliensis*, ed. E. O. Blake, 426–432.

A specimen entry from IE, with translation and references to the corresponding entries in DB, is given opposite. For some corresponding entries in ICC, see above, ICC sample.

BVRGVM de GRENTEBRIGE. p uno HVNDRET

se defend. T.R.E. In hoc burgo fuer 7 funt

dece cuftodiæ. In prima cuftodia. L.IIII. ma

furæ. ex his. II. funt waftæ. In hac pma cuftodia hĩ

Alan com. v. burgenfes nichil reddentes. Comes mori

tonienfis de tra Judichel hĩ. III. mafuras. 7 ibi fuɴ. III.

burgenfes q̃ T.R.E. reddeƀ. v. fol 7. VIII. den 7 I. obolũ.

m̃ nichil redduɴ. Radulf de bans. hĩ. III. burg.

nichil reddent. Roger hõ epi Remigij. III. burg.

nil redd. Erchenger hĩ. I. burg. nichil reddit.

Hæc ead una cuftodia p duabʒ cõputabat. T.R.E.

fed p caftro funt deftructæ. xxvII. dom.

In Scda cuftodia fuer. xLvIII. mafuræ. T.R.E. ex his

duæ funt waftæ. De his. xIII. mafuræ nichil reddt.

reliq. xxxII. reddt oms cfuetudines. De his hĩ Alan com

v. burg nil redd. 7 IX. maneɴ in tris Angloʒ.

In Tcia cuftodia. T.R.E. fuer. xLI. mafura. Ex his fuɴ

xI. waftæ. reliquæ. xxx. redduɴ oms confuetudines.

In Quarta cuftodia. T.R.E. fuer. xLv. mafuræ. Ex his

xxIIII. fuɴ waftæ. refiduæ. xxI. redd oms cfuetud.

In Quinta cuftodia. T.R.E. fuer. L. mafuræ. Vna ex his

e wafta. aliæ oms reddunt cfuetudines fuas.

In Septima cuftodia T.R.E. fuer. xxxvII. mafuræ. Tres

★ francig hñt de his. III. mafuras. fʒ nichil reddt.

In Octaua cuftodia. T.R.E. fuer. xxxvII. mafuræ. Ex his

q̃dã pƀr unã tenet. 7 nichil reddit. ⌈ fuɴ. III. waftæ.

In Nona cuftodia. T.R.E. fuer. xxx.II. mafuræ. De his

In Decima cuftodia. T.R.E. fuer. xxIx. mafuræ. Ex

his fuɴ. vI. waftæ. tam fe defenduɴ.

CAMBRIDGESHIRE

B
1 The Borough of CAMBRIDGE
answered for a Hundred before 1066. In this borough there
were and are ten wards.
> In the first ward, 54 dwellings; 2 of them are derelict.
> In this first ward, Count Alan has 5 burgesses who
> pay nothing.
> The Count of Mortain has 3 dwellings of the land of
> Judicael. 3 burgesses who paid 5s 8½d before
> 1066 now pay nothing.
> Ralph Banks has 3 burgesses who pay nothing.
> Roger, Bishop Remigius's man, (has) 3 burgesses;
> they pay nothing.
> Erchenger has 1 burgess; he pays nothing.
> This single ward was accounted as two before 1066 but
> 27 houses have been destroyed for the castle.

2 In the second ward were 48 dwellings before 1066;
> 2 of them are derelict. 13 of these dwellings pay nothing;
> the remaining 32 pay all dues.
> Count Alan has 5 of the burgesses who pay nothing
> and 9 who dwell on the lands of the English.

3 In the third ward were 41 dwellings before 1066;
> 11 of them are derelict. The remaining 30 pay all dues.

4 In the fourth ward were 45 dwellings before 1066;
> 24 of them are derelict. The 21 left pay all dues.

5 In the fifth ward were 50 dwellings before 1066;
> One of these is derelict. All the others pay their dues.

6 In the seventh ward were 37 dwellings before 1066.
> 3 Frenchmen have 3 of these dwellings but pay nothing.

7 In the eighth ward were 37 dwellings before 1066.
> A priest holds one of them and pays nothing.

8 In the ninth ward were 32 dwellings before 1066;
> 3 of them are derelict.

9 In the tenth ward were 29 dwellings before 1066;
> 6 of them are derelict, but they still answer.

De consuetudinib҃ huj̉ uillæ . vii . lib̄ p̄ annū . 7 de
Landgable . vii . lib̄ . 7 ii . oræ . 7 duo den̉.

Burgenſes . T . R . E . accōmodaba̅ꝛ uicecomiti carrucas
ſuas ter in anno . modo nouē uicib҃ exigunt̉.

Nec aueras nec curr̉ . T . R . E . inueniebaꝛ . quæ m̅ fa
ciuꝛ p̄ conſuetudinē impoſitā . Reclamaꝛ autē ſup
picotū uicecomitē . cōmunē paſturā ſibi p̄ eū ablatā.

Ipſe Picot fecit ibi . iii . molend̉ . q̃ aufer̄ paſturā 7 plures
domos deſtruuꝛ 7 mol̄ unum abbis de Elẏ . 7 alterū
Alani comitis . Ipſa molend̉ reddt̄ ix . lib̄ p̄ annū.

De harieta Lagemānoꝛ habuit iſdē picot . viii . lib̄
7 unū palefridū . 7 uni militis arma.

Aluric̉ Godricſone q̃do fuit uicecomes . habuit
harietā unius iſtoꝛ . xx . ſolid̉.

10 From the dues of this town £7 a year;
from the land-tribute £7, 2 *ora*, 2d.

11 Before 1066 the burgesses lent their ploughs to the Sheriff
three times a year, now they are demanded on nine occasions.
Before 1066 they found neither cartage nor carts;
they now do so through an imposed due.
They also claim back for themselves from Picot the Sheriff
the common pasture taken away through him and by him.

12 Picot himself has made 3 mills there which diminish the
pasture and (which) have destroyed many houses.
Also a mill of the Abbot of Ely, and another of Count Alan.
The mills themselves pay £9 a year.

13 Picot also had £8, a riding-horse, and arms for 1 man-at-arms
from the heriot of lawmen.

14 When he was Sheriff, Aelfric Godricson had 20s as the heriot of
1 of them.

.I. WILLELM⁹ REX.

.II. Eᵖs Wintonienſis.

.III. Eᵖs Lincolienſis.

.IIII. Eᵖs Rofenſis.

.V. Abbas de Elẏ.

.VI. Abbas de S̄ Edmundo.

.VI. Abƀ de Rameſẏ.

.VII. Abƀ de Torni.

.VIII Abƀ de Croiland.

.X. Abƀ S̄ Wandregiſili.

.XI Abbatiſſa de Cietriz.

.XI. Comes moritonienſis.

.XII. Comes Rogerius.

.XIII. Comes Alanus.

.XV. Comes Euſtachius.

.XVI. Canonici baiocenſes.

XVI. Walteri⁹ Gifard.

.XVI. Wiƚƚs de Warenna.

.XIX. Ricard fili⁹ Gisleƀti.

.XX. Roƀtus de Todeni.

.XXI. Roƀtus gernon.

XXII. Goisfrid⁹ de mãneuile.

.XXII. Giſleƀtus de Gand.

.XXIII. Giſleƀtus fili⁹ Turaldi.

.XXV Eudo dapifer.

.XXVI. Harduin⁹ de Scalers.

.XXVI. Hugo de Berneres.

.XXVII Hugo de port.

.XXVIII Albericus de uer.

.XXX. Euſtachi⁹ de Huntedune.

.XXXI. Wido de Reinbecurt.

.XXXII. Petrus de Valoinges.

.XXXIII. Picot de grantebrige.

.XXXIII. Rannulf⁹ fr̄ Ilgerij.

.XXXV. Johes filius Waleranni.

.XXXVI. Wiƚƚs filius Anſculfi.

.XXXVI. Wiƚƚs de Cahainges.

.XXXVII. Roƀtus fafiton.

.XXXVIII Dauid de argentom.

.XL. Duo carpentarij regis.

.XLI. Judita comitiſſa.

.XLII. Azelina uxor Rad talleƀ.

.XLII! Vxor Boſelini de diue.

.XLIIII. Erchenger piſtor

1 King William
2 The Bishop of Winchester
3 The Bishop of Lincoln
4 The Bishop of Rochester
5 The Abbot of Ely
6 The Abbot of St. Edmund's
7 The Abbot of Ramsey
8 The Abbot of Thorney
9 The Abbot of Crowland
10 The Abbot of St. Wandrille's
11 The Abbess of Chatteris
12 The Count of Mortain
13 Earl Roger
14 Count Alan
15 Count Eustace
16 The Canons of Bayeux
17 Walter Giffard
18 William of Warenne
19 Richard son of Count Gilbert
20 Robert of Tosny
21 Robert Gernon
22 Geoffrey de Mandeville
23 Gilbert of Ghent
24 Gilbert son of Thorold
25 Eudo the Steward
26 Hardwin of Scales
27 Hugh of Bernières
28 Hugh of Port
29 Aubrey de Vere
30 Eustace of Huntingdon
31 Guy of Raimbeaucourt
32 Picot of Cambridge
33 Peter of Valognes
34 Ranulf brother of Ilger
35 John son of Waleran
36 William son of Ansculf
37 William of Keynes
38 Robert Fafiton
39 David of Argenton
40 Two of the King's carpenters
41 Countess Judith
42 Azelina wife of Ralph Tallboys
43 The wife of Boselin of Dives
44 Erchenger the baker

SAHAM Maneriũ regis . p . ix . hid 7 dim̃ fe

defd . Tra . ẽ . xiiii . carucis . Ibi fuɴ . xvi . uitti . 7 xvi .

bord cũ . xii . car . In dñio . ii . car . 7 iiii . ferui . 7 ii . mold

. xxiiii . fot . De pifcar . iii . mitt 7 ð. anguitt . Ptũ

xiiii . car . Paftura ad pecuñ uillæ . Ibi . vii . pifcatores

reddentes regi p̃fentation pifciũ ter in anno fcdm qd

poffuɴ . In totis ualentijs redd p annũ . xxv . lib arfas

7 penfatas . 7 xiii . lib 7 viii . fot 7 iiii . den ad numerũ

de albis denar . p frumto . brafio . melle 7 alijs minutis

c̃fuetudinibʒ . T.R.E. reddeb . xxv . lib ad numerũ .

189 c

7 p . iii . dies firmã de frumto . melle 7 brafio . 7 de alijs oĩibʒ

Hoc M̃ habuit rex . E . femp in dñio .

M̃ FORDEHĀ dñica uilla regis . p . v . hid 7 dim̃ fe defd .

Tra . ẽ . x . car . In dñio . ii . car . 7 iiii . adhuc pofs fieri .

Ibi . vi . uitti 7 xv . bord de xv . acris . cũ . iiii . car .

Ibi . i . ferũ . 7 ii . molini . xvi . folid . 7 ii . porc pafcuɴ p

annũ . Ptũ . vi . car . Paftura ad pec uillæ . Reddit

x . lib arfas 7 penfatas . 7 xiii . lib 7 viii . fot 7 iiii . den

de albo argento . p melle . frumto 7 brafio . T.R.E. red

debat . x . lib ad numer . 7 firmã triũ derũ int mel fru

mentũ 7 brafiũ . Hoc M̃ fẽp habuit rex . E . in dñio .

In hac uilla qdã fochs ten . i . hid de foca regis . Hic . T.R.E.

potuit dare trã fuã cui uoluit . fʒ tam̃ fẽp inuenit

auerã uel . viii . den in feruitio regis . 7 forisfacturã

emdabat uicecomiti .

M̃ GISLEHĀ dñica uilla regis . p vi . hid 7 xl . acris træ

fe defd . Tra . ẽ . x . car . In dñio funt duæ . 7 xvi . uitti . 7 x .

bord cũ . viii . car . Ibi . iii . molini 7 dim̃ de xxii . folid

7 viii . den . 7 mille 7 cc.l . anguitt . Ptũ . x . car . Paftura

LAND OF THE KING

In STAPLOE Hundred

1   SOHAM is a manor of the King's. It answers for 9½ hides.
     Land for 14 ploughs.
         16 villagers and 16 smallholders with 12 ploughs;
             In lordship 2 ploughs;
             4 slaves; 2 mills at 24s; from fisheries 3,500 eels; meadow for
                 14 ploughs; pasture for the village livestock.
             7 fishermen there, who pay to the King a presentation
                 of fish three times a year, according to what they can.
     In total value, it pays £25 a year assayed and weighed, and
     £13 8s 4d at face value in white pence for corn, malt,
     honey and other small customary dues. Before 1066 it paid   189 c
     £25 at face value, and three days' revenue in corn, honey,
     malt and everything else.
         King Edward always had this manor in lordship.

2 M. FORDHAM is a lordship village of the King's. It answers
     for 5½ hides. Land for 10 ploughs. In lordship 2 ploughs;
     a further 4 possible.
         6 villagers and 15 smallholders with 15 acres, with
             4 ploughs.
         1 slave; 2 mills, 16s, feed 2 pigs a year; meadow for 6
             ploughs; pasture for the village livestock.
     It pays £10 assayed and weighed, and £13 8s 4d in white
     silver for honey, corn and malt; before 1066 it paid £10
     at face value and three days' revenue in honey, corn and malt.
         King Edward always had this manor in lordship.
             In this village a Freeman, Bruman, holds 1 hide of the King's
             jurisdiction; before 1066 he could grant his land to whom
             he would, but, however, he always found cartage or 8d in
             the King's service and made good his fine to the
             Sheriff.

3 M. ISLEHAM is a lordship village of the King's. It answers
     for 6 hides and 40 acres of land. Land for 10 ploughs.
     In lordship 2;
         16 villagers and 10 smallholders with 8 ploughs.
         3½ mills at 22s 8d and 1,250 eels; meadow for 10 ploughs;
             pasture for the village livestock.

ad pecuñ uillæ . Reddit . x . liƀ arſas 7 penſatas . 7 xiii.

liƀ 7 viii . ſolid 7 iiii . deñ de aƚbo argento ꝓ melle . fru

m̄to 7 braſio . 7 alijs c̄ſuetud minutis . Hoc m̄ ſemp habuit

rex . E . in dn̄io . In hoc m̄ fueř . iiii . ſocħi regis . E . 7 de

hac tra|7 xl ac̄s habueř . cui uolueř dare 7 uendere

potueř . ſ̧ Auerā ƚ viii . deñ in ſeruitio regis ſep̄ inueneř.

7 forisfac̄turā ſuā uicecom̄iti emendabant.   ꝼ HVND.

m̄ CHAVELAI dn̄ica uilla ꝛegis . ꝓ . viii . hiđ IN CHAVELAI

7 xl . acris ſe defđ . Tra . ē xii . cař . In dn̄io ſuꝥ . ii . 7 iii.

poteſt fieri . Ibi xii . uiƚƚi 7 vii . borđ cū . viii . cař . 7 ix.

poteſt fieri . P̊tū . i . cař . Silua . xx . porc̄ . Paſta ad pec̄

uiƚƚæ . Redđ . x . liƀ arſas 7 penſatas . 7 xiii . liƀ 7 . viii . ſoƚ

7 iiii . deñ de albis nūmis . ꝓ melle . frum̄to 7 braſio.

T.R.E. reddeƀ . xv . liƀ ad numerū . Hoc m̄ habuit ſep̄

rex . E . in dn̄io.   IN STANES HVND.

m̄ WITBORHĀ dn̄ica uilla regis . ē Ibi . ii . hidæ . 7 Tra

viii . cař . In dn̄io eſt una . 7 iii . adhuc fieri poſſuꝥ . Ibi . v.

uiƚƚi 7 v . borđ cū . v . cař . Ibi . ii . ſerui . 7 i . moliñ . x . ſoƚ . 7 ii.

oræ de theloneo . P̊tū . viii . cař . Redđ . x . liƀ arſas et

penſatas . 7 xiii . liƀ 7 viii . ſoƚ 7 iiii . deñ de albo argento

ꝓ melle frum̄to 7 braſio . Firma regis . E . fuit . xiiii . liƀ ad

numerū . ꝓ om̄ibꝫ reƀ ad firmā ꝓtinentiƀ . Hoc m̄ fuit

ſemp̄ in dn̄io regis.   IN WEDERLAI HVND.

m̄ TVBERTONE eſt dn̄ica uilla regis . Ibi . ii . hidæ 7 dim.

Tra . ē . v . cař . In dn̄io ſunt . ii . 7 iii . poteſt fieri . Ibi . vii.

189 d   ꝼ uiƚƚi

7 v . borđ cū . ii . çař . P̊tū . ii . cař . Reddit . c . ſoƚ ad nu

merū . 7 tn̄td reddeƀ . T.R.E. Ħ tra fuit ſep̄ de firma

regis . Cū his . ii . hiđ eſt dim uirg . quātten un̄ ſocħs.

qui n̄ fuit ibi . T.R.E. 7 tc̄ ualeƀ . ii . ſoƚ . m̄ . xii . deñ.

Iſte ħo fuit ſub Wallef comite.

It pays £10 assayed and weighed, and £13 8s 4d in white
silver for honey, corn, malt and other small customary
dues.

King Edward always had this manor in lordship.

In this manor were 4 Freemen of King Edward's; they had 1
hide and 40 acres of this land. They could grant and sell to
whom they would, but they always found cartage or 8d in
the King's service, and made good their fine to the
Sheriff.

In CHEVELEY Hundred

4 M. CHEVELEY is a lordship village of the King's. It answers
for 8 hides and 40 acres. Land for 12 ploughs.
In lordship 2; a third possible.
    12 villagers and 7 smallholders with 8 ploughs; a ninth possible.
    Meadow for 1 plough; woodland, 20 pigs; pasture for
        the village livestock.
It pays £10 assayed and weighed, and £13 8s 4d in white
coin for honey, corn and malt. Before 1066 it paid £15
at face value.
    King Edward always had this manor in lordship.

In STAINE Hundred

5 M. WILBRAHAM is a lordship village of the King's. 2 hides.
Land for 8 ploughs. In lordship 1; a further 3 possible.
    5 villagers and 5 smallholders with 5 ploughs.
    2 slaves; 1 mill, 10s; 2 *ora* from toll; meadow for 8
        ploughs.
It pays £10 assayed and weighed, and £13 8s 4d in white
silver for honey, corn and malt. King Edward's revenue was
£14 at face value for everything that belonged to the revenue.
    This manor was always in the King's lordship.

In WETHERLEY Hundred

6 M. COMBERTON is a lordship village of the King's. 2½ hides.
Land for 5 ploughs. In lordship 2; a third possible.
    7 villagers and 5 smallholders with 2 ploughs.   189 d
    Meadow for 2 ploughs.
It pays 100s at face value; before 1066 it paid as much.
    This land was always in the King's revenue.
With these 2 hides is ½ virgate which a Freeman holds who was not
there before 1066. Value then 2s, now 12d.
This man was under Earl Waltheof.

In *HASLINGEFELD* ten̄ Rex . VII . hid̄ 7 I . uirg̅ . Tra . e̅ . VIII .

car̄ . In dn̄io funt . II . 7 III . pot̄ fieri . Ibi XI . uilłi 7 IX . bord̄

cū . IIII . car̄ . 7 v̅ . pot̄ fieri . P̄tū . III . car̄ . Nem ad fepes refic̅ .

7 II . ferui . Redd̄ x . lib̄ arfas 7 penfatas . 7 XIII . lib̄ 7 VIII . fot̄

7 IIII . den̄ de alb̄ nūmis ꝑ melle frūmto 7 brafio . 7 alijs c̅fuet̄ .

T.R.E . reddeb̄ x . lib̄ ad numer̅ . 7 q̅tū oportebat c̅t̅ hoc

frūmti . brafij . 7 mellis . H̅ tra fuit fe̅p de firma regis .

In *CHINGESTONE* ten̄ Rex . I . hid̄ 7 III . uirg̅ . *IN STOV HD̄ .*

T̅ra . e̅ . II . car̄ . In dn̄io . e̅ una . 7 un uiłłs 7 III . bord̄ cū . I . car̄ .

Ibi un feru . Redd̄ . xL . fot̄ ad numer̅ T.R.E . Lx . fot̄ reddeb̄

H̅ tra fuit de firma regis fe̅p *IN CESTRETONE HVND̄ .*

CESTRETONE dn̄ica uilla regis . ꝑ xxx . hid̄ fe defd̄ . T̅ra

e̅ . XVI . car̄ . In dn̄io fu̅n . III . 7 IX . adhuc poſſ fieri . Ibi . II .

uilłi 7 XVI . bord̄ 7 VI . cot̄ cū . IIII . car̄ . P̄br h̅t̅ . I . uirg̅ tra̅e

P̄tū . VIII . car̄ . De marefch . mille anguiłł . Redd̄ xv . lib̄

arfas 7 penfatas . 7 XIII . lib̄ 7 VIII . fot̄ 7 IIII . den̄ de alb̄ nūmis .

ꝑ melle frūmto 7 brafio . 7 alijs c̅fuetudinib̄ T . R . E . redd

xv . lib̄ ad numer̅ . 7 c̅tra hoc c̅fuetudine̅ q̅tū oportebat .

In Witelesfeld hund̄ . In hiftetone jacet Wara de I hida

* 7 dimid̄ . de ꝑ ceftreforde . 7 eſt in Exfeffe apꝑciata

hanc tra̅ tenuit Algar comes . *IN CHAVELAI HVND̄ .*

ꝑ *DITONE* ꝑ x . hid̄ fe defd̄ . T.R.E . 7 m̊ ꝑ una hida . T̅ra

e̅ . XVI . car̄ . In dn̄io . II . car̄ . 7 VII . uiłłi 7 III . bord̄ cū . III . car̄

7 adhuc XIII . car̄ poſſ fieri . Ibi . III . ferui . Paftura ad pec̅

uillæ . Silua . ccc . porc̄ . De herbagia uillæ . VI . fot̄ . 7 VIII den̄

In totis ualent̄ ual̄ . XII . lib̄ . Q̊do recep̅ . xv . lib̄ 7 tm̄d̄ T R E

Hoc ꝑ ten̄ Wiłłs de nonueres ad firma̅ de rege .

Hoc ꝑ jacuit in æccła S̅ Edeldridæ de Ely̅ T.R.E . fed

Stigand archiep̅s eū inde fup̅fit . ho̅es de Hund̄ nefciu̅n

Rō q̅m̊ .

189 d

7 M. In HASLINGFIELD the King holds 7 hides and 1 virgate.
Land for 8 ploughs. In lordship 2; a third possible.
   11 villagers and 9 smallholders with 4 ploughs; a fifth possible.
   Meadow for 3 ploughs; wood for repairing fences; 2 slaves.
It pays £10 assayed and weighed, and £13 8s 4d in white
coin for honey, corn, malt and other customary dues;
before 1066 it paid £10 at face value, and in proportion to this,
as much corn, malt and honey as was needed.
   This land was always in the King's revenue.

In LONGSTOW Hundred
8   In KINGSTON the King holds 1 hide and 3 virgates.
Land for 2 ploughs. In lordship 1;
   1 villager and 3 smallholders with 1 plough.
    1 slave.
It pays 40s at face value; before 1066 it paid 60s.
   This land was always in the King's revenue.

In CHESTERTON Hundred
9   CHESTERTON is a lordship village of the King's. It answers for 30
hides. Land for 16 ploughs. In lordship 3; a further 9 possible.
   2 villagers, 16 smallholders and 6 cottagers with 4 ploughs.
    A priest has 1 virgate of land.
   Meadow for 8 ploughs; from the marsh 1,000 eels.
It pays £15 assayed and weighed, and £13 8s 4d in white
coin for honey, corn, malt and other customary dues;
before 1066 it paid £15 at face value and, in proportion to this,
as much customary dues as was needed.

In WHITTLESFORD Hundred
10   In HINXTON lies the defence obligation of 1½ hides of
   Chesterford Manor; it is assessed in Essex.
Earl Algar held this land.

In CHEVELEY Hundred
11 M. WOODDITTON answered for 10 hides before 1066; now for 1 hide.
Land for 16 ploughs. In lordship 2 ploughs;
   7 villagers and 3 smallholders with 3 ploughs; a further 13
   ploughs possible.
   3 slaves; pasture for the village livestock; woodland, 300 pigs;
   from the village grazing 6s 8d.
Total value £12; when acquired £15; before 1066 as much.
   William of Noyers holds this manor for the King at a revenue.
   This manor lay in (the lands of) the Church of St. Etheldreda
of Ely before 1066, but Archbishop Stigand took it away;
the men of the Hundred do not know how.

In *ESSELINGE* hᵉ rex W *IN STAPLEHOV HVND.*

XIII. hid 7 dim. Tra. e̅. xxxIIII.| In dn̄io suꝫ VII. car. 7 adhuc

III. poſſ fieri. Ibi xxxv. uilli 7 xxxIIII. bord̄ cū xxIIII.

car̄. Ibi. VII. ſerui. 7 III. molini. xx. ſolid̄. 7 VII. mil anguill

P̄tū. IIII. car̄. In totis ualent̄ ual. LIII lib̄. Q̄do Godric

recep̄. XII. lib̄. T.R.E. LVI. lib̄. Hoc ꝳ tenuit Edeua pulcra

7 in hoc ꝳ fuer̄. VII. ſochi hōes ej̄d Edeuæ. 7 recede abſꝗ

ej̄ licentia potuer̄. ipſa ū habuit ſoca eoꝫ 7 unqſꝗ

in ſeruitio regis inuenit Auera. ł VIIᵗᵒI. den ł mancipiū.

Iɴ Sahā hᵉ rex. W. VI. hid 7 XL. aᶜs in breue ſuo.

190 a

Iɴ Flamingdice Hund. In Fuleberne ten̄ Picotus

. xxvI. ſochos. qui hn̄t. IIII. hid ſub manu regis.

Tra. e̅ ibi. VI. car̄. 7 ibi ſunt. P̄tū carucis. Redduꝴ

p ann̄. VIII. lib̄ arſas 7 penſatas. 7 unoꝗꝗ Anno. XII.

equos. 7 XII. inguardos ſi rex in uicecomitatu ueniret.

Si n̄ ueniret. XII. ſol 7 VIII. den̄. T.R.E. n̄ reddebaꝴ

uicecomiti niſi Averas 7 inguardos. ł XII. ſolid 7 VIII. den.

7 ſup plus inuaſit Picot ſup rege. *IN CILDEFORD HD.*

Iɴ Badburghā ten̄ Picot dim̄ hid 7 dim uirḡ de rege.

H̄ tra jacet in Ceſtreforde. 7 ibi. e̅ app̄ciata. xxx. ſol

in Exſeſſe. Wluin hanc tr̄a tenuit ſub Algaro. non com᾽

potuit recede nec uende.

Iɴ Abintone ten̄ Picot ſub manu regis. 7 un ſochs ꝯ Sagar

de eo dim uirḡ. Val XII. den̄. Hanc tr̄a tenuit Elmar

T.R.E. 7 dare 7 uende potuit. Hanc inuaſit Alberic de Ver ꝯ

ſup rege. 7 picot deratiocinauit ea. c̄t eū. De pecu

nia quā inde ſūpſit Albic adhuc retinet. CCCC. oues

xx. min. 7 unā carucā. ut hōes de hund teſtant̄.

Iɴ Eſcelforde ten̄ Petrus de ualong *IN REPELAV HD*

III. hid de firma regis in Neuport. Tra. e̅. IIII. car̄.

In STAPLOE Hundred

12   In EXNING King William has 13½ hides. Land for 34 ploughs.
In lordship 7 ploughs; a further 3 possible.
35 villagers and 34 smallholders with 24 ploughs.
7 slaves; 3 mills, 20s and 7,000 eels; meadow for 4 ploughs.
Total value £53; when Godric acquired it £12; before 1066 £56.
Edeva the Fair held this manor, and in this manor were 7
Freemen, Edeva's men; they could withdraw without
her permission, but she had jurisdiction of them herself;
each of them found cartage in the King's service, or 8d
or a pledge.

13   In SOHAM King William has 6 hides and 40 acres, in his writ.

In FLENDISH Hundred   190 a
14   In FULBOURN Picot holds 26 Freemen who have 4 hides, under the
King's hand.
Land for 6 ploughs; they are there.
Meadow for the ploughs.
They pay £8 a year assayed and weighed, and each year 12 horses
and 12 escorts if the King comes into the Sheriffdom; if he does
not come, 12s 8d; before 1066 they only paid the Sheriff cartages
and escorts or 12s 8d; Picot annexed the excess in the King's
despite.

In CHILFORD Hundred
15   In BABRAHAM Picot holds ½ hide and ½ virgate from the King.
This land lies in (the lands of) Chesterford and is assessed there,
at 30s, in Essex.
Wulfwin held this land under Earl Algar; he could
not withdraw or sell.

16   In ABINGTON Picot holds under the King's hand; Sigar, a
Freeman, holds ½ virgate from him.
Value 12d.
Aelmer held this land before 1066; he could grant
and sell. Aubrey de Vere appropriated it in the King's despite;
and Picot adjudged it against him. Of the stock which he
took from it, Aubrey still keeps 400 sheep, less 20, and 1 plough,
as the men of the Hundred testify.

In THRIPLOW Hundred
17   In SHELFORD Peter of Valognes holds 3 hides of the King's
revenue in Newport. Land for 4 ploughs. In lordship 1;
a second possible;

In dñio . ē una . 7 altera poť fieri . 7 v . uiłłi 7 vi . borđ
hñt . ii . car . ptū . iiii . car . Redđ . iiii . lib arſas 7
penſas . 7 xx . ſolid p numerū . Ħ tra . ē bereuuicha
in Neuport . ſȝ Wara ej jacet in Grantebrige . Hanc
teñ trā com Heraldus . *IN ERNINGFORD HVNĐ.*

Iñ *LIDLINTONE* teñ Wiłłs camerarius 7 Otho aurifab
de rege ad firmā . iiii . hid |7 dim uirg . Tra . ē . x . car .
In dñio . ii . hid 7 iii . car . Ibi xxvi . uiłłi 7 x . borđ cū
. vii . car . Ibi . vi . ſerui . Ptū . ii . car . Silua . xxx . porc .
In totis ualent uał 7 ualuit ſemp . xxii . lib .
Hoc ꝏ tenuit Algar . Ħoes huj ꝏ reddeƀ War
pennā uicecomiti regis . aut cuſtodiā faciebant .
Iñ Abintone teñ Rex dim hiđ quæ jacet in Lidling
tone . Tra . ē . i . car . 7 ibi eſt . atqȝ cū eod ꝏ apꝓciata .
Iñ Abintone teñ Aluuin bedell dim v de rege .
Tra . ē dim car . 7 ibi eſt . Vał . v . ſoł . T . R . E . x . ſolid .
Iſđ tenuit . T . R . E . nec dare nec uendė potuit . In Iche
lintone jacuit .   *IN PAPEWORD HĐ.*

Iñ Draitone teñ . ii . ſochi dim hiđ de rege . Tra . ē
iiii . boƀ 7 ptū . Vał 7 ualuit ſēp . ii . ſoł . Idē ipſi tenueř .
7 dare 7 uendė potueř .

~~Iñ Witelesf hđ . In hiſtetune jac Wara de hđa 7 dim .~~
~~De Ceſtres man . 7 ē . apꝓciata in exexę . Algar ten .~~
Picot hť ſub manu Reg . i . hiđ . hanc tenƀant . vii .
Schi . T . R . E . 7 uenđ potant .

190 b

.II. **W** TERRA EPI WINTON .   *IN ERNINGFORD HĐ*
ꝏ   ALCHELIN eps Wintonienſis teñ Mordune .
p . viii . hiđ ſe defđ . Tra . ē . xvi . car . In dñio . iiii . hidæ .
7 ibi ſuɴ . v . car . 7 xv . uiłłi 7 xv . borđ cū . xi . car .
Ibi . xi . ſerui . 7 i . molin de . xvi . den . 7 alij . ii . molini
de . xxxii . den . ptū . xvi . car . Paſtura ad pec uillæ .

5 villagers and 6 smallholders have 2 ploughs.
Meadow for 4 ploughs.
It pays £4 assayed and weighed and 20s in face value.
This land is an outlier in Newport but its defence obligations
lie in Cambridge. Earl Harold held this land.

In ARMINGFORD Hundred
18 In LITLINGTON William the Chamberlain and Otto the Goldsmith
hold 4½ hides and ½ virgate from the King, at a revenue. Land
for 10 ploughs. In lordship 2 hides and 3 ploughs.
26 villagers and 10 smallholders with 7 ploughs.
6 slaves; meadow for 2 ploughs; woodland, 30 pigs.
The total value is and always was £22.
Earl Algar held this manor. The men of this manor paid
guard-penny to the King's Sheriff, or kept guard.

19 In ABINGTON (Pigotts) the King holds ½ hide which lies in
(the lands of) Litlington. Land for 1 plough; it is there;
and it is assessed with that same manor.

20 In ABINGTON (Pigotts) Alwin Cock the beadle holds ½ virgate
from the King. Land for ½ plough; it is there.
Value 5s; before 1066, 10s.
The same man held it before 1066; he could not grant or sell.
It lay in (the lands of) Ickleton.

In PAPWORTH Hundred
21 In (Fen) DRAYTON 2 Freemen hold ½ hide from the King.
Land for 4 oxen, and meadow.
The value is and always was 2s.
The very same men held it; they could grant and sell.

In WHITTLESFORD Hundred
22 *In HINXTON lies the defence obligation of 1½ hides of
Chesterford Manor; it is assessed in Essex. Earl
Algar held it.*

23 Picot holds 1 hide under the King's hand. 7 Freemen held it
before 1066; they could sell.

2   LAND OF THE BISHOP OF WINCHESTER   190 b

In ARMINGFORD Hundred
1 M. Bishop Walkelin of Winchester holds (Steeple) MORDEN. It answers for 8
hides. Land for 16 ploughs. In lordship 4 hides; 5 ploughs there.
15 villagers and 15 smallholders with 11 ploughs.
11 slaves; 1 mill at 16d and 2 other mills at 32d; meadow for 16
ploughs; pasture for the village livestock.

In totis ualent ual . xx . lib . Q̆do recep̄ . x . lib . T.R.E.

xvi . lib . Hoc M̃ jacet 7 jacuit in æccła S̃ PETRI Wintoñ.

In Cloptune teñ iſdē eps . iii . hid 7 dim . Tra . ē

.v . car . In dñio . i . hida 7 iii . uirg . 7 ibi . ē una car.

Ibi . vi . uiłłi 7 v . borđ cū . iiii . car . 7 iiii . pot fieri.

P̃tū . v . car . Paſtura ad pec uillæ . Ual . lx . ſol.

Q̆do recep̄ . xl . ſol . T.R.E. iiii . lib . H̃ tra jacuit

in dñio æcclæ S̃ PETRI Wintonienſis.

In Abintone teñ Hugo de . W . epo . ii . hid 7 dim

7 dim uirg . Tra . ē . v . car . In dñio . iii . car . 7 ix . borđ

unqſq̃ de . v . acris . cū . ii . car . P̃tū . v . car . 7 ii . ſolid.

Ual . vii . lib . Q̆do recep̄ . iii . lib . T.R.E. viii . lib.

Hoc M̃ jacuit 7 jacet in æccła S̃ Petri Wintoñ.

7 ibi uñ ſochs tenuit dim uirg ſub archiepo

Stigando . 7 potuit abſq̃ licentia ej recedere.

In Baſingborne teñ iſđ ep̄s . i . hid . 7 ii . uirg 7 dim.

Tra . ē . iii . car . In dñio . i . hid . 7 ibi . ē . i . car . Ibi uñ

uiłłs 7 iiii . borđ cū . i . car . 7 altera pot fieri . Ibi

ii . molini de xx . ſol . P̃tū . i . car . Ual . lx . ſol . Q̆do

recep̄ . xl . ſol . T.R.E. lx . ſol . H̃ tra jacuit 7 jacet

in æccła S̃ PETRI Wintoñ . 7 ibi fuit . i . ſochs hō . S.

Archiepi . dimid uirg tenuit . 7 dare 7 uende potuit.

ETERRA EP̄I LINCOLIENSIS. *IN WITELESFORD HD̄.*

.III. Ep̄s Lincolienſis teñ in Hiſtetone . ii . hid.

7 Robt de eo . Tra . ē . ii . car . Vna . ē ibi . 7 alia pot

fieri . Ibi . ii . uiłłi . 7 ii . borđ . P̃tū . ii . car . 7 i . mol

de . viii . ſol . Ual . xl . ſol . Q̆do recep̄ . xx . ſol . T.R.E.

iiii . lib . Hanc tra tenuit Siuuarđ de Heraldo.

7 potuit dare cui uoluit. *IN NORESTOV HD̄.*

In Madinglei . teñ picot de epo . R . i . uirg træ

7 dim . Ual 7 ualuit . v . ſol . T.R.E. x . ſol . Hanc trā

Total value £20; when acquired £10, before 1066 £16.
This manor lies and lay in (the lands of) St. Peter's Church,
Winchester.

2 In CLOPTON the Bishop also holds 3½ hides. Land for 5 ploughs.
In lordship 1 hide and 3 virgates; 1 plough there.
6 villagers and 5 smallholders with 3 ploughs; a fourth
possible.
Meadow for 5 ploughs; pasture for the village livestock.
Value 60s; when acquired 40s; before 1066 £4.
This land lay in the lordship of St. Peter's Church,
Winchester.

3 In ABINGTON (Pigotts) Hugh holds 2½ hides and ½ virgate from Bishop
W(alkelin). Land for 5 ploughs. In lordship 3 ploughs;
9 smallholders, each with 5 acres, with 2 ploughs.
Meadow for 5 ploughs, and 2s too.
Value £7; when acquired £3; before 1066 £8.
This manor lay and lies in (the lands of) St. Peter's Church,
Winchester. One Freeman held ½ virgate there under Archbishop
Stigand; he could withdraw without his permission.

4 In BASSINGBOURN the Bishop also holds 1 hide and 2½ virgates.
Land for 3 ploughs. In lordship 1 hide; 1 plough there.
1 villager and 4 smallholders with 1 plough; a second possible.
2 mills at 20s; meadow for 1 plough.
Value 60s; when acquired 40s; before 1066, 60s.
This land lay and lies in (the lands of) St. Peter's Church,
Winchester. 1 Freeman, Archbishop Stigand's man, was there
and held ½ virgate; he could grant and sell.

3   LAND OF THE BISHOP OF LINCOLN

In WHITTLESFORD Hundred
1 The Bishop of Lincoln holds 2 hides in HINXTON, and Robert
from him. Land for 2 ploughs; 1 there; another possible.
2 villagers; 2 smallholders.
Meadow for 2 ploughs; 1 mill at 8s.
Value 40s; when acquired 20s; before 1066 £4.
Siward held this land from Earl Harold; he could grant
to whom he would.

In NORTHSTOW Hundred
2 In MADINGLEY Picot holds 1½ virgates of land from Bishop R(emigius).
The value is and was 5s; before 1066, 10s.

tenuit Blacuin hō regis. E. 7 recedĕ potuit . f; foca
Wluuio epo remanfit.   *IN CESTRETONE HD.*

ᛗ *HISTONE* . ꝓ xxvi . hiđ 7 dim̄ fe defđ . Hoc ᛗ eft
unū de duodeci Manerijs dn̄icis epifcopat Lin
colienfis . Ibi ten̄ . R . eꝑs . xvii . hiđ . i . uirg mi̇n.
Tra . ē . xiii . caŕ . In dn̄io . viii . hidæ . 7 ibi fuɴ̃ . ii . caŕ.
7 iii . pot fieri . Ibi xviii . uiłłi . 7 xviii . borđ cū . ix . caŕ.

190 c
7 decima caŕ pot fieri . Ibi . iiii . cot . 7 iiii . ferui . Ƥtū
xiii . caŕ . Paftura ad pec uillæ . In totis ualent
uał . x . liƀ . Qdo receꝑ xii . liƀ . T . R . E . xiiii . liƀ.
De xxvi . hiđ 7 dim . ten Picot de epo . ix . hidas
7 iii . uirg . Tra . ē . vi . caŕ . In dn̄io . i . caŕ . 7 altera
pot fieri . Ibi . x . uiłłi 7 xix . cot cū . ii . caŕ . 7 aliæ
duæ poſ fieri . Ƥtū . vi . caŕ . Pafta ad pec uillæ.
Vał . iiii . liƀ . Qdo receꝑ vi . liƀ . T . R . E . vii . liƀ.
Hanc trā . ix . fochi tenueŕ . 7 uendĕ potueŕ . fed
foca remanfit epo.
In eađ uilla ten̄ . R . eꝑs . i . hid 7 i . uirg . 7 duas
part uni uirg . Tra . ē . i . caŕ . f; n̄ eft caŕ . Ibi un̄
uiłłs 7 i . cotar . Ƥtū . i . caŕ . Vał . v . foł . Qdo receꝑ
. x . foł . T . R . E . xx . foł . Hanc trā tenuit Wluuin
hō abƀis de Elẏ . 7 reddeƀ in anno fextariū mellis.
Hanc trā inuafit eꝑs . R . fuꝑ abƀem . ut hunđ teftaꞇ.
Picot uicecom de epo tenꝭt.
In Cildrelai ten̄ Rogeri de epo . R . iii . hiđ . Tra . ē
ii . caŕ 7 dim . In dn̄io . ē una . 7 i . uiłłs 7 v . borđ cū . i . caŕ.
7 dim caŕ pot fieri . Ibi . i . cot . 7 iii . ferui . Nem ad fepes.
Vał . l . foł . Qdo receꝑ xl . foł . T . R . E . c . foł . Hoc ᛗ te
nuit Siuuarđ hō Heraldi . 7 uendĕ potuit.

Blackwin, King Edward's man, held this land; he could
withdraw; but the jurisdiction remained with Bishop Wulfwy.

In CHESTERTON Hundred

3 M. HISTON answers for 26½ hides. This manor is one of the 12
lordship manors of the Bishopric of Lincoln. Bishop R(emigius)
holds 17 hides less 1 virgate. Land for 13 ploughs. In
lordship 8 hides; 2 ploughs there; a third possible.
18 villagers and 18 smallholders with 9 ploughs;
a tenth plough possible.
4 cottagers; 4 slaves.   190 c
Meadow for 13 ploughs; pasture for the village livestock.
Total value £10; when acquired £12; before 1066 £14.

4 Of the 26½ hides Picot holds 9 hides and 3 virgates from the Bishop.
Land for 6 ploughs. In lordship 1 plough; a second possible.
10 villagers and 19 cottagers with 2 ploughs; another 2
possible.
Meadow for 6 ploughs; pasture for the village livestock.
Value £4; when acquired £6; before 1066 £7.
9 Freemen held this land; they could sell, but the
jurisdiction remained with the Bishop.

5 In the same village Bishop R(emigius) holds 1 hide and 1 virgate
and 2 parts of 1 virgate. Land for 1 plough, but the plough
is not there.
1 villager; 1 cottager.
Meadow for 1 plough.
Value 5s; when acquired 10s; before 1066, 20s.
Wulfwin, the Abbot of Ely's man, held this land; he paid
a sester of honey a year. Bishop R(emigius) annexed this
land in the Abbot's despite, as the Hundred testifies.
Picot the Sheriff holds (it) from the Bishop.

6 In CHILDERLEY Roger holds 3 hides from Bishop R(emigius).
Land for 2½ ploughs. In lordship 1;
1 villager and 5 smallholders with 1 plough; [another] ½ plough
possible.
1 cottager; 3 slaves.
Wood for fences.
Value 50s; when acquired 40s; before 1066, 100s.
Siward, Earl Harold's man, held this manor; he could sell.

TERRA EPI DE ROVECESTRE. *IN STAPLEHOV*

.IIII. Eps Rofenſis ten jn Giſlehā . I . hid 7 dim . 7 xx aĉs
ſub Archiepo Lanfranco . Tra . ē . III . caʀ . In dñio . I . caʀ.
7 XI . uilli cū . II . caʀ . Ibi dim molend . II . ſol 7 VIII . den.
7 ccc . anguill . Ptū . III . caʀ . 7 II . mil anguill . Paſta ad
pecun uillæ . Val 7 ualuit XL . ſol . T.R.E. ʟx . ſol . De hac
tra tenuit Wluuin uenator regis . E . dim hid 7 xx . aĉs.
7 XII . ſochi habueʀ . I . hid . ſub Turбto 7 dare 7 uende potueʀ.

TERRA ABBATIE DE ELȲG. *IN RADEFELLE HVND.*

.V. ᛗ Abbas De Elȳ ten *STVVICESWORDE* . Ibi ħt VIII . hid
7 dim . 7 dim uirg . Tra . ē XII . caʀ . In dñio . III . hid 7 dim.
7 ibi ſuɴ . III . caʀ . 7 duæ adhuc poſſ fieri . Ibi . XVI . uilli
7 V . borđ cū . VI . caʀ . 7 VII ma . poteſt fieri . Ibi . IIII . ſerui.
Silua ad . cc.ʟx . porc . Paſta ad pecun uillæ . Int
totū ual . x . lib . 7 tntđ qdo recep . T.R.E. XII . lib.
H tra jacuit 7 jacet in dñio æcclæ de Elȳ.
In ead uilla ten Harduin de Eſcalers . I . uirg de abбe.
Tra . ē . II . bob . Valuit ſēp . V . ſol . Hanc tra tenuit
Goduin . ſʒ ñ poterat uende . Dim hid pti ħt abб
de Elȳ in dñio in ipſa uilla . De hoc ᛗ ſūpſit Seric
de Odburcuilla . I . uirg 7 dim de dñica firma abбis
de Elȳ . 7 poſuit in ᛗ S Wandregiſili . ut hunđ teſtaʀ.
190 d
In *WESLAI* . ten abб . III . hiđ . Tra . ē . V . caʀ . Ibi ſuɴ . II.
7 adhuc . III . poſſ . ēe . Ibi . IIII . uilli 7 V . borđ . 7 II . ſerui.
Ptū . II . bob . Val 7 ualuit . x . ſol . T.R.E. c . ſol . H tra
jacet 7 jacuit ſēp in dñio æcclæ de Elȳ . teſtante hund.
ᛗ Ipſe abб ten *WARATINGE* . Ibi . IIII . hid 7 dim . Tra . ē
VII . caʀ . In dñio . III . hid . 7 ibi . II . caʀ . 7 adhuc . II . poſſ
fieri . Ibi . VI . uilli 7 III . borđ cū . III . caʀ . Ibi . III . ſerui.
7 ptū . I . caʀ . Silua . xx . porc . Paſta ad pecun uillæ.

4   LAND OF THE BISHOP OF ROCHESTER

In STAPLOE Hundred
1   The Bishop of Rochester holds 1½ hides and 20 acres in ISLEHAM
under Archbishop Lanfranc. Land for 3 ploughs. In lordship 1 plough;
   11 villagers with 2 ploughs.
   ½ mill, at 2s 8d and 300 eels; meadow for 3 ploughs, and
     2,000 eels; pasture for the village livestock.
The value is and was 40s; before 1066, 60s.
   Of this land Wulfwin, King Edward's Huntsman, held ½ hide
and 20 acres; 12 Freemen had 1 hide under Thorbert; they could
all grant and sell.

5   LAND OF THE ABBOT OF ELY

In RADFIELD Hundred
1 M. The Abbot of Ely holds STETCHWORTH. He has 8½ hides and ½ virgate.
   Land for 12 ploughs. In lordship 3½ hides; 3 ploughs there;
a further 2 possible.
   16 villagers and 5 smallholders with 6 ploughs; a seventh possible.
   4 slaves; woodland for 260 pigs; pasture for the village livestock.
In total, value £10; when acquired, as much; before 1066 £12
   This land lay and lies in the lordship of the Church of Ely.

2   In the same village Hardwin of Scales holds 1 virgate from the Abbot.
Land for 2 oxen.
The value always was 5s.
   Godwin held this land, but he could not sell. The Abbot of Ely
also has ½ hide of meadow in lordship in this village.
   Saeric of Auberville took 1½ virgates of this manor away from the
Abbot of Ely's lordship revenue and placed them in St. Wandrille's
manor, as the Hundred testifies.

3   In WESTLEY (Waterless) the Abbot holds 3 hides. Land for   190 d
5 ploughs; 2 there; a further 3 possible.
   4 villagers; 5 smallholders; 2 slaves.
   Meadow for 2 oxen.
The value is and was 10s; before 1066, 100s.
   This land lies and always lay in the lordship of the Church of Ely,
as the Hundred testifies.

4 M. The Abbot holds (West)WRATTING himself. 4½ hides. Land for
7 ploughs. In lordship 3 hides; 2 ploughs there; a further 2 possible.
   6 villagers and 3 smallholders with 3 ploughs.
   3 slaves; meadow for 1 plough; woodland, 20 pigs; pasture for the
   village livestock.

Int totū uat.IIII.lib.Q̇do recep̄.́xl.fot.T.R.É.́c.fot.

Hoc ꝳ jacet 7 jacuit sep̄ in dnio æcctæ de Elẏ.

In ead uilla ten Harduin de abbe.III.hid.Tra.ē.IIII.

car.In dnio.II.car.7 v.uitti 7 IIII.bord cū.II.car.Ibi

IIII.ferui.7 IIII.ac̄ p̄ti.Silua.XII.porc̄.Vat.IIII.lib.

Q̇do recep̄.́xx.fot.T.R.É.́xl.fot.Hanc trā tenuer̄

x.fochi.hoēs abbis fuer̄.7 abſq̣ ej licentia trā ſuā

uende n̄ potuer̄.Hoꝣ.vi.inueniec̄ Aueras.7 IIII.inū

jnguard.fi rex ueniret in fcẏra.Si non.vIII.den ꝓ auera.

7 IIII.ꝓ Inguard.reddebant.

ꝳ Ipſe abb ten BELESHA.Ibi funt.IX.hidæ.Tra.XIX.

car.In dnio.v.hidæ.7 ibi ſuꝥ.v.car.7 II.plus poſſ eſſe.

Ibi.XII.uitti 7 XII.bord cū XII.car.Ibi.II.ferui.7 uñ

molin.IIII.folid.Silua.cc.porc̄.7 XII.ac̄ p̄ti.De paſta

XXXII.den.In totis ualent uat.XVII.lib.Q̇do recep̄.́

x.lib.T.R.É.́xII.lib.Hoc ꝳ jacet 7 jacuit in dnio æcctæ

In ead uilla ten Harduin de abbe q̄ter.xx.ac̄s.Tra eſt

.I.car.7 ibi eſt.Vat 7 ualuit sep̄.XIII.fot 7 IIII.den.Hanc

trā tenuer̄.III.fochi hoēs abbis de Elẏ.n̄ potuer̄ dare

nec uende abſq̣ ej licentia trā ſuā.tam inueniec̄ auerā

In Saham ten iſd abb   IN STAPLEHOV HVND.£7 inguard.

dim hid.Tra.ē.II.car.In dnio.ē una.7 III.uitti 7 x.bord

cū.I.car.P̄tū.II.car.Paſtura ad pecuñ uillæ.7 una

nauis quæ pifcat in mara ꝓ c̄fuetud.Vat.XXX.fot.Q̇do

recep̄.́xx.fot.T.R.É.́xxx.fot.H̄ tra jacuit sep̄ in æccta.

In SVAFAM ten iſdē abb.III.hid. IN STANES HVND.

Tra.ē.v.car.In dnio.I.hida 7 III.uirg.7 ibi ſuꝥ.II.car.

7 v.uitti 7 II.bord cū.III.car.Ibi.II.ferui.7 de theloneo

retis.́vI.fot.De marefc.́.vI.den.Vat 7 ualuit sep̄.c.fot.

H̄ tra jacet 7 jacuit sep̄ in æccta.

190 d

In total, value £4; when acquired 40s; before 1066, 100s.
This manor lies and always lay in the lordship of the Church of Ely.

6 In the same village Hardwin holds 3 hides from the Abbot. Land for
4 ploughs. In lordship 2 ploughs;
    5 villagers and 4 smallholders with 2 ploughs.
    4 slaves; meadow, 4 acres; woodland, 12 pigs.
Value £4; when acquired 20s; before 1066, 40s.
    10 Freemen held this land; they were the Abbot's men and could
not sell their land without his permission. 6 of them found cartages
and 4 found escorts if the King came into the Shire; if not, they
paid 8d for cartage and 4[d] for escorts.

6 M. The Abbot holds BALSHAM himself. 9 hides. Land for 19 ploughs.
In lordship 5 hides; 5 ploughs there; 2 more possible.
    12 villagers and 12 smallholders with 12 ploughs.
    2 slaves; 1 mill, 4s; woodland, 200 pigs; meadow, 12 acres;
        from pasture 32d.
Total value £17; when acquired £10; before 1066 £12.
This manor lies and always lay in the lordship of the Church of Ely.

7 In the same village Hardwin holds 80 acres from the Abbot. Land
for 1 plough; it is there.
The value is and always was 13s 4d.
    3 Freemen, the Abbot of Ely's men, held this land; they could not
grant or sell their land without his permission; however, they found
cartage and escort.

In STAPLOE Hundred

8 In SOHAM the Abbot also holds ½ hide. Land for 2 ploughs. In
lordship 1.
    3 villagers and 10 smallholders with 1 plough.
    Meadow for 2 ploughs; pasture for the village livestock;
        1 boat which fishes in the Mere by customary right.
Value 30s; when acquired 20s; before 1066, 30s.
This land always lay in (the lands of) the Church.

In STAINE Hundred

9 In SWAFFHAM the Abbot also holds 3 hides. Land for 5 ploughs.
In lordship 1 hide and 3 virgates; 2 ploughs there;
    5 villagers and 2 smallholders with 3 ploughs;
    2 slaves; from the fish-net toll 6s; from the marsh 6d.
The value is and always was 100s.
This land lies and always lay in (the lands of) the Church.

In ead uilla ten̄ Harduin̄ ſub abbe . ii . hid 7 iii . uirg.

Tra . ē . iii . car̄ . In dn̄io . i . car̄ . 7 ii . uilti cū . ii . car̄ . P̄tū
ii . bob . Val 7 ualuit ſēp . Lxx . ſol . Hanc tr̄a tenuer̄ . iiii.
ſochi . nec potuer̄ recede ſine licentia Abbis.

In Coeia ten̄ Picot ſub abbe . iii . hid 7 iii . uirg . Tra . ē
iiii . car̄ . In dn̄io . ii . car̄ . 7 v . uilti cū . ii . car̄ . Ibi . i . ſeruus.

191 a
7 dim molin̄ . xL . den.

P̄tū . iiii . car̄ . Val . vi . lib . Q̄do recep̄ . 7 T . R . E . iiii . lib.
Hanc tr̄a tenuer̄ . ii . ſochi ſub abbe . n̄ potuer̄ recede
ſine ej licentia.   IN FLĀMINDIC HVND.

In Fuleberne ten̄ iſd abb . iiii . hid 7 dim . Tra . ē . vi . car̄.
In dn̄io . iii . hidæ . ubi poſs . ee . iii . car̄ . ſƷ nulla ibi habet.
Ibi . viii . uilti 7 vi . bord cū . iii . car̄ . p̄tū car̄ . Val &
ualuit . xx . ſol . T . R . E . vi . lib . H̄ tra jacet & jacuit ſēp
in dn̄io æcclæ de Elȳ ad firmā.

In Teuerſhā ten̄ iſd abb . i . hid . Tra . ē . i . car̄ 7 dim.
In dn̄io . ē una car̄ . 7 ii . uilti 7 ii . bord . Val 7 ualuit
xx . ſol . T . R . E . xL . ſol . H̄ tra jacuit ſēp in æccla.

ⱮHorningesie ꝑ vii . hid ſe defd . Tra . ē . xvii . car̄.
In dn̄io . iii . hidæ 7 dim . 7 ibi . viii . car̄ 7 dim . Ibi xxii.
uilti 7 xiiii . bord cū . ix . car̄ . Ibi . xv . ſerui . 7 i . molin̄
de . x . ſol . 7 mille anguilt . P̄tū car̄ . In totis ualent
ual xviii . lib . Q̄do recep̄ . xiiii . lib . 7 tntd . T . R . E.
H̄ tra jacuit ſēp 7 jacet in dn̄io æcclæ de Elȳ . ⌐HVND.

In Wichehā ten̄ iſd abb . i . hid 7 dim . IN CILDEFORD
Tra . ē . iiii . car̄ . In dn̄io dim hlda . 7 ibi . ii . car̄ 7 dim.
Ibi . vi . uilti 7 ii . bord cū . ii . car̄ . Ibi . ii . ſerui . 7 iiii . ac̄
p̄ti . Silua . L . porc . Val . Lxv . ſol . Q̄do recep . Lx . ſol.
T . R . E . xL . ſol . H̄ tra jacet 7 jacuit ſēp in dn̄io æcclæ Elȳ.

10 In the same village Hardwin holds 2 hides and 3 virgates under
the Abbot. Land for 3 ploughs. In lordship 1 plough;
   2 villagers with 2 ploughs.
   Meadow for 2 oxen.
The value is and always was 70s.
   4 Freemen held this land; they could not withdraw without the
Abbot's permission.

11 In QUY Picot holds 3 hides and 3 virgates under the Abbot.
Land for 4 ploughs. In lordship 2 ploughs;
   5 villagers with 2 ploughs.   191 a
   1 slave; ½ mill, 40d; meadow for 4 ploughs.
Value £6; when acquired and before 1066 £4.
   2 Freemen held this land under the Abbot; they could not withdraw
without his permission.

  In FLENDISH Hundred
12 In FULBOURN the Abbot also holds 4½ hides. Land for 6 ploughs.
In lordship 3 hides, where 3 ploughs are possible, but none is
recorded there.
   8 villagers and 6 smallholders with 3 ploughs.
   Meadow for the ploughs.
The value is and was 20s; before 1066 £6.
   This land lies and always lay in the lordship of the Church of Ely,
at a revenue.

13 In TEVERSHAM the Abbot also holds 1 hide. Land for 1½ ploughs.
In lordship 1 plough;
   2 villagers; 2 smallholders.
The value is and was 20s; before 1066, 40s.
   This land always lay in (the lands of) the Church.

14 M. HORNINGSEA answers for 7 hides. Land for 17 ploughs. In
lordship 3½ hides; 8½ ploughs there.
   22 villagers and 14 smallholders with 9 ploughs.
   15 slaves; 1 mill at 10s and 1,000 eels; meadow for the ploughs.
Total value £18; when acquired £14; before 1066 as much.
   This land always lay and lies in the lordship of the Church
of Ely.

  In CHILFORD Hundred
15 In (West) WICKHAM the Abbot also holds 1½ hides. Land for 4 ploughs.
In lordship ½ hide; 2½ ploughs there.
   6 villagers and 2 smallholders with 2 ploughs.
   2 slaves; meadow, 4 acres; woodland, 50 pigs.
Value 65s; when acquired 60s; before 1066, 40s.
   This land lies and always lay in the lordship of the Church
of Ely.

In Berchehã ten un focĥs dim uirg̃ fub abbe. Valet
7 ualuit. xl. den. Hic inueniebat Inguard uicecomiti. T.R.E.
In Badburhã ten Harduin fub abbe dim uirg̃ træ.
Val 7 ualuit. xl. den. ii. fochi tenuer. ñ potuer recedẽ.
In Pampefuuorde ten ifd abb. ii. hid 7 iii. uirg̃ 7 dim.
Tra. ẽ. vi. car. In dñio. i. hida. 7 i. uirg̃ 7 dim. 7 ibi fuɴ
ii. car. Ibi. xii. uilli 7 v. bord cũ. iiii. car. Ibi. iiii. feryi.
7 uñ moliñ de. xx. fol. Ptũ. i. car. Val 7 ualuit fẽp
vii. lib. Ĥ tra jacuit fẽp 7 jacet in dñio æcclæ de Elẏ.
In ead uilla ten Harduin de abbe. x. acs. Tra. i. bou.
Val. xii. den. Hanc trã tenuit Snellinc de abbe. fed
non potuit recedere.   IN ƦEPESLAV HVND.
Ipfe abb ten vi. hid 7 dim in Trepeflau. Tra. ẽ. viii.
car. In dñio. iii. hide 7 ibi fuɴ. iii. car. Ibi. xii. uilli
7 v. bord. cũ. v. car. Ibi. v. ferui. 7 ptũ. i. car. Paftura
ad pecuñ uillæ. In totis ualent ual 7 ualuit xi. lib.
T.R.E. xii. lib. Ĥ tra jacet 7 jacuit fẽp in dñio æcclæ.
In ead uilla ten Harduin fub abbe p qddã refpectũ
ipfius abbis de dñico uictu monachoʒ. i. hidã. donec
cũ rege inde loquat. Tra. ẽ. i. car. Val 7 ualuit fẽp
xx. fol. Ĥ tra jacuit fẽp in dñio æcclæ de Elẏ. T.R.E.
In ead uilla tenebat Harduin. ii. acs de tra abbis.
191 b
de quibʒ non ht aduocatũ nec libatorẽ. fed oc
cupauit fup abbem ut hões de hund teftantur.
ᴍ HAVOCHESTVN. p. viii. hid 7 dim fe defd. Tra
ẽ. xii. car. In dñio. v. hidæ. 7 ibi fuɴ. iiii. car.
7 xvi. uilli 7 iiii. bord cũ. viii. car. Ibi. iii. ferui. 7 ii.
molini de. l. fol. Ptũ. iiii. car. Pafta ad pec uillæ.
In totis ualent ual 7 ualuit. xiii. lib. T.R.E. xiiii. lib.
Hoc ᴍ jacet 7 jacuit fẽp in dñio æcclæ de Elẏ.

16   In BARHAM 1 Freeman holds ½ virgate under the Abbot.
The value is and was 40d; before 1066 he found escort for the
Sheriff.

17   In BABRAHAM Hardwin holds ½ virgate of land under the Abbot.
The value is and was 40d.
      2 Freemen held it; they could not withdraw.

18   In PAMPISFORD the Abbot also holds 2 hides and 3½ virgates.
Land for 6 ploughs. In lordship 1 hide and 1½ virgates; 2 ploughs
there.
      12 villagers and 5 smallholders with 4 ploughs.
      3 slaves; 1 mill at 20s; meadow for 1 plough.
The value is and always was £7.
      This land always lay and lies in the lordship of the Church
of Ely.

19   In the same village Hardwin holds 10 acres from the Abbot.
Land for 1 ox.
Value 12d.
      Snelling held this land from the Abbot, but he could not withdraw.

   In THRIPLOW Hundred

20   The Abbot holds 6½ hides in THRIPLOW himself. Land for 8 ploughs.
In lordship 3 hides; 3 ploughs there.
      12 villagers and 5 smallholders with 5 ploughs.
      5 slaves; meadow for 1 plough; pasture for the village livestock.
The total value is and was £11; before 1066 £12.
      This land lies and always lay in the Church's lordship.

21   In the same village Hardwin holds 1 hide of the lordship supplies
of the monks under the Abbot through a deferment of the Abbot
until he speaks with the King about it. Land for 1 plough.
The value is and always was 20s.
      This land always lay in the lordship of the Church
of Ely before 1066.

22   In the same village Hardwin held 2 acres of the Abbot's land,
for which he does not have a patron nor a deliverer, but he   191 b
appropriated it in the Abbot's despite, as the men of the
Hundred testify.

23 M. HAUXTON answers for 8½ hides. Land for 12 ploughs. In
lordship 5 hides; 4 ploughs there;
      16 villagers and 4 smallholders with 8 ploughs.
      3 slaves; 2 mills at 50s; meadow for 4 ploughs; pasture
        for the village livestock.
The total value is and was £13; before 1066 £14.
      This manor lies and always lay in the lordship of the Church
of Ely.

In Herleſtone ten̑ Picot . I . hid̑ 7 dim̄ de abbate

juſſu regis . 7 eſt ap̄pciata in Herleſtone.

hanc tr̄a tenu̇it q̇d̄a ſocħs ſub abƀe de Elẏ . T.R.E.

potuit recede̅ ſine licentia ej̇ . ſed ſoca remanſit abƀi.

Ⓜ ＥＳＣＥＬＦＯＲＤＥ . ꝑ IX . hid̑ 7 XXIIII . acris ſe defd̑.

Tr̄a . ē . XI . caȓ . In dn̄io . v . hidæ . 7 ibi ſunt . III . caȓ.

Ibi . XX . uiłłi 7 VIII . bord̑ cū . VIII . caȓ . Ibi . VII . ſerui.

7 II . moł de . XLV . ſoł . 7 II . porc̑ redd̑ . Ptū . IIII . caȓ.

In totis ualent̑ ual 7 ualuit . XII . liƀ . T.R.E . XIIII . liƀ.

In ead̑ uilla ten̑ Harduin̑ . II . hid̑ 7 dim̑ . 7 IX . ac̊s.

7 un̄ monaſteriū de dn̄ica firma monachoʒ de Elẏ.

7 ibi fuer̄ . T.R.E . ut hund̑ teſtat̑ . m̄ non ħt abƀ.

In ead̑ uilla ten̑ VII . ſocħi . I . hid̑ 7 dim̑ 7 VI . ac̊s.

de ſoca abƀis. | potuer̄ recede̅ cū tr̄a . ſ; ſoca rema∕ de Elẏ.

nebat æcclæ de Elẏ . Hoc Ⓜ jacuit 7 jacet ſēp in dn̄io æcclæ

Ⓜ ＳＴＡＰＬＥＦＯＲＤＥ . ꝑ x . hid̑ ſe defd̑ . Tr̄a . ē XI . caȓ.

In dn̄io . VI . hid̑ 7 dim̑ . 7 ibi . IIII . caȓ . Ibi XVI . uiłłi

7 IIII . bord̑ . cū . VII . caȓ . Ibi . VII . ſerui . 7 p̄tū . v . caȓ.

Paſta ad pecun̑ uillæ . Silua ad ſepes refic̑ . In totis

ualent̑ ual 7 ualuit XII . liƀ . T.R.E ⁝ XIII . liƀ . Hoc Ⓜ

jacet 7 jacuit ſēp in dn̄io æcclæ de Elẏ.

In Wadone . ten̑ Harduin̑ . II . hid̑ 7 dim̑ . Tr̄a . ē . III . caȓ.

In dn̄io . I . hid̑ . 7 I . caȓ . Ibi . VI . uiłłi 7 XV . cot cū . I . caȓ

7 dim̑ . 7 alia dim̑ poteſt fieri . Ptū . II . caȓ . Paſta

ad pecun̑ uillæ . Ħ tr̄a ap̄pciata . ē cū tr̄a Harduini.

De hac tr̄a ten̑ uit Turbern̑ . I . hid̑ de abƀe . n̄ poterat

ſeparare ab æccła ext firm̄a monachoʒ . T.R.E . nec

in die mortis ej̇ . 7 XII . ſocħi habuer̄ . I . hid̑ 7 dimid̑.

uende̅ potuer̄ . ſed ſoca remanſit abƀi.

In Melrede . ten̑ Hard̑ . I . uirg̑ de ſoca abƀis.

24 In HARSTON Picot holds 1½ hides from the Abbot by the King's
command; it is assessed in Harston. A Freeman held
this land under the Abbot of Ely before 1066; he could
withdraw without his permission, but the jurisdiction remained
with the Abbot.

25 M. SHELFORD answers for 9 hides and 24 acres. Land for 11 ploughs.
In lordship 5 hides; 3 ploughs there.
20 villagers and 8 smallholders with 8 ploughs.
7 slaves; 2 mills at 45s pay 2 pigs; meadow for 4 ploughs.
The total value is and was £12; before 1066 £14.

26 In the same village Hardwin holds 2½ hides and 9 acres and a
monastery, of the lordship revenue of the monks of Ely. They
were there before 1066, as the Hundred testifies; now the Abbot
does not have them.

27 In the same village 7 Freemen hold 1½ hides and 6 acres of
the Abbot's jurisdiction; they could not withdraw with the land,
but the jurisdiction remained with the Church of Ely. This manor
always lay and lies in the lordship of the Church of Ely.

28 M. STAPLEFORD answers for 10 hides. Land for 11 ploughs.
In lordship 6½ hides; 4 ploughs there.
16 villagers and 4 smallholders with 7 ploughs.
7 slaves; meadow for 5 ploughs; pasture for the village livestock;
woodland for repairing fences.
The total value is and was £12; before 1066 £13.
This manor lies and always lay in the lordship of the Church
of Ely.

[In ARMINGFORD Hundred]
29 In WHADDON Hardwin holds 2½ hides. Land for 3 ploughs. In
lordship 1 hide and 1 plough.
6 villagers and 15 cottagers with 1½ ploughs; another ½ possible.
Meadow for 2 ploughs; pasture for the village livestock.
This land is assessed with Hardwin's land. Thorbern White held
1 hide of this land from the Abbot; he could not separate it from
the Church outside the monks' revenue before or in 1066.
12 Freemen had 1½ hides; they could sell, but the jurisdiction
remained with the Abbot.

30 In MELDRETH Hardwin holds 1 virgate of the Abbot's jurisdiction.

In ead uilla ten abb̄.ii.hid 7 iii.uirg̓.Tra.ē.vii.

caŕ.In dn̄io,i.hid 7 dim̓.7 i.caŕ 7 dim̓.7 dim̄ pot

fieri.Ibi   .x.bord̄.cū.iii.caŕ.Ibi.iii.ſerui.

7 i.molin̄.iii.ſol.P̊tū.v.caŕ.Val 7 ualuit.c.ſol.

T.R.E.'vi.lib̄.H̄ tra jacet 7 jacuit sēp in dn̄io æcclæ.

In ead uilla ten̓ Harduin.i.hid 7 dim̄.7 i.monaſteriū

191 c

Q̄ In ead uill̄ ten̓ Wido de Rebutcurt.x.ſochos.

ex his.i.n̄ potat uende tēp.R.E.alij potant.H̄ test' h̄d.

de dn̄ica firma monachoȝ qd̄ tenebaɴ 7 in uita 7 in

morte.R.E.ut hōēs de hund̄ teſtantur.   Q̄

In Melleburne ten̓ abb̄ de Ely: ii.hid̄ 7 i.uirg̓ træ.

Tra.ē.v.caŕ.In dn̄io.i.hid 7 i.uirg̓.7 ibi.i.caŕ 7 dim̄.

7 dim̄ poteſt fieri.Ibi.vi.uilli 7 ix.bord̄ cū.iii.caŕ.

Ibi.iii.cot.7 i.molin̄ de.ii.ſol 7 viii.den̓.P̊tū.v.caŕ.

Paſta ad pecun̄ uillæ.Val 7 ualuit.c.ſol.T.R.E.'vi.lib̄.

h̄ tra jacet 7 jacuit sēp in dn̄io æcclæ de Ely.

In Eſceprid dim̄ uirg̓ ten̓ Harduin.que die mortis

.E.regis erat in æccla de Ely. *IN STOV HVND̓.*

In Harduic ten̓ abb̄ de Ely.iii.hid 7 i.uirg̓.7 xii.

acs.Tra.ē.vi.caŕ.In dn̄io.i.hid 7 dim̄ 7 xii.acræ.

7 ibi ſuɴ.ii.caŕ.Ibi.vii.uilli cū.iiii.caŕ.Ibi.iiii.ſerui.

p̊tū.iiii.caŕ.Nem̄ ad ſepes.Val.c.ſol 7 ualuit.T.R.E.'

vi.lib̄.h̄ tra jacet 7 jacuit sēp in dn̄io æcclæ de Ely.

In ead uilla ten̓ Radulf de abb̄e.x.acs Tra.i.bou.

Val 7 ualuit xii.den̓.H̄ tr̄a tenuit Cabe ſub abb̄e.

nec potuit ab eo recedere.

31 In the same village the Abbot holds 2 hides and 3 virgates. Land
for 7 ploughs. In lordship 1½ hides and 1½ ploughs; [another]
½ [plough] possible.
... 10 smallholders with 3 ploughs.
3 slaves; 1 mill, 3s; meadow for 5 ploughs.
The value is and was 100s; before 1066 £6.
This land lies and always lay in the lordship of the Church.

32 In the same village Hardwin holds 1½ hides and a monastery of
the lordship revenue of the monks before and in 1066, as the   191 c
men of the Hundred testify.

33 ⊖ In the same village Guy of Raimbeaucourt holds 10 Freemen.
One of them could not sell before 1066; the others could; this the
Hundred testifies.

34 In MELBOURN the Abbot of Ely holds 2 hides and 1 virgate of land.
Land for 5 ploughs. In lordship 1 hide and 1 virgate; 1½ ploughs
there; [another] ½ possible.
6 villagers and 9 smallholders with 3 ploughs.
3 cottagers;
1 mill at 2s 8d; meadow for 5 ploughs; pasture for the village
livestock.
The value is and was 100s; before 1066 £6.
This land lies and always lay in the lordship of the Church
of Ely.

[In WETHERLEY Hundred]
35 In SHEPRETH Hardwin holds ½ virgate, which was in (the lands of)
the Church of Ely in 1066.

In LONGSTOW Hundred
36 In HARDWICK the Abbot of Ely holds 3 hides, 1 virgate
and 12 acres. Land for 6 ploughs. In lordship 1½ hides
and 12 acres; 2 ploughs there.
7 villagers with 4 ploughs.
4 slaves; meadow for 4 ploughs; wood for fences.
The value is and was 100s; before 1066 £6.
This land lies and always lay in the lordship of the Church
of Ely.

37 In the same village Ralph holds 10 acres from the Abbot.
Land for 1 ox.
The value is and was 12d.
Cabe held this land under the Abbot; he could not withdraw
from him.

Ⓜ *GRATEDENE* ꝑ.v.hiđ ſe defđ.Tra.ē.ıx.caŕ.

In đñio.ıı.hidæ 7 dim.7 ibi.ē.ı.caŕ.7 ıı.poſſ fieri.

Ibi.vııı.uiłłi 7 ıııı.borđ cū.vı.caŕ.Ibi.ıııı.ſerui.

P̊tū.ııı.caŕ.Paſta ad pecuñ uillæ.Silua ad.Lx.

porc.7 de c̄ſuetuđ ſiluæ.ıı.ſoł.In totis ualent uał

vııı.lib.Q̇đo recep.ıx.lib.T.R.E.xv.lib.Hoc Ⓜ

jacet 7 jacuit ſēp in đñio æcclæ de Elẏ. *IN PAPEWORD*

Ⓜ *WIVELINGHA* ꝑ vıı.hiđ ſe defđ.Tra.ē   *HVND.*

vıı.caŕ.In đñio.ıııı.hidæ.7 ibi.ıı.caŕ.Ibi.xıı.uiłłi

cū.v.caŕ.Ibi.vııı.cot 7 ı.ſerů.P̊tū.vıı.caŕ.Paſta

ad pecuñ uillæ.De maris.vı.ſoł.In totis ualentijs

uał 7 ualuit.c.ſoł.T.R.E.vııı.lib.Hoc Ⓜ jacet 7 ſēp

jacuit in đñio æcclæ de Elẏ.   *IN NORESTOV HVND.*

In Hochinton teñ Aluiet.xv.ac̄s.de abƀe.Tra eſt

.ı.boui.Vał 7 ualuit ſēp.ııı.ſoł.Iſtemet tenuit T.R.E.

7 dare potuit.ſoca ū remanſit abƀi.

Ⓜ *EPINTONE* ꝑ.vı.hiđ 7 dim ſe defđ.Tra.ē.vı.caŕ.

In đñio.ııı.hiđ 7 dim.7 ibi.ē dim caŕ.7 ı.caŕ 7 dim **pot**

★ fieri.Ibi.ı.uiłłs 7 vııı.borđ cū.ıı.caŕ.7 ıı.poſſ fieri.

Ibi.vıı.cot 7 ı.ſerů.p̊tū.ıı.caŕ.Vał 7 ualuit.xL.ſoł.

T.R.E.vııı.lib.Hoc Ⓜ jacet 7 jacuit ſēp in đñio æcclæ de Elẏ.

Ⓜ *COTEHA* ꝑ.x.hiđ ſe defđ.   *IN CESTRETONE HVND.*

Tra.ē.vııı.caŕ.In đñio.vı.hiđ.7 ı.caŕ.Ibi.xvı.uiłłi

7 x.cot.cū.vı.caŕ.Ibi.ıı.ſerui.P̊tū.vııı.caŕ.Paſta

ad pecuñ uillæ.In totis ualent uał 7 ualuit.c.ſoł.

T.R.E.vııı.lib.Hoc Ⓜ jacet 7 jacuit in æcclæ đñio de Ely.

191 c

38 M. (Little) GRANSDEN answers for 5 hides. Land for 9 ploughs. In
lordship 2½ hides; 1 plough there; [another] 2 possible.
8 villagers and 3 smallholders with 6 ploughs.
4 slaves; meadow for 3 ploughs; pasture for the village livestock;
woodland for 60 pigs; from customary dues on the woodland 2s.
Total value £8; when acquired £9; before 1066 £15.
This manor lies and always lay in the lordship of the Church
of Ely.

In PAPWORTH Hundred
39 M. WILLINGHAM answers for 7 hides. Land for 7 ploughs. In
lordship 4 hides; 2 ploughs there.
12 villagers with 5 ploughs.
8 cottagers; 1 slave.
Meadow for 7 ploughs; pasture for the village livestock;
from marshes 6s.
The total value is and was 100s; before 1066 £8.
This manor lies and always lay in the lordship of the Church
of Ely.

In NORTHSTOW Hundred
40 In OAKINGTON Alfgeat the priest holds 15 acres from the Abbot.
Land for 1 ox.
The value is and always was 3s.
The very same man held it before 1066; he could grant, but the
jurisdiction remained with the Abbot.

41 M. IMPINGTON answers for 6½ hides. Land for 6 ploughs. In
lordship 3½ hides. ½ plough there; [another] 1½ ploughs possible.
1 villager and 8 smallholders with 2 ploughs; [another] 2 possible.
7 cottagers; 1 slave.
Meadow for 2 ploughs.
The value is and was 40s; before 1066 £8.
This manor lies and always lay in the lordship of the Church
of Ely.

In CHESTERTON Hundred
42 M. COTTENHAM answers for 10 hides. Land for 8 ploughs. In lordship
6 hides and 1 plough.
16 villagers and 10 cottagers with 6 ploughs.
2 slaves; meadow for 8 ploughs; pasture for the village livestock.
The total value is and was 100s; before 1066 £8.
This manor lies and lay in the lordship of the Church of Ely.

In Hiſtone ten abb̄ . I . hid̄ 7 III . uirg̃ . H̄ tra . ē app̄ciata
cū Epintone . IN DVOB̄ HVND DE ELẏ . QVI CONVEÑIVN̄

Ⓜ WITESIE ꝑ . II . hid̄ ten̄ æccła   Ⱶ AP WICEFORDE .
de Elẏ . Tra . ē . IIII . car̃ 7 dim̄ . In dn̄io . I . hida . 7 ibi . I . car̃
7 dim̄ . Ibi . VIII . uiłłi 7 IIII . cot cū . III . car̃ . Ibi . III . ſerui .
P̃tū . I . car̃ . Paſta ad pecun̄ uillæ . De gurgite . II . ſoł .
Vał . IIII . lib̄ . Qdo recep̄ᷓ III . lib̄ . T . R . E . ᷓ c . ſoł . Hoc Ⓜ jacet
7 jacuit sēp in æccła de Elẏ . in dn̄ica firma .

Ⓜ DODINTON ten̄ abb̄ de Elẏ ꝑ . v . hid̄ . Tra . ē . VIII . car̃ .
In dn̄io . II . hidæ 7 dim̄ . 7 ibi . III . car̃ . Ibi . XXIIII . uiłłi
cū . v . car̃ . Ibi . VIII . ſochi . de . I . hida . 7 VIII . cot . 7 I . ſeruuſ .
p̃tū . VIII . car̃ . Paſta ad pecun̄ uillæ . Silua . CC . L . porc̃ .
De piſcarijs . XXVII . mił anguiłł 7 CL . De p̃ſentationib̄ .
XX . IIII . ſoł . In totis ualent uał . XVI . lib̄ . Qdo recep̄ᷓ
x . lib̄ . T . R . E . ᷓ XII . lib̄ . Hoc Ⓜ jacet 7 jacuit in dn̄io   ^{de Elẏ.} æccłæ
Ad hoc Ⓜ jacet . I . bereuuicha . Mercha . ubi ſuꞃ̃ ^{cł} XII . uiłłi
q̃ſꝗ̨ de . XII . acris . H̄ app̄ciata . ē cū Ⓜ .

In Cetriz ten̄ iſd abb̄ . II . hid̄ 7 dim̄ uirg̃ . Tra . ē . III . car̃ .
In dn̄io dim̄ hid̄ . 7 ibi . VI . boues . Ibi . VI . uiłłi . 7 II . bord̄ .
★ 7 II . cot cū . II . car̃ . 7 II . ^{ob'} bob̄ . P̃tū . II . car̃ . Silua . XX . porc̃ .
De piſcar̃ mille 7 q̃ngen̄ anguiłł . Vał . XL . ſoł . Qdo
recep̄ᷓ XXX . ſoł . T . R . E . ᷓ L . ſoł . H̄ tra jacuit 7 jacet in
dn̄io æccłæ de Elẏ .

Ⓜ LITELPORT ten̄ abb̄ de Elẏ . ꝑ . II . hid̄ 7 dim̄ . Tra . ē . VI .
car̃ . In dn̄io . I . hida . 7 ibi . II . car̃ . Ibi . XV . uiłłi 7 VIII . ^{to}
cot cū . IIII . car̃ . Ibi . VIII . ſerui . 7 p̃tū . VI . car̃ . Paſta
ad pecun̄ uillæ . De piſcar̃ . XVII . mił anguiłł . De p̃ſen
tation̄ piſciū . ᷓ XII . ſoł 7 IX . den̄ . In totis ualent uał . x .
lib̄ . Qdo recep̄ᷓ VII . lib̄ . T . R . E . ᷓ VI . lib̄ . Hoc Ⓜ jacet
7 jacuit sēp in æccła de Elẏ . in dn̄io

43   In HISTON the Abbot holds 1 hide and 3 virgates. This land is   191 d
assessed with Impington.

In the two Hundreds of ELY which meet at Witchford
[E1]

44 M. Ely Church holds WHITTLESEY for 2 hides. Land for 4½ ploughs.
In lordship 1 hide; 1½ ploughs there.
    8 villagers and 4 cottagers with 3 ploughs.
    3 slaves; meadow for 1 plough; pasture for the village livestock;
        from the weir 2s.
Value £4; when acquired £3; before 1066, 100s.
    This land lies and always lay in the lordship revenue of the
Church of Ely.

45 M. The Abbot of Ely holds DODDINGTON for 5 hides. Land for 8 ploughs.
In lordship 2½ hides; 3 ploughs there.
    24 villagers with 5 ploughs.
    8 Freemen with 1 hide; 8 cottagers; 1 slave.
    Meadow for 8 ploughs; pasture for the village livestock; woodland,
        250 pigs; from fisheries 27,150 eels; from presentations 24s.
Total value £16; when acquired £10; before 1066 £12.
    This manor lies and lay in the lordship of the Church of Ely. With
this manor lies 1 outlier, MARCH, where there are 12 villagers with
12 acres each; it is assessed with the manor.

46   In CHATTERIS the Abbot also holds 2 hides and ½ virgate.
Land for 3 ploughs. In lordship ½ hide; 6 oxen there.
    6 villagers, 2 smallholders and 2 cottagers with 2 ploughs
        and 2 oxen.
    Meadow for 3 ploughs; woodland, 20 pigs; from fisheries 1,500 eels.
Value 40s; when acquired 30s; before 1066, 50s.
    This land lay and lies in the lordship of the Church of Ely.

47 M. The Abbot of Ely holds LITTLEPORT for 2½ hides. Land for 6 ploughs.
In lordship 1 hide; 2 ploughs there.
    15 villagers and 8 cottagers with 4 ploughs.
    8 slaves; meadow for 6 ploughs; pasture for the village livestock;
        from fisheries 17,000 eels; from presentations of fish 12s 9d.
Total value £10; when acquired £7; before 1066 £6.
    This manor lies and always lay in the lordship of the Church of Ely.

In Stuntenei teñ abb̄.ɪ.hid 7 dim.Tra.ē.ɪɪɪ.car̄.In
dn̄io.ɪ.hid 7 ɪ.car̄.Ibi.vɪ.uilli 7 v.cot̄ 7 ɪɪɪ.serui.cū.ɪɪ.
car̄.P̄tū.ɪɪɪ.car̄.Pasta ad pec̄ uillæ.De piscar̄.xxɪɪɪɪ.
mil Anguill.De p̄sent̄.xvɪɪɪ.sol̄.Int totū ual 7 ualuit
x.lib̄.7 xɪɪɪɪ.sol̄.T.R.E.˒xɪɪ.lib̄.H̄ tra.ē Berew de m̄ de Elẏ.
Isd abb̄ teñ Liteltedford.ɪ.hid̄.Tra.ē.ɪ.car̄.│Ibi.ɪ.uill
de vɪ.acris.7 ɪɪɪɪ.cot̄.P̄tū.ɪ.car̄.Pasta ad pec̄ uillæ.De
pisc̄ q̄ngent anguill.De p̄sent̄.ɪɪɪɪ.den̄ 7 dim.Val.xʟ.sol̄.
Q̄do recep̄.˒xx.sol̄.T.R.E.˒xxx.sol̄.H̄ tra.ē Berew de Elẏ.
m̄ STRADHĀ.p̄.v.hid̄ se defd̄.Tra.ē.ɪx.car̄.In dn̄io.
ɪɪɪ.hid̄.7 ibi.ɪɪɪɪ.car̄.Ibi xɪɪ.uilli.q̄sq̄ x.ac̄s.7 xɪ.uilli
de.ɪ.hida.hi hn̄t.v.car̄.Ibi.x.cot̄.7 ɪɪ.serui.P̄tū.ɪx.car̄.
Pasta ad pec̄ uillæ.De piscar̄.ɪɪɪ.mil anguill.7 cc.ʟ.
De p̄sent̄.vɪɪ.sol̄ 7 vɪɪ.den̄.In totis ual ualet.ɪx.lib̄.
192 a
Q̄do recep̄.˒vɪ.lib̄.T.Ŗ.E.˒xɪɪ.lib̄.Hoc m̄ jacet & ja
cuit sēp in dn̄io æcclæ de Elẏ.
m̄ WILBERTONE teñ abb̄ de Elẏ.Ibi.v.hidæ.Tra.ē.vɪɪ.
car̄.In dn̄io.ɪɪɪ.hid̄ 7 ɪ.uirḡ.7 ibi.ɪɪɪ.car̄.Ibi.ɪɪɪɪ.sochi
qui ñ potuer̄ nec poss recede.7 ɪx.uilli.cū.ɪɪɪɪ.car̄.
Ibi.vɪɪɪɪ.cot̄ 7 vɪɪɪ.serui.P̄tū.vɪɪ.car̄.Pasta ad pec̄
uillæ.De junc̄.xvɪ.den̄.Int tot̄ ual.vɪɪ.lib̄.Q̄do
recep̄.˒ɪɪɪɪ.lib̄.T.R.E.˒x.lib̄.Hoc m̄ jacet 7 jacuit sēp iñ
dn̄io æcclæ de Elẏ.
m̄ LINDONE teñ abb̄ de Elẏ.Ibi.ɪɪɪɪ.hid̄.Tra.ē.vɪ.car̄.
In dn̄io.ɪɪ.hidæ 7 dim.7 ibi.ɪɪɪɪ.car̄.Ibi.ɪɪ.sochi qui
ñ potuer̄ neq̄ poss recede.7 xɪɪɪɪ.uilli.cū.ɪɪ.car̄.
Ibi.ɪx.cot̄.7 ɪ.bord̄ 7 x.serui.De piscar̄.ɪɪɪ.mil an
guill.7 ccc.7 xxxɪɪɪ.De p̄sent̄.ɪɪɪɪ.sol̄.P̄tū.vɪ.car̄.
Pasta ad pec̄ uillæ.Int tot̄ ual.vɪɪɪ.lib̄.Q̄do recep̄.˒
ɪɪɪɪ.lib̄.T.R.E.˒ɪx.lib̄.Hoc m̄ jacet 7 jacuit in dn̄io æcclæ.
HELLE teñ abb̄ de Elẏ.Ibi.ɪɪ.hidæ.Tra.ē.v.car̄.In
dn̄io.ɪ.hid̄ 7 ɪ.uirḡ 7 x.ac̄.7 ibi.ɪɪɪ.car̄.Ibi.x.uilli
cū.ɪɪ.car̄.Ibi.ɪɪɪɪ.cot̄.7 v.serui.P̄tū.v.car̄.Pasta ad

48   In STUNTNEY the Abbot holds 1½ hides. Land for 3 ploughs.
In lordship 1 hide and 1 plough.
>   6 villagers, 5 cottagers and 3 slaves with 2 ploughs.
>   Meadow for 3 ploughs; pasture for the village livestock;
>   from fisheries 24,000 eels; from presentations 18s.
The total value is and was £10 14s; before 1066 £12.
This land is an outlier of Ely Manor.

49   The Abbot also holds LITTLE THETFORD. 1 hide. Land for 1 plough;
it is there, in lordship.
>   1 villager with 6 acres; 4 cottagers.
>   Meadow for 1 plough; pasture for the village livestock; from
>   fisheries 500 eels; from presentations 4½d.
Value 40s; when acquired 20s; before 1066, 30s.
This land is an outlier of Ely.

50 M. STRETHAM answers for 5 hides. Land for 9 ploughs. In lordship
3 hides; 4 ploughs there.
>   12 villagers, 10 acres each; 11 villagers with 1 hide; they have
>   5 ploughs. 10 cottagers; 2 slaves.
>   Meadow for 9 ploughs; pasture for the village livestock; from
>   fisheries 3,250 eels; from presentations 7s 7d.
Total value £9; when acquired £6; before 1066 £12.   192 a
This manor lies and always lay in the lordship of the Church
of Ely.

51 M. The Abbot of Ely holds WILBURTON. 5 hides. Land for 7 ploughs.
In lordship 3 hides and 1 virgate; 3 ploughs there.
>   4 Freemen who could not and cannot withdraw; 9 villagers
>   with 4 ploughs. 9 cottagers; 8 slaves.
>   Meadow for 7 ploughs; pasture for the village livestock; from
>   reeds 16d.
Total value £7; when acquired £4; before 1066 £10.
This manor lies and always lay in the lordship of the Church
of Ely.

52 M. The Abbot of Ely holds LINDEN (End). 4 hides. Land for 6 ploughs.
In lordship 2½ hides; 4 ploughs there.
>   2 Freemen who could not and cannot withdraw; 14 villagers
>   with 2 ploughs. 9 cottagers; 1 smallholder; 10 slaves.
>   From fisheries 3,333 eels; from presentations 4s; meadow for
>   6 ploughs; pasture for the village livestock.
Total value £8; when acquired £4; before 1066 £9.
This manor lies and lay in the Church's lordship.

53   The Abbot of Ely holds HILL (Row). 2 hides. Land for 5 ploughs.
In lordship 1 hide and 1 virgate and 10 acres. 3 ploughs there.
>   10 villagers with 2 ploughs.
>   4 cottagers; 5 slaves.

pecun uillæ. 7 de portu. III. socos. Val. c. sol. Q̃do recep̃:
XL. sol. T.R.E: VI. lib. H̃ tra. ẽ bereuuicha de Lindone.

Hadrehã ten VII. sochi sub abbe. q̃ n̄ potuer̃ neq;
poss recede. Ibi. III. hidæ. Tra. ẽ. V. car̃. 7 ibi sunt.
Ibi. VIII. uitti q̃sq; dim uirg. 7 IIII. bord q̃sq; . V. acs.
Ibi. VI. cot. P̃tũ. V. car. Pasta ad pec uillæ. Val 7 ualuit
VIII. lib. T.R.E: XII. lib. HVCVSQ; VN̄ HVND. NVNC ALT.

M̃ *Wisbece*. ten abb de Ely. Ibi. X. hide. Tra. ẽ. X.
car. In dn̄io. I. hida. 7 I. uirg. 7 ibi sunt. II. car̃. Ibi. XV.
uitti q̃sq; X. ac. 7 XIII. sochi de. II. hid 7 dim. q̃ non
potuer̃ nec poss recede. hi om̃s. VIII. car̃. Ibi. XVII.
cot 7 II. serui. De piscar. mill 7 q̃ngent anguill. p̃tũ
X. car. Pasta ad pec uillæ. Int̃ tot ual 7 ualuit. c.
sol. T. R. E: VI. lib. Hoc M̃ jacet 7 jacuit in dn̄io æcclæ.
In ead uilla. II. piscat redd abbi. XIIII. mill anguil.
7 de p̃sent. XIII. sol 7 IIII. den. Sup om̃s hoẽs huj
uille ht̃ abb Socam.

M̃ *Ely* p. X. hid se desd. Tra. ẽ XX. car̃. In dn̄io. V.
hidæ. 7 ibi. V. car. 7 VI. pot fieri. Ibi. XL. uitti. q̃sq;
XV. acs. cũ. XIIII. car̃. Ibi. XXVIII. cot 7 XX. serui.
De pisc. III. mil 7 DCC 7 L. anguill. De p̃sent. II. sol
7 III. den. P̃tũ. XX. car. Pasta ad pec uillæ. Ibi. III. ar
pendi uineæ. In totis ualent ual. XXX. lib. Q̃do recep̃:
XX. lib. T. R. E: XXX. III. lib. Tot hoc M̃ fuit 7 Semp est dn̄ium.
Haneia. ẽ. I. insula. in qua. ẽ træ dim hida. H̃ geldũ
192 b non dat. nec unq dedit T.R.E.

M̃ *Dvnehã* ten abb de Ely. Ibi. IIII. hidæ. Tra. ẽ. VIII. car.
In dn̄io. II. hidæ 7 dim. 7 ibi. IIII. car. Ibi XV. uitti q̃sq; de
XII. acris. cũ. IIII. car. Ibi. VIII. cot. 7 VIII. serui. P̃tũ. VIII.
car. Pasta ad pec uillæ. De piscar. CCC. Anguill. 7 II. solid.
Silua. c. porc. In totis ualent ual. X. lib Q̃do recep̃: c. sol.
T.R.E: XII. lib. Hoc M̃ jacet 7 jacuit sep̃ in dn̄io æcclæ de Ely.

Meadow for 5 ploughs; pasture for the village livestock; from
    the port 3 ploughshares.
Value 100s; when acquired 40s; before 1066 £6.
This land is an outlier of Linden (End).

54 7 Freemen hold HADDENHAM under the Abbot; they could not
and cannot withdraw. 3 hides. Land for 5 ploughs; they are there.
    8 villagers, ½ virgate each; 4 smallholders, 5 acres each.
    6 cottagers.
Meadow for 5 ploughs; pasture for the village livestock.
The value is and was £8; before 1066 £12.

Thus far, one Hundred [E1] ; now the other [E2]
55 M. The Abbot of Ely holds WISBECH. 10 hides. Land for 10 ploughs.
In lordship 1 hide and 1 virgate; 2 ploughs there.
    15 villagers, 10 acres each; 13 Freemen with 2½ hides, who could
      not and cannot withdraw; all of them, 8 ploughs.
    17 cottagers; 2 slaves.
From fisheries 1,500 eels; meadow for 10 ploughs; pasture for
    the village livestock.
The total value is and was 100s; before 1066 £6.
This manor lies and lay in the Church's lordship.

56 In the same village 2 fishermen who pay 14,000 eels to the Abbot,
and 13s 4d from presentations.
The Abbot has jurisdiction over all the men of this village.

57 M. ELY answers for 10 hides. Land for 20 ploughs. In lordship 5 hides;
5 ploughs there; a sixth possible.
    40 villagers, 15 acres each, with 14 ploughs.
    28 cottagers; 20 slaves.
From fisheries 3,750 eels; from presentations 2s 3d; meadow
    for 20 ploughs; pasture for the village livestock. 3 *arpents*
    of vines.
Total value £30; when acquired £20; before 1066 £33.
The whole of this manor always was and is in lordship.

58 HAINEY is an island, in which there is ½ hide of land. It does not
give tax and never did before 1066.   192 b

59 M. The Abbot of Ely holds DOWNHAM. 4 hides. Land for 8 ploughs.
In lordship 2½ hides; 4 ploughs there.
    15 villagers, 12 acres each, with 4 ploughs.
    8 cottagers; 8 slaves.
Meadow for 8 ploughs; pasture for the village livestock; from
    fisheries 300 eels and 2s; woodland, 100 pigs.
Total value £10; when acquired 100s; before 1066 £12.
This manor lies and always lay in the lordship of the Church
of Ely.

Ⓜ *WICEFORD* ten abb̃ de Ely̆. Ibi . iii . hid . Tra . ē . vii . car̃.
In dñio . i . hida 7 dim̃ . 7 ibi . ii . car̃ . 7 iii . pot fieri . Ibi . v.
ſocħi de dim̃ hida. | 7 xvii . uilli q̃ſq̃ de . vii . acris . Hi om̃s
^{qui n̄ potuer̃ nec poſſunt recedere.}
ſimul . iiii . car̃ . Ibi . vii . cot . 7 viii . ſerui . P̊tū . vii . car̃ . Paſta
ad pecun̄ uillæ . In totis ualent ual . x . lib̃ Q̃do recep̃ . viii . lib̃.
T . R . E . xii . lib̃ . Hoc Ⓜ fuit 7 eſt de dñio æcclæ .

Ⓜ *WINTEWORDE* ten abb̃ de Ely̆. Ibi . iii . hid 7 dimidia .
Tra . ē . vii . car̃ . In dñio . i . hida . 7 ibi . ē . i . car̃ . 7 alta pot
fieri . Ibi . ix . uilli q̃ſq̃ de . x . ac . 7 ii . ſocħi de . i . hida . qui
n̄ potuer̃ nec poſſ uende ſine abb̃is lictia . 7 un̄ ſocħs de . i .
uirg ad eund̃ modū . 7 ſub his ſocħis . ix . uilli q̃ſq̃ de . x . ac . hi om̃s . v . car̃ .
Ibi . xvii . cot . 7 p̃tū . vii . car̃ . Paſta ad pecun̄ uillæ .
Silua . xx . porc̃ . In totis ualent ual . x . lib̃ 7 x . ſol . 7 tntd̃
q̃do recep̃ . T . R . E . xii . lib̃ . Hoc Ⓜ jacet 7 jacuit ſep̃ in dñio ^{æcclæ.}

Ⓜ *WICEHA* ten abb̃ de Ely̆ . Ibi . iiii . hid 7 i . uirg . Tra . ē
vii . car̃ . In dñio . ii . hid . 7 ibi . ii . car̃ . 7 iii . pot fieri . Ibi . xii .
^{or}
ſocħi de . ii . hid dim̃ uirg min . q̃ n̄ potuer̃ nec poſſ dare
abſq̃ abb̃is lictia . Ibi . ii . uilli de . x . acris . 7 ii . bord̃ q̃ſq̃
de . v . ac . Hi om̃s . iiii . car̃ . Ibi . iiii . cot . 7 v . ſerui . P̊tū
vii . car̃ . Paſta ad pec̃ uillæ . Val 7 ualuit . c . ſol . T . R . E .
vii . lib̃ . Hoc Ⓜ fuit 7 eſt de dñio æcclæ de Ely̆ .

Ⓜ *SVDTONE* . ten abb̃ de Ely̆ . Ibi . v . hidæ . Tra . ē . x . car̃ .
^{in dñio}
| . ii . hidæ . 7 ibi . iii . car̃ . 7 iiii . pot . ēē . Ibi . ix . ſocħi de . ii .
^{ab́}
hid . q̃ n̄ potuer̃ nec poſſ recede ſine lictia abb̃is . 7 viii .
uilli quiſq̃ de vii . ac 7 dim̃ . 7 xv . cot . Hi om̃s cū . vi .
car̃ . Ibi . vii . ſerui . p̃tū . x . car̃ . Paſta ad pecun̄ uillæ .
De piſcar̃ . xl . iiii . ſol . Silua . v . porc̃ . In totis ualent
ual 7 ualuit . xii . lib̃ . T . R . E . xvi . lib̃ . Hoc Ⓜ fuit 7 . ē
de dñio æcclæ de Ely̆ .

60 M. The Abbot of Ely holds WITCHFORD. 3 hides. Land for 7 ploughs.
In lordship 1½ hides; 2 ploughs there; a third possible.
   5 Freemen with ½ hide, who could not and cannot withdraw;
      17 villagers with 7 acres each: all of them together, 4 ploughs.
         7 cottagers, 8 slaves.
   Meadow for 7 ploughs; pasture for the village livestock.
Total value £10; when acquired £8; before 1066 £12.
This manor was and is in the Church's lordship.

61 M. The Abbot of Ely holds WENTWORTH. 3½ hides. Land for 7 ploughs.
In lordship 1 hide; 1 plough there; a second possible.
   9 villagers with 10 acres each; 2 Freemen with 1 hide, who could
      not and cannot sell without the Abbot's permission;
      1 Freeman with 1 virgate in the same manner; under these
      Freemen 9 villagers with 10 acres each; all of them, 5 ploughs.
         17 cottagers;
   meadow for 7 ploughs; pasture for the village livestock;
      woodland, 20 pigs.
Total value £10 10s; when acquired, as much; before 1066 £12.
This manor lies and always lay in the Church's lordship.

62 M. The Abbot of Ely holds WITCHAM. 4 hides and 1 virgate.
Land for 7 ploughs. In lordship 2 hides; 2 ploughs there;
a third possible.
   12 Freemen with 2 hides less ½ virgate, who could not and
      cannot grant without the Abbot's permission. 2 villagers
      with 10 acres; 2 smallholders with 5 acres each; all of
      them, 4 ploughs.
         4 cottagers; 5 slaves.
Meadow for 7 ploughs; pasture for the village livestock.
The value is and was 100s; before 1066 £7.
This manor was and is of the lordship of the Church of Ely.

63 M. The Abbot of Ely holds SUTTON. 5 hides. Land for 10 ploughs.
In lordship 2 hides; 3 ploughs there; a fourth possible.
   9 Freemen with 2 hides, who could not and cannot withdraw
      without the Abbot's permission; 8 villagers with 7½ acres
      each; 15 cottagers; all of them with 6 ploughs.
   7 slaves; meadow for 10 ploughs; pasture for the village
      livestock; from fisheries 44s; woodland, 5 pigs.
The total value is and was £12; before 1066 £16.
This manor was and is of the lordship of the Church of Ely.

TERRA SCI EADMVNDI.

.VI. **A**BBAS de S Eadmundo ten in.II'. hund de Ely in
Merche.XVI.aĉs.Tra.ē dim car.7 ibi.ē cū.III'.bord.
p̄tū.IIII.car.Silua.IIII.porc.Val 7 ualuit sēp.III.sol.
7 jacet 7 jacuit sēp in dūio æcclæ S Eadmundi.
In Wisbece hī isd abb.I.piscatorē redd.v.mil anguill.
In Sahā ten ipse abb.VI.acras træ.Ibi.ē un piscator
hūs.I.sagenā in Lacu ejd uillæ.Val 7 ualuit.IIII.sol.T.R.E.
.v.sol.H tra jacet 7 jacuit sēp in æccla S Eadmundi.

192 c

VII. **A**BBAS **TERRA ÆCCLÆ DE RAMESYG.** *IN STOV HVND.*
de Ramesy ten in Brone.I.hid.7 II.mili
tes ten de eo.Tra.ē.I.car.Ibi.II.bord.p̄tū.I.car.
Val 7 ualuit sēp.X.sol.7 jacet 7 jacuit sēp in æccla S
Benedicti de Ramesy.7 ē Bereuu de Stou.
ⓜ In *Stov* ten Wido sub abbe ipso.II.hid.Tra.ē.v.
car.In dūio.II.car sunt.7 v.uilli 7 vI.bord.cū.III.
car.Ibi.I.cot.7 p̄tū.II.car.Pasta ad pecun uillæ.
Nem ad sepes 7 domos.Int totū ual.L.sol.Qdo recep̄.
IIII.lib.T.R.E.vI.lib.Hoc ⓜ jacet 7 jacuit in dūio
æcclæ S Benedicti de Ramesy. *IN PAPEWORD HVND.*
ⓜ *Gravelei* ten abb de Ramesy.Ibi.v.hid.Tra.VII.
car.In dūio.II.hid 7 dim.7 ibi suɴ.II.car.Ibi.VIII.
uilli 7 VIII.bord.cū.v.car.Ibi.IIII.serui.Nem ad sepes.
7 domos.Val 7 ualuit.vI.lib.T.R.E.VIII.lib.Hoc ⓜ
jacet 7 jacuit sēp in æccla S Benedicti.

6   LAND OF SAINT EDMUND

In the Two Hundreds of ELY

[E1]
1   The Abbot of St. Edmund's holds 16 acres in MARCH. Land for
½ plough; it is there, with
     3 smallholders.
     Meadow for 4 ploughs or oxen; woodland, 4 pigs.
     The value is and always was 3s.
     It lies and always lay in the lordship of St. Edmund's Church.

[E2]
2   In WISBECH the Abbot also has 1 fisherman who pays 5,000 eels.

[In STAPLOE Hundred]
3   In SOHAM the Abbot holds 6 acres of land himself.
     1 fisherman who has 1 fishing-net in the village mere.
     The value is and was 4s; before 1066, 5s.
     This land lies and always lay in the lordship of St. Edmund's
Church.

7   LAND OF RAMSEY CHURCH   192 c

In LONGSTOW Hundred
1   The Abbot of Ramsey holds 1 hide in BOURN; 2 men-at-arms
hold from him. Land for 1 plough.
     2 smallholders.
     Meadow for 1 plough.
     The value is and always was 10s.
     It lies and always lay in (the lands of) St. Benedict's
Church, Ramsey; it is an outlier of Longstowe.

2 M. In LONGSTOWE Guy holds 2 hides under the Abbot. Land for
5 ploughs. In lordship 2 ploughs;
     5 villagers and 6 smallholders with 3 ploughs.
       1 cottager;
     meadow for 2 ploughs; pasture for the village livestock;
       wood for fences and houses.
In total, value 50s; when acquired £4; before 1066 £6.
     This manor lies and lay in the lordship of St. Benedict's
Church, Ramsey.

In PAPWORTH Hundred
3 M. The Abbot of Ramsey holds GRAVELEY. 5 hides. Land for
7 ploughs. In lordship 2½ hides; 2 ploughs there.
     8 villagers and 8 smallholders with 5 ploughs.
     4 slaves; wood for fences and houses.
     The value is and was £6; before 1066 £8.
     This manor lies and always lay in (the lands of) St. Benedict's
Church.

ᴍ *ELESWORDE* ten abb de Rameſy . Ibi . ıx . hıd . 7 ı . uirg.
7 v . ac . Tra . ē . xxıı . car . In dnio . ıııı . hidæ . 7 ibi . ııı . car.
7 ıııı . pot fieri . lbi . xıx . uilli . 7 xvıı . bord 7 ı . franc
hns . ııı . uirg . Hi ſimul . xvıııı . car hnt . Ibi . v . cot.
ptu . ıııı . car . 7 ıııı . ſerui . Paſta ad pec uillæ . Nem ad
domos curiæ . In totis ualent ual . xvı . lib . Qdo recep:
xıııı . lib . T.R.E: xx . lib . Hoc ᴍ jacuit ſep 7 jacet in
dnio æcclæ S Benedicti.

ᴍ *CHENEPEWELLE* ten abb S Benedicti . Ibi . v . hide.
Tra . ē . vııı . car . In dnio . ı . hida 7 dim . 7 ibi ſuɴ . ıı . car.
Ibi . vııı . uilli . 7 ıııı . ſochi hntes . ı . hid 7 dim . 7 ıııı . bord
qſq̸ de . v . acris . Ibi . ıııı . cot . 7 ıııı . ſerui . Nem ad ſepes.
ptu . ıı . car . In totis ualent ual 7 ualuit . vı . lib . T.R.E:
vııı . lib . Hoc ᴍ jacet 7 jacuit ſep in dnio æcclæ S Bened.
Supdicti . ıııı ſochi tra ſuã potuer dare 7 uende . T.R.E.
abſq̸ lictia abbis . ſed Soca abbi remãſit.
Iu Bocheſuuorde ten iſd abb dim hid . Tra . ē dim car.
ptu dim car . Val 7 ualuit . ıııı . ſol . H tra jacet 7 jacuit
in dnio æcclæ.
In Draitone ten iſd abb . ııı . uirg . Tra . ē . ıııı . bob . 7 ibi
ſuɴ . ptu . ıııı . bob . Ibi . ıı . ſerui . Val 7 ualuit ſep . ııı . ſol.
H tra jacet 7 jacuit ſep in dnio æcclæ.

ᴍ *OVRE* ten abb de Rameſy . Ibi . x . hidæ . 7 ııı . uirg.
Tra ē x . car 7 dim . In dnio . vı . hidæ . 7 ibi . ē . ı . car.
7 altera pot fieri . Ibi . xıııı . uilli . 7 ıı . bord . 7 ııı . cot
cũ . vı . car . 7 adhuc . ıı . car 7 dim poſs fieri . Ibi . ıı . ſerui.
ptu . x . car 7 dim . Paſta ad pecun uillæ . De mareſch.
vı . ſol 7 ıııı . den . In totis ualent ual . vııı . lib . Qdo recep:
192 d
vı . lib . T.R.E: x . lib . Hoc ᴍ jacet 7 jacuit ſep in
dnio æcclæ S Benedicti.

4 M. The Abbot of Ramsey holds ELSWORTH. 9 hides, 1 virgate and
5 acres. Land for 22 ploughs. In lordship 4 hides; 3 ploughs
there; a fourth possible.
19 villagers, 17 smallholders and 1 Frenchman who has
3 virgates; together they have 18 ploughs.
5 cottagers.
Meadow for 4 ploughs; 4 slaves; pasture for the village
livestock; wood for the court's houses.
Total value £16; when acquired £14; before 1066 £20.
This manor always lay and lies in the lordship of St. Benedict's
Church.

5 M. The Abbot of St. Benedict's holds KNAPWELL. 5 hides. Land for
8 ploughs. In lordship 1½ hides; 2 ploughs there.
8 villagers and 4 Freemen, who have 1½ hides; 4 smallholders
with 5 acres each. 4 cottagers; 4 slaves.
Wood for fences; meadow for 2 ploughs.
The total value is and was £6; before 1066 £8.
This manor lies and always lay in the lordship of St. Benedict's
Church. Before 1066 the said 4 Freemen could grant and sell
their land without the Abbot's permission, but the jurisdiction
remained with the Abbot.

6 In BOXWORTH the Abbot also holds ½ hide. Land for ½ plough.
Meadow for ½ plough.
The value is and was 4s.
This land lies and lay in the Church's lordship.

7 In (Fen) DRAYTON the Abbot also holds 3 virgates. Land for 4 oxen;
they are there.
Meadow for 4 oxen.
2 slaves.
The value is and always was 3s.
This land lies and always lay in the Church's lordship.

8 M. The Abbot of Ramsey holds OVER. 10 hides and 3 virgates.
Land for 10½ ploughs. In lordship 6 hides; 1 plough there;
a second possible.
14 villagers, 2 smallholders and 3 cottagers with 6 ploughs;
a further 2½ ploughs possible.
2 slaves; meadow for 10½ ploughs; pasture for the village
livestock; from the marsh 6s 4d.
Total value £8; when acquired £6; before 1066 £10.   192 d
This manor lies and always lay in the lordship of St. Benedict's
Church.

Ƕ *BVREWELLE* ten abb de Ramesy. Ibi . x . hid 7 i. uirg.

Tra . e . xvi . car . In dnio . iii . hide 7 xl . ac . 7 ibi . iiii .

car . Ibi . xl.ii . uitti 7 dim. cu . xii . car . Ibi . viii . ſerui .

ptu . x . car . Paſta ad pecun uille. 7 ii . molini . de . vi .

ſot 7 viii . den . In totis ualent uat 7 ualuit . xvi . lib .

T.R.E. xx. lib . Hoc Ƕ jacet 7 jacuit ſep in dnio æcclæ

S Benedicti.   *IN NORESTOV HVND.*

GRETONE ten abb de Ramesy . Ibi . viii . hidæ. 7 ii .

uirg 7 dim. Tra. e . vi . car . In dnio . iii . hide. 7 ibi. e

una car . 7 alia pot fieri . Ibi . vii . uitti 7 vi . bord

cu . iiii . car . Ibi . ii . ſerui . Ptu . vi . car . In totis ua

lent uat . iiii . lib . Qdo recep. vi . lib . T.R.E. viii . lib .

Hoc Ƕ jacet 7 jacuit in æccta S Benedicti .

In duobz Hund de Ely . ten abb de Ramesy in Cetriz

iii . hid. dim uirg min . Tra . e . iiii . car . In dnio . i . hida

7 dim. 7 ibi. e . i . car. 7 x . uitti 7 v . bord cu . iii . car .[^7.ii.ſerui]

Ptu . iiii . car . Silua . c . porc . De piſcar . iii . mit anguitt .

De pſentat . xxvii . den . Vat . lx . ſot . Qdo recep. xx .

ſot . T.R.E. iiii . lib . H tra jacet 7 jacuit in eccta S Bened .

In Wiſbece ht abb de Rameſi . viii . piſcatores . redd

v . mit 7 cc.lx . anguitt .

VIII.   TERRA ECCLE DE TORNYG. *IN.* ii. HVND DE ELY.

Abbas de Torny . ten In *WITESIE* . iiii . hid . Tra

e . vi . car . In dnio . ii . hid. 7 ibi . ii . car . 7 xvi . uitti

qſq . viii . acs . 7 vi . cot cu . iiii . car . Ibi . i . ſeruus . Ptu

vi . car . Paſta ad pecun uillæ . De gurgit . iiii . ſot .

7 de piſcib pt hoc . xx . ſot . In totis ualent uat . vi .

lib . Qdo recep. xx . ſot . T.R.E. vii . lib . Hoc Ƕ jacuit

7 jacet in dnio ecclæ de Torny . ſed Soca ht abb de Ely .

In STAPLOE Hundred
9 M. The Abbot of Ramsey holds BURWELL. 10 hides and 1 virgate.
Land for 16 ploughs. In lordship 3 hides and 40 acres; 4 ploughs
there.
    42½ villagers with 12 ploughs.
    8 slaves; meadow for 10 ploughs; pasture for the village livestock;
      2 mills at 6s 8d.
The total value is and was £16; before 1066 £20.
This manor lies and always lay in the lordship of St. Benedict's
Church.

In NORTHSTOW Hundred
10   The Abbot of Ramsey holds GIRTON. 8 hides and 2½ virgates.
Land for 6 ploughs. In lordship 3 hides; 1 plough there;
a second possible.
    7 villagers and 6 smallholders with 4 ploughs.
    2 slaves; meadow for 6 ploughs.
Total value £4; when acquired £6; before 1066 £8.
This manor lies and lay in (the lands of) St. Benedict's Church.

In the Two Hundreds of ELY
[E1]
11   The Abbot of Ramsey holds 3 hides less ½ virgate in CHATTERIS.
Land for 4 ploughs. In lordship 1½ hides; 1 plough there;
    10 villagers and 5 smallholders with 3 ploughs;
      2 slaves.
    Meadow for 4 ploughs; woodland, 100 pigs; from fisheries
      3,000 eels; from presentations 27d.
Value 60s; when acquired 20s; before 1066 £4.
This land lies and lay in (the lands of) St. Benedict's Church.

[E2]
12   In WISBECH the Abbot of Ramsey has 8 fishermen who pay 5,260 eels.

8   LAND OF THORNEY CHURCH

In the Two Hundreds of ELY
[E1]
1   The Abbot of THORNEY holds 4 hides in WHITTLESEY. Land for
6 ploughs. In lordship 2 hides; 2 ploughs there;
    16 villagers, 18 acres each; 6 cottagers with 4 ploughs.
    1 slave; meadow for 6 ploughs; pasture for the village livestock;
      from the weir 4s and besides this 20s from fish.
Total value £6; when acquired 20s; before 1066 £7.
This manor lay and lies in the lordship of the Church of Thorney.
but the Abbot of Ely has the jurisdiction.

.IX. Abbas de Croilant ten In *Hochinton*. vii . hid

7 dim̅ . Tra . e̅ . viii . car̅ . In dn̅io . iiii . hid̅ . 7 ibi fuṅ . ii .

car̅ . Ibi . xiiii . uiłłi . 7 iii . bord̅ cū . vi . car̅ . Ibi . iiii . cot̅ .

7 iii . ſerui . P̊tū . ii . car̅ . In totis ualent̅ ual 7 ualuit

vi . lib̅ . T.R.E. viii . lib̅ . Hoc m̅ fuit 7 e̅ in dn̅io æcclæ S Guth ᵍˡᵃᶜⁱ·

m̅ *Coteha* ten ab̅b̅ de Croiland . *In Cestretone Hd.*

Ibi . xi . hidæ . Tra . e̅ . viii . car̅ . In dn̅io . vi . hidæ . 7 ibi . e̅

una car̅ . 7 altera pot fieri . Ibi . xii . uiłłi 7 viii . bord̅

cū . vi . car̅ . Ibi . i . ſeru̅ . P̊tū . viii . car̅ . Paſt̅a ad pecuṅ

uillæ . De mareſch . q̇ngent̅ anguiłł . 7 de p̅ſentat

xii . den̅ . In totis ualent̅ ual 7 ualuit . vi . lib̅ . T.R.E.

viii . lib̅ . Hoc m̅ fuit ſe̅p 7 e̅ in dn̅io æcclæ S Gutlaci .

193 a

In Draitone ten ab̅b̅ de Croiland . vii . hid̅ 7 dim̅ . Tra

e̅ . vi . car̅ . In dn̅io . iiii . hidæ 7 iii . uirg̅ . 7 ibi . i . car̅ . 7 alta

pot fieri . Ibi . xi . uiłłi 7 v . bord̅ . cū . iii . car̅ . 7 iiii . ᵗᵃ pot fieri .

Ibi . iiii . cot̅ . p̊tū : ii . car̅ . Val : ⁷ ᵘᵃˡᵘⁱᵗ iiii : lib̅ 7 x . ſol . T.R.E. c . ſol .

H̅ tra jacet 7 jacuit in dn̅io æcclæ S Guthlaci . *In* ᶠˡᵗ̅ *Hvnd*

In Wiſbece h̅t ab̅b̅ de Croilant . iii . piſcat̅ redd̅ . iiii .

.X. mił anguiłł . TERRA SC̅I WANDREGISILI.

Abbas s̅ Wandregiſili *In Radefelle Hvnd*

ten de rege . *Dvllingeha̅* . Ibi . vi . hide . Tra . e̅ . xii .

car̅ . In dn̅io . iii . hide . 7 ibi . iii . car̅ . Ibi . xvii . uiłłi

7 x . bord̅ . cū . ix . car̅ . Ibi : ii . ſeru̅ . 7 p̊tū . i . car̅ . Silua

c . porc̅ . Paſt̅a ad pecuṅ . In totis ualent̅ ual . xii . lib̅ .

Q̇do recep̅ . xv . lib̅ . T.R.E. xv : lib̅ . Hanc tra̅ Algar̅

com tenuit .

9   LAND OF CROWLAND CHURCH

In NORTHSTOW Hundred
1   The Abbot of Crowland holds 7½ hides in OAKINGTON. Land for
     8 ploughs. In lordship 4 hides; 2 ploughs there.
         14 villagers and 3 smallholders with 6 ploughs.
             4 cottagers; 3 slaves.
         Meadow for 2 ploughs.
     The total value is and was £6; before 1066 £8.
     This manor was and is in the lordship of St. Guthlac's Church.

In CHESTERTON Hundred
2 M. The Abbot of Crowland holds COTTENHAM. 11 hides. Land for
     8 ploughs. In lordship 6 hides; 1 plough there; a second possible.
         12 villagers and 8 smallholders with 6 ploughs.
             1 slave; meadow for 8 ploughs; pasture for the village livestock;
             from the marsh 500 eels; from presentations 12d.
     The total value is and was £6; before 1066 £8.
     This manor always was and is in the lordship of St. Guthlac's
     Church.

3   The Abbot of Crowland holds 7½ hides in (Dry) DRAYTON.   193 a
     Land for 6 ploughs. In lordship 4 hides and 3 virgates;
     1 plough there; a second possible.
         11 villagers and 5 smallholders with 3 ploughs; a fourth possible.
             4 cottagers.
         Meadow for 2 ploughs.
     The value is and was £3 10s; before 1066, 100s.
     This land lies and lay in the lordship of St. Guthlac's Church.

In ELY Hundred
     [E1]
4   In WISBECH the Abbot of Crowland has 3 fishermen who pay 4,000 eels.

10   LAND OF ST. WANDRILLE'S

In RADFIELD Hundred
1   The Abbot of St. Wandrille's holds DULLINGHAM from the King.
     6 hides. Land for 12 ploughs. In lordship 3 hides; 3 ploughs there.
         17 villagers and 10 smallholders with 9 ploughs.
             2 slaves; meadow for 1 plough; woodland, 100 pigs; pasture
             for the livestock.
     Total value £12; when acquired £15; before 1066 £15.
         Earl Algar held this land.

TERRA ÆCCLÆ DE CETRIZ.

Abbatissa de CIETRIZ teñ de rege *IN ŘEPESLAV·HVNĎ.*
in *FOXETVNE* ꞉v꞉hid 7 xl ꞉ acs . Tra . e͂꞉viii . car.

In dn͂io꞉i . hida 7 xl . ac͂꞉7 ibi funt . ii . car . Ibi . xvi . uilli
7 xi . borđ . cu͂ . vi . car . Ibi dim molin͂ . de x . fol 7 viii^{to}.
den͂ . p͂tu͂ om͂ib car . Val 7 ualuit . vi . liƀ . T.R.E.꞉vii . liƀ.
H͂ tra jacuit sep 7 jacet in dn͂io æcclæ. *IN STAPLEHOV*
In Buruuella teñ moniales de cietriz . dim^{cecelie}   ꞁ *HVNĎ.*
hid͂ . Tra dim car͂ . 7 ibi . e͂ . P͂tu͂ . ii . bob . Val 7 ualuit sep
x . fol . H͂ tra fuit 7 e͂ de dn͂io æcclæ. *IN WEDRELAI.*
In Barentone teñ æccla de Cietriz . ii . hid͂ .   ꞁ *HVNĎ.*
Tra . e͂ . iii . car . In dn͂io . i . hida . 7 ibi . i . car . Ibi . viii .
borđ . 7 v . cot cu͂ . ii . car . Ibi . iii . ferui . 7 i . molin͂ . xxv .
fol . 7 iiii . den͂ . P͂tu͂ . iii . car . Val 7 ualuit . iii . liƀ ꞉ T.R.E.꞉
iiii . liƀ . H͂ tra jacuit 7 jacet in dn͂io æcclæ de Cietriz.
In Efceprid teñ ead æccla . i . hid͂ 7 i . uirg 7 dim͂ .
Tra . e͂ . i . car 7 dim . In·dn͂io dim hida . 7 ibi dim car .
Ibi . i . uilts 7 . iii . borđ 7 iiii . cot^{or} . cu͂ . i . car . Ibi . i . feru͂ .
7 i . molin͂ de . v . folid . 7 iiii . den͂ . P͂tu͂ . i . car 7 dim .
Val 7 ualuit . xxx . fol . T.R.E.꞉ xl . fol . H͂ tra jacet
7 jacuit sep in æcclæ dn͂io de Cietriz.
In Oreuuelle teñ ead æccla . iiii^{ta} . part uni͂ uirg .
Tra . e͂ dim boui . 7 ual xii . den͂ ꞉ Ad æcclam^{seper}͂ptinuit.
In Oure teñ ead æccla . i . hida͂ . Tra . e͂ . i . car . 7 ibi . e͂ .
cu͂ . iiii . uiltis . P͂tu͂ . i . car . Pafta ad pec . Val 7 ualuit
xvi . fol . H͂ tra jacuit sep 7 jacet in dn͂io æcclæ^{cietriz.} de

In THRIPLOW Hundred
1 The Abbess of Chatteris holds 5 hides and 40 acres from the King in FOXTON. Land for 8 ploughs. In lordship 1 hide and 40 acres; 2 ploughs there.
   16 villagers and 11 smallholders with 6 ploughs.
   ½ mill at 10s 8d; meadow for all the ploughs.
   The value is and was £6; before 1066 £7.
   This land always lay and lies in the Church's lordship.

In STAPLOE Hundred
2 In BURWELL the nuns of Chatteris Church hold ½ hide. Land for ½ plough; it is there.
   Meadow for 2 oxen.
   The value is and always was 10s.
   This land was and is of the Church's lordship.

In WETHERLEY Hundred
3 In BARRINGTON Chatteris Church holds 2 hides. Land for 3 ploughs. In lordship 1 hide; 1 plough there.
   8 smallholders and 5 cottagers with 2 ploughs.
   3 slaves; 1 mill, 25s 4d; meadow for 3 ploughs.
   The value is and was £3; before 1066 £4.
   This land lay and lies in the lordship of Chatteris Church.

4 In SHEPRETH the Church also holds 1 hide and 1½ virgates. Land for 1½ ploughs. In lordship ½ hide; ½ plough there.
   1 villager, 3 smallholders and 4 cottagers with 1 plough.
   1 slave; 1 mill at 5s 4d; meadow for 1½ ploughs.
   The value is and was 30s; before 1066, 40s.
   This land lies and always lay in the lordship of Chatteris Church.

5 In ORWELL the Church also holds the fourth part of 1 virgate. Land for ½ ox.
   Value 12d.
   It always belonged to the Church.

[In PAPWORTH Hundred]
6 In OVER the Church also holds 1 hide. Land for 1 plough; it is there, with
   4 villagers.
   Meadow for 1 plough; pasture for the livestock.
   The value is and was 16s.
   This land always lay and lies in the lordship of Chatteris Church.

.XII.   COMES MORITON: *IN WITELESFORD HD̃.*

Comes Moritonienſis ten.ii.hiđ in Salſiton.7 abb
de Greſtain de eo: Tra.e̅.iii.car.In dn̅io.e̅ una.7 vi.
uilli 7 iii.borđ hn̅t.ii.car.Ibi.i.molin.xxvi.ſol.7 ii.deñ.
P̃tũ.iii.car.Val 7 ualuit ſep:vi.lib.Hanc tr̅a tenuit
Orgar ſub Haroldo comite.7 cui uoluit dare potuit.

In Bertone ten Robt de comite *IN WEDERLAI.HD̃.*
:i.hiđ.Tra.e̅.i.car.7 ibi.e̅ cũ.ii.borđ 7 i.ſeruo.P̃tũ
.i.car.Val 7 ualuit.xl.ſol.T.R.E:l.ſol.Hanc tr̅a
tenuit Judichel uenator.E.R.7 cui uoluit dare pot.

In Granteſeta ten iſđ Robt de com.i.uirg.Tra.e̅.iiii.
bob.7 ibi ſunt.p̃tũ.ii:bob.Val 7 ualuit.v.ſol.Hanc
tr̅a tenuit Judichel uenator.7 cui uoluit dare potuit.

In Gretone ten Morin de comite *IN NORESTOV HD̃.*
ii.hiđ 7 dim.7 dim uirg.Tra.e̅.ii.car 7 dim.In dn̅io
eſt.i.car.7 dim poteſt fieri.Ibi.i.uills.7 v.borđ.7 iii.
cot cu.i.car.P̃tũ.i.car.Val 7 ualuit.xl.ſol.T.R.E:
iiii.lib.Hanc tr̅a tenuit Judichel.7 cui uoluit uenđe pot.

In Hiſtone ten Morin de comite *IN CESTRETONE HD̃.*
.i.uirg 7 x.ac̅s.H̅ tra app̃ciata.e̅ in Gretone.

XIII.   TERRA ROGERIJ COMITIS *IN ERNINGFORD HVND'*

Rogerivs Comes ten In Mordune.i.hiđ 7 iiii.
parte:i.uirg.Tra.e̅.ii.car.In dn̅io dim hida.7 iiii.
pars.i.uirg.7 ibi.e̅.i.car.7 vi:borđ cũ.i.car.P̃tũ.ii:
car.Paſta ad pec uillæ:Val 7 ualuit.xl.ſol.T.R.E:
l.ſol.Hanc tr̅a tenuit Goda de Algaro.7 potuit dare

LAND OF THE COUNT OF MORTAIN

In WHITTLESFORD Hundred

1 The Count of Mortain holds 2 hides in SAWSTON, and the Abbot of
   Grestain from him. Land for 3 ploughs. In lordship 1;
      6 villagers and 3 smallholders have 2 ploughs.
      1 mill, 26s 2d; meadow for 3 ploughs.
   The value is and always was £6.
      Ordgar held this land under Earl Harold; he could grant to
   whom he would.

In WETHERLEY Hundred

2 In BARTON Robert holds 1 hide from the Count. Land for 1 plough;
   it is there, with
      2 smallholders; 1 slave.
      Meadow for 1 plough.
   The value is and was 40s; before 1066, 50s.
      Judicael, King Edward's Huntsman, held this land; he could
   grant to whom he would.

3 In GRANTCHESTER Robert also holds 1 virgate from the Count.
   Land for 4 oxen; they are there, with
      1 villager.
      Meadow for 2 oxen.
   The value is and was 5s.
      Judicael the Huntsman held this land; he could grant to
   whom he would.

In NORTHSTOW Hundred

4 In GIRTON Morin holds 2½ hides and ½ virgate from the Count.
   Land for 2½ ploughs. In lordship 1 plough; [another] ½ possible.
      1 villager, 5 smallholders and 3 cottagers with 1 plough.
      Meadow for 1 plough.
   The value is and was 40s; before 1066 £4.
      Judicael held this land; he could sell to whom he would.

In CHESTERTON Hundred

5 In HISTON Morin holds 1 virgate and 10 acres from the Count.
      This land is assessed in Girton.

13 LAND OF EARL ROGER

In ARMINGFORD Hundred

1 Earl Roger holds 1 hide and the fourth part of 1 virgate in
   (Steeple) MORDEN. Land for 2 ploughs. In lordship ½ hide
   and the fourth part of 1 virgate; 1 plough there;
      6 smallholders with 1 plough.
      Meadow for 2 ploughs; pasture for the village livestock.
   The value is and was 40s; before 1066, 50s.
      Goda held this land from Earl Algar; she could grant to whom
   she would.

In alia Mordune ten̄ dim̄ hid̄ 7 dim̄ uirḡ.Tra̅.e̅.I.car̄.

7 II.bob̄.In dn̄io.I.uirḡ træ.7 ibi suŋ.II.boues.Ibi.IIII.

bord̄.cū.I.car̄.P̄tū.I.car̄.Val̄ 7 ualuit sēp.xx.fol̄.

Hanc trā tenuit Goda fub Algaro.7 p̄tinet ad Scelgei.

De hac trā occupauit Harduin de Scalers.IIII.ac̄s.

fup comite.ut hund̄ teftat̄.

In Crauuedene ten comes.R.III.uirḡ træ.Tra̅.e̅.VI.

bob̄.7 p̄tū totid̄ bob̄.Val̄ 7 ualuit sēp.x.fol̄.Hanc trā

tenuit Almar hō Wallef comitis.7 uende potuit.

SCELGEI ten Rog comes.p.V.hid̄ fe defd̄.Trā.e̅

VI.car̄,In dn̄io.III.hidæ.7 ibi funt.II.car̄.Ibi.XI.bord̄.

7 VII.cot cū.IIII.car̄.7 I.molin̄ de.x.fol̄.P̄tū.VI.car̄.

7 de reddita p̄ti.II.fol̄.Pafta ad pec uillæ.In totis

ualent ual̄ 7 ualuit.VII.lib̄.T.R.E.XIIII.lib̄.Hanc

trā tenuit Goda fub Algaro.

In Abintone ten com̄ Rog.I.uirḡ træ quæ jacet in

Scelgei fuo p̄po M̄.Val̄ 7 ualuit sēp XIII.fol̄ 7 IIII.den̄.

Hanc trā tenuit Goda fub Algaro comite.

193 c

In Melrede ten abb̄ de S Ebrulfo de com̄ Rogerio

II.hid̄.Tra̅.e̅.V.car̄.In dn̄io.II.car̄.7 V.uilli 7 III.bord̄.

cū.III.car̄.Ibi.II.ferui.7 II.molini de.XV.fol̄ 7 IIII.den̄.

P̄tū.II.car̄.Int totū ual̄.VI.lib̄.Q̄do recep̄.XL.fol̄.

T.R.E.VIII.lib̄.Hanc trā Goda fub Algaro.pot uende.

In Melleburne ten ift̄ abb̄ de comite R.dim̄ hid̄.

IIII.part uni uirḡ min̄.Tra̅.e̅ dim̄ car̄.7 ibi.e̅ cū.I.

uillo.p̄tū dim̄ car̄.Val̄ 7 ualuit sēp.V.fol̄.Hanc

tra Goda tenuit de Algaro.7 uende potuit.

In Orduuelle ten.R.comes.I.hid̄ 7 I.uirḡ.7 III.

part uni uirḡ.Tra̅.e̅.I.car̄ 7 dim̄.In dn̄io dim̄ hida

7 ibi dim̄ car̄.7 II.uilli 7 III.bord̄ cū.I.car̄.Ibi un̄

2 In the other (Guilden) MORDEN Earl Roger holds ½ hide and
½ virgate. Land for 1 plough and 2 oxen. In lordship 1 virgate of
land; 2 oxen there.
    4 smallholders with 1 plough.
    Meadow for 1 plough.
The value is and always was 20s.
    Goda held this land under Earl Algar; it belongs to Shingay.
Hardwin of Scales appropriated 4 acres of this land in the Earl's
despite, as the Hundred testifies.

3 In CROYDON Earl Roger holds 3 virgates of land. Land for 6 oxen;
    pasture for as many oxen.
The value is and always was 10s.
    Aelmer, Earl Waltheof's man, held this land; he could sell.

4 Earl Roger holds SHINGAY. It answers for 5 hides. Land for
6 ploughs. In lordship 3 hides; 2 ploughs there.
    11 smallholders and 7 cottagers with 4 ploughs;
    1 mill at 10s; meadow for 6 ploughs; from the payments of the
        meadow 2s; pasture for the village livestock.
The total value is and was £7; before 1066 £14.
    Goda held this land under Earl Algar.

5 In ABINGTON (Pigotts) Earl Roger holds 1 virgate of land which lies
in his own manor of Shingay.
The value is and always was 13s 4d.
    Goda held this land under Earl Algar.

6 In MELDRETH the Abbot of St. Evroul holds 2 hides from   193 c
Earl Roger. Land for 5 ploughs. In lordship 2 ploughs;
    5 villagers and 3 smallholders with 3 ploughs.
    2 slaves; 2 mills at 15s 4d; meadow for 2 ploughs.
Total value £6; when acquired 40s; before 1066 £8.
    Goda held this land under Earl Algar; she could sell.

7 In MELBOURN the Abbot also holds from Earl Roger ½ hide less the
fourth part of 1 virgate. Land for ½ plough; it is there, with
    1 villager.
    Meadow for ½ plough.
The value is and always was 5s.
    Goda held this land from Earl Algar; she could sell.

[In WETHERLEY Hundred]
8 In ORWELL Earl Roger holds 1 hide and 1 virgate and the third part
of 1 virgate. Land for 1½ ploughs. In lordship ½ hide; ½ plough
there;
    2 villagers and 3 smallholders with 1 plough.

feruus.7 ptū.ı.car.7 nem ad fepes reficiendas.

Vaɫ.xx.foɫ.Qdo recep:xxx.foɫ.T.R.E.ʹL.folid.

Hanc trā tenueꞃ.vı.fochi.7 dare 7 uendē trā.fuā

potueꞃ.Vn eoꝗ hō regis.E.fuit.7 inuuardū inuenit

uicecomiti.Tres iftoꝗ fochoꝗ accōmodauit picot

Rogerio comiti.ppꞇ placita fua tenenda.fꝗ poftea

occupaueꞃ eos hēes comitis 7 retinueꞃ cū tris fuis:

fine libatore.7 rex inde feruitiū n̄ habuit nec hꞇ.

fic ipfe uicecomes dicit.

In Werateuuorde ten Comes.ıı.hiđ.7 ıı.part uni

uirg.Tra.ē.ııı.caꞃ.In dn̄io.ı.hida 7 ıı.part.ı.uirg.

7 dim caꞃ ē ibi.7 alia dim pot fieri.Ibi.ıı.cot 7 xv.

borđ cū.ıı.caꞃ.Ibi.ıı.ferui.7 ptū.ıı.caꞃ.Vaɫ 7 ua

luit.xL.foɫ.T.R.E.ʹLx.foɫ.Hanc trā tenueꞃ.vı.fochi.

7 cui uolueꞃ trā fuā uendē potueꞃ.

In Witeuuelle ten R.cōm.ı.uirg træ.7 ııı.part

uni uirg.Tra.ē.ıııı.bob.Vaɫ 7 ualuit.ıı.foɫ.Hanc

trā.ııı.fochi tenueꞃ.7 cui uolueꞃ uendē potueꞃ.

ᛗ In ERNINGTVNE ten Rog cōm.ııı.hiđ 7 dim.

Tra.ē.vııı.caꞃ.In dn̄io.ıı.hidæ.7 ibi fuꝫ.ıı.caꞃ.

7 ıııı.pot fieri.Ibi.vı.uiɫɫi 7 vı.cot.cū.ıııı.caꞃ.

Ibi.ııı.ferui.7 ptū.ıı.caꞃ.7 nem ad fepes.Int totū

uaɫ.ıx.liɓ.Qdo recep:x.liɓ.T.R.E.ʹxı.liɓ.Hoc

ᛗ tenuit Aluric teign.R.E.7 ibi fueꞃ.ııı.fochi

un eoꝗ hō Wallef cōm.7 alt hō abɓis de Elẏ.7 ııı.

hō Robti.f.Wimarc.7 recedē potueꞃ quo uolueꞃ.

In Chingeftone ten comes.ıı.part IN STOV HD.

uni uirg.Tra.ē.ıı.bob.Vaɫ 7 ualuit.ıı.foɫ.Hanc

trā tenuit Almar hō Wallef cōm.7 dare po

tuit cui uoluit.

1 slave; meadow for 1 plough; wood for repairing fences. Value 20s; when acquired 30s; before 1066, 50s.

6 Freemen held this land; they could grant and sell their land. One of them was King Edward's man; he found escort for the Sheriff. Picot lent 3 of these men to Earl Roger for holding his pleas, but afterwards the Earl's men appropriated them and retained them with their lands, without a deliverer; the King has not had, nor has, any service thence, as the Sheriff himself says.

9 In WRATWORTH the Earl holds 2 hides and 2 parts of 1 virgate. Land for 3 ploughs. In lordship 1 hide and 2 parts of 1 virgate; ½ plough there; another ½ possible.

2 cottagers and 15 smallholders with 2 ploughs.

2 slaves; meadow for 2 ploughs.

The value is and was 40s; before 1066, 60s.

6 Freemen held this land; they could sell their land to whom they would.

10 In WHITWELL Earl Roger holds 1 virgate of land and the third part of 1 virgate. Land for 4 oxen.

The value is and was 2s.

3 Freemen held this land; they could sell to whom they would.

11 M. In ARRINGTON Earl Roger holds 3½ hides. Land for 8 ploughs. In lordship 2 hides; 3 ploughs there; a fourth possible.

6 villagers and 6 cottagers with 4 ploughs.

3 slaves; meadow for 2 ploughs; wood for fences.

Total value £9; when acquired £10; before 1066 £11.

Aelfric, King Edward's thane, held this manor. 3 Freemen were there; one of them was Earl Waltheof's man, the second the Abbot of Ely's man, and the third a man of Robert son of Wymarc; they could withdraw whither they would.

In LONGSTOW Hundred

12 In KINGSTON the Earl holds 2 parts of 1 virgate. Land for 2 oxen. The value is and was 2s.

Aelmer, Earl Waltheof's man, held this land; he could grant to whom he would.

.XII .II. TERRA ALANI COMITIS. *In Flamidinc Hvnd.*

Comes Alanvs ten In Fuleberne viii.hid.Tra.ē
xiii.car.In dnio.iiii.hidæ.7 ibi fuɳ.iii.car.7 adhuc
poſs fieri duæ.Ibi.xvi.uiłłi 7 x.bord cū viii.car.Ibi
iiii.ſerui.7 i.moliñ de xx.ſoł.P̄tū car.In totis ualent
uał 7 ualuit ſēp.xv.lib.Hoc ꟿ tenuit Goduiñ cilt
hō Eddeuæ pulchræ.ñ potuit recedere.

ꟿ *Hintone* ten Alan com.Ibi.vii.hidæ.Tra.ē xiii.
car.In dnio.iii.hidæ 7 dim.7 ibi fuɳ.iiii.car.Ibi.xix.
uiłłi 7 xxii.bord cū.ix.car.Ibi⹏iiii.ſerui.7 p̄tū.iii.car.
7 iiii.moliñ de xxv.ſoł.Paſta ad pec uillæ.7 iiii.ſocos.
De mareſc.xxv.den.7 de currib.vi.den.In totis ua
lent.uał 7 ualuit.xviii.lib.T.R.E.ʼxii.lib.Hoc ꟿ
tenuit Eddeue pulchra⹏7 ibi fuer.viii.ſochi.qui.ii.
Aueras 7.iiii.ineuuard inueniebant uicecomiti.

In Teureſhā ten.A.com.i.hid 7 dim.Tra.ē.ii.car.
ſed ñ ſunt ibi.H̄ tra.ē appciata cū Hintone ꟿ com.
Hanc tenuer.ii.ſochi hōes Eddeue.ñ potuer recede.
7 i.auerā 7 i.ineuuard inuen uicecomiti.

In ead uilla ten Robt de.A.com.i.hid.Tra.ē.i.car.
7 ibi.ē.7 p̄tū.i.car.Vał 7 ualuit ſēp.x.ſoł.Hanc tra
tenuer.v.hōes Eddeue.nec ab ea potuer recede.7 iii.
ineuuard inuen uicecomiti. *In Cildeford Hvnd.*

In Horſei ten.A.com.ii.hid 7 ii.uirg 7 dim.Tra.ē
v.car.7 ibi ſunt cū.viii.uiłłis 7 v.bord.Vał.c.ſoł.
Qdo recep.ʼiiii.lib.T.R.E.ʼc.ſoł.Hanc tra tenuit
Eddeua 7 ii.ſochi hōes ej.un inuen auerā.alt Ineuuard.

In ead uilla ten Aluuin de com.A.ūnā uirg tre.
Tra.ē.vi.bob.Ibi.ii.bord 7 Silua.xx.porc.Vał 7 ua
luit.v.ſoł.Hanc tra tenuit Goduiñ hō Eddeue.non
potuit recede.

193 d

In FLENDISH Hundred

1   Count Alan holds 8 hides in FULBOURN. Land for 13 ploughs.
In lordship 4 hides; 3 ploughs there; a further 2 possible.
      16 villagers and 10 smallholders with 8 ploughs.
      4 slaves; 1 mill at 20s; meadow for the ploughs.
The total value is and always was £15.
      Young Godwin, Edeva the Fair's man, held this manor; he could
not withdraw.

2 M. Count Alan holds (Cherry) HINTON. 7 hides. Land for 13 ploughs.
In lordship 3½ hides; 4 ploughs there.
      19 villagers and 22 smallholders with 9 ploughs.
      4 slaves; meadow for 3 ploughs; 4 mills at 25s; pasture for the
           village livestock; 4 ploughshares; from marshes 25d; from carts 6d.
The total value is and was £18; before 1066 £12.
      Edeva the Fair held this manor. 8 Freemen were there, who
·found 2 cartages and 4 escorts for the Sheriff.

3   In TEVERSHAM Count Alan holds 1½ hides. Land for 2 ploughs,
but they are not there.
      This land is assessed with the Count's manor of (Cherry) Hinton.
      2 Freemen, Edeva's men, held it; they could not withdraw from her;
they found 1 cartage and 1 escort for the Sheriff.

4   In the same village Robert holds 1 hide from Count Alan. Land
for 1 plough; it is there;
      meadow for 1 plough.
The value is and always was 10s.
      5 men of Edeva's held this land and could not withdraw from
her; they found 3 escorts for the Sheriff.

In CHILFORD Hundred

5   In HORSEHEATH Count Alan holds 2 hides and 2½ virgates. Land
for 5 ploughs; they are there, with
      8 villagers; 5 smallholders.
Value 100s; when acquired £4; before 1066, 100s.
      Edeva held this land. 2 Freemen, her men, [were there] ; one
found cartage, the other (found) escort.

6   In the same village Alwin holds 1 virgate of land from Count Alan.
Land for 6 oxen.
      2 smallholders;
      woodland, 20 pigs.
The value is and was 5s.
      Godwin, Edeva's man, held this land; he could not withdraw.

In Wicheham̃ ten̆.A.com.II.hid̃.Tra.ē.v.car̃.In dñio

★ .I.hid̃ 7 dim̃|7 IIII.uilti 7 IIII.bord̃ cū.III.car̃.Ibi.IIII.

ferui.7 p̃tū.II.car̃.Silua.c.porc̃.Int tot uat 7 ualuit

x.lib̃.T.R.E.′viii.lib̃.Hanc tr̃a tenuit Eddeua.7 ĩi.

foc̃hi hões ej.I.auer̃a 7 I.jneuuard̃ inuener̃.⌐XII.deñ.

Ibid̃.I.foc̃hs ten̄ fub comite.IIII.part uni uirg̃.Vat

I̊n Berchehã ten̆ Anfchitil de.A.com.III.hid̃.dim̃

uirg̃ min̄.Tra.ē.v.car̃.In dñio fuɲ.III|7 VI.uilti.

7 IIII.bord̃ cū.II.car̃.Ibi.VI.ferui.P̃tū.II.car̃.7 uñ

molin̄ de.v.fot.Int tot uat 7 ualuit.IX.lib̃.

I̊n ead̃ uilla ten̄ Morin̄ fub comite.I.hid̃ 7 dimid̃.

T̊ra.ē.III.car̃ 7 dim̃.In dñio funt.II.7 VI.uilti 7 II.

bord̃ cū.I.car̃ 7 dim̃.p̃tū.I.car̃.7 I.molin̄ de.II.fot.

194 a

Vat 7 ualuit.LX.fot.Has.II.tras tenuit Eddeua.

I̊n ead̃ uilla ten̄.I.foc̃hs.I.uirg̃ fub comite.Tra.ē.IIII.bob.

7 ibi funt.H̃ tra uat 7 ualuit.IIII.fot.Iftemet tenuit fub

Eddeua.7 inuen̄ ineuuardũ.

Ⓜ LINTONE.ten̆.A.com.Ibi.III.hid̃ 7 III.uirg̃.Tra.ē.VIII.

car̃.In dñio.II.hidæ.7 ibi fuɲ.III.car̃.Ibi xvi.uilti 7 v.

bord̃ cū.v.car̃.Ibi.VI.ferui.7 II.molin̄ de xvi.fot.P̃tū

II.car̃.Silua.xxx.porc̃.Int tot uat XII.lib̃.Qdo receb̃.

7 T.R.E.′xv.lib̃.Ibid̃ uñ foc̃hs ten̄.I.uirg̃ fub comite.

7 eft app̃ciata cū Lintone.Hanc tr̃a tenuit Eddeua.

7 ibi.I.foc̃hs fuit.q̃ inuen̄ Auer̃a uicecomiti.

I̊n Grentebrige h̃t.A.com.x.burgenfes.

Ⓜ Alĩa LINTONE ten̆.A.com.Ibi.II.hid̃ 7 dim̃.Tra.ē.v.

car̃.In dñio.I.hid̃ 7 dim̃.7 ibi.|II.car̃.Ibi.VIII.uilti.

7 II.bord̃,Ibi.IIII.ferui.7 I.molin̄ de.VIII.fot.P̃tū.I.car̃.

Silua.xx.porc̃.Int tot uat.VII.lib̃.Qdo receb̃.7 T.R.E.′

c.fot.Hoc Ⓜ tenuit Eddeua pulchra.

7   In (West) WICKHAM Count Alan holds 2 hides. Land for 5 ploughs.
In lordship 1½ hides; 2 ploughs there;
    4 villagers and 4 smallholders with 3 ploughs.
    4 slaves; meadow for 2 ploughs; woodland, 100 pigs.
The total value is and was £10; before 1066 £8.
    Edeva held this land. 2 Freemen, her men, [were there] ;
they found 1 cartage and 1 escort.
    There 1 Freeman also holds the fourth part of 1 virgate
under the Count; value 12d.

8   In BARHAM Ansketel holds 3 hides less ½ virgate from Count Alan.
Land for 5 ploughs. In lordship 3 ploughs;
    6 villagers and 4 smallholders with 2 ploughs.
    6 slaves; meadow for 2 ploughs; 1 mill at 5s.
The total value is and was £9.

9   In the same village Morin holds 1½ hides under the Count.
Land for 3½ ploughs. In lordship 2;
    6 villagers and 2 smallholders with 1½ ploughs.
    Meadow for 1 plough; 1 mill at 2s.
The value is and was 60s.   194 a
    Edeva held this two lands.

10   In the same village 1 Freeman holds 1 virgate under the Count.
Land for 4 oxen; they are there.
The value of this land is and was 4s.
    He himself held it under Edeva; he found escort.

11 M. Count Alan holds LINTON. 3 hides and 3 virgates. Land for
8 ploughs. In lordship 2 hides; 3 ploughs there.
    16 villagers and 5 smallholders with 5 ploughs.
    6 slaves; 2 mills at 16s; meadow for 2 ploughs; woodland, 30 pigs.
Total value £12; when acquired and before 1066 £15.
    There 1 Freeman also holds 1 virgate under the Count; it is
assessed with Linton. Edeva held this land; 1 Freeman was there,
who found cartage for the Sheriff.

12   In CAMBRIDGE Count Alan has 10 burgesses.

13 M. Count Alan holds the other (Little) LINTON. 2½ hides. Land for
5 ploughs. In lordship 1½ hides; 2 ploughs there.
    8 villagers and 2 smallholders with 3 ploughs.
    4 slaves; 1 mill at 8s; meadow for 1 plough; woodland, 20 pigs.
Total value £7; when acquired and before 1066, 100s.
    Edeva the Fair held this manor.

ⓂIpſe com̄ ten̄ Abintone.Ibi.v.hidæ.Tra.ē.viii.car̄.

In dn̄io.ii.hid 7 dim̄.7 ibi ſunt.iii.car̄.Ibi.xi.uilli.7 v.bord̄.

cū.v.car̄.Ibi.iiii.ſerui.7 i.mol̄ de.vi.ſol̄ 7 viii.denar̄.

P̄tū.ii.car̄.Silua.xx.porc̄.Int tot̄ ual̄ 7 ualuit.x.lib̄.

Hoc Ⓜ tenuit Eddeua.

In Badburgh ten̄ Brien ſub.A.comite.ii.hid̄ 7 dim̄.

7 xx.iiii.acs̄.Tra.ē.iiii.car̄.In dn̄io.ē una.7 xvii.uilli

7 iii.bord̄ cū.iii.car̄.Ibi.i.ſeru.7 p̄tū.iiii.bob.Valet

7 ualuit.l.ſol̄.Hanc tr̄a tenuer̄.vi.ſochi.ſub Eddeua.

n̄ potuer̄ recedē abſq̄ eȷ licentia.Hi.iiii.Aueras inue

ner̄.7 ii.Ineuuardos.

In ead uilla ten̄ Radulf ſub comite.i.hid̄ dim̄ uirg min̄.

Tra.ē.i.car̄.7 ibi.ē.P̄tū.i.car̄.7 iii.uilli 7 iii.bord̄.7 un̄

molin̄ de.v.ſol̄ 7 iiii.den̄.Val̄ 7 ualuit.xx.ſol̄.Hanc

tr̄a tenuit Alric p̄br ſub Eddeua.n̄ potuit recedē ab ea.

In Pampeſuuorde ten̄.ii.milit̄ ſub comite.i.hid̄ 7 xx

ii.acs̄.Tra ē.ii.car̄ 7 ii.bob̄.In dn̄io.i.car̄.7 ii.uilli

7 v.bord̄ cū.i.car̄.P̄ti.ii.acs̄ 7 dim̄.Val̄ xxx.ſol̄.Q̄do

recep̄.x.ſol̄.T.R.E.xxx.ſol̄.Hanc tr̄a tenuit Almar

ſub Eddeua.7 recedē potuit.ſ̧ ſoca Æideue remanſit.

In Witeleſforde ten̄ Girard de com̄.   *IN WITELESFORD HD.*

dim̄ uirg tre.Val̄ 7 ualuit.ii.ſol̄.De.i.uirg 7 dim̄

ten̄ ipſe ſacā 7 ſocā de comite.quā uirg

dimid̄ ten̄ un̄ hō comitis.Eddeua tenuit

In Dodeſuuorde ten̄ Girard de comite.vi.hid̄ de

~~comite~~.Tra.ē.vi.car̄.In dn̄io ſunt.ii,7 iiii.uilli.7 v.

bord̄ cū.iiii.car̄.Ibi.i.ſeruus.7 p̄tū.ii.car̄.Int totū

194 b

ual̄ 7 ualuit.c.ſol̄.T.R.E.vii.lib̄.Hanc tr̄a tenuit Eddeua.

In Fugeleſmara ten̄.ii.milites *IN KEPESLAV HD.*

de.A.comite.i.hid̄.Tra.ē.i car̄.7 ii.boū.p̄tū.i.car̄.

14 M. The Count holds ABINGTON himself. 5 hides. Land for 8 ploughs.
In lordship 2½ hides; 3 ploughs there.
11 villagers and 5 smallholders with 5 ploughs.
4 slaves; 1 mill at 6s 8d; meadow for 2 ploughs; woodland, 20 pigs.
In total, the value is and was £10.
Edeva held this manor.

15 In BABRAHAM Brian holds 2½ hides and 24 acres under Count Alan.
Land for 4 ploughs. In lordship 1;
17 villagers and 3 smallholders with 3 ploughs.
1 slave; meadow for 4 oxen.
The value is and was 50s.
6 Freemen held this land under Edeva; they could not withdraw
without her permission. They found 4 cartages and 2 escorts.

16 In the same village Ralph holds 1 hide less ½ virgate under the
Count. Land for 1 plough; it is there. Meadow for 1 plough;
3 villagers; 3 smallholders;
1 mill at 5s 4d.
The value is and was 20s.
Alric the priest held this land under Edeva; he could not
withdraw from her.

17 In PAMPISFORD 2 men-at-arms hold 1 hide and 22 acres under the
Count. Land for 2 ploughs and 2 oxen. In lordship 1 plough;
2 villagers and 5 smallholders with 1 plough.
Meadow, 2½ acres.
Value 30s; when acquired 10s; before 1066, 30s.
Aelmer held this land under Edeva; he could withdraw, but
the jurisdiction remained with Edeva.

In WHITTLESFORD Hundred
18 In WHITTLESFORD Gerard holds ½ virgate of land from the Count.
The value is and was 2s.
He himself holds from the Count the full jurisdiction of 1½
virgates. A man of the Count's holds the 1½ virgates. Edeva
held them.

19 In DUXWORTH Gerard holds 6 hides from the Count. Land for
6 ploughs. In lordship 2;
4 villagers and 5 smallholders with 4 ploughs.
1 slave; meadow for 2 ploughs.
In total, the value is and was 100s; before 1066 £7.   194 b
Edeva held this land.

In THRIPLOW Hundred
20 In FOWLMERE 2 men-at-arms hold 1 hide from Count Alan.
Land for 1 plough and 2 oxen.
Meadow for 1 plough.

Val 7 ualuit xx. fot. T.R.E. xxv. fot. Hanc tra

tenuit Eddeua. 7 h tra inuenieb. 11. Ineuuard uicec.

In Herleftone ten Odo de com. v. uirg tre 7 dim.

Tra. e. 1. car 7 dim. 7 ibi. e. car 7 dim. cu uno uillo

7 111. bord. Val xx. fot. Qdo recep. xv. T.R.E. xxx. fot.

De hac tra. 1111. uirg 7 dim. tenuer. 1111. fochi fub Eddeua.

7 inuenieb. 11. jnew uicecom. 7 tam recede potuer.

7 un pbr fub Orgaro. 1. uirg tenuit. un Ineuuard

inuen. 7 recede potuit.

In Efcelford ten Harduin de comite. 1. hid 7 dim.

7 vi. acs. Tra. e. 11. car. 7 ibi fuñ cu. vi. uiltis. 7 11. bord.

ptu. 11. car. Val. xxx. fot. Qdo recep. xx. T.R.E. xl. fot.

Hanc tra. vi. fochi fub Eddeua tenuer. 1111. jnew

inuener. 7 recede potuer. *In Erningford Hd*

In Atelai. ten Almar de comite. 1. hid 7 111. uirg

Tra. e. 111. car. In dnio. e una car. 7 11. uilti 7 v. bord

cu. 111. car. Ibi. 111. ferui. Ptu. 1. car. Silua ad fepes.

Val 7 ualuit. xl. fot. T.R.E. lx. fot. Iftemet tenuit

T.R.E. fub Eddeua. 7 1. ineuuard inuen. 7 recede potuit.

In Crauuedene. ten Almar fub comite. 11. uirg 7 dim.

Tra. e. vi. bou. 7 ibi funt cu. 1. bord 7 1. cot. Val 7 ua

luit. x. fot. T.R.E. xv. fot. Hanc tra tenuit Godeue

fub Eddeua. 7 recede potuit.

In ead uilla ten Fulchei de comite. 1. uirg træ. Val

7 ualuit. v. fot. Hanc tenuit Leueue fub Eddeue. et

recede potuit.

In Wandrie ten Odo de com. A. 1111. hid 7 111. uirg.

Tra. e. vi. car. In dnio fuñ. 11. 7. vi. uilti 7 v. bord

cu. 1111. car. Ibi. 1111. ferui. 7 11. molini de. xlv. fot.

Ptu. vi. car. Nem ad fepes. Int tot ual. viii. lib.

Qdo recep. vi. lib. T.R.E. x. lib. De hac tra. 1. hid

tenuer. vi. fochi fub Eddeua 7 recede potuer.

The value is and was 20s; before 1066, 25s.
Edeva held this land; this land found 2 escorts for the Sheriff.

21 In HARSTON Odo holds 5½ virgates of land from the Count.
Land for 1½ ploughs; 1½ ploughs there, with
    1 villager; 3 smallholders.
Value 20s; when acquired 15 [s] ; before 1066, 30s.
    4 Freemen held 4½ virgates of this land under Edeva; they
found 2 escorts for the Sheriff; however, they could withdraw.
A priest held 1 virgate under Ordgar; he found 1 escort and
could withdraw.

22 In SHELFORD Hardwin holds 1½ hides and 6 acres from the Count.
Land for 2 ploughs; they are there, with
    6 villagers; 2 smallholders.
    Meadow for 2 ploughs.
Value 30s, when acquired 20s; before 1066, 40s.
    6 Freemen held this land under Edeva, they found 4 escorts
and could withdraw.

In ARMINGFORD Hundred
23 In (East) HATLEY Aelmer holds 1 hide and 3 virgates from the Count.
Land for 3 ploughs. In lordship 1 plough;
    2 villagers and 5 smallholders with 3 ploughs.
    3 slaves; meadow for 1 plough; woodland for fences.
The value is and was 40s; before 1066, 60s.
    He held it himself under Edeva before 1066; he found 1 escort
and could withdraw.

24 In CROYDON Aelmer holds 2½ virgates under the Count.
Land for 6 oxen; they are there, with
    1 smallholder; 1 cottager.
The value is and was 10s; before 1066, 15s.
    Godiva held this land under Edeva; she could withdraw.

25 In the same village Fulkwy holds 1 virgate of land from the Count.
The value is and was 5s.
    Leofeva held it under Edeva; she could withdraw.

26 In WENDY Odo holds 4 hides and 3 virgates from Count Alan.
Land for 6 ploughs. In lordship 2;
    6 villagers and 5 smallholders with 4 ploughs.
    4 slaves; 2 mills at 45s; meadow for 6 ploughs; wood for fences.
In total, value £8; when acquired £6; before 1066 £10.
    6 Freemen held 1 hide of this land under Edeva; they could
withdraw.

꟒ Ipſe.A.comes ten̄ *In Basingborne*.vii.hid̄

7 i.uirḡ 7 dim̄.Tra.ē.xviii.car̄.In dn̄io.iiii.hid̄.

7 ibi ſuꝗ.v.car̄.7 adhuc.ii.poſſ.ēē.Ibi.viii.uitti

7 xi.bord̄ 7 x.cot.cū.xi.car̄.Ibi.iiii.ſerui.7 ii.

molini de.xx.ſot.Ptū.v.car̄.In totis ualent

uat.xxx.liƀ.Q̄do recep̄.xxvi.liƀ 7 tn̄td̄ T.R.E.

Hoc ꟒ tenuit Eddeua.7 ibi fuer̄ x.ſocħi.7 viii.eoꝗ

hōēs Eddeue trā ſuā potuer̄ uende ſꝫ ſoca ei remanſit.

7 alij.ii.hōēs Aꝉgari.iiii.jneward uicecō inuener̄.

            ⌜7 ipſi trā ſuā uende potuer̄.

194 c

Īn Wadune ten̄ Colſuaṅ de.A.com dim̄ hid̄.Tra

ē.i.car̄ 7 dim̄.In dn̄io.i.car̄.7 i.uitts ħt dim̄ car̄.

Vat 7 ualuit xx.ſot.T.R.E.xl.ſot.Iſtemet tenuit

de Eddeua.T.R.E.7 uend̄e potuit.

Īn ead uilla ten̄ Radulf de cō.ii.hid̄ 7 i.uirḡ.træ.

Tra.ē.iiii.car̄.In dn̄io ſuꝗ.ii.7 ii.uitti 7 i.bord̄ cū.ii.

car̄.Ibi.iiii.ſerui.7 i.molin̄ de xii.den̄.Ptū.i.car̄.

Paſta ad pec uillæ.Int tot uat 7 ualuit.vi.liƀ.

T.R.E.viii.liƀ.Hanc trā tenuit Leuui.hō Aſgari.

ſtalre.7 cui uoluit dare 7 uend̄e potuit.

Īn ead ten̄.ii.hōēs de comite.i.uirḡ.Tra.ē dim̄ car̄.

Vat 7 ualuit.iiii.ſot.T.R.E.vi.ſot.Hanc trā tenuer̄

ii.ſocħi.ui hō Colſuan fuit.alt de ſoca S̄ Edeldrid̄.

7 uend̄e potuit.ſoca·ū æcctæ remanſit.

Īn ead ten̄ Odo de cō.ii.hid̄ 7 i.uirḡ.Tra.ē.iii.

car̄.In dn̄io.ē.i.car̄ 7 dim̄.7 ii.uitti 7 dim̄ cū.iiii.

bord̄ hn̄t.i.car̄ 7 dim̄.Ibi.ii.ſerui.Ptū.i.car̄.Vat

c.ſot.Q̄do recep̄.xxx.ſot.T.R.E.vi.liƀ.Hanc tram

tenuit Eddeua.In ipſa tra fuit 7 eſt.i.ſocħs teneꝹ

dim̄ uirḡ.Tra.ē.ii.boū.Vat 7 ualuit.ii.ſot.Hō Ed

Īn Melrede ten̄ Colſuan de cō.i.uirḡ. ⌜deue tenuit.

27 M. In BASSINGBOURN Count Alan himself holds 7 hides and 1½ virgates. Land for 18 ploughs. In lordship 4 hides; 5 ploughs there; a further 2 possible.
 8 villagers, 11 smallholders and 10 cottagers with 11 ploughs.
 3 slaves; 2 mills at 20s; meadow for 5 ploughs.
Total value £30; when acquired £26; before 1066 as much.
 Edeva held this manor. 10 Freemen were there. 8 of them, Edeva's men, could sell their land, but the jurisdiction remained with her. The other 2, Earl Algar's men, found 4 escorts for the Sheriff; they could sell their land.

28 In WHADDON Colswein holds ½ hide from Count Alan. Land   194 c
for 1½ ploughs. In lordship 1 plough;
 1 villager has ½ plough.
The value is and was 20s; before 1066, 40s.
 He held it himself from Edeva before 1066; he could sell.

29 In the same village Ralph holds 2 hides and 1 virgate of land from the Count. Land for 4 ploughs. In lordship 2;
 2 villagers and 1 smallholder with 2 ploughs.
 4 slaves; 1 mill at 12d; meadow for 1 plough; pasture for
  the village livestock.
In total, the value is and was £6; before 1066 £8.
 Leofwy, Asgar the Constable's man, held this land; he could grant and sell to whom he would.

30 In the same (village) 2 men hold 1 virgate from the Count. Land for ½ plough.
The value is and was 4s; before 1066, 6s.
 2 Freemen held this land. One was Colswein's man. The other (was) of St. Etheldreda's jurisdiction; he could sell, but the jurisdiction remained with the Church.

31 In the same (village) Odo holds 2 hides and 1 virgate from the Count. Land for 3 ploughs. In lordship 1½ ploughs;
 2½ villagers with 4 smallholders have 1½ ploughs.
 2 slaves; meadow for 1 plough.
Value 100s; when acquired 30s; before 1066 £6.
 Edeva held this land.
 In this land there was and is 1 Freeman who holds ½ virgate. Land for 2 oxen.
The value is and was 2s.
 Edeva's man held it.

32 In MELDRETH Colswein holds 1 virgate from the Count. Land for

Tra.ē.ı.car.7 ibi.ē.cū.ıı.cot.7 ibi.ıı.molini de.xvɪɪɪ.

ſoł.p̄tū.ıı.caī.Vał.xxx.ſoł.Q̇do recep̄ʳxx.ſoł.T.R.E.ʳ

xʟ.ſoł.Iſtemet tenuit ſub Eddeua.7 dare potuit.

In Melleborne teñ Colſuan de comite.ıɪɪ.uirg̓ træ.

T̓ra.ē.ı.caī 7 dim̓.7 ibi ſuɴ̓ cū.ɪɪɪ.borđ 7 ı.ſeruo.

p̊tū.ɪɪɪɪ.bob.Vał xx.ſoł.Q̇do recep̄ʳxv.ſoł.T.R.E.ʳ

xʟ.ſoł.Iſtemet tenuit ſub Eddeua.7 recedē pot ab ea.

In Granteſete teñ Gollan ſub cōm *IN WEDERLAI HD.*

.ı.uirg̓ 7 dim̓.T̓ra.ē.ı.caī.7 ibi.ē cū.ı.uiłło 7 ɪɪɪ.cot.

7 ı.ſeruo.P̊tū.ɪɪɪɪ.bob.Vał 7 ualuit.xx.ſoł.Hanc

t̓ra tenuit Gogan hō Eddeue.n̄ potuit ſine lictia recedē.

In hoc eod Hunđ teñ Alan cōm.ıı.moliñ de.c.ſoł.

quos recep̄ .p.vɪɪɪ.lib.T.R.E.ualeƀ.vɪ.lib.Eddeua

In Haſlingefelde teñ Roƀt de comite ꝼ tenuit.

.ı.hiđ 7 dim uirg̓.T̓ra.ē.ı.caī 7 dim̓.In dn̄io.ē.�.

caī.7 ɪɪɪɪ.uiłłi cū.ı.borđ hn̄t dim caī.P̊tū.ɪɪɪɪ.bob.

Vał.xx.ſoł.Q̇do recep̄ʳxxɪɪ.ſoł.7 tn̄tđ T.R.E.

Hanc t̓ra tenuit Eldred ſub Eddeua.n̄ potuit recedē

ſine licentia ꝯ̓.

In ead uilla teñ ipſe cōm dim̓ hidā in dn̄io.quæ ptiñ

ad Suaueſy̓.ꝏ ſuū.T̓ra.ē dim̓ caī.Vał 7 ualuit.vɪɪɪ.ſoł.

Eddeua pulchra tenuit. ꝼ Meruin tenuit de Eddeua.

In ead uilla teñ Roƀt de cōm.xɪɪ.ac̓s træ.Vał 7 ualuit.ɪɪ.

194 d

In Barentone teñ Picot de cōm dim̓ uirg̓.T̓ra.ē.ɪɪ.

bob.7 ibi ſunt cū.ıı.borđ.p̄tū.ıı.bob.Vał 7 ualuit

ɪɪ.ſoł.T.R.E.ʳxxxɪɪ.deñ.Hanc t̓ra uñ hō regis.E.tenuit.

unū jneuuard uicecōm inueñ.7 cui uoluit dare potuit.

1 plough; it is there, with
   2 cottagers.
   2 mills at 18s; meadow for 2 ploughs.
Value 30s; when acquired 20s; before 1066, 40s.
   He held it himself under Edeva; he could grant.

33 In MELBOURN Colswein holds 3 virgates of land from the Count.
Land for 1½ ploughs; they are there, with
   3 smallholders; 1 slave.
   Meadow for 4 oxen.
Value 20s; when acquired 15s; before 1066, 40s.
   He held it himself under Edeva; he could withdraw from her.

In WETHERLEY Hundred

34 In GRANTCHESTER Godlamb holds 1½ virgates under the Count.
Land for 1 plough; it is there, with
   1 villager; 3 cottagers; 1 slave.
   Meadow for 4 oxen.
The value is and was 20s.
   Godman, Edeva's man, held this land; he could not withdraw
without her permission.

35 In this same Hundred Count Alan holds 2 mills at 100s, which
he acquired for £8; before 1066 they were worth £6. Edeva
held them.

36 In HASLINGFIELD Robert holds 1 hide and ½ virgate from the Count.
Land for 1½ ploughs. In lordship 1 plough;
   4 villagers with 1 smallholder have ½ plough.
   Meadow for 4 oxen.
Value 20s; when acquired 22s; before 1066 as much.
   Aldred held this land under Edeva; he could not withdraw
without her permission.

7 In the same village the Count holds ½ hide himself in lordship;
it belongs to Swavesey, his manor. Land for ½ plough.
The value is and was 8s.
   Edeva the Fair held it.

8 In the same village Robert holds 12 acres of land from the Count.
The value is and was 2s.
   Merwin held (it) from Edeva; he could grant.

9 In BARRINGTON Picot holds ½ virgate from the Count. Land   194 d
for 2 oxen; they are there, with
   2 smallholders.
   Meadow for 2 oxen.
The value is and was 2s; before 1066, 32d.
   A man of King Edward's held this land; he found 1 escort for
the Sheriff, and could grant to whom he would.

In Escepride . teñ Rainald de com . i . uirg 7 dim . Tra eſt
dim car . 7 ibi . ē cū . i . uitto . 7 vi . part . i . mol redd . xiiii . den .
p̄tū . iiii . boƀ . Val . viii . ſot . Q̇do recep̄ . v . ſot . T.R.E. viii . ſot .
Hanc trā tenuit Haminc hō regis . E . jneūuard inuenit .
7 uendē trā ſuā potuit .

In Oreduuelle teñ picot de com . iii . uirg 7 iiii . partē
uni uirg . 7 v . ac̄s . Tra . ē . i . car 7 dim . 7 ibi ſuɴ cū . vi . borđ .
p̄tū . i . car . Val 7 ualuit . xx . ſot . T.R.E. xxx . ſot . Hanc trā
tenuit Turƀn ſub Eddeua . 7 recedē potuit ab ea .

In Warateuuorde teñ ipſe com . i . uirg 7 iii . part . i . uirg
Tra . ē dim car . p̄tū . iiii . boƀ . cū . i . uitto . Val 7 ualuit . viii .
ſot . T.R.E. x . ſot . Hanc trā tenuit . i . ſocħs ſub Eddeua .
7 dare 7 uendē potuit .

In Witeuuelle teñ Fulcui de com đim hiđ . Tra . ē . i . car .
7 ibi . ē cū . iii . cot . P̄tū đim car . 7 nem ad ſepes . Val 7 ua
luit . x . ſot . T.R.E. xx . ſot . Hanc trā tenuit Goduui
ſub Eddeua . 7 recedē potuit ab ea .

In Winepole teñ ipſe com . ii . hid 7 ii . uirg 7 dim . Tra . ē
iii . car . In dñio . ii . hide . 7 ibi . i . car . 7 adhuc đim poteſt
fieri . Ibi . ii . uitti cū . i . borđ hñt . i . car 7 dim . Ibi . vi . cot .
7 ii . ſerui . P̄tū đim car . Int tot ual vii . liƀ . Q̇do recep̄ . vi .
liƀ . T.R.E. viii . liƀ . Hanc trā tenuit Eddeua pulchra .

In Erningtone teñ Fulcui de com đim hiđ . Tra . ē đim
car . 7 ibi . ē cū . ii . uittis . P̄tū . iiii . boƀ . Silua ad ſepes . Val
7 ualuit . x . ſot . T.R.E. xx . ſot . Hanc trā tenuit Leueue
ſub Eddeua . 7 . potuit recedē ab ea . IN STOV HVND .

In Aueresdone teñ Roƀt 7 ii . Angli de com . i . hiđ . Tra
ē . ii . car . 7 ibi ſuɴ cū . ii . uittis 7 iii . borđ 7 i . cot . p̄tū . ii .

40   In SHEPRETH Reginald holds 1½ virgates from the Count. Land
for ½ plough; it is there, with
    1 villager;
    the sixth part of 1 mill, which pays 14d; meadow for 4 oxen.
Value 8s; when acquired 5s; before 1066, 8s.
    Heming, King Edward's man, held this land; he found escort,
and could sell his land.

41   In ORWELL Picot holds 3 virgates and the fourth part of 1 virgate
and 5 acres from the Count. Land for 1½ ploughs; they are
there, with
    6 smallholders.
    Meadow for 1 plough.
The value is and was 20s; before 1066, 30s.
    Thorbern held this land under Edeva; he could withdraw from her.

42   In WRATWORTH the Count holds 1 virgate and the third part of
1 virgate himself. Land for ½ plough.
    Meadow for 4 oxen, with
    1 villager.
The value is and was 8s; before 1066, 10s.
    1 Freeman held this land under Edeva; he could grant and sell.

43   In WHITWELL Fulkwy holds ½ hide from the Count. Land for 1 plough;
it is there, with
    3 cottagers.
    Meadow for ½ plough; wood for fences.
The value is and was 10s; before 1066, 20s.
    Godwy held this land under Edeva; he could withdraw from her.

44   In WIMPOLE the Count holds 2 hides and 2½ virgates himself. Land
for 3 ploughs. In lordship 2 hides; 1 plough there; a further ½
possible.
    2 villagers with 1 smallholder have 1½ ploughs.
      6 cottagers; 2 slaves.
    Meadow for ½ plough.
In total, value £7; when acquired £6; before 1066 £8.
    Edeva the Fair held this land.

45   In ARRINGTON Fulkwy holds ½ hide from the Count. Land for
½ plough; it is there, with
    2 villagers.
    Meadow for 4 oxen; woodland for fences.
The value is and was 10s; before 1066, 20s.
    Leofeva held this land under Edeva; she could withdraw from her.

In LONGSTOW Hundred

46   In EVERSDEN Robert and 2 Englishmen hold 1 hide from the Count.
Land for 2 ploughs; they are there, with
    2 villagers; 3 smallholders; 1 cottager.

cár.7 nem ad fepes.Val.xxv.fol.Qdo recep.x.fol.

T.R.E.xx.fol.Hanc trã tenueř.11.fochi.hões Eddeuæ.

7 potueř dare 7 uendere.

In Chingeftone ten Almar de com.1.uirg.Tra.ẽ.11.

bob.7 ibi fuṅ.ptũ.11.bob.Val 7 ualuit.11.fol.Hanc

trã tenuit Aluiet hõ comit Algari.7 uende potuit.

In Tofth ten com.11.hið 7 1.uirg.7 viii.acs.Tra.ẽ.iiii.

    cár.In dñio.1.hið 7 viii.ac.7 ibi.ẽ.1.cár.

    Ibi.v.uilli cũ.11.cot.hñt.iiii.cár.Ibi

11.ferui.Ptũ.11.cár.7 nem ad fepes.Int toť ual

iiii.lib.Qdo recep.iii.lib.T.R.E.xl.fol.H̃ tra.ẽ BER

in Suauefỹ,Eddẹua tenuit.

In Brunam ten Almar de com.iiii.hið 7 1.uirg.

Tra.ẽ.v.cár 7 dim.In dñio.ẽ.1.cár 7 adhuc dim̃

pot fieri.Ibi.1x.uilli cũ xiii.bord hñt.111.cár.

7 iiii.pot fieri.Ibi.11.ferui.Ptũ.v.cár.7 dim.Pafta

ad fuã pecun.Nem ad domos 7 fepes.Val 7 ualuit

iiii.lib.T.R.E.c.fol.Hanc trã 7 alias.111.quæ fecunt.

tenuit Almar qui nẽ tenet.hõ Eddeue fuit.7 1.ine

warð inuen,7 recede fine licentia potuit.7 dare

7 uende trã fuã cui uoluit.

In Caldecote ten Almar de com dim hið.Tra.ẽ

.1.cár 7 dim.In dñio.ẽ.1.cár.7 111.bord cũ dim cár.

Ibi.11.ferui.7 ptũ.1.cár 7 dim.Nem ad dom 7 fepes.

Val 7 ualuit fẽp.xxx.fol.

In Stou ten Almar de com.1.uirg tre 7 dim̃.Tra

ẽ.vi.bob.7 ibi fuṅ.Ibi.11.ferui.7 ptũ.vi.bob.Pafta

ad pec uillæ.Nem ad fepes 7 domos.Val.xxx.fol.

Qdo recep.x.fol.T.R.E.xxx.fol.

In Hatelai ten Almar de com.1.uirg.Tra.ẽ.11.bob.

Val 7 ualuit fẽp.11.fol 7 iiii.denar.

Meadow for 2 ploughs; wood for fences.
Value 25s; when acquired 10s; before 1066, 20s.
2 Freemen, Edeva's men, held this land; they could grant and sell.

47 In KINGSTON Aelmer holds 1 virgate from the Count. Land for 2 oxen; they are there.
Meadow for 2 oxen.
The value is and was 2s.
Alfgeat, Earl Algar's man, held this land; he could sell.

48 In TOFT the Count holds 2 hides and 1 virgate and 8 acres. Land for 4 ploughs. In lordship 1 hide and 8 acres; 1 plough there.
5 villagers with 2 cottagers have 4 ploughs.
2 slaves; meadow for 2 ploughs; wood for fences.
In total, value £4; when acquired £3; before 1066, 40s.
This land is an outlier in Swavesey. Edeva held (it).

49 In BOURN Aelmer holds 4 hides and 1 virgate from the Count.   195 a
Land for 5½ ploughs. In lordship 1 plough; a further ½ possible.
9 villagers with 13 smallholders have 3 ploughs; a fourth possible.
2 slaves; meadow for 5½ ploughs; pasture for their livestock;
   wood for houses and fences.
The value is and was £4; before 1066, 100s.
Aelmer held this land and the other 3 which follow; he holds them now. He was Edeva's man and found 1 escort. He could withdraw without permission and grant and sell his land to whom he would.

50 In CALDECOTE Aelmer holds ½ hide from the Count. Land for 1½ ploughs. In lordship 1 plough.
3 smallholders with ½ plough.
2 slaves; meadow for 1½ ploughs; wood for houses and fences.
The value is and always was 30s.

51 In LONGSTOWE Aelmer holds 1½ virgates of land from the Count.
Land for 6 oxen; they are there.
2 slaves; meadow for 6 oxen; pasture for the village livestock;
   wood for fences and houses.
Value 30s; when acquired 10s; before 1066, 30s.

52 In HATLEY (St. George) Aelmer holds 1 virgate from the Count.
Land for 2 oxen.
The value is and always was 2s 4d.

ꟿ Ipſe comes.teñ *PAPEWORDE*. Ibi.v.hidæ.Tra.ē
vii.cař.In dñio.ii.hidæ 7 dim.7 ibi fuɴ.ii.cař.Ibi
x.uilli 7 v.borđ cũ.v.cař.Ibi.iiii.ſerui.Ptũ.ii.
cař.Nem ad ſepes 7 domos.In totis ualent ual.viii.
liɓ.Qdo recep.ix.liɓ.7 tñtđ T.R.E.Hoc ꟿ tenuit
Goda ſub Eddeua.7 uendē potuit.

In Bocheſuuorde teñ.ii.ſochi ſub com.i.hiđ.Tra
ē.i.cař.7 ibi.ē.Ptũ.i.cař.Val 7 ualuit xviii.ſol
7 viii.deñ.T.R.E.xxvi.ſol.Iſtimet tenuer ſub Eddeua.
7 uendē potuer.

ꟿ Ipſe comes teñ *SVAVESYE*. Ibi xiii.hidæ.Tra.ē
xiiii.cař.In dñio.vi.hide.7 ibi fuɴ.iii.cař.7 iiii.
pot.eē.Ibi x.uilli cũ xix.borđ 7 viii.ſochi tenent
iii.hiđ de ipſa tra.Hi ſimul hñt.x.cař.Ibi.xvii.
cot.7 ii.ſerui.7 i.molin de.xl.ſol.De piſcař.iiii.
mill anguil.cc.l.min.Ptũ.xiiii.cař.Paſta ad
pecun uillæ.In totis ualent ual.xvi.liɓ.Qdo re
cep.viii.liɓ.T.R.E.xviii.liɓ.Hoc ꟿ tenuit Eddeua.
7 ipſi.viii.ſochi potuer uendē tra ſua ſine ej lictia.

In Draitone teñ.v.ſochi de com.iiii.hiđ 7 dim.
Tra.ē.ii.cař.7 ibi fuɴ cũ.i.uillo 7 v.borđ.7 iii.cot.
ptũ.ii.cař.paſta ad pecun uillæ.Val 7 ualuit xx.
ſol.T.R.E.xxvii.ſol.Ipſimet ſochi tenuer ſub Eddeua.
7 potuer uendē cui uoluer.

In Wiuelinghā teñ.i.ſochs de com.i.uirg træ.

195 b

Tra.ē.ii.boɓ.Ptũ.ii.boɓ.Val 7 ualuit ſēp.iii.ſoli
Hanc tra tenuit Oſulf hõ Eddeuæ.uendē potuit.ſed
ſoca remanſit Abbatiæ de Elẏ. *IN NORESTOV HVND.*
In Stantune teñ Picot.iiii.hiđ.7 i.uirg 7 dim.Tra.ē

In PAPWORTH Hundred

53 M. The Count holds PAPWORTH himself. 5 hides. Land for 7 ploughs.
In lordship 2½ hides; 2 ploughs there.
10 villagers and 5 smallholders with 5 ploughs.
4 slaves; meadow for 2 ploughs; wood for fences and houses.
Total value £8; when acquired £9; before 1066 as much.
Goda held this manor under Edeva; he could sell.

54 In BOXWORTH 2 Freemen hold 1 hide under the Count.
Land for 1 plough; it is there.
Meadow for 1 plough.
The value is and was 18s 8d; before 1066, 26s.
They held it themselves under Edeva; they could sell.

55 M. The Count holds SWAVESEY himself. 13 hides. Land for 14 ploughs.
In lordship 6 hides; 3 ploughs there; a fourth possible.
10 villagers with 19 smallholders and 8 Freemen hold 3 hides
of this land. Together they have 10 ploughs.
17 cottagers; 2 slaves;
1 mill at 40s; from fisheries 4,000 eels less 250;
meadow for 14 ploughs; pasture for the village livestock.
Total value £16; when acquired £8; before 1066 £18.
Edeva held this manor. The 8 Freemen could sell their land
themselves without her permission.

56 In (Fen) DRAYTON 5 Freemen hold 4½ hides from the Count.
Land for 2 ploughs; they are there, with
1 villager; 5 smallholders; 3 cottagers.
Meadow for 2 ploughs; pasture for the village livestock.
The value is and was 20s; before 1066, 27s.
The Freemen held (it) themselves under Edeva; they could
sell to whom they would.

57 In WILLINGHAM 1 Freeman holds 1 virgate of land from the Count.
Land for 2 oxen.   195 b
Meadow for 2 oxen.
The value is and always was 3s.
Oswulf, Edeva's man, held this land; he could sell, but the
jurisdiction remained with Ely Abbey.

In NORTHSTOW Hundred

58 In LONGSTANTON Picot holds 4 hides and 1½ virgates from the Count.

.v.car̅.In dn̅io.ii.car̅.7 iiii.uilti 7 xii.bord 7 vi.cot

hn̅t.vi.car̅.Ibi.i.feru 7 p̅tū.ii.car̅.Val 7 ualuit; c.fot̅;

T.R.E.′viii.libɓ.Hanc tra̅ tenue̅r.xiii.fochi.Ex his

un̅ ho̅ fuit Wluui epi.reliq fue̅r hoe̅s Eddeuæ.om̅s

tra̅ fua̅ dare 7 uende̅ potue̅r.

I̅n Bece ten̅ Walter de com̅.iiii.hid̅ 7 dim̅.xii.ac̅s

min̅.Tra.e̅.iiii.car̅.In dn̅io.i.hid̅ 7 dim̅.7 xviii.ac̅s;

7 ibi.e̅.i.car̅.Ibi.iii.uilti cu̅ xiii.bord hn̅t.iiii.car̅.

Ibi.xvii.cot̅.p̅tū.vi.car̅.Pafta ad pec̅ uillæ.Marefch;

cccc.l.anguitt.In totis ualent.ual.vi.libɓ.7 x.fot̅.Q̲do

rece̅p.′vi.libɓ.T.R.E.′iii.libɓ.Hoc m̅ tenuit Eddeua.7 ibi

tenuit.i.fochs fub ea.ii.hid̅ 7 i.uirg̅.Potuit dare cui uoluit;

f̅z de uirg̅ habuit abb de Ely̅ faca̅ 7 foca̅.

I̅n Draitone ten̅ monachi de Suauefy̅ fub comite.A.

iii.hid̅.Tra.e̅.iii.car̅.In dn̅io.e̅.i.car̅.7 v.uilti cu̅.ii.cot

hn̅t.ii.car̅.P̅tū.i.car̅.Val 7 ualuit xl.fot̅.T.R.E.′lx.fot̅.

Hanc tra̅ tenuit Eddeua.   *IN CHAVELAI HVND.*

m̅ *Ditone* ten̅ Wighen de com̅.A.p.v.hid̅ fe defd̅

T.R.E.7 m̅ p.iii.hid̅.Tra.e̅.x.car̅.In dn̅io.iiii.car̅.

Ibi.x.uilti cu̅.viii.bord hn̅t.vi.car̅.Ibi.iiii.ferui.

Pafta ad pecun̅ uillæ.Silua.c.l.porc̅.In totis ua

lent ual.x.libɓ.Q̲do rece̅p.′xiiii.libɓ.T.R.E.′vii.libɓ.

Hoc m̅ tenuit Eddeua.

I̅n Chauelai ten̅ Enifant de com̅.i.hid̅ 7 dim̅.7 xx.ac̅s.

Tra.e̅.iii.car̅.7 ibi funt.in dn̅io.ii.7 iiii.bord cu̅.i.car̅.

Ibi.i.feru.Silua.xii.porc̅.Pafta ad pec̅ uillæ.Val

7 ualuit fe̅p.xl.fot̅.Hanc tra̅ tenuit Herulf ho̅ Eddeue.

dare 7 uende̅ potuit.   *IN STANES HVND.*

I̅n Suafam.ten̅ Goisfrid de com̅.i.hid̅ 7 iii.uirg̅.Tra

e̅.iiii.car̅.In dn̅io.e̅ una.7 iii.uilti hn̅t.iii.car̅.Ibi

Land for 5 ploughs. In lordship 2 ploughs;
4 villagers, 12 smallholders and 6 cottagers have 6 ploughs.
1 slave; meadow for 2 ploughs.
The value is and was 100s; before 1066 £8.
13 Freemen held this land. One of them was Bishop Wulfwy's
man; the rest were Edeva's men; all could grant and sell their land.

59   In LANDBEACH Walter holds 4½ hides less 12 acres from the Count.
Land for 4 ploughs. In lordship 1½ hides and 18 acres; 1 plough there.
3 villagers with 13 smallholders have 3 ploughs.
    17 cottagers.
Meadow for 6 ploughs; pasture for the village livestock;
    marsh, 450 eels.
Total value £6 10s; when acquired £6; before 1066 £3.
Edeva held this manor. 1 Freeman held 2 hides and 1 virgate
under her. He could grant to whom he would, but Ely Abbey had
full jurisdiction of the virgate.

[In CHESTERTON Hundred]
60   In (Dry) DRAYTON the monks of Swavesey hold 3 hides under Count
Alan. Land for 3 ploughs. In lordship 1 plough;
5 villagers with 2 cottagers have 2 ploughs.
Meadow for 1 plough.
The value is and was 40s; before 1066, 60s.
Edeva held this land.

In CHEVELEY Hundred
61 M. Wighen holds WOODDITTON from Count Alan. It answered for 5 hides
before 1066, and now for 3 hides. Land for 10 ploughs. In lordship
4 ploughs.
10 villagers with 8 smallholders have 6 ploughs.
4 slaves; pasture for the village livestock; woodland, 150 pigs.
Total value £10; when acquired £14; before 1066 £7.
Edeva held this manor.

62   In CHEVELEY Enisant holds 1½ hides and 20 acres from the Count.
Land for 3 ploughs; they are there. In lordship 2;
4 smallholders with 1 plough.
1 slave; woodland, 12 pigs; pasture for the village livestock.
The value is and always was 40s.
Horwulf, Edeva's man, held this land; he could grant and sell.

In STAINE Hundred
63   In SWAFFHAM Geoffrey holds 1 hide and 3 virgates from the Count.
Land for 4 ploughs. In lordship 1;
3 villagers have 3 ploughs.

ii . ſerui . 7 i . molin̄ de . iiii . ſot 7 iiii . den . 7 c . anguiłł.

P̊tū . i . car̓ . Paſta ad ſuā pecun̓ . Vał xl . ſot . Q̣do recep̓.

xx . ſot . T.R.E. ſimilit̓ . Hanc trā tenuer̓ . vi . ſochi ſub

Eddeua . n̄ potuer̓ ſine ej licītia recede̓ . ſ̧ inuenieb̓

uicecomiti . iii . jneuuard 7 i . Auerā p annum.

In ead uilla ten̓ . iii . milit̓ de com̓ . iii . hid̓ 7 i . uirg̓.

Tra . ē . iiii . car̓ . 7 ibi ſunt . cū . iii . uittis 7 ii . ſeruis . P̊tū

ii . car̓ . Vał c . ſot . Q̣do recep̓ . lv . ſot . T.R.E. ſimilit̓.

De hac trā tenuit Huſcarl hō regis . E . iii . uirg̓ . 7 auerā

inuen̓ . Trā ſuā dare 7 uende̓ potuit . ſ̧ ſoca regi remanſit.

195 c

De ead̓ trā tenuit Eddeua . i . hid̓ 7 i . uirg̓ . 7 Wluui hō ej̓

. i . hid̓ 7 i . uirg̓ . Socā ej habuit Eddeua.

Odo ten̓ de . A . com̓ . iiii . hid̓ . Tra . ē . ix . car̓ . In dn̄io

ſunt . ii̊ . 7 viii . uitti cū . vii . bord hn̄t . vii . car̓ . Ibi

. vi . ſerui . 7 i . molin̄ . v . ſot 7 iiii . den̓ . P̊tū . ix . car̓.

Paſta ad pecun̓ uillæ . In totis ualent uał 7 ualuit

xii . lib̄ . T.R.E. x . lib̄ . Hanc trā tenuit Ordmær̓

hō Eddeue . 7 potuit dare cui uoluit.

Odo ten̓ de com̓ . i . hidā . Tra . ē . ii . car̓ . 7 ibi . ē cū

iii . bord̓ . P̊tū . i . car̓ . 7 i . molin̄ . xviii . ſot . Valet

xl . ſot . Q̣do recep̓ . xx . ſot . T.R.E. xl . ſot . Hanc

trā tenuit Gr̊ibald̓ hō Eddeue . n̄ potuit dare nec uende̓.

BELLINGEHĀ ten̓ Ordmær de com̓ . IN STAPLEHOV HĎ.

p . iii . hid̓ 7 dim̄ ſe defd̓ . T . R . E . 7 m̊ p . ii . hid̓ 7 dim̄.

Tra . ē . vi . car̓ . In dn̄io ſunt . ii . 7 ix . uitti cū . vi . bord̓

hn̄t . iiii . car̓ . Ibi . vi . ſerui . 7 ii . molini . Vn̄ redd̓ . vi . ſot.

7 alt moliturā de dn̄io . P̊tū . ii . car̓ . Paſta ad pec̓ uillæ.

In totis ualent̓ uał 7 ualuit . lx . ſot . T.R.E. c . ſot . Hoc

Ⓜ tenuit Ordmær ſub Eddeua . 7 potuit dare cui uoluit.

2 slaves; 1 mill at 4s 4d and 100 eels; meadow for 1 plough;
     pasture for their livestock.
Value 40s; when acquired 20s; before 1066 the same.
     6 Freemen held this land under Edeva; they could not withdraw
without her permission, but they found 3 escorts and 1 cartage a
year for the Sheriff.

64   In the same village 3 men-at-arms hold 3 hides and 1 virgate from
the Count. Land for 4 ploughs; they are there, with
     3 villagers; 2 slaves.
     Meadow for 2 ploughs.
Value 100s; when acquired 55s; before 1066 the same.
     Huscarl, King Edward's man, held 3 virgates of this land;
he found cartage. He could grant and sell his land, but the
jurisdiction remained with the King. Edeva held 1 hide and   195 c
1 virgate of this land and Wulfwy, her man, 1 hide and 1 virgate;
Edeva had its jurisdiction.

65   Odo holds 4 hides from Count Alan. Land for 9 ploughs.
In lordship 2;
     8 villagers with 7 smallholders have 7 ploughs.
     6 slaves; 1 mill, 5s 4d; meadow for 9 ploughs; pasture for the
          village livestock.
The total value is and was £12; before 1066 £10.
     Ordmer, Edeva's man, held this land; he could grant to whom
he would.

66   Odo holds 1 hide from the Count. Land for 2 ploughs; it is there,
with
     3 smallholders.
     Meadow for 1 plough; 1 mill, 18s.
Value 40s; when acquired 20s; before 1066, 40s.
     Grimbald, Edeva's man, held this land; he could not grant or sell.

In STAPLOE Hundred
67   Ordmer holds BADLINGHAM from the Count. It answered for 3½ hides
before 1066, now for 2½ hides. Land for 6 ploughs. In lordship 2;
     9 villagers with 6 smallholders have 4 ploughs.
     6 slaves; 2 mills, 1 pays 6s, the other (pays) milling from the
          lordship; meadow for 2 ploughs; pasture for the village livestock.
In total, the value is and was 60s; before 1066, 100s.
     Ordmer held this manor under Edeva; he could grant to whom he
would.

In Effellinge ten̄ Wihomarc de com̄.1.hiđ 7 dim̄.

Tra.ē.111.car̄.In dn̄io suɴ.11.car̄.7 1111.uitłi hn̄t.1.car̄.

Ibi.v111.ſerui.7 1.molin̄.v.soliđ 7 1111.den̄.Piſcar̄.mitł

7 cc.anguitł.p̄tū.11.car̄.Paſta ad pecun̄ uillæ.Val 7 ua

luit.L.ſoł.T.R.E.́LX.ſoł.Hanc tr̄a tenuit Alſi hō Eddeuæ.

7 potuit abſq̷ ej licentia recedē.

In Buruuelle ten̄ Alan̄ de.A.com̄.11.hiđ 7 dim̄.Tra ē

v.car̄.In dnio ſunt.11.7 1111.uitłi hn̄t.111.car̄.Ibi.1111.ſerui.

7 11.molini de.v1.soliđ 7 v111.den̄.P̄tū.111.car̄.Paſta

ad pecun̄ uillæ.Val.1111.liƀ.Q̱do recep̄.́111.liƀ.T.R.E.́

v1.liƀ.Hanc tr̄a tenuer̄ ſub Eddeua.11.sochi.potuer̄

ſine lictia ej recedē.Vn̄ hoȝ inuen̄ jneuuard in ſeru regis.

In ead uilla ten̄ Goisfriđ.1.hiđ 7 1.uirg.de.A.comite.

Tra.ē.11.car̄.7 ibi ſunt in dn̄io cū.111.uitłis 7 11.ſeruis.

P̄tū.1.car̄.Paſta ad pecun̄ uillæ.Val.XL.ſoł.Q̱do recep̄.́

xxx.ſoł.T.R.E.́XL.ſoł.Hanc tr̄a tenuit.1.sochs ſub

Eddeua.potuit recedē ſine ej licentia.

In Forh̄a.ten̄ Wihomarc de com̄.111.hiđ 7 dim̄.Tra.ē

1111.car̄.In dn̄io.1.hida.7 1.car̄.7 sochi hn̄t.111.car̄.

p̄tū.1.car̄.Paſta ad pec uillæ.Val.1111.liƀ.Q̱do recep̄.́

111.liƀ.T.R.E.́LXX.ſoł.Hanc tr̄a tenuer̄.111.sochi.quoȝ

11.hoēs Eddeue.tcius hō Algari.potuer̄ recedē ſine

licentia eoȝ.Jneuuard 7 Auer̄a uicecomiti inuenieƀ.

In Giſłeh̄a ten̄ Gaufriđ de com̄.XL.ac̄s træ.Tra eſt

1111.boƀ.P̄tū ipſis boƀ.7 11.uitłi.Val.x.ſoł.Q̱do recep̄.́v.ſoł.

195 d

T.R.E.́x.ſoł.Hanc tr̄a tenuer̄.11.sochi.hoēs.R.E.

fuer̄.recedē potuer̄.Auer̄a ł ineuuard inunieƀ uicecom̄.

68   In EXNING Wymarc holds 1½ hides from the Count. Land for 3 ploughs.
In lordship 2 ploughs;
    4 villagers have 1 plough.
    8 slaves; 1 mill, 5s 4d; a fishery, 1,200 eels; meadow for 2 ploughs;
        pasture for the village livestock.
The value is and was 50s; before 1066, 60s.
    Alfsi, Edeva's man, held this land; he could withdraw without her
permission.

69   In BURWELL Alan holds 2½ hides from Count Alan. Land for 5 ploughs.
In lordship 2.
    4 villagers have 3 ploughs.
    4 slaves; 2 mills at 6s 8d; meadow for 3 ploughs; pasture for the
        village livestock.
Value £4; when acquired £3; before 1066 £6.
    2 Freemen held this land under Edeva; they could withdraw
without her permission. One of them found escort or 4d in the
King's service.

70   In the same village Geoffrey holds 1 hide and 1 virgate from Count
Alan. Land for 2 ploughs; they are there in lordship, with
    3 villagers; 2 slaves.
    Meadow for 1 plough; pasture for the village livestock.
Value 40s; when acquired 30s; before 1066, 40s.
    1 Freeman held this land under Edeva; he could withdraw
without her permission.

71   In FORDHAM Wymarc holds 3½ hides from the Count. Land for
4 ploughs. In lordship 1 hide and 1 plough;
    Freemen have 3 ploughs.
    Meadow for 1 plough; pasture for the village livestock.
Value £4; when acquired £3; before 1066, 70s.
    3 Freemen held this land; 2 of them were Edeva's men, the third
Earl Algar's man; they could withdraw without their permission.
They found escort and cartage for the Sheriff.

72   In ISLEHAM Geoffrey holds 40 acres of land from the Count.
Land for 4 oxen.
    Meadow for these oxen;
    2 villagers.
Value 10s; when acquired 5s; before 1066, 10s.   195 d
    2 Freemen held this land; they were King Edward's men;
they could withdraw. They found cartage or escort for the Sheriff.

In Sahā teñ Adeſtan̄.ɪ.hid̄.de coɱ.Tra.e.ɪɪɪɪ.car̄.

In dñio.ɪ.car̄.7 vɪ.uiłłi cū.vɪɪɪ.bord̄ hñt.ɪɪ.car̄.7 ɪɪɪ.

pot̄ fieri.Ptū.ɪɪɪ.car̄.Paſta ad pec uillæ.7 ɪ.milleñ

★ 7 dim anguiłł.7 in mara de Sahā.ɪ.ſagenā c̄ſuetud̄.

Vał.ʟx.ſoł.Qdo recep̄.vɪ.lib̄.7 tñtd̄ T.R.E.Hanc trā

tenuit Alſi ſub Eddeua.7 potuit recede ſine ej licentia.

Ipſe comes teñ *WICHA*.p.vɪɪ.hid̄ ſe defd̄ T.R.E.7 m̄

p.v.hid̄.Tra.xɪɪ.car̄.In dñio.ɪɪɪ.hide.7 ɪɪɪ.car̄.7 ɪɪɪɪ.

pot̄ fieri.Ibi xɪ.uiłłi cū vɪɪɪ.bord̄.hñt.vɪɪɪ.car̄.

Ibi.v.ſerui.7 ɪɪɪ.molini de xxvɪɪɪ.ſoł.7 ɪɪɪɪ.mił 7 cc

7 ʟ.anguiłł.Ptū.xɪɪ.car̄.Paſta ad pecun uillæ.7 p

conſuetud̄.ɪɪɪ.ſagenas in mara de Sahā.In totis ua

lentijs uał 7 ualuit.xɪɪɪɪ.lib̄.T.R.E.vɪ.lib̄.Hoc m̄

tenuit Eddeua pulchra. *IN RADEFELLE HVND̄.*

In Dulinghā teñ.ɪɪ.milites de coɱ.ɪɪ.hid̄ 7 x.ac̄s.

Tra.e.ɪɪ.car̄.7 ibi ſunt cū.ɪɪ.uiłłis 7 ɪx.bord̄.7 ɪɪ.ſeruis.

Ptū.ɪɪ.bob̄.Vał 7 ualuit ſēp xʟɪɪɪɪ.ſoł.Hanc trā

tenuer̄.ɪɪɪ.ſochi.ñ potuer̄ recede.

In Sticeſuuorde teñ.A.coɱ dim hid̄.Tra.e dim car̄.

7 ibi.e.Vał 7 ualuit ſēp.x.ſoł.Hanc tenuit Grim hō

Eddeue.ñ potuit recede

In Weſlai teñ.ɪɪ.milites de coɱ.ɪ.hid̄.Tra.e.ɪɪ.car̄.

7 ibi ſuꝗ cū.ɪɪɪɪ.bord̄.Vał 7 ualuit ſēp.xx.ſoł.Hanc

trā tenuer̄.vɪɪ.ſochi ſub Eddeua.Aueras.ɪɪɪɪ.inuenieb̄.

in ſeruitio regis.ñ potuer̄ recede ſine lic̄tia dñæ.

m̄ Ipſe comes teñ *BVRCH*.Ibi.v.hid̄.Tra.e.vɪɪɪ.car̄.In

dñio.ɪɪɪ.hidæ.7 ibi ſuꝗ.ɪɪɪɪ.car̄.Ibi.vɪɪ.uiłłi cū.x.bord̄

hñt.ɪɪɪɪ.car̄.Ibi.ɪɪ.ſerui.7 ɪɪɪɪ.ac̄ pti.Parcus beſtiarū

ſiluatic̄.In totis ualent uał.ɪx.lib̄.Qdo recep̄.vɪɪɪ.lib̄.

T.R.E.x.lib̄.Hanc trā tenuit Eddeua.

73   In SOHAM Adestan holds 1 hide from the Count. Land for 4 ploughs.
In lordship 1 plough;
    6 villagers with 8 smallholders have 2 ploughs; a third possible.
    Meadow for 3 ploughs; pasture for the village livestock;
      1½ thousand eels; in Soham Mere 1 fishing-net [for]
      customary dues.
Value 60s; when acquired £6; before 1066 as much.
    Alfsi held this land under Edeva; he could withdraw without
her permission.

74   The Count holds WICKEN himself. It answered for 7 hides before
1066, now for 5 hides. Land for 12 ploughs. In lordship 3 hides
and 3 ploughs; a fourth [plough] possible.
    11 villagers with 8 smallholders have 8 ploughs.
    5 slaves; 3 mills at 28s and 4,250 eels; meadow for 12 ploughs;
      pasture for the village livestock; 3 fishing-nets in Soham
      Mere for customary dues.
In total, the value is and was £14; before 1066 £6.
    Edeva the Fair held this manor.

  In RADFIELD Hundred

75   In DULLINGHAM 2 men-at-arms hold 2 hides and 10 acres from the
Count. Land for 2 ploughs; they are there, with
    2 villagers; 9 smallholders; 2 slaves.
    Meadow for 2 oxen.
The value is and was 44s.
    3 Freemen held this land; they could not withdraw.

76   In STETCHWORTH Count Alan holds ½ hide. Land for ½ plough;
it is there.
The value is and always was 10s.
    Grim, Edeva's man, held it; he could not withdraw.

77   In WESTLEY (Waterless) 2 men-at-arms hold 1 hide from the Count.
Land for 2 ploughs; they are there, with
    4 smallholders.
The value is and always was 20s.
    7 Freemen held this land under Edeva. They found 4 cartages
in the King's service; they could not withdraw without their
lady's permission.

78 M. The Count holds BURROUGH (Green) himself. 5 hides. Land for
8 ploughs. In lordship 3 hides; 4 ploughs there.
    7 villagers with 10 smallholders have 4 ploughs.
    2 slaves; meadow, 4 acres; a park for woodland beasts.
In total, value £9; when acquired £8; before 1066 £10.
    Edeva held this land.

In Carlentone ten Wihomarc de com.i.uirg træ.

Quidã fochs tenuit.7 auerã inuenit.

Ifdē Wihomarc ten de com.i.hid 7 dim.Tra.e.iii.
car.In dnio fuɴ.ii.7 iii.uilti cũ.iii.bord hnt.i.car.
Ibi.iii.serui.Ptũ.ii.bob.Silua.x.porc.Val 7 ualuit
iii.lib.Hanc trã tenuit Goduin sub Eddeua.ñ pot recede.

In Waratinge ten Almar de com.i.hid 7 dim.Tra.e
iiii.car.In dnio.fuɴ.ii.7 iii.uilti cũ.i.bord hnt.ii.car.
Ibi.i.feruus.7 Silua.viii.porc.Val lx.fol.Qdo recep.
xx.fol.T.R.E.similit.Hanc trã tenuer.ii.fochi sub Eddeua.
ñ potuer recede ab ea.Vñ eoʒ inuen Averã uicecom.

In Belefhã ten Almar de com.xl.acs træ.Ħ appciat cũ
alia tra.Leflet tenuit sub Eddeua.ñ potuit recede ab ea.

196 a

XXV. TERRA EVSTACHIJ COMITIS. *IN WITELESFORD HD.*

Comes EVSTACHIVS ten *HICHELINTONE*.ꝑ xix.hid
7 dim se defd.Tra.e.xxiiii.car.In dnio.ix.hidæ.7 ibi
iii.car.7 iiii.pot fieri.Ibi.xxx.uilti cũ.x.bord hnt xvi.
car.7 iiii.adhuc poff fieri.Ibi.iii.serui.7 ii.molini.xxx.folid.
Ptũ.iii.car.Int tot ual xx.lib.Qdo recep.xx.iiii.lib.
7 T.R.E.similit.Hoc ᛘ tenuit Alfi teign.R.E.

In Dochefuuorde.ten ipfe com.v.hid 7 iii.uirg.Tra.e
vi.car.In dnio.e.i.car.7 ii.plus poff fieri.Ibi.ii.uilti
cũ.vi.bord hnt.ii.car.7.iii.pot fieri.Ibi.i.molin de
xii.fol fuit.ɱ confract fʒ pot restaurari.Ptũ.ii.car.
Int tot ual.c.fol.Qdo recep.vii.lib.7 tntd T.R.E.
Hanc trã ten Hernulf de com.E.Herulf tenuit de
rege.E.vii.uirg.7 Stigand archieps.iii.hid 7 dim.
De hac tra ten Wido de com E.dim hid 7 i.molin
ad firmã.Int tot ual.xx.viii.fol 7 viii.den.Hanc trã
tenuit Ingara·de rege.E.7 potuit uendere.

79   In CARLTON Wymarc holds 1 virgate of land from the Count.
A Freeman held it; he found cartage.

80   Wymarc also holds 1½ hides from the Count. Land for 3 ploughs.
In lordship 2;
    3 villagers with 3 smallholders have 1 plough.
    3 slaves; meadow for 2 oxen; woodland, 10 pigs.
The value is and was £3.
    Young Godwin held this land under Edeva; he could not
withdraw.

81   In (West) WRATTING Aelmer holds 1½ hides from the Count.
Land for 4 ploughs. In lordship 2;
    3 villagers with 1 smallholder have 2 ploughs.
    1 slave; woodland, 8 pigs.
Value 60s; when acquired 20s; before 1066 the same.
    2 Freemen held this land under Edeva; they could not withdraw
from her. One of them found cartage for the Sheriff.

82   In BALSHAM Aelmer holds 40 acres of land from the Count. It is
assessed with the other land. Leofled held (it) under Edeva; she
could not withdraw from her.

25 [15]   **LAND OF COUNT EUSTACE**   196 a

In WHITTLESFORD Hundred

1   Count Eustace holds ICKLETON. It answers for 19½ hides. Land for
24 ploughs. In lordship 9 hides; 3 ploughs there; a fourth possible.
    30 villagers with 10 smallholders have 16 ploughs; a further 4
      possible.
    3 slaves; 2 mills, 30s; meadow for 3 ploughs.
In total, value £20; when acquired £24; before 1066 the same.
    Alfsi, King Edward's thane, held this manor.

2   In DUXFORD the Count holds 5 hides and 3 virgates himself. Land
for 6 ploughs. In lordship 1 plough; 2 more possible.
    2 villagers with 6 smallholders have 2 ploughs; a third possible.
    1 mill at 12s was there; now it is broken, but it can be repaired.
      Meadow for 2 ploughs.
In total, value 100s; when acquired £7; before 1066 as much.
    Arnulf holds this land from Count Eustace. Horwulf held 7
virgates from King Edward, and Archbishop Stigand (held) 3½ hides.
    Guy holds ½ hide of this land and 1 mill at a revenue from Count
Eustace.
In total, value 28s 8d.
    Ingvar held this land from King Edward and could sell.

In Trūpintone ten Ernulf de arda ſub comite.ɪɪ.hiđ
7 ɪ.uirg 7 dim.Tra.ē.ɪɪ.car 7 dim.In dñio.ē.ɪ.7 dim.
7 ɪɪɪ.uiłłi hñt.ɪ.car.Ibi.ɪ.ſeru.7 p̃tū carr.Int toꞇ uał
7 ualuit.ɪɪɪɪ.liɓ.T.R.E.c.ſoł.Hanc trā tenuit Herulf
teign.R.E.potuit dare cui uoluit. *IN WEDERLAI HVNⱵ.*
In Granteſete ten.ɪɪ.milit de com.ɪɪ.hiđ 7 ɪɪɪ.uirg.
Tra.ē.ᴠɪ.car.In dñio ſunt.ɪɪɪ.7 ɪɪɪ.uiłłi 7 dim cū.xɪɪɪ.
borđ 7 xᴠɪ.coꞇ hñt.ɪɪɪ.car.Ibi.ɪ.moliñ de xʟ.ſoł.P̃tū
ɪɪɪɪ.car.Int toꞇ uał.ᴠɪɪɪ.liɓ.Q̧do recep̃.x.liɓ.7 tñtđ
T.R.E.Hanc trā tenuer.ɪɪɪ.ſochi.quoꝗ.ɪɪ.hōes regis.E.
uendē potuer.7 ɪɪɪ.hō Aſgari ſtalri dim hiđ habuit.
7 auerā inuen.uendē tam trā ſuā potuit.

XXVI **C**TERRA CANONICOꝗ BAIOCENSIᴠ. *IN STOV HVNⱵ.*
anonici baiocenſes ten in Hecteſlei.ɪɪɪ.hiđ.Tra.ē.ɪx.
car.In dñio.ɪ.hiđ 7 dim.7 ibi ſunt.ɪɪɪ.car.7 ᴠɪ.uiłłi
cū.x.borđ hñt.ᴠɪ.car.Ibi.ᴠ.coꞇ 7 ᴠɪ.ſerui.P̃tū.ɪɪɪɪ.
car.Silua.xx.porc.In totis ualent uał 7 ualuit ſēp
xɪɪɪ.liɓ.Hoc ʍ tenuit com Algarus.

XXVII. **W**TERRA WALTERIJ GIFARD. *IN STANES HVNⱵ.*
ALTERIVS Gifard ten *BODICHESSHA*.p.x.hiđ
ſe defđ.Tra.ē.xx.car.In dñio.ᴠ.hidæ.7 ibi.ſunt ᴠɪ.car.Ibi
xxᴠ.uiłłi cū.xɪɪ.borđ.hñt.xɪɪɪɪ.car.Ibi.xɪɪɪɪ.ſerui.
7 ɪɪɪɪ.moł de xɪɪɪɪ.ſoł.P̃tū.ᴠɪ.car.De mareſc.ɪɪɪ.ſocos.
7 cccc.Anguiłł.In totis ualent uał 7 ualuit.xx.liɓ.
T.R.E.xᴠɪ.liɓ.De hoc ʍ tenuit Harold.ᴠɪɪɪ.hiđ.
7 Alricus monach habuit.ɪɪ.hiđ.q̃s ñ potuit dare uel
uendē abſꝗ licentia abɓis de Rameſy.cuj hō erat.

In THRIPLOW Hundred

3   In TRUMPINGTON Arnulf of Ardres holds 2 hides and 1½ virgates
under the Count. Land for 2½ ploughs. In lordship 1½;
    3 villagers have 1 plough.
    1 slave; meadow for the ploughs.
In total, the value is and was £4; before 1066, 100s.
    Horwulf, King Edward's thane, held this land and could grant
to whom he would.

In WETHERLEY Hundred

4   In GRANTCHESTER 2 men-at-arms hold 2 hides and 3 virgates from
the Count. Land for 6 ploughs. In lordship 3;
    3½ villagers with 13 smallholders and 16 cottagers have
        3 ploughs.
    1 mill at 40s; meadow for 4 ploughs.
In total, value £8; when acquired £10; before 1066 as much.
    3 Freemen held this land, 2 of whom, King Edward's men,
could sell. The third, Asgar the Constable's man, had ½ hide
and found cartage; however, he could sell his land.

26 [16]   LAND OF THE CANONS OF BAYEUX

In LONGSTOW Hundred

1   The Canons of Bayeux hold 3 hides in ELTISLEY. Land for 9 ploughs.
In lordship 1½ hides; 3 ploughs there;
    6 villagers with 10 smallholders have 6 ploughs.
        5 cottagers; 6 slaves.
    Meadow for 3 ploughs; woodland, 20 pigs.
The total value is and always was £13.
    Earl Algar held this manor.

27 [17]   LAND OF WALTER GIFFARD

In STAINE Hundred

1   Walter Giffard holds BOTTISHAM. It answers for 10 hides. Land for
20 ploughs. In lordship 5 hides; 6 ploughs there.
    25 villagers with 12 smallholders have 14 ploughs.
    14 slaves; 4 mills at 14s; meadow for 6 ploughs; from the marsh
        3 ploughshares and 400 eels.
The total value is and was £20; before 1066 £16.
    Earl Harold held 8 hides of this manor; Alric the monk had
2 hides which he could not grant or sell without the permission of
the Abbot of Ramsey, whose man he was.

In Suafhā teñ Hugo dē Walterio . vii . hid 7 dim . 7 x.

acs . Tra . ē . xi . car . In dñio . funt . iii . 7 xii . uilli cū . iiii.

bord hñt . viii . car . Ibi . iii . ferui . 7 iii . mol de xxx . fol

iiii . deñ min . 7 ccc . Anguill . Ptū . iii . car . Pafta ad pec

uillæ . In totis ualent ual . xii . lib . Qdo recep . x . lib . 7 tñtd

T.R.E. Hoc ꟿ tenuit Aluui harpari . iii . hid 7 i . moliñ

de dñica firma monachoꝛ de Elẏ . 7 ipfi habeb 7 in uita

7 in morte regis . E . ñ potuit recede abfq̨ licția abbis.

7 iii . fochi hões abbis tenueř . ii . hid|7 x . acs . nec ifti potueř

recede abfq̨ licția abbis . 7 xix . fochi hões regis . E . tenueř

ii . hid . ñ potueř recede abfq̨ licția dñi fui . fed fēp

inuenieb auerā 7 ineuuard uicecomiti regis.

In ead uilla teñ Hugo de Walto . iii . uirg . Tra . ē . i . car.

7 ibi . ē cū . iiii . bord . Ptū . i . car . Val 7 ualuit x . fol.

T.R.E. xx . fol . Hanc trā tenuit Wluuiñ hō abbis de Elẏ.

ñ potuit recede ab æccła fine eꝭ licentia . *IN WEDERLAI HD.*

In Herletone teñ Walter . f . albici de Walterio . iiii . hid.

Tra . ē . vi . car . In dñio funt . ii . 7 vii . uilli cū . ix . bord hñt

iiii . car . Ibi . ii . ferui . 7 dim moliñ de xiii . fol 7 iiii . deñ.

7 c . anguill . Ptū . iii . car . Int tot redd . vii . lib . Qdo

recep . vi . lib . T.R.E. viii . lib . Hanc trā tenuit Achi

teign regis . E . 7 ibi . v . fochi fueř . 7 v . ineuuard inueneř.

7 trā fuā uende potueř.

In Barenton teñ ifd Walt de Walterio . xl . acs . Tra

ē . vi . bob . 7 ibi funt . cū . ii . cot . Ptū . vi . bob . Val 7 ua

luit fēp . x . fol . Hanc trā tenuit Achi hō Heraldi.

7 dare 7 uende potuit.

In Orduuelle teñ Walt de Walterio . i . uirg . Tra . ē

ii . bob . Ibi funt . iii . bord . Val 7 ualuit fēp . ii . fol . Hanc

trā tenuit Achi hō Heraldi . Ħ ꝑtiñ ad herletone.

2   In SWAFFHAM (Bulbeck) Hugh holds 7½ hides and 10 acres from   196 b
    Walter. Land for 11 ploughs. In lordship 3;
        12 villagers with 4 smallholders have 8 ploughs.
        3 slaves; 3 mills at 30s less 4d and 300 eels; meadow for 3
            ploughs; pasture for the village livestock.
    Total value £12; when acquired £10; before 1066 as much.
        Alwy the Harper held this manor; 3 hides and 1 mill of the
    household revenue of the monks of Ely; they held (them) them-
    selves before and in 1066; he could not withdraw without the
    Abbot's permission.
        3 Freemen, the Abbot's men, held 2½ hides and 10 acres;
    these men could not withdraw without the Abbot's permission.
        19 Freemen, King Edward's men, held 2 hides; they could not
    withdraw without their lord's permission, but they always found
    cartage and escort for the King's Sheriff.

3   In the same village Hugh holds 3 virgates from Walter. Land for
    1 plough; it is there, with
        4 smallholders.
        Meadow for 1 plough.
    The value is and was 10s; before 1066, 20s.
        Wulfwin, the Abbot of Ely's man, held this land; he could not
    withdraw from the Church without his permission.

    In WETHERLEY Hundred
4   In HARLTON Walter son of Aubrey holds 4 hides from Walter
    Giffard. Land for 6 ploughs. In lordship 2;
        7 villagers with 9 smallholders have 4 ploughs.
        2 slaves; ½ mill at 13s 4d and 100 eels; meadow for
            3 ploughs.
    In total, it pays £7; when acquired £6; before 1066 £8.
        Aki, King Edward's thane, held this land. 5 Freemen were
    there; they found 5 escorts and could sell their land.

5   In BARRINGTON Walter also holds 40 acres from Walter Giffard.
    Land for 6 oxen; they are there, with
        2 cottagers.
        Meadow for 6 oxen.
    The value is and always was 10s.
        Aki, Earl Harold's man, held this land; he could grant and sell.

6   In ORWELL Walter holds 1 virgate from Walter Giffard. Land for
    2 oxen.
        3 smallholders.
    The value is and always was 2s.
        Aki, Earl Harold's man, held this land. It belongs to Harlton.

WILLELM de Warenna ten̄ In Carlentone . ii . hid̄
7 vii . ac̄s 7 dim̄ . Walt de Grantcurt ten̄ de eo . Tra . ē . iiii .
car̄ . In dn̄io funt . iii . 7 un uil̄ls 7 dim̄ cū . iii . bord̄ hn̄t
. i . car̄ . Ibi . iii . ſerui . P̄tū . ii . bob . Silua . xii . porc̄ . Val̄
7 ualuit ſēp . iiii . lib̄ . Hoc M̄ tenuit Tochi teign̄ . R . E .

In ead̄ uilla ten̄ abb̄ de Cluniaco . iiii . hid̄ 7 ii . ac̄s
de Wil̄lo . Tra . ē . vii . car̄ . In dn̄io funt . iii . 7 iiii . uil̄li
cū . xiiii . bord̄ hn̄t . iii . car̄ . Ibi . iii . ſerui . Silua . c . porc̄ .
Val̄ 7 ualuit ſēp . viii . lib̄ . Hanc tr̄a tenuit Algar

M̄ Ipſe Wil̄ls ten̄ *WESTONE* . p . vii . hid̄ ſe defd̄ . Tra . ē
xv . car̄ . In dn̄io . iiii . hide . 7 ibi funt . ii . car̄ . 7 iii . pot
fieri . Ibi . xix . uil̄li cū . vii . bord̄ . hn̄t xii . car̄ . Ibi
v . ſerui . 7 iiii . ac̄ p̄ti . Silua . ccc . porc̄ . Int totum

196 c

val̄ . xvi . lib̄ . 7 i . unc̄ auri . Q̄do recep̄ : x lib̄ . 7 tn̄td̄
T . R . E . Hanc tr̄a tenebat Tochi de abb̄e de Ely die
qua rex . E . fuit uiuus 7 mortuus . ita qd̄ n̄ poterat eā
ſeparare ab æccl̄a . q̄m dn̄ica firma erat de abbatia .
ut hōes de Hund̄ teſtant̄ . In hac tr̄a fuer̄ . ii . ſochi
un̄ inuen̄ Auerā 7 alt̄ Ineuuard̄ . Hōes Goduini eraɴ .
nec ab eo recede poterant . In ead̄ uilla ten̄ Walt . i . uirḡ .
In Waratinge ten̄ Lanb̄t . iii . uirḡ de Wil̄lo . ᚠ de Wil̄lo .
Tra . ē dim̄ car̄ . 7 ibi . ē . cū . i . uil̄lo . 7 dim̄ ac̄ p̄ti . Val̄
7 ualuit . ſēp . v . ſol̄ . Hanc tr̄a tenuit Tochi de rege . E .
7 i . Auerā inueniebat .   *IN CILDEFORD HVND.*

In Wichehā ten̄ Lanb̄t de Wil̄lo . i . hid̄ . Tra . ē . iii . car̄
7 dim̄ . In dn̄io funt . ii . 7 x . bord̄ hn̄t . i . car̄ 7 dim̄ .
Ibi . iii . ſerui . 7 p̄tū . i . car̄ . Silua . xii . porc̄ . Val̄ 7 ua
luit ſēp . c . ſol̄ . Hanc tr̄a tenuit Tochi . 7 i . ſochs ibi
fuit qui Auerā inuenieb̄ .

196 b, c

LAND OF WILLIAM OF WARENNE

In RADFIELD Hundred

1   William of Warenne holds 2 hides and 7½ acres in CARLTON.
Walter of Grand-court holds from him. Land for 4 ploughs.
In lordship 3;
    1½ villagers with 3 smallholders have 1 plough.
    3 slaves; meadow for 2 oxen; woodland, 12 pigs.
The value is and always was £4.
    Toki, King Edward's thane, held this manor.

2   In the same village the Abbot of Cluny holds 4 hides and 2 acres
from William. Land for 7 ploughs. In lordship 3;
    4 villagers with 14 smallholders have 3 ploughs.
    3 slaves; woodland, 100 pigs.
The value is and always was £8.
    Earl Algar held this land.

3 M. William holds WESTON (Colville) himself. It answers for 7 hides.
Land for 15 ploughs. In lordship 4 hides; 2 ploughs there; a
third possible.
    19 villagers with 7 smallholders have 12 ploughs.
    5 slaves; meadow, 4 acres; woodland, 300 pigs.
In total, value £16 and 1 ounce of gold; when acquired £10;   196 c
before 1066 as much.
    Toki held this land from the Abbot of Ely in 1066, on condition
that he could not separate it from the Church, it being in the Abbey's
household revenue, as the men of the Hundred testify.
    There were 2 Freemen on this land; one found cartage and the
other escort. They were Young Godwin's men; they could not
withdraw from him.

4   In the same village Walter holds 1 virgate from William.

5   In (West) WRATTING Lambert holds 3 virgates from William. Land
for ½ plough; it is there, with
    1 villager;
    meadow, ½ acre.
The value is and always was 5s.
    Toki held this land from King Edward; it found 1 cartage.

In CHILFORD Hundred

6   In (West) WICKHAM Lambert holds 1 hide from William. Land for
3½ ploughs. In lordship 2;
    10 smallholders have 1½ ploughs.
    3 slaves; meadow for 1 plough; woodland, 12 pigs.
The value is and always was 100s.
    Toki held this land.
    1 Freeman was there who found cartage.

In Trûpinton ten̅ Witts . IIII . hiꝺ 7 dim̅ . Tra . e̅ . v . car̅.

In dn̅io funt . II . 7 IX . uitti cū . IIII . borꝺ hn̅t . III . car̅.

Ibi . I . molin de . xx . fot . Ptū . v . car̅ . Pafta ad peꞓ uillæ.

7 IIII . focos . Vat 7 ualuit . vI . liƀ . T.R.E. vII . liƀ . Hanc

tra̅ tenuit Tochi de æccta de Elẏ . die q̃ rex . E . fuit uiu̅

7 mortuus . n̅ potuit dare nec uende nec ab æccta fepa

rare . Hanc tra̅ poftea habuit Frederi fr̅ Witti.

ꞏℳꞏ CHENET . T.R.E . fe defꝺ ꝑ . III . hiꝺ . | *IN STAPLEHOV HꝹ.*

7 m̊ ꝑ . II . hiꝺ 7 dim̅ . Tra . e̅ . x . car̅ . Nicol ten̅ de Witto.

In dn̅io fuꝕ . v . car̅ . 7 vII . uitti cū . v . borꝺ hn̅t . v . car̅.

Ibi . xII . ferui . 7 I . molin̅ nit redꝺ . Ptū . II . car̅ . Pafta

ad pecun̅ uillæ . In totis ualent uat . xII . liƀ . Qꝺo

receꝑ. IX . liƀ . T.R.E. xII . liƀ . Hoc ℳ tenuit Tochit

teign̅ regis . E . 7 ibiꝺ . I . foctis . I . uirg̅ fub eo habuit.

Auera̅ ɫ . vIII . den inuen̅ . tra̅ fua̅ ta̅m dare 7 uende.

In Wifbece ht̅ Witts . vI . pifcatores . *IN HVNꝹ DE ELẎ.*

reddtes . III . mitt Anguitt 7 dim̅ . 7 v . fot.

Ꞃ TERRA RICARDI FILIJ GISLEBERT *IN PAPEWORD HVNꝹ.*

.XXV. ꞀICARꝺ fit Giftebti ten̅ in Papeuuorde . I . uirg̅ træ.

7 Witts de eo . Tra . e̅ . IIII . boƀ . 7 ptū totiꝺ boƀ . Vat . IIII.

fot . Qꝺo receꝑ. v . fot . T.R.E. vIII . fot . Hanc tra̅ tenuit

Aluriꞓ ꝑƀr de aƀƀe de Elẏ . 7 ab eo recede n̅ potuit.

Soca etia̅ fep in æccta jacuit . Hanc tra̅ Ricarꝺ fuꝑ

rege̅ occupauit . 7 de ea . xx . fot pecuniæ accepit.

In Horfei ten̅ Wlueua dim̅ uirg̅ *IN CILDEFORD HVNꝹ.*

de Ricarꝺo . Tra . e̅ . IIII . boƀ . Vat 7 ualuit . v . fot.

In Wicheha̅ ten̅ Wlueua de Ricarꝺo dim̅ uirg̅ . 7 uat

v . fot . 7 un̅ foctis . IIII . part . I . uirg̅ . 7 uat xII . denar̅.

In THRIPLOW Hundred

7 In TRUMPINGTON William holds 4½ hides. Land for 5 ploughs.
In lordship 2;
    9 villagers with 4 smallholders have 3 ploughs.
    1 mill at 20s; meadow for 5 ploughs; pasture for the village
      livestock; 4 ploughshares.
The value is and was £6; before 1066 £7.
    Toki held this land from the Church of Ely in 1066; he could
not grant, sell or separate (it) from the Church. Afterwards,
Frederick, William's brother, had this land.

In STAPLOE Hundred

8 M. KENNETT answered for 3½ hides before 1066; now for 2½ hides.
Land for 10 ploughs. Nicholas holds from William. In lordship
5 ploughs;
    7 villagers with 5 smallholders have 5 ploughs.
    12 slaves; 1 mill which pays nothing; meadow for 2 ploughs;
      pasture for the village livestock.
Total value £12; when acquired £9; before 1066 £12.
    Toki, King Edward's thane, held this manor. 1 Freeman
also had 1 virgate under him there; he found cartage or 8d;
however, he could grant and sell his land.

In the Hundred of ELY
[E2]

9 In WISBECH William has 6 fishermen who pay 3,500 eels and 5s.

25 [19]   LAND OF RICHARD SON OF COUNT GILBERT

In PAPWORTH Hundred

1 Richard son of Count Gilbert holds 1 virgate of land in PAPWORTH,
and William from him. Land for 4 oxen;
    pasture for as many oxen.
Value 4s; when acquired 5s; before 1066, 8s.
    Aelfric the priest held this land from the Abbot of Ely and could
not withdraw from him. The jurisdiction also always lay in (the lands
of) the Church. Richard appropriated this land in the King's despite,
and received 20s of stock from it.

In CHILFORD Hundred

2 In HORSEHEATH Wulfeva holds ½ virgate from Richard. Land for
4 oxen.
The value is and was 5s.

3 In (West) WICKHAM Wulfeva holds ½ virgate from Richard.
Value 5s.
    1 Freeman (holds) the fourth part of 1 virgate. Value 12d.

In Wadune ten Harduin̅ *In Erningford Hd.*

de Ricardo . 1 . uirg̅ træ . Tra . e̅ . 1111 . bob . Val 7 ualuit

v . fol . T.R.E. xv . fol . Hanc tr̅a tenuit Sageua fub

Eddeua pulc̅ . 7 potuit dare cui·uoluit . H̅ n̅ ptinuit

ad Anteceffore̅ Ricardi . nec unq̟ de ea faifit fuit .

fed Radulf eā tenebat die quó c̅tra rege̅ deliq̅t . .
^{Waders}

R TERRA ROBERTI DE TODENI. *In Witelesford Hd.*

OTBERT de Todeni in Dochefuuorde ten̅ . 1111 .

hid 7 dim̅ . Giflebt ten de eo . Tra . e̅ . v . car̅ . In dn̅io . e̅ . 1 .

7 11 . pl pofs . ee̅ . 7 1111 . uilti cū . v . bord hn̅t . 11 . car̅ .

Ibi . 11 . ferui . 7 11 . molini de . L . fol . P̅tu . 11 . car̅ . Valet

v11 . lib̅ 7 x . fol Q̇do recep̅. c 7 x . fol . T.R.E. v111 . lib̅ .

Hanc tr̅a tenuit Vlf teig̅ regis . E .

R TERRA ROBERTI GERNON . *In Cildeford Hvnd.*

OTBERT Gernon ten̅ . 11 . hid in C̅apas . 7 Turftin̅ de eo .

Tra . e̅ . v1 . car̅ . In dn̅io fuṅ . 11 . 7 v111 . uilti cū . v111 . bord .

hn̅t . 1111 . car̅ . Ibi . v1 . ferui . p̅tu . 11 . car̅ . Silua . x11 . porc̅ .

Val . 1111 . lib̅ . Q̇do recep̅. xxx . fol . T . R . E. xl . fol . Hanc

tr̅a tenuit Lepfi fub Heraldo . 7 potuit recede̅ fine lic̅tia ej̅ .
^{comite}

In Dochefuuorde ten Rob̅t dim hid . Val 7 ualuit

v . fol . T.R.E. v1 . fol . Hanc tenuit Aluric de . E . rege .

7 potuit recede̅ . *In Re₁slav Hvnd.*
^{PE}

Ipfe Rob̅t ten Fuglemære . p x . hid fe defd . Tra . e̅ x1 .

car̅ . In dn̅io . v . hidæ . 7 ibi funt . 11 . car̅ 7 dim . Ibi . xx11 .

uilti cū . x . bord . hn̅t . v111 . car̅ 7 dim . Ibi . 1111 . ferui .

7 1 . molin̅ de x . fol 7 v111 . den̅ . P̅tu om̅ib̅ car̅ . Pafta

ad pecun̅ uillæ . 7 x . den̅ . In totis ualent ual 7 ualuit

fēp . x11 . lib̅ . Hoc M̅ tenuit Aluric cap̅ de . E . rege .

In ARMINGFORD Hundred 196 d

4 In WHADDON Hardwin holds 1 virgate of land from Richard.
Land for 4 oxen.
The value is and was 5s; before 1066, 15s.
Saevia held this land under Edeva the Fair; she could grant to whom she would. This did not belong to Richard's predecessor, nor was he ever put in possession of it, but Ralph Wader held it on the day he rebelled against the King.

[20] LAND OF ROBERT OF TOSNY

In WHITTLESFORD Hundred

1 Robert of Tosny holds 4½ hides in DUXFORD. Gilbert holds from him.
Land for 5 ploughs. In lordship 1; 2 more possible;
4 villagers with 5 smallholders have 2 ploughs.
2 slaves; 2 mills at 50s; meadow for 2 ploughs.
Value £7 10s; when acquired 110s; before 1066 £8.
Ulf, King Edward's thane, held this land.

[21] LAND OF ROBERT GERNON

In CHILFORD Hundred

1 Robert Gernon holds 2 hides in CAMPS, and Thurstan from him.
Land for 6 ploughs. In lordship 2;
8 villagers with 8 smallholders have 4 ploughs.
6 slaves; meadow for 2 ploughs; woodland, 12 pigs.
Value £4; when acquired 30s; before 1066, 40s.
Leofsi held this land under Earl Harold, and could withdraw without his permission.

[In WHITTLESFORD Hundred]

2 In DUXFORD Robert holds ½ hide.
The value is and was 5s; before 1066, 6s.
Aelfric held it from King Edward and could withdraw.

In THRIPLOW Hundred

3 M. Robert holds FOWLMERE himself. It answers for 10 hides. Land for 11 ploughs. In lordship 5 hides; 2½ ploughs there.
22 villagers with 10 smallholders have 8½ ploughs.
4 slaves; 1 mill at 10s 8d; meadow for all the ploughs; pasture for the village livestock and 10d.
The total value is and always was £12.
Aelfric Kemp held this manor from King Edward.

In Herleſtone ten Rannulf de Roḃto . i . hiđ 7 i . uirg.

Tra.ē.i.caŕ 7 ii.bob.7 ibi ſunt cū . iii.borđ 7 i.cot.

p̃tū.i.caŕ.Val xxx.ſoł.Qđo receṕ.́xx.ſoł.T.R.E.́xxx.ſoł.

Hanc trā tenuit.i.ſocħs ſub.E.rege   .7 i.ineuuarđ

inueń.7 trā ſuā uendé potuit.f̢ ſoca regi remanſit.

In Barentone ten Roḃt vii.hiđ *In Wederlai Hvnđ.*

7 ii.uirg 7 dim.Tra.ē xi.caŕ.In dn̄io.iii.hiđ 7 dim.

7 ii.part uni uirg.7 ibi.ē.i.caŕ 7 alta pot fieri.Ibi

xx.uiłłi cū.vii.borđ 7 iii.cot hn̄t.ix.caŕ.Ibi.ii.ſerui.

7 i.molin̄ 7 dim de xxx.ii.ſoł.P̃tū.vi.caŕ.In totis

ualent ual.xii.liḃ.Qđo receṕ.́viii.liḃ.T.R.E.́xvi.liḃ.

In hac trā fueŕ.xv.ſocħi tenent de rege.E.iiii.hiđ

7 i.uirg 7 dim.7 inueń uicecomiti.xii.aueras 7 dim.

7 iiii.Ineuuarđ.7 alij.iiii.hōēs Al̄gari tenueŕ.ii.hiđ 7 dim v.

7 alij.iii.hōēs Aſgari.ten.i.hiđ.Om̄s hi potueŕ trā ſuā

dare 7 uendé.De hac q̇q̢ trā tenuit Edric pur

197 a

iii.uirg ſub rege.E.7 uendé potuit.7 dim v tenuit

iſđ Edericus.quæ die mortis.E.regis jacebat in æcc̄la

de Cetriz.Hanc inuaſit Roḃt gernon ſuṗ abbatiſsā.

ut teſtant hōes de hundret.

In Orduuelle ten Roḃt.i.uirg.Tra.ē.iii.bob.7 ibi ſuɴ.

cū.ii.borđ.p̃tū.ii.bob.7 i.molin̄ de.xii.ſoł.Val 7 sēp

ualuit xviii.ſoł 7 viii.den.Hanc trā tenuit.i.ſocħs

regis.E.7 unā Auerā inueń.7 tam̄ trā ſuā uendé potuit.

In Contone ten Picot de Roḃto *In Pape^Sword Hđ.*

i.hiđ 7 i.uirg.Tra.ē.i.caŕ.7 ibi.ē cū.iii.borđ.P̃tū

.i.caŕ 7 dim.Val xvi.ſoł.Qđo receṕ.́xx.ſoł.7 tntđ

T.R.E.Hanc trā tenuit.i.hō Wallef com̄.Soca jacuit

In Bocheſuuorde ten Picot de Roḃto Γ in Stantone.

iii.hiđ 7 dim.Tra.ē.iii.caŕ.In dn̄io ſunt.ii.7 iii.uiłłi

196 d, 197 a

4 In HARSTON Ranulf holds 1 hide and 1 virgate from Robert.
Land for 1 plough and 2 oxen; they are there, with
   3 smallholders; 1 cottager.
   Meadow for 1 plough.
Value 30s; when acquired 20s; before 1066, 30s.
   1 Freeman held this land under King Edward and found
1 escort; he could sell his land, but the jurisdiction remained
with the King.

In WETHERLEY Hundred
5 In BARRINGTON Robert holds 7 hides and 2½ virgates. Land
for 11 ploughs. In lordship 3½ hides and 2 parts of 1 virgate;
1 plough there; a second possible.
   20 villagers with 7 smallholders and 3 cottagers have
      9 ploughs.
   2 slaves; 1½ mills at 32s; meadow for 6 ploughs.
Total value £12; when acquired £8; before 1066 £16.
   There were 15 Freemen in this land who held 4 hides and
1½ virgates from King Edward and who found 12½ cartages
and 4 escorts for the Sheriff; 4 others, Earl Algar's men, held
2 hides and ½ virgate; 3 others, Asgar the Constable's men,
held 1 hide. All these men could grant and sell their land.
   Of this land also Edric Snipe held 3 virgates under King
Edward and could sell. Edric also held ½ virgate which in 1066
lay in (the lands of) the Church of Chatteris. Robert Gernon
annexed this (land) in the Abbess's despite, as the men of the
Hundred testify.

197 a

6 In ORWELL Robert holds 1 virgate. Land for 3 oxen; they are
there, with
   2 smallholders.
   Meadow for 2 oxen; 1 mill at 12s.
The value is and always was 18s 8d.
   A Freeman of King Edward's held this land and found
1 cartage; however, he could sell his land.

In PAPWORTH Hundred
7 In CONINGTON Picot holds 1 hide and 1 virgate from Robert.
Land for 1 plough; it is there, with
   3 smallholders.
   Meadow for 1½ ploughs.
Value 16s; when acquired 20s; before 1066 as much.
   A man of Earl Waltheof's held this land; his jurisdiction
lay in Longstanton.

8 In BOXWORTH Picot holds 3½ hides from Robert. Land for
3 ploughs. In lordship 2;

cū . iii . cot hñt . i . cař . Ibi . ii . ſerui . P̊tū . iii . cař . Valet
xxx . ſoł . Q̣do recep̄ʔ x . ſoł . T.R.E.ʔ lx . ſoł . Hanc t̃ra te
nuit Lefsi hō Wallef comit̃ . 7 uendere potuit.

In Suaueſẏ . teñ Picot de Rob̃to . i . hiđ . T̃ra . ē . i . cař.
7 ibi . ii . borđ . P̊tū . i . cař . Vał 7 ualuit . v . ſoł . T.R.E.ʔ
xx . ſoł . Hanc t̃ra tenuit Lefsi hō Wallef comitis.
7 dare 7 uendẽ potuit . Has t̃ras   teñ Picot uicec
de Rob̃to gernon . in maritagio feminæ ſuæ.

.XX. **G**TERRA GOISFR̃ DE MĀNEVILE. *IN FLAMIDINC HVŃD.*
OISFRIḊ de Manneuille teñ . ii . hiđ 7 dim̃ in Fule
berne . T̃ra . ē . iii . cař . Wilłs teñ de eo . Ibi ſuɴ̃ . iii . cař.
p̊tū . i . cař . Vał . L . ſoł . Q̣do recep̄ʔ . lx . ſoł . 7 tñtđ T.R.E.
Hanc t̃ra tenuit Alſi de Aſgaro . 7 dare potuit abſq̨ eȷ̇ liẗia.

In Salſiton teñ Rogeri̇ de Goisfrido *IN WITELESFORD*
ii . hiđ . T̃ra . ē . ii . cař . 7 ibi ſuɴ̃ cū . vi . uiłłis 7 iiii. ⌈ HVŃD̨. or
borđ . Ibi . i . ſerũ . 7 p̊tū . ii . cař . 7 i . moliñ de . xxvi . ſoł.
7 viii . deñ . Vał 7 ualuit ſēp . c . ſoł . Hanc t̃ra tenuit Sigar
de Aſgaro ſtalro . 7 dare 7 uendẽ potuit abſq̨ eȷ̇ liẗia.

In Trepeſlau teñ Sigar . i . hiđ 7 dim̃ *IN R̃EPESLAV HD̃.*
de Goisfrido . T̃ra . ē . ii . cař . In dñio . una . 7 iiii . uiłłi hñt or
alterā . Ibi . i . ſerũ . Paſta ad pecuñ . Vał 7 ualuit ſēp xl . ſoł.
Iſtemet Sigar tenuit ſub Aſgaro . 7 dare ł uendẽ ſine li
centia eȷ̇ potuit . Soca ũ dño remanſit.

In Foxetune teñ Sigar de Goisfr̃ . iii . hiđ 7 dim̃ . 7 xx . ačs.
T̃ra . ē . v . cař . In dñio ſunt . īi . 7 v . uiłłi cū . x . borđ hñt
iii . cař . Ibi . i . ſerũ . 7 p̊tū . v . cař . Vał 7 ualuit ſēp . iiii . lib̃.
Iſtemet Sigar tenuit ſub Aſgaro . uendẽ 7 dare potuit.
ſoca ũ dño remanſit.

3 villagers with 3 cottagers have 1 plough.
2 slaves; meadow for 3 ploughs.
Value 30s; when acquired 10s; before 1066, 60s.
Leofsi, Earl Waltheof's man, held this land and could sell.

9   In SWAVESEY Picot holds 1 hide from Robert. Land for 1 plough.
2 smallholders.
Meadow for 1 plough.
The value is and was 5s; before 1066, 20s.
    Leofsi, Earl Waltheof's man, held this land; he could grant and
sell. Picot the Sheriff holds these lands from Robert Gernon, in
his wife's marriage portion.

20 [22]   LAND OF GEOFFREY DE MANDEVILLE

In FLENDISH Hundred
1   Geoffrey de Mandeville holds 2½ hides in FULBOURN.   Land for 3
ploughs. William holds from him. 3 ploughs there.
    Meadow for 1 plough.
Value 50s; when acquired 60s; before 1066 as much.
    Alfsi held this land from Asgar, and could grant without his
permission.

In WHITTLESFORD Hundred
2   In SAWSTON Roger holds 2 hides from Geoffrey. Land for 2 ploughs;
they are there, with
    6 villagers; 4 smallholders.
    1 slave; meadow for 2 ploughs; 1 mill at 26s 8d.
The value is and always was 100s.
    Sigar held this land from Asgar the Constable; he could grant
and sell without his permission.

In THRIPLOW Hundred
3   In THRIPLOW Sigar holds 1½ hides from Geoffrey. Land for 2 ploughs.
In lordship 1;
    4 villagers have the other.
    1 slave; pasture for the livestock.
The value is and always was 40s.
    Sigar held it himself under Asgar; he could grant or sell without
his permission, but the jurisdiction remained with the lord.

4   In FOXTON Sigar holds 3½ hides and 20 acres from Geoffrey. Land
for 5 ploughs. In lordship 2;
    5 villagers with 10 smallholders have 3 ploughs.
    1 slave; meadow for 5 ploughs.
The value is and always was £4.
    Sigar held it himself under Asgar; he could sell and grant, but
the jurisdiction remained with the lord.

᠎

ſ teſtant.

In eaď uilla . ē dim moliñ redď.x|viii . deñ . qūe occụ
pauit Roƀt gernon ſuꝑ Goisfriđ . ut hōēs de hunď

197 b

Ⓜ Chipehā ꝑ x . hiđ ſe defendeƀ In Staplehov Hvnđ.
T.R.E . Sed qđā uicecom miſit eas ad . v . hiđ . ꝑ conceſ
ſione ejđ regis . qa firma ej̄ eū grauabat.7 m̄ ſe deſđt
ꝑ v . hiđ . Tra . ē . xvii ; car . Goisfriđ teñ de rege . In dn̄io
ſuꝗ . iii . hidæ . 7 ibi . iii . car . Ibi . xix . uiłłi cū . xiii . borđ
hn̄t . xiiii . car . Ibi . vi . ſerui . Ptū . iii ; car . Paſta ad peç
uillæ . De piſc miłł 7 q̄ngeut anguiłł . In totis ualent ual
xx . liƀ . Qďo receꝑ; xvi . liƀ . T.R.E; xii . liƀ . Hoc Ⓜ tenuit
Orgar uicecom regis . E . qui poſtea fuit hō Aſgari ſtalri.
De hac tra fuer . v . hidæ in firmā regis . E . 7 ii . ſochi ha
buer . ii . hiđ de rege . 7 tr̄ā ſuā cui uoluer dare potuer.
7 tam̄ unquiſqᷤ inuenieƀ . viii . deñ ł unū equū in ſeruitio
regis . 7 ꝑ forisfactura ſua faciebaꝗ rectitudiñ in Forhā.
Ipſe Orgar uicecom habuit . iii . hiđ de hac tra . 7 potuit
dare cui uoluit . Hanc tr̄ā poſuit Orgar in uadimonio.
ꝑ vii . mark auri 7 ii . uncijs . ut hōēs Goisfridi dn̄t.
Sed hōēs de hunđ neqᷦ breue aliqđ neqᷦ legaƀ . R.E.
inde uider . neqᷦ teſtimoniū ꝑhibent . In Erningford Hđ.
In Mordune teñ Ricarđ de Goisfrido . iii . uirg træ.
Tra . ē . ii . car . In dn̄io . i . car . 7 un uiłłs cū . v . cot hn̄t . i . car,
Ibi alij . iii . cot ſuꝗ . 7 ptū . iiii . boƀ . Paſta ad pecuñ.
Val xx . ſol . Qďo receꝑ; xv . ſol . T.R.E; xl . ſol . Hanc
tram tenuit Goduin de Aſgaro . 7 uende potuit.
In Haſlingefelde teñ Roger . v . hiđ In Wederlai Hvnđ
de Goisfrido . Tra . ē . vi . car . In dn̄io ſunt . ii . 7 viii . uiłłi
cū . xviii . cot hn̄t . iiii . car . Ptū . ii . car . Int totū ual
vii . liƀ . Qďo receꝑ 7 T.R.E; vi . liƀ . Hanc tr̄ā tenuit Sigar
hō Aſgari . 7 potuit dare ł uende . ſ; ſoca dn̄o remanſit.

197 a, b

5   In the same village is ½ mill, which pays 10s 8d, which Robert
Gernon appropriated in Geoffrey's despite, as the men of the
Hundred testify.

In STAPLOE Hundred
6 M. CHIPPENHAM answered for 10 hides before 1066. But a Sheriff put
them at 5 hides, through King Edward's concession, because its
revenue oppressed him; it now answers for 5 hides. Land for 17
ploughs. Geoffrey holds from the King. In lordship 3 hides;
3 ploughs there.
      19 villagers with 13 smallholders have 14 ploughs.
      6 slaves; meadow for 3 ploughs; pasture for the village
         livestock; from the fish pond 1,500 eels.
Total value £20; when acquired £16; before 1066 £12.
      Ordgar, King Edward's Sheriff, who was later Asgar the
Constable's man, held this manor. 5 hides of this land were in
King Edward's revenue; 2 Freemen had 2 hides from the King
and could grant their land to whom they would; however,
each found 8d or 1 horse in the King's service, and for their
fines they did justice in Fordham.
      Ordgar the Sheriff had 3 hides of this land himself and
could grant to whom he would. Ordgar placed this land in
pledge for 7 marks and 2 ounces of gold, as Geoffrey's men
state; but the men of the Hundred have seen thereon neither
any writ nor commissioner of King Edward, nor do they offer
witness.

In ARMINGFORD Hundred
7   In (Guilden) MORDEN Richard holds 3 virgates of land from
Geoffrey. Land for 2 ploughs. In lordship 1 plough;
      1 villager with 5 cottagers have 1 plough.
         3 other cottagers there;
      meadow for 4 oxen; pasture for the livestock.
Value 20s; when acquired 15s; before 1066, 40s.
      Godwin held this land from Asgar the Constable and could sell.

In WETHERLEY Hundred
8   In HASLINGFIELD Roger holds 5 hides from Geoffrey. Land for
6 ploughs. In lordship 2;
      8 villagers with 18 cottagers have 4 ploughs.
      Meadow for 2 ploughs.
In total, value £7; when acquired and before 1066 £6.
      Sigar, Asgar the Constable's man, held this land and could
grant or sell; but the jurisdiction remained with the lord.

In Esceprid ten̅ Sigar de Goisfr̅.i.hid.T̅ra.ē.i.car̅.7 ibi.ē
cū.i.uitto 7 ii.bord.7 ii.molini de.x.fol 7 viii.den.p̅tu̅
i.car̅.Vat 7 ualuit.xx.fol.T.R.E.′xxiii.fol.Iftemet
de Afgaro tenuit.7 dare t́ uende̅ potuit.

In Ordeuuelle ten̅ Sigar de Goisf̅.i.uirg̅.7 iii.part tiā ē7
uni uirg̅.T̅ra.ē.iiii.bob.7 ibi funt.p̅tu̅.ii.bob.cū.i.uitto,
Vat 7 ualuit.viii.fot.T.R.E.′x.fot.Iftemet tenuit fub
Afgaro.7 uende̅ potuit.

.XXI. G TERRA GISLEBERTI DE GAND. *In Papeword hvnd̅.*
Gislebert̅ de Gand ten̅.i.virg̅ 7 dim̅ in Papeuuorde.
Aluuold ten̅ de eo.T̅ra.ē.iiii.bob.7 ibi funt.cū.i.uitto.
P̅tu̅.iiii.bob.Vat 7 ualuit.v.fol.T.R.E.′x.fot.Hanc
t̅rā tenuit Vlf teign regis.E.7 jacet in Stantone.

In Elefuuorde ten.ii.fochi de Giftebto dim̅ hid.v.ac̅s
min̅.T̅ra.ē.vi.bob.7 ibi fuɲ.7 p̅tu̅.vi.bob.Vat 7 ualuit
sēp.vi.fot 7 viii.den.Hanc t̅rā tenuē.ii.fochi hōes Vlf.

197 c
unus eoʒ ineuuard ind̅.n̅ uicecomiti.Ambo tam̅ re
cede̅ cū tra fua potuit.

In Cunitone ten̅.viii.fochi de Giftebto.ii.hid.7 iii.
uirg̅.T̅ra.ē.ii.car̅ 7 dim̅.7 ibi fuɲ.cū.viii.cot.p̅tu̅
ii.car̅ 7 dim̅.Vat 7 ualuit.xxv.fol.T.R.E.′xxx.fot.
Iftimet tenuē de Vlf.7 dare 7 uende potueruɲ.

In Bochefuuorde ten̅.vi.fochi de Giftebto.i.hid 7 i.uirg̅.
T̅ra.ē.i.car̅.7 ibi.ē.P̅tu̅.i.car̅.Vat.x.fot.Qdo recep.′
xvi.fot.T.R.E.′xx.fot.Iftimet tenuē de Vlf.7 uen
dere potuē.Soca eoʒ jacuit in Stantone.

197 b, c

9   In SHEPRETH Sigar holds 1 hide from Geoffrey. Land for 1 plough;
it is there, with
1 villager; 2 smallholders.
2 mills at 10s 8d; meadow for 1 plough.
The value is and was 20s; before 1066, 23s.
He held it himself from Asgar and could grant or sell.

10 In ORWELL Sigar holds 1 virgate and the third part of 1 virgate
from Geoffrey. Land for 4 oxen; they are there.
Meadow for 2 oxen, with 1 villager.
The value is and was 8s; before 1066, 10s.
He held it himself under Asgar and could sell.

21 [23]   LAND OF GILBERT OF GHENT

In PAPWORTH Hundred

1   Gilbert of Ghent holds 1½ virgates in PAPWORTH. Alfwold holds
from him. Land for 4 oxen; they are there, with
1 villager.
Meadow for 4 oxen.
The value is and was 5s; before 1066, 10s.
Ulf, King Edward's thane, held this land; it lies in (the lands
of) (Fen) Stanton.

2   In ELSWORTH 2 Freemen hold ½ hide less 5 acres from Gilbert.
Land for 6 oxen; they are there;
meadow for 6 oxen.
The value is and always was 6s 8d.
2 Freemen, Ulf's men, held this land; one of them found   197 c
escort for the Sheriff; however, both could withdraw with their
land.

3   In CONINGTON 8 Freemen hold 2 hides and 3 virgates from Gilbert.
Land for 2½ ploughs; they are there, with
8 cottagers.
Meadow for 2½ ploughs.
The value is and was 25s; before 1066, 30s.
They held it themselves from Ulf; they could grant and sell.

4   In BOXWORTH 6 Freemen hold 1 hide and 1 virgate from Gilbert.
Land for 1 plough; it is there.
Meadow for 1 plough.
Value 10s; when acquired 16s; before 1066, 20s.
They held it themselves from Ulf and could sell; their
jurisdiction lay in (Fen) Stanton.

In Suauefy . ten Giflebt . i . hid . Tra . e̅ . i . car . 7 ibi . e̅.

cu̅ . ii . uiłłis . 7 iii . borđ 7 ii . cot . De marefch . ccxxv.

anguiłł . Vał 7 ualuit . x . foł . T.R.E. xx . foł . Hanc

tra̅ tenuit Vlf teign̅ regis . E.

In Draitone ten Giflebt . iii . hid 7 i . uirg . Tra . e̅ . i . car

7 dim . In d̅n̅io . i . hida . 7 un̅ fochs hn̅s . i . hid 7 i . uirg.

7 ibi . iiii . uiłłi . P̊tu̅ . i . car 7 dim . Pafta ad pec uillæ.

Vał 7 ualuit . x . foł . T.R.E. xx . foł . Hanc tra̅ tenuit

Vlf teign̅ . E . regis . 7 ipfe un̅ fochs fuit ho̅ ej . tam̅ tra̅

fua̅ potuit dare 7 uende abfq̅ licentia ej.

.XXII. **GTERRA GISLEBTI FILIJ TVRALDI** *IN NORESTOV HĐ*

GISLEBERT fił Turaldi In Stantone ten . iiii . hid

7 dim . Tra . e̅ . vi . car . Hugo ten de eo . In d̅n̅io fuɴ . ii.

car . 7 vii . uiłłi cu̅ . ix . borđ 7 xiii . cot hn̅t . iiii . car.

Ibi . iii . ferui . P̊tu̅ . ii . car . De marefch . iii . miłł 7 cc . angłł

7 ii . foł 7 viii . den̅ . Vał 7 valuit . vi . liƀ . T.R.E. viii . liƀ.

Hanc tra̅ tenuit Sexi teign̅ regis . E . 7 dare ɫ uende pot.

.XXIII. **ETERRA EVDON FILIJ HVBERTI .** *IN CILDEFORD HVND.*

EVDO dapifer In Badburgha̅ ten . i . uirg tre 7 dim

7 Pirot ten de eo . Tra . e̅ dim car . Ibi . ii . uiłłi . Vał 7 ua

luit . ii . ores . Hanc tra̅ tenuit Aluric 7 dare 7 uende potuit.

In Pa̅pefuuorde ten̅ Pirot . v . acs de Eud . Vał 7 ualuit

vi . den̅ . Burro tenuit de Alurico ca̅pe . 7 recede potuit.

In Salfitone ten̅ Pirot de Eud iiii . hid . *IN WITELESFORD HĐ.*

Tra . e̅ . v . car . In d̅n̅io funt . ii . 7 xi . uiłłi cu̅ . vi . borđ hn̅t

iii . car . Ibi . i . feru̅ . 7 ii . molini de . xxx . foł 7 viii . den̅ . P̊tu̅

v . car . Vał 7 ualuit fe̅p . viii . liƀ . Hanc tra̅ tenuit Aluric

de rege . 7 fub eo . iii . fochi fuer . 7 recede n̅ potuer.

5 In SWAVESEY Gilbert holds 1 hide. Land for 1 plough; it is there, with
2 villagers; 3 smallholders; 2 cottagers.
From the marsh 225 eels.
The value is and was 10s; before 1066, 20s.
Ulf, King Edward's thane, held this land.

6 In (Fen) DRAYTON Gilbert holds 3 hides and 1 virgate. Land for
1½ ploughs. In lordship 1 hide;
1 Freeman who has 1 hide and 1 virgate. 4 villagers.
Meadow for 1½ ploughs; pasture for the village livestock.
The value is and was 10s; before 1066, 20s.
Ulf, King Edward's thane, held this land; the one Freeman was
his man; however, he could grant and sell his land without his
permission.

22 [24] LAND OF GILBERT SON OF THOROLD

In NORTHSTOW Hundred

1 Gilbert son of Thorold holds 4½ hides in LONGSTANTON. Land for 6
ploughs. Hugh holds from him. In lordship 2 ploughs;
7 villagers with 9 smallholders and 13 cottagers have 4 ploughs.
3 slaves; meadow for 2 ploughs; from the marsh 3,200 eels and
2s 8d.
The value is and was £6; before 1066 £8.
Saxi, King Edward's thane, held this land and could grant or sell.

23 [25] LAND OF EUDO SON OF HUBERT

In CHILFORD Hundred

1 Eudo the Steward holds 1½ virgates of land in BABRAHAM; Pirot holds
from him. Land for ½ plough.
2 villagers.
The value is and was 2 *ora*.
Aelfric held this land; he could grant and sell.

2 In PAMPISFORD Pirot holds 5 acres from Eudo.
The value is and was 6d.
Burro held from Aelfric Kemp and could withdraw.

In WHITTLESFORD Hundred

3 In SAWSTON Pirot holds 4 hides from Eudo. Land for 5 ploughs.
In lordship 2;
11 villagers with 6 smallholders have 3 ploughs.
1 slave; 2 mills at 30s 8d; meadow for 5 ploughs.
The value is and always was £8.
Aelfric held this land from the King; 3 Freemen were under him
and could not withdraw.

In Cloptune ten Hunfrid de Eud *IN ERNINGFORD HD*.
.I. hid 7 dim. Tra.ē.II. car. 7 ibi fuɲ. cū. VII. bord. Ptū
II. car. Silua ad fepes refic. Val. IIII. lib. Q̃do recep.'xl.
fol. 7 tñtd T.R.E. Hanc trã tenuit Guerd comes.
In Hatelai ten Hunfrid de Eudone. I. hid 7 I. uirg.
Tra.ē.I. car. 7 ibi. II. bord. Ptū. I. car. Val 7 ualuit. xx. fol.

197 d

T.R.E.'xxx. fol. Hanc trã tenuit Almar hō Rotbti.f.Wim.
7 dare 7 uende trã fuã potuit.
In Crauuedene ten Hunfrid de Eud. II. hid. Tra.ē.II.car.
7 ibi funt cū. VI. uittis 7 dim. Ptū. II. car. Val 7 ualuit
fēp xL. fol. Hanc trã tenuit Guerd comes.
In Winepol ten Hunfrid de Eudone. *IN WEDERLAI HD*.
.I. hid. 7 I. uirg 7 dim. Tra.ē.II. car. 7 ibi fuɲ in dñio.
7 un uitts 7 I. feru. Ptū. I. car. Silua ad fepes. Valet
7 ualuit fēp c. fol. Hanc trã tenuit Guerd comes.
In Chingeftone ten Hunfrid de Eud *IN STOV HVND.*
x. acs træ. Tra.ē.I. boui. Val 7 ualuit fēp. VIII. den.
Hanc trã tenuit Almar hō Wallef.7 recede potuit.
In *GAMELINGE*. ten Eudo. XVIII. hid. Tra.ē XVIII. car.
In dñio. IX. hidæ. 7 ibi funt. III. car. Ibi xxx. uitti cū XII.
bord hñt. xv. car. Ibi. I. francig ht dim hid. 7 XII. cot.
7 IIII. ferui. ptū XII. car. Silua. x. porc. Pafta ad pecun
uillæ. In totis ualent ual. XVIII. lib. Q̃do recep.'x. lib. 7 tñtd
T.R.E. Hoc ᴍ tenuit Vlmer de Etone. 7 ibi fuer. IX. fochi
qui tenuer. IIII. hid. 7 dare 7 uende potuer. 7 fup has hid
.I. uirg tenuer. quæ.ē de Grantedene ᴍ abbis de Elỳ. quã
occupauit Lifois de mofteriis fup abbem. fic Hund teftat.

In ARMINGFORD Hundred

4 In CLOPTON Humphrey holds 1½ hides from Eudo. Land for 2 ploughs; they are there, with
7 smallholders.
Meadow for 2 ploughs; woodland for repairing fences.
Value £4; when acquired 40s; before 1066 as much.
Earl Gyrth held this land.

5 In (East) HATLEY Humphrey holds 1 hide and 1 virgate from Eudo.
Land for 1 plough.
2 smallholders.
Meadow for 1 plough.
The value is and was 20s; before 1066, 30s.   197 d
Aelmer, Robert son of Wymarc's man, held this land; he could grant and sell his land.

6 In CROYDON Humphrey holds 2 hides from Eudo. Land for 2 ploughs; they are there, with
6½ villagers.
Meadow for 2 ploughs.
The value is and always was 40s.
Earl Gyrth held this land.

In WETHERLEY Hundred

7 In WIMPOLE Humphrey holds 1 hide and 1½ virgates from Eudo.
Land for 2 ploughs; they are there, in lordship;
1 villager; 1 slave.
Meadow for 1 plough; woodland for fences.
The value is and always was 100s.
Earl Gyrth held this land.

In LONGSTOW Hundred

8 In KINGSTON Humphrey holds 10 acres of land from Eudo. Land for 1 ox.
The value is and always was 8d.
Aelmer, Earl Waltheof's man, held this land and could withdraw.

9 In GAMLINGAY Eudo holds 18 hides. Land for 18 ploughs. In lordship 9 hides; 3 ploughs there.
30 villagers with 12 smallholders have 15 ploughs. 1 Frenchman has ½ hide; 12 cottagers; 4 slaves.
Meadow for 12 ploughs; woodland, 10 pigs; pasture for the village livestock.
Total value £18; when acquired £10; before 1066 as much.
Wulfmer of Eaton held this manor. 9 Freemen were there who held 4 hides; they could grant and sell; in addition to these hides they held 1 virgate which belongs to (Little) Gransden, the Abbot of Ely's manor, and which Lisois of Moutiers appropriated in the Abbot's despite, as the Hundred testifies.

In Hatelai.teñ Eudo.I.hidā.Tra.ē.I.car.sed ñ habet ibi.

In dñio suñ.III.uirg 7 x.acre.cū.III.bord de xx.acris.

Nem ad sepes.Val.v.sol.Q̇do recep.x.sol.T.R.E.xx.sol.

Hanc trā tenuer.II.sochi Robti filij Wimarc.7 uende potuer.

H TERRA HARDVINI DE SCALERS. *IN STANES HVND.*

Hardviñ de Scalers teñ.I.uirg træ in Suafham.

Tra.ē.II.boū.Val 7 ualuit sep.v.sol.Hanc trā tenuer

VI.sochi.Quoᵹ.III.inuener Auerā.7 alij.III.jnewardos.

In Staplehou hund teñ Hard dim hid de rege.Tra est

IIII.boū.7 ibi sunt.ptū ipsis bobᵹ.Val xx.sol.Q̇do recep.

XVI.sol.T.R.E.xx.sol.Hanc trā tenuit Turch hō abbis

de Ramesy.ñ potuit sine licentia ej recede.7 tam inueñ

jn seruitio regis ₺ jneuuard uel.IIII.denar. *IN RADEFELLE*

In Dullinghā teñ Hard.II.hid.xx.acs miñ. *[*HVND.*

Tra.ē.II.car.7 ibi sunt.cū.VII.uillis 7 I.bord.Silua.IIII.

porc.Val 7 ualuit sep XL.sol.Hanc trā inuener xvi.

sochi.7 dare 7 uende trā suā potuer.7 tam Aueras inuener.

In Weslai teñ Hard xv.acs træ.Val 7 ualuit sep xvi.

den.Duo sochi comitis Heroldi tenuer.7 recede ñ potuer.

In Carletone teñ.II.milites de Hard dim hid.III.acs miñ.

Tra.ē dim car.7 ibi.ē.Val 7 ualuit sep.x.sol.De hac

tra tenuer sub heraldo.II.sochi.xxxvIII.acs.7 inuenieb

.I.jneuuard uicecom.Tcius ū de Algaro com.vIII.acs

tenuit.7 auerā inuenit.fᵹ recede non potuit.

197 d

10 In HATLEY (St. George) Eudo holds 1 hide. Land for 1 plough; but
it is not recorded there. In lordship 3 virgates and 10 acres, with
   3 smallholders with 20 acres.
   Wood for fences.
Value 5s; when acquired 10s; before 1066, 20s.
   2 Freemen of Robert son of Wymarc held this land and could sell.

24 [26]　　　　　LAND OF HARDWIN OF SCALES

In STAINE Hundred
1 Hardwin of Scales holds 1 virgate of land in SWAFFHAM. Land for 2
oxen.
The value is and always was 5s.
   6 Freemen held this land, 3 of whom found cartage and the other
3 (found) escorts.

In STAPLOE Hundred
2 Hardwin holds ½ hide from the King. Land for 4 oxen; they are there.
   Meadow for these oxen.
Value 20s; when acquired 16s; before 1066, 20s.
   Thork, the Abbot of Ramsey's man, held this land; he could not
withdraw without his permission; however, he found either escort or
4d in the King's service.

In RADFIELD Hundred
3 In DULLINGHAM Hardwin holds 2 hides less 20 acres. Land for 2
ploughs; they are there, with
   7 villagers; 1 smallholder.
   Woodland, 4 pigs.
The value is and always was 40s.
   16 Freemen held this land; they could grant and sell their land;
however, they found cartages.

4 In WESTLEY (Waterless) Hardwin holds 15 acres of land.
The value is and always was 16d.
   2 Freemen of Earl Harold's held (it) and could not withdraw.

5 In CARLTON 2 men-at-arms hold ½ hide less 3 acres from Hardwin.
Land for ½ plough; it is there.
The value is and always was 10s.
   2 Freemen held 38 acres of this land under Harold and found
1 escort for the Sheriff; a third held 8 acres from Earl Algar and
found cartage, but he could not withdraw.

Ĭn Weſtone teń Durand de Hard. 1 .hid .Tra .ē. 1 . car.

7 ibi.ē.7 p̃tū car .Silua. xii .porc .Val .xx . ſol. Qdo

recep.́ x . ſol.7 tntd T.R.E. Hanc trā tenuit Turgar

hō Algari comitis . ñ potuit recede abſq̧ lictia ejus.

Ĭn ead uilla teń Hard . 1 .uirg træ in dñio .Tra .ē . 11 .bob.

Val 7 valuit sēp .v . ſol. H̃ tra inuen Auerā 7 Jneuuard.

Hanc . 11 . ſocħi ſub Haroldo tenuer.7 recede ñ potuer.

Ĭn Waratinge teń Hard .1 .uirg træ . 11 .bob .ē terra.

Ibi ſuɴ .́ 11 . bord .Val 7 ualuit . 111 . ſol.Hanc tenueŕ Tochi

7 Wigar .uń inuen Auerā 7 alt inueń Jnward. IN CILDEFORD

Ĭn Horſei teń .v .uilli de Hard dim hid .Tra .ē   ꝼHVND.

.1 .car.7 ibi.ē 7 p̃tū .Silua .xxiiii .porc .Val 7 ualuit

sēp .xxv . ſol. De hac tra tenueŕ iiii .hões..1 .uirg 7 dimid

de rege.7 tam .1 .auerā 7 11.ĩnew inuenieb .7 Ledmar dim

uirg tenuit ſub anteceſſore Alberici de uer .ñ potuit

fine ej lictia recede.

Ĭn Wicheħā teń Hard .1 .uirg de rege .Tra .ē dim car.7 ibi.ē.

cū .111 .bord.7 dim ac̃ p̃ti .Val 7 ualuit .xl .deń .T.R.E.́

v . ſol 7 iiii .deń .Tres ſocħi tenueŕ .7 1 . Auerā inueneŕ.

Ĭn Badburgħā teń Durand ſub hard dim hid .Tra .ē

dim car.7 ibi.ē cū .iiii .bord .Val 7 ualuit xviii .ſol

7 viii .deń .Hanc trā tenueŕ.iiii .ſocħi .iiii . Aueras inue

neruɴ .nec recede potueŕ. H̃ tra .ē de feudo regis.

Ĭn P̃apeſuuorde teń Hard .1 .uirg .Val 7 ualuit sēp

lxv .deń.Duo ſocħi de rege tenueŕ.nec recede potueŕ.

6 In WESTON (Colville) Durand holds 1 hide from Hardwin. Land for 198 a
1 plough; it is there;
    meadow for the plough; woodland, 12 pigs.
Value 20s; when acquired 10s; before 1066 as much.
    Thorgar, Earl Algar's man, held this land; he could not withdraw
without his permission.

7 In the same village Hardwin holds 1 virgate of land in lordship.
Land for 2 oxen.
The value is and always was 5s.
    This land found cartage and escort. 2 Freemen held it under
Earl Harold and could not withdraw.

8 In (West) WRATTING Hardwin holds 1 virgate of land. Land for
2 oxen.
    2 smallholders there.
The value is and was 3s.
    Toki and Withgar held it; one found cartage and the other found
escort.

In CHILFORD Hundred

9 In HORSEHEATH 5 villagers hold ½ hide from Hardwin. Land for 1
plough; it is there;
    meadow; woodland, 24 pigs.
The value is and always was 25s.
    4 men held 1½ virgates of this land from the King; however,
they found 1 cartage and 2 escorts.
    Ledmer held ½ virgate under Aubrey de Vere's predecessor; he
could not withdraw without his permission.

10 In (West) WICKHAM Hardwin holds 1 virgate from the King. Land
for ½ plough; it is there, with
    3 smallholders;
    meadow, ½ acre.
The value is and was 40d; before 1066, 5s 4d.
    3 Freemen held (it), and found 1 cartage.

11 In BABRAHAM Durand holds ½ hide under Hardwin. Land for ½
plough; it is there, with
    4 smallholders.
The value is and was 18s 8d.
    4 Freemen held this land; they found 4 cartages, and could not
withdraw. This land is of the King's Holding.

12 In PAMPISFORD Hardwin holds 1 virgate.
The value is and always was 65d.
    2 Freemen held (it) from the King, and could not withdraw.

İn Witelesforde teñ Harð . ı . uirg̔. *IN WITELESFORD HD̄.*

Tra̅.e̅.ıı.bob̥.Val̄ 7 ualuit.xxx.ıı.deñ.Hanc tenuit
un hō Guerd.uendē ñ potuit.

İn Hiſtetone teñ Durand de Harð.ı.hið.Tra̅.e̅.ı.car̔.
7 ibi.e̅.cū.ıı.ſeruis.7 p̃tū.ı.car̔.Val̄ xx.ſol̄.Q̣do recep̄:
x.ſol̄.7 tn̄tð T.R.E.Hanc tr̄a tenuit Eſtred ſub Algaro.
potuit dare 7 uendē cui uoluit.

İn Inchelintone teñ Durand de harð dim̄ hið.Tra̅.e̅
ıııı.bob̥.Val̄ xxxıı.deñ.Q̣do recep̄: xıı.deñ.T.R.E:
v.ſol̄.Hanc tenuit Eſtred ſub Algaro.7 uendē potuit.

İn Docheſuuorde teñ Pagan̄.ııı.hið 7 ı.uirg̔ de
Harð.Tra̅.e̅.ııı.car̔ 7 ıı.bob̥.In dn̄io ſunt.ıı.car̔.
.7 ı.uil̄ls cū.ıııı.borð hn̄t.ı.car̔ 7 ıı.bou.Ibi.ıııı.ſerui̥
P̃tū.ı.car̔.De paſt̄a.ı.ſocc.Val̄.L.ſol̄.Q̣do recep̄:
ᴌx.ſol̄.T.R.E:c.ſol̄.Hanc tr̄a tenuer̄.xııı.ſochi.
Quoᵹ.xı.fuer̄ hōes.R.E.7 ıı.Aueras 7 ıx.Jneẃ
uicecomiti inuener̄.tam̄ tras ſuas uendē potuer̄.
7 ıı.reliq̊.ı.hið 7 dim̄ tenuer̄.un hō Algari̥.alt̄
hō Eddeue.ſᵹ tr̄a ſuā uendere‖potuer̄. *IN KEPESLAV*

İn Hauocheſtone teñ Harð.ı.hið 7 dim̄.   *HVND.*
Tra̅.e̅.ıı.car̔.7 ibi ſunt cū.ıııı.borð.In dn̄io.e̅ una
hida 7 dim̄.7 ı.mol̄ de.xx.ſol̄.P̃tū.ıı.car̔.paſtura
ad pecun̄ uillæ.Val̄ 7 ualuit.ᴌx.ſol̄.T.R.E:ıııı.lib̥.

198 b
De hac tra tcnuit Bundi.ııı,uirg̔ de abbe de Elẏ.7 uendē
potuit.ſoca u̥ remanſit abbi.7 alt̄ ſochs Algari comit̥.
ııı.uirg̔ tenuit.7 cū tra ſua recedē potuit.

İn Eſcelforde teñ Harð.vı.hið 7 ı.uirg̔.7 vıı.ac̄s.Tra̅.e̅
.vı.car̔.7 ıı.bob̥.7 ibi ſunt.vııı.car̔.In dn̄io.ı.hida.
7 ibi.e̅.ı.car̔.7 xııı.uil̄li cū.ıııı.borð hn̄t.vıı.car̔.

In WHITTLESFORD Hundred

13 In WHITTLESFORD Hardwin holds 1 virgate. Land for 2 oxen.
The value is and was 32d.
A man of Earl Gyrth's held it; he could not sell.

14 In HINXTON Durand holds 1 hide from Hardwin. Land for 1 plough;
it is there, with
2 slaves;
meadow for 1 plough.
Value 20s; when acquired 10s; before 1066 as much.
Estred held this land under Earl Algar; he could grant and sell
to whom he would.

15 In ICKLETON Durand holds ½ hide from Hardwin. Land for 4 oxen.
Value 32d; when acquired 12d; before 1066, 5s.
Estred held it under Earl Algar and could sell.

16 In DUXFORD Payne holds 3 hides and 1 virgate from Hardwin. Land
for 3 ploughs and 2 oxen. In lordship 2 ploughs;
1 villager with 4 smallholders have 1 plough and 2 oxen.
3 slaves; meadow for 1 plough; from the pasture 1 ploughshare.
Value 50s; when acquired 60s; before 1066, 100s.
13 Freemen held this land, 11 of whom were King Edward's
men and found 2 cartages and 9 escorts for the Sheriff; however,
they could sell their lands. The remaining 2, one Earl Algar's man,
the other Edeva's man, held 1½ hides; but they could not sell their
land.

In THRIPLOW Hundred

17 In HAUXTON Hardwin holds 1½ hides. Land for 2 ploughs; they are
there, with
4 smallholders.
In lordship 1½ hides;
1 mill at 20s; meadow for 2 ploughs; pasture for the village
livestock.
The value is and was 60s; before 1066 £4.
Bondi held 3 virgates of this land from the Abbot of Ely and   198 b
could sell; but the jurisdiction remained with the Abbot.
Another Freeman of Earl Algar's held 3 virgates and could
withdraw with his land.

18 In SHELFORD Hardwin holds 6 hides, 1 virgate and 7 acres. Land
for 6 ploughs and 2 oxen; 8 ploughs there. In lordship 1 hide;
1 plough there;
13 villagers with 4 smallholders have 7 ploughs.

Ptu̅.IIII.car̅.Pasta ad pecuñ.Val 7 ualuit.VI.lib.

T.R.E.'VIII.lib.De hac tra.II.hidæ 7 dim̅.7 IX.acræ.

7 uñ monasteriu̅.fuer̅ in dñio eccłæ de Elẏ.T.R.E.7 in

die quo isd rex obijt.7 suɴ de dñica firma m̅ ut hund testat.

De hac tra adhuc teñ.VII.sochi.I.hid 7 dim̅ 7 VI.acs.

de Soca abbis de Elẏ.n̅ pot recede cu̅ tra.s̡ soca rema

nebat æcclæ Elẏ.De ead̅ tra.III.sochi tenuer̅ dim̅ hid.

sub comite Guerd.n̅ potuer̅ sine lictia ej recede.Soca

eoȥ jacuit in Witelesforde.Alsi tenuit dim̅ hid de Algaro.com'

potuit dare ł uende.soca u̅ comiti remanebat.7 I.inew

inuen̅.Duo sochi.I.uirg 7 VII.acs tenuer̅ de comite Heraldo.

n̅ potuer̅ recede absfȥ licentia.7 V.sochi.III.uirg 7 dim

tenuer̅ sub.E.rege.7 I.auera̅ 7 II.inew inuen̅ uicecom̅.

tra̅ sua̅ uende potuer̅.sed soca eoȥ regi remansit.

In Mordune teñ Hard.I.hid. *IN ERNINGFORD HVND.*

IIII.part.I.uirg min̅.Tra.e̅.II.car̅.7 ibi sunt.Ibi.II.moł

de.IIł.ores.p̅tu̅.II.car̅.pasta ad pec uillæ.Val 7 ualuit

XXX.soł.T.R.E.'XL.soł.Modo teñ hanc tra̅ VII.sochi

de Hard.7 ipsimet tenuer̅.T.R.E.dare 7 uende tra̅ sua̅

potuer̅.s̡ soca remansit in Mordune.

In Mordune teñ Aluerad de hard dim uirg.Tra.e̅ dim

car̅.Ibi.e̅.I.cot 7 I.ac p̅ti.Val 7 ualuit.V.soł.T.R.E.'x.soł.

Hanc tra̅ tenuit Winterled de Algaro.n̅ potuit uende.com̅

Ħ tra jacet in Litingtone.

In Crauuedene teñ.II.milites de Hard.III.hid 7 I.uirg.

Tra.e̅.IIII.car̅.Ibi sunt.III.c̅.7 IIII.pot fieri.Ibi.VIII.

bord.7 p̅tu̅.I.car̅.Val 7 ualuit se̅p.LXV.soł.De hac

★ tra tenuit Alflet.I.hida̅.com̅data.S.Arch.7 dare et

uende potuit.De rege.E.tenuer̅.IIII.sochi.I.hida̅.7 IIII.or

inew inuener̅ uicecomiti.tra̅ u̅ sua̅ dare ł uende potuer̅.

7 uñ ho̅ Asgari stalri.V.uirg tenuit.7 dare 7 uende potuit.

Meadow for 4 ploughs; pasture for the livestock.
The value is and was £6; before 1066 £8.

2½ hides and 9 acres of this land and a monastery were in the
lordship of the Church of Ely before and in 1066, and are now of
the household revenue, as the Hundred testifies.

7 Freemen held a further 1½ hides and 6 acres of this land, of
the Abbot of Ely's jurisdiction; they could not withdraw with
the land, but the jurisdiction remained with the Church of Ely.

3 Freemen held ½ hide of the same land under Earl Gyrth;
they could not withdraw without his permission. Their
jurisdiction lay in Whittlesford.

Alfsi held ½ hide from Earl Algar; he could grant or sell, but
the jurisdiction remained with the Earl; he found 1 escort.

2 Freemen held 1 virgate and 7 acres from Earl Harold; they
could not withdraw without permission.

5 Freemen held 3½ virgates under King Edward; they found
1 cartage and 2 escorts for the Sheriff; they could sell their land,
but their jurisdiction remained with the King.

In ARMINGFORD Hundred

19   In (Steeple) MORDEN Hardwin holds 1 hide less the fourth part of
1 virgate. Land for 2 ploughs; they are there.
2 mills at 2 *ora*; meadow for 2 ploughs; pasture for the village
    livestock.
The value is and was 30s; before 1066, 40s.
Now 7 Freemen hold this land from Hardwin; they held it
themselves before 1066; they could grant and sell their land,
but the jurisdiction remained in (Steeple) Morden.

20   In (Guilden) MORDEN Alfred holds ½ virgate from Hardwin. Land
for ½ plough.
1 cottager;
meadow, 1 acre.
The value is and was 5s; before 1066, 10s.
Winterled held this land from Earl Algar; he could not sell.
This land lies in (the lands of) Litlington.

21   In CROYDON 2 men-at-arms hold 3 hides and 1 virgate from Hardwin.
Land for 4 ploughs. 3 ploughs there; a fourth possible.
8 smallholders;
meadow for 1 plough.
The value is and always was 65s.
Alfled, under the patronage of Archbishop S(tigand), held
1 hide of this land; she could grant and sell.
4 Freemen held 1 hide from King Edward and found 4 escorts
for the Sheriff, but they could grant or sell their land.
A man of Asgar the Constable's held 5 virgates; he could grant
and sell.

In Wandei ten Alured de Harð.i.uirg.Tra.ē.iii.bob.

★ Val 7 ualuit sēp.v.fol.Hanc trā tenuit Goda cōmdata
Algari. potuit dare 7 uende cui uoluit.

In Lidtingtone ten Adelulf de Harð ad firmā.ii.uirg
7 dim.Tra.ē.i.car.Ibi.ē dim.7 dim pot fieri.Ibi.i.borð.
Val 7 ualuit xv.fol.T.R.E.xl.fol.De hac trā tenuit
Algar hō Stigand Arch.dim hið.7 Aluui hō Algari
dim uirg.n̄ potuit foras mittere de Inchelintone.

In Abintone ten.ii.milit de harð.i.hið.7 i,uirg.7 dim.
Tra.ē.ii.car.7 ibi funt.cū.v.borð.Ptū.iiii.bob.Val
lv.fol.Qdo recep.xxv.fol.T.R.E.lx.fol.De hac tra
tenuit.i.uirg un hō.R.E.7 unā Auerā inuen uicecomiti.

198 c

7 alij.ii.fochi hōes Algari comitis.potueꝛ dare trā
fuā 7 uende cui uolueꝛ.

In Bafingborne ten Leuing de Harð.i.hið.Tra.ē.i.
car.7 ibi.ē cū.ii.borð.Ptū.ii.bob.Val 7 ualuit.xxx.fol.
T.R.E.xl.fol.Hanc trā tenueꝛ.ii.fochi Algari.potueꝛ
dare 7 uende cui uolueꝛ.

In Wadone ten Harð.i.hið 7 iii.uirg.Tra.ē.ii.car.
In dn̄io.i.hida.7 ibi.ē.i.car.7 iii.uilti cū.v.cot hn̄t.i.car.
Pafta ad pecun uillæ.Ptū.i.car.Val.iiii.lib.7 xv.fol
Qdo recep.lx.fol.T.R.E.iiii.lib 7 xv.fol.Hanc trā tenu
eruꝼ.ii.fochi.un hō Stigandi arch.alt hō Algari comit.
7 recede potueꝛ.

In Wadone ten Harð.ii.hið 7 dim.Tra.ē.iii.car.
In dn̄io.i.hida.7 ibi.ē.i.car.Ibi.vi.uilti 7 xv.cot hn̄t
.i.car 7 dim.7 adhuc dim pot fieri.Ptū.ii.car.Pafta
ad pec uillæ.Val|ualuit lxx.fol.T.R.E.iiii.lib.De haç tra

198 b, c

22 In WENDY Alfred holds 1 virgate from Hardwin. Land for 3 oxen. The value is and always was 5s.

Goda, under the patronage of Earl Algar, held this land; she could grant and sell to whom she would.

23 In LITLINGTON Aethelwulf holds 2½ virgates from Hardwin at a revenue. Land for 1 plough. ½ plough there; [another] ½ possible.

1 smallholder.

The value is and was 15s; before 1066, 40s.

Algar, Archbishop Stigand's man, held ½ hide of this land, and Alfwy, Earl Algar's man, ½ virgate; he could not put (it) outside Ickleton.

24 In ABINGTON (Pigotts) 2 men-at-arms hold 1 hide and 1½ virgates from Hardwin. Land for 2 ploughs; they are there, with

5 smallholders.

Meadow for 4 oxen.

Value 55s; when acquired 25s; before 1066, 60s.

A man of King Edward's held 1 virgate of this land and found 1 cartage for the Sheriff. 2 other Freemen, Earl Algar's men, could grant their land and sell to whom they would.   198 c

25 In BASSINGBOURN Leofing holds 1 hide from Hardwin. Land for 1 plough; it is there, with

2 smallholders.

Meadow for 2 oxen.

The value is and was 30s; before 1066, 40s.

2 Freemen of Earl Algar held this land; they could grant and sell to whom they would.

26 In WHADDON Hardwin holds 1 hide and 3 virgates. Land for 2 ploughs. In lordship 1 hide; 1 plough there;

3 villagers with 5 cottagers have 1 plough.

Pasture for the village livestock; meadow for 1 plough.

Value £4 15s; when acquired 60s; before 1066 £4 15s.

2 Freemen, one Archbishop Stigand's man, the other Earl Algar's man, held this land and could withdraw.

7 In WHADDON Hardwin holds 2½ hides. Land for 3 ploughs. In lordship 1 hide; 1 plough there.

6 villagers and 15 cottagers have 1½ ploughs; a further ½ possible.

Meadow for 2 ploughs; pasture for the village livestock.

The value is and was 70s; before 1066 £4.

tenuit Turbern̅ . I . hid̃ ſub abb̃e de Elẏ . ita qd̃ n̄ poterat
dare nec ab æccła ſeparare . ext̃ dñicā firmā monachoᵹ̃ .
tēpore . R.E. 7 in morte ej̃ . 7 XII . ſochi hões abb̃is de Elẏ
. I . hid̃ 7 dim̃ tenuer̃ . potuer̃ dare 7 uende̅ cui uoluer̃ .
ſed ſoca remanſit æcclæ.

In ead̃ uilla ten̅ Hard̃ dim̃ uirg̃ . Tra . ē . II . bob̃ . Val̃ 7 ua
luit ſēp . II . ſol̃ . Hanc tenuit Danemund hõ Aſgari ſtalri.
In Melrede ten̅ Hard̃ . I . uirg̃ . Tra . ē ⌐ 7 uende̅ potuit
dim̃ car̃ . Val̃ 7 ualuit ſēp . II . ſol̃ . Hanc tenuit Almar̃
ſub abb̃e de Elẏ . 7 uende̅ potuit . ſᵹ ſoca æcclæ remanſit.
In ead̃ uilla ten̅ Hugo de Hard̃ . I . hid̃ 7 dim̃ . Tra . ē . II .
car̃ . 7 ibi ſuᶮ cū . III . cot̃ 7 I . ſeruo . Ibi . I . monaſteriũ
7 I . molin̅ de . V . ſol̃ 7 IIII . den̅ . P̃tū . II . car̃ . Paſta ad
pecun̅ uillæ . Val̃ 7 ualuit XL . ſol̃ . T.R.E. IIII . lib̃ . H̃ tra
jacuit in æccła de Elẏ in dñio monachoᵹ̃ . 7 in uita 7 in
morte regis . E . ut hões de hund̃ teſtant̃.

In Melleburne ten̅ Durand de Hard̃ . I . hid̃ 7 I . uirg̃ .
Tra . ē . I . car̃ 7 dim̃ . Ibi . ē una . 7 dim̃ pot̃ fieri . Ibi eſt
. I . uił̃s cū . II . bord̃ 7 III . cot̃ . P̃tū . I . car̃ . Paſta ad pec̃ .
Val̃ XXV . ſol̃ . Q̃do recep̃ XXX . ſol̃ . T.R.E. XL . ſolid̃ .
Hanc tr̃a tenuit Sired hõ Algari . 7 dare 7 uende̅ pot̃ .
In Eſceprid ten̅ Hard̃ . II . hid̃ 7 dim̃ uirg̃ . Tra . ē . II .
car̃ . 7 II . bob̃ . 7 ibi ſunt cū . II . uił̃is 7 IX . cot̃ . 7 I . ſeruo.
P̃tū om̃ibᵹ car̃ . Hanc tr̃a ten̅ . I . miles 7 II . Angli ſub
eo . Ibi . I . molin̅ de . VII . ſol̃ . II . den̅ min̅ . Val̃ 7 ualuit
XL.II . ſol̃ . T.R.E. L . ſol̃ . Hanc tr̃a tenuer̃ . V . ſochi . un̅
hoᵹ̃ hõ Algari . 7 alij hões regis . E . fuer̃ . 7 II . Aueras
7 II . Ineuuard̃ inuener̃ . 7 tam̅ tr̃a ſua uende̅ potuer̃ .
In Eſceprid ten̅ Hugo de Hard̃ dim̃ uirg̃ . Tra . ē . II .
bob̃ . 7 p̃tū . II . bob̃ . Val̃ 7 ualuit ſēp . II . ſol̃ . H̃ tra ja
cuit in dñio æcclæ de Elẏ . 7̃ in uita 7 in morte . R.E.
ut hões de hund̃ teſtantur.

Thorbern held 1 hide of this land under the Abbot of Ely before and in 1066 on condition that he could not grant it or separate it from the Church, outside the monks' household revenue.

12 Freemen, the Abbot of Ely's men, held 1½ hides; they could grant and sell to whom they would, but the jurisdiction remained with the Church.

28 In the same village Hardwin holds ½ virgate. Land for 2 oxen. The value is and always was 2s.

Danemund, Asgar the Constable's man, held it and could sell.

29 In MELDRETH Hardwin holds 1 virgate. Land for ½ plough. The value is and always was 2s.

Aelmer held it under the Abbot of Ely and could sell; but the jurisdiction remained with the Church.

30 In the same village Hugh holds 1½ hides from Hardwin. Land for 2 ploughs; they are there, with
3 cottagers; 1 slave.
1 monastery; 1 mill at 5s 4d; meadow for 2 ploughs; pasture for the village livestock.
The value is and was 40s; before 1066 £4.

This land lay in (the lands of) the Church of Ely, before and in 1066, in the monks' lordship, as the men of the Hundred testify.

31 In MELBOURN Durand holds 1 hide and 1 virgate from Hardwin. Land for 1½ ploughs. 1 there; [another] ½ possible.
1 villager with 2 smallholders and 3 cottagers.
Meadow for 1 plough; pasture for the livestock.
Value 25s; when acquired 30s; before 1066, 40s.

Sired, Earl Algar's man, held this land; he could grant and sell.

[In WETHERLEY Hundred]
32 In SHEPRETH Hardwin holds 2 hides and ½ virgate. Land for 2 ploughs and 2 oxen; they are there, with
2 villagers; 9 cottagers; 1 slave.
Meadow for all the ploughs.
1 man-at-arms holds this land, and 2 Englishmen under him.
1 mill at 7s less 2d.
The value is and was 42s; before 1066, 50s.

5 Freemen held this land; one of them was Earl Algar's man; the others were King Edward's men and found 2 cartages and 2 escorts; however, they could sell their land.

33 In SHEPRETH Hugh holds ½ virgate from Hardwin. Land for 2 oxen; meadow for 2 oxen.
The value is and always was 2s.

This land lay in the lordship of the Church of Ely before and in 1066, as the men of the Hundred testify.

Ịn Orduuelle teñ Durand de Harđ. iii. uirg 7 iii. part
unius uirg. Tra. ē. i. car. 7 vi. boues ibi funt. cū. iiii.
cot. 7 i. moliñ de. viii. fol. Ptū. vi. boƀ. Nem ad
fepes clauđ. Val 7 ualuit xx. fol. T.R.E. xl. fol. Hanc
trā tenueř. ii. fochi. uñ hō Wallef. iii. uirg tenuit.
alt hō regis. iii. part. i. uirg tenuit. Duos Inewarđ
inueneř. 7 recede potueruɴ.

Ịn Warateuuorde teñ. ii. milit de Harđ. iii. uirg.
Tra. ē. i. car. Ibi. vi. cot 7 ptū. i. car. Val 7 ualuit
xxv. fol. T.R.E. l. fol. Hanc trā tenueř. ii. fochi.
uñ hō Wallef 7 alt hō Roƀti filij Wimarc. 7 dare
7 uende potueř.

Ịn Wateuuelle teñ R. caluus de Harđ. ii. hiđ.
Tra. ē. ii. car. In dñio. ē. i. car. 7 i. borđ cū. iiii. cot
hñt. i. car. Ptū. i. car. Nem ad clauđ fepes. Valet
xxx. fol. Qdo recep. xx. fol. T.R.E. xl. fol. Hanc
trā tenueř. viii. fochi. Hoʒ. vi. hōēs regis fueř.
7 v. uirg tenueř. 7 iii. Aueras 7 iii. Inew inueneř.
7 vii. hō. R. fil Wimarc dim hiđ habuit. 7 viii.
hō Algari. i. uirg tenuit. Ōms hi recede potueř.

Ịn Aurefdone teñ Durand de Harđ *IN STOV HVND.*
. i. uirg. Tra. ē. iii. boƀ. 7 ibi funt. cū. i. uilło. ptū
iii. boƀ. Val 7 ualuit fep. viii. fol. Hanc trā
tenuit. i. foħs Algari. 7 recede potuit.

Ịn Chingeftone teñ. ii. milit de Harđ. i. uirg.
Tra. ē. iii. boƀ. 7 ptū. Val 7 ualuit fep. ii. fol.
Hanc trā tenuit Goding. hō Eddeuæ pulchræ 7 pot
Ịn eađ uilla teñ Roƀt caluus de Harđ Ⅎ recede.
ix. acs. Tra. ē dim boui. Val 7 ualuit fep vi. den.

34 In ORWELL Durand holds 3 virgates and the third part of 1
    virgate from Hardwin. Land for 1 plough. 6 oxen there, with
      4 cottagers;
      1 mill at 8s; meadow for 6 oxen; wood for making fences.
    The value is and was 20s; before 1066, 40s.
      2 Freemen held this land. One, Waltheof's man, held 3
    virgates; the other, the King's man, held the third part of 1
    virgate. They found 2 escorts and could withdraw.

35 In WRATWORTH 2 men-at-arms hold 3 virgates from Hardwin.
    Land for 1 plough.
      6 cottagers;
      meadow for 1 plough.
    The value is and was 25s; before 1066, 50s.
      2 Freemen, one Waltheof's man, the other Robert son of
    Wymarc's man, held this land; they could grant and sell.

36 In WHITWELL R(obert) the Bald holds 2 hides from Hardwin.
    Land for 2 ploughs. In lordship 1 plough;
      1 smallholder with 4 cottagers have 1 plough.
      Meadow for 1 plough; wood for making fences.
    Value 30s; when acquired 20s; before 1066, 40s.
      8 Freemen held this land. 6 of them were the King's men
    and held 5 virgates; they found 3 cartages and 3 escorts. The
    seventh, Robert son of Wymarc's man, had ½ hide; the eighth,
    Earl Algar's man, held 1 virgate. All these could withdraw.

  In LONGSTOW Hundred
37 In EVERSDEN Durand holds 1 virgate from Hardwin. Land for
    3 oxen; they are there, with
      1 villager.
      Meadow for 3 oxen.
    The value is and always was 8s.
      A Freeman of Earl Algar's held this land and could withdraw.

38 In KINGSTON 2 men-at-arms hold 1 virgate from Hardwin. Land
    for 3 oxen;
      meadow.
    The value is and always was 2s.
      Goding Thorbert, Edeva the Fair's man, held this land and
    could withdraw.

39 In the same village Robert the Bald holds 9 acres from Hardwin.
    Land for ½ ox.
    The value is and always was 6d.

Hanc t̄rā tenuit Wĺmer h̄o Rob̄ti filij Wimarc.7 dare
In Caldecote ten̄.ii.milit de Harđ ⌐potuit.
iii.uirg 7 x.ac̄s.Tra.ē.ii.car̄.7 ibi funt.cū.vi.
borđ.p̄tū.ii.car̄.Vaĺ 7 ualuit.lii.foĺ.Hanc
t̄rā tenuer̄.ii.foch̄i fub Eddeua.7 potuer̄ recedē.
In Stou ten̄ un̄ miles 7 ii.Angli.iii.uirg 7 dim̄.
Tra.ē.i.car̄ 7 dim̄.7 ibi funt cū.iiii.borđ.P̄tū
.i.car̄ 7 dim̄.Nem ad fepes.Vaĺ.xl.ii.foĺ.Q̣do
recep̄.xxx.foĺ.T.R.E.xl.ii.foĺ.Hanc t̄rā te
nuer̄.iiii.fochi.un̄ ho₂ h̄o Stigand Arch̄.7 alij
iii.h̄oēs abb̄is de Ramefy.dare 7 uendē potuer̄.
℧ Ipfe Harduin̄ ten̄ Cauftone.p x.hiđ fe defđ
T.R.E.7 m̄ p.vi.hiđ.Tra.ē.xii.car̄.In dn̄io
.v.hidæ.7 ibi funt.iiii.car̄.Ibi.xvii.uilti cū.viii.
borđ 7 x.cot h̄ntes.viii.car̄.p̄tū.xii.car̄.
Nem ad fepes 7 domos.Int totū uaĺ.xi.lib̄.Q̣do
recep̄.vi.lib̄.T.R.E.xiiii.lib̄.Hoc ℧ tenuit
Turgar teign̄ regis.E.7 ibi fuer̄.xxii.fochi.
Ho₂.iiii.h̄oēs regis.E.fuer̄.i.hiđ 7 dim̄ uirg

tenuer̄.H̄ dim̄ uirg.iii.Ineward inueniebat.
★ Ifte t̄ras fuas dare 7 uendē potuer̄.Alij.xviii.
h̄oēs Algari comitis fuer.7 de hac t̄ra vi.hiđ dim̄
uirg minus habuer̄.
In Crocheftone ten̄ Adelulf.i.hiđ de Harđ.
Tra.ē.i.car̄ 7 dim̄.7 ibi funt.In dn̄io.i.car̄.7 v.borđ
cū.ii.cot h̄nt dim̄ car̄.P̄tū.i.car̄ 7 dim̄.Pafta
ad pecun̄.Vaĺ.xx.foĺ.Q̣do recep̄.xiii.foĺ.T.R.E.
xl.foĺ.Hanc t̄rā.ii.fochi h̄oēs regis.E.tenuer̄.
7 ii.aueras uicecomiti inuener̄. IN PAPEWORD HD̄.
In Papeuuorde ten̄ Pagan̄ de Harđ.i.uirg 7 dim̄.

Wulfmer, Robert son of Wymarc's man, held this land and could grant.

40 In CALDECOTE 2 men-at-arms hold 3 virgates and 10 acres from Hardwin. Land for 2 ploughs; they are there, with
6 smallholders.
Meadow for 2 ploughs.
The value is and was 52s.
2 Freemen held this land under Edeva and could withdraw.

41 In LONGSTOWE 1 man-at-arms and 2 Englishmen hold 3½ virgates. Land for 1½ ploughs; they are there, with
4 smallholders.
Meadow for 1½ ploughs; wood for fences.
Value 42s; when acquired 30s; before 1066, 42s.
4 Freemen held this land. One of them was Archbishop Stigand's man, the other 3 were the Abbot of Ramsey's men; they could grant and sell.

42 M. Hardwin holds CAXTON himself. Before 1066 it answered for 10 hides; now for 6 hides. Land for 12 ploughs. In lordship 5 hides; 4 ploughs there.
17 villagers with 8 smallholders and 10 cottagers who have 8 ploughs.
Meadow for 12 ploughs; wood for fences and houses.
In total, value £11; when acquired £6; before 1066 £14.
Thorgar, King Edward's thane, held this manor. 22 Freemen were there. 4 of them were King Edward's men; they held 1 hide and ½ virgate; this ½ virgate found 3 escorts; these men could grant and sell their lands. The other 18 were Earl Algar's men; they had 6 hides less ½ virgate of this land.

199 a

43 In CROXTON Aethelwulf holds 1 hide from Hardwin. Land for 1½ ploughs; they are there. In lordship 1 plough;
5 smallholders with 2 cottagers have ½ plough.
Meadow for 1½ ploughs; pasture for the livestock.
Value 20s; when acquired 13s; before 1066, 40s.
2 Freemen, King Edward's men, held this land; they found 2 cartages for the Sheriff.

In PAPWORTH Hundred
44 In PAPWORTH Payne holds 1½ virgates from Hardwin. Land for

Tra.̄e.iiii.bob.7 ibi funt.cū.iiii.borđ.P̊tū.iiii.

bob.Val 7 ualuit fēp.v.fol.Hanc trā.ii.fochi

hōes regis.E.tenuer.7 ii.ineuuarđ inueneꝝ7 uende

In Elefuuorde teñ Pagan de harđ.i.uirg. ⌠ potuer.

Tra.̄e dim car.7 ibi.̄e cū.i.uilło,.P̊tū dim car.Val

7 ualuit.iiii.fol.T.R.E.́v.fol.Hanc trā,ii.fochi.R.E.

tenuer.7 i.Jneẘ inueneꝝ7 uende potuer.

In Cunitone teñ Pagan de Harđ.ii.hiđ.Tra.̄e,ii.

car,In dñio.i.car,7 i.uilłs cū.iiii.borđ hꝑ.i.car.

Ibi.ii.ferui.P̊tū,ii.car.Val.xx.fol.Q̊do recēp.́xvi.

fol.7 tūtđ T.R.E.Hanc trā tenuer.iii.fochi.R.E.

7 ii.aueras.7 i.jneuuarđ inueneꝝ7 recede potuer.

In Bochefuuorde teñ Pagan de Harđ.iiii.hiđ

7 dim.Tra.̄e.iiii.car.In dñio.i.car.7 viii.uilłi cū

vi.borđ 7 iii.cot hñt.iii.car.Ibi.ii.ferui.7 p̊tū

iiii.car.Val 7 ualuit fēp lx.fol.Hanc trā tenuit

.i.teigñ regis.E.iii.hiđ 7 dim.7 uende pot cui uoł.

7 vii.fochi regis.E.i.hiđ habuer.7 iii.Aueras 7 iii.

ineẘ uicecomiti inuenieƀ.7 uende pot trā fuā.

In Oure teñ Radulf de Harđ.ii.hiđ 7 i.uirg.

Tra.̄e.ii.car 7 dim.7 ibi funt.cū.iii.uilłis 7 i.borđ.

7 iii.cot.P̊tū.ii.car 7 dim.Pafta ad pecuñ.Val

7 ualuit.xxx.fol.T.R.E.́l.fol.Hanc trā tenuer.

De hac trā tenuit.i.fochs fub abƀe de Elẏ dim

hiđ.ñ potuit dare ꝉ uende ext æcclam fine lictia

abƀis.7 alij.ii.fochi.iii.uirg habuer.uende po

tueruꝗ.foca remanfit abbati de Elẏ.

7 alij.vii.habuer.i.hiđ.hōes abƀis de Ramefẏ

fuer.uende potuer.fine foca.

4 oxen; they are there, with
    4 smallholders.
    Meadow for 4 oxen.
The value is and always was 5s.
    2 Freemen, King Edward's men, held this land; they found
2 escorts and could sell.

45   In ELSWORTH Payne holds 1 virgate from Hardwin. Land for
½ plough; it is there, with
    1 villager.
    Meadow for ½ plough.
The value is and was 4s; before 1066, 5s.
    2 Freemen of King Edward's held this land; they found
1 escort and could sell.

46   In CONINGTON Payne holds 2 hides from Hardwin. Land for
2 ploughs. In lordship 1 plough;
    1 villager with 4 smallholders have 1 plough.
    2 slaves; meadow for 2 ploughs.
Value 20s; when acquired 16s; before 1066 as much.
    3 Freemen of King Edward's held this land; they found
2 cartages and 1 escort, and could withdraw.

47   In BOXWORTH Payne holds 4½ hides from Hardwin. Land for
4 ploughs. In lordship 1 plough;
    8 villagers with 6 smallholders and 3 cottagers have 3 ploughs.
    2 slaves; meadow for 4 ploughs.
The value is and always was 60s.
    A thane of King Edward's held 3½ hides of this land and
could sell to whom he would.
    7 Freemen of King Edward's had 1 hide; they found 3
cartages and 3 escorts for the Sheriff, and could sell their land.

48   In OVER Ralph holds 2 hides and 1 virgate from Hardwin. Land
for 2½ ploughs; they are there, with
    3 villagers; 1 smallholder; 3 cottagers.
    Meadow for 2½ ploughs; pasture for the livestock.
The value is and was 30s; before 1066, 50s.
    [10 Freemen] held this land. 1 Freeman held ½ hide of this
land under the Abbot of Ely; he could not grant or sell outside
the Church without the Abbot's permission. 2 other Freemen
had 3 virgates; they could sell; the jurisdiction remained with
the Abbot of Ely. The other 7 had 1 hide; they were the Abbot
of Ramsey's men; they could sell without the jurisdiction.

In Draitone ten Pagan de Harð . v . hið 7 iii . uirg.

Tra . e̅ . v . car . In d̅n̅io . ii . car . 7 ix . uilti cu̅ . iii . borð

hn̅t . ii . car . 7 iii . pot fieri . Ibi . vii . cot . 7 p̃tu̅ . ii . car .

H̅ tra ual . iiii . liƀ . Q̲do recep . c . fol . T . R . E . vi . liƀ .

Hanc tr̅a tenuer̅ . xix . fochi . Sex ho₂ ho̅es R . E .

ii . hið dim̅ uirg min̅ habuer̅ . 7 vi . inew uicecom

inuener̅ . 7 tr̅a fua dare potuer̅ . 7 alij . iiii . ho̅es Eddeue

i . hið 7 dim̅ habuer̅ . 7 recede potuer̅ fine Soca .

199 b

7 alij . v . ho̅es abƀis de Ely̅ fuer̅ . Quo₂ . iiii . tenuer̅

. i . hið 7 uende potuer̅ abfq₂ foca . Quint u̅

dim̅ uirg habuit fub abƀe . f₂ n̅ potuit uendere .

7 alij . iiii . ho̅es sc̅i Guthlaci fuer̅ . i . hið 7 i . uirg te

nuer̅ de d̅n̅ica firma æccl̅æ . *In Radefelle Hvnd̅.*

In Stiuicefuuorde ten Harð . i . uirg . Tra . e̅ . ii . boƀ .

Val 7 ualuit fe̅p . v . fol . Hanc tr̅a tenuit Goduin̅

ho̅ abƀis de Ely̅ . n̅ potuit uendere . *In Weslai Hvnd̅.*

★ In Waratinge ten Harð . iii . hið . Tra . e̅ . iiii . car . In d̅n̅io

funt . ii . 7 v . uilti cu̅ . iiii . borð hn̅t . ii . car . Ibi . iiii . ferui .

7 iiii . ac̅ p̃ti . Silua . xii . porc . Val . vi . liƀ . Q̲do recep .

xx . fol . T . R . E . xl . fol . Hanc tr̅a tenuer̅ x . fochi ho̅es

abƀis de Ely̅ . uende n̅ potuer̅ .

In *Belesshā* ten Harð   qt xx . ac̅s de tra

abƀis . Tra . e̅ . i . car . 7 ibi eft . Val 7 ualuit . xiii . fol 7 iiii .

den̅ . Hanc tr̅a tenuer̅ . iii . fochi . uende n̅ potuer̅ .

In Suafhā ten Harð . ii . hið 7 iii . uirg . Tra . e̅ . iii . car . *In Stanes*

In d̅n̅io . e̅ . i . 7 ii . uilti hn̅t . ii . car . P̃tu̅ . ii . boƀ . Valet   *Hvnd̅.*

7 ualuit fe̅p . lxx . fol . Hanc tr̅a tenuer̅ . iiii . fochi abƀis

de Ely̅ . n̅ potuer̅ uendere . *In Flamiding Hvnd̅*

In Badburghā ten Harð de rege dim̅ uirg de tra

In CHESTERTON Hundred

49 In (Dry) DRAYTON Payne holds 5 hides and 3 virgates from Hardwin. Land for 5 ploughs. In lordship 2 ploughs;
9 villagers with 3 smallholders have 2 ploughs; a third possible.
7 cottagers;
meadow for 2 ploughs.
Value of this land £4; when acquired 100s; before 1066 £6.
19 Freemen held this land. 6 of them, King Edward's men, had 2 hides less ½ virgate; they found 6 escorts for the Sheriff and could grant their land. 4 others, Edeva's men, had 1½ hides; they could withdraw without the jurisdiction. 5 others were the Abbot 199 b of Ely's men; 4 of them held 1 hide and could sell without the jurisdiction; the fifth had ½ virgate under the Abbot, but could not sell. The other 4 were St. Guthlac's men; they held 1 hide and 1 virgate from the Church's household revenue.

In RADFIELD Hundred

50 In STETCHWORTH Hardwin holds 1 virgate. Land for 2 oxen.
The value is and always was 5s.
Godwin, the Abbot of Ely's man, held this land; he could not sell.

In WESTLEY Hundred

51 In (West) WRATTING Hardwin holds 3 hides. Land for 4 ploughs. In lordship 2;
5 villagers with 4 smallholders have 2 ploughs.
4 slaves; meadow, 4 acres; woodland, 12 pigs.
Value £6; when acquired 20s; before 1066, 40s.
10 Freemen, the Abbot of Ely's men, held this land; they could not sell.

52 In BALSHAM Hardwin holds 80 acres of the Abbot's land. Land for 1 plough; it is there.
The value is and was 13s 4d.
3 Freemen held this land; they could not sell.

In STAINE Hundred

53 In SWAFFHAM Hardwin holds 2 hides and 3 virgates. Land for 3 ploughs. In lordship 1;
2 villagers have 2 ploughs.
Meadow for 2 oxen.
The value is and always was 70s.
4 Freemen of the Abbot of Ely's held this land; they could not sell.

In FLENDISH Hundred

54 In BABRAHAM Hardwin holds from the King ½ virgate of the Abbot's land.

abƀis. Vał 7 ualuit xɴ. deꞑ. Duo focħi tenueꞃ de

abƀe de Elẏ. Non potueꞃ recedere.

Ɪn Pāpeſuuorde teꞑ Harđ. x. aĉs. Tra. ē. uno boui.

Vał 7 ualuit. xɪɪ. deꞑ. Snelinc tenuit hanc trā de

abƀe de Elẏ. ꞇ potuit recedere. *Iɴ Ʀepeslav hꝺ*

Ɪn Trepeſlai teꞑ Harđ de rege. ɪ. hiđ. de dꞑico uiĉtu

monachoʒ. Tra. ē. ɪ. caꞃ. 7 ibi eſt. Vał 7 ualuit ſēp xx. ſoł.

Ħ tra fuit de dꞑio æcċæ de Elẏ.

Ɪn eađ uilla tenebat Harđ. ɪɪ. aĉs de tra abƀis. de qꝺ

ꞇ ħt aduocatū ꞇ liƀatoꝛē. ſed occupauit ſuꝑ abƀem.

ut hōes de hunđ teſtanꞇ.

.XXV. **H**TERRA HVGONIS DE BERNERES. *Iɴ Stov hvɴd.*

Hvɢo de Berneres teꞑ de rege In Eureſdone. ɪ. hiđ.

Tra. ē. ɪ. caꞃ. 7 ibi eſt. cū. ɪ. uiłło 7 ɪ. ſeruo. Ꝑtū. ɪ. caꞃ.

Nem ad ſepes. Vał. xɪɪɪ. ſoł. Qdo recep. x. ſoł. T.R.E.

xx. ſoł. Hanc trā tenuit Eduui hō abƀis de Elẏ. po

tuit dare ꞇ uendė ſine liĉtia ej. ſʒ ſocā habuit Algar.

.XXVI **H**TERRA HVGONIS DE PORTH. *Iɴ Staplehov hꝺ.*

Hvɢo de Porth teꞑ in Giſlehā. ɪ. hiđ 7 dimiđ

7 xx. aĉs. Tra. ē. ɪɪɪ. caꞃ. In dꞑio. ē una. 7 ɪɪ. uiłti cū

ɪɪɪ. borđ hꞑt. ɪɪ. caꞃ. Ibi. ɪɪ. ſerui. Ꝑtū. ɪ. caꞃ. Paſta

ad pecuꞑ uille. Vał 7 ualuit. xɴ. ſoł. T.R.E. ɴx. ſoł.

Hoc ꝏ tenuit Orgaꞃ uicecōm R.E. potuit recedere

abſqʒ liĉtia dꞑi ſui.

Ɪpſe Hugo teꞑ de feudo eꝑi baioc Snellewelle. ꝑ. v. hiđ

ſe defđ ſēp. Tra. ē. x. caꞃ. In dꞑio ſunt. ɪɪ. 7 ɪɪɪ. pot

fieri. Ibi. vɪ. focħi. 7 vɪɪɪ. uiłti. 7 ɪɪɪ. borđ. 7 ɪɪɪ. ſerui.

The value is and was 40d.
   2 Freemen held (it) from the Abbot of Ely; they could not withdraw.

55 In PAMPISFORD Hardwin holds 10 acres. Land for 1 ox.
The value is and was 12d.
   Snelling held this land from the Abbot of Ely; he could not withdraw.

In THRIPLOW Hundred
56 In THRIPLOW Hardwin holds from the King 1 hide of the monks' lordship supplies. Land for 1 plough; it is there.
The value is and always was 20s.
   This land was of the lordship of the Church of Ely.

57 In the same village Hardwin held 2 acres of the Abbot's land, for which he did not have a patron or a deliverer; but he appropriated it in the Abbot's despite, as the men of the Hundred testify.

25 [27]   LAND OF HUGH OF BERNIÈRES

In LONGSTOW Hundred
1 Hugh of Bernières holds 1 hide in EVERSDEN from the King.
Land for 1 plough; it is there, with
   1 villager; 1 slave.
   Meadow for 1 plough; wood for fences.
Value 13s; when acquired 10s; before 1066, 20s.
   Edwy, the Abbot of Ely's man, held this land; he could grant or sell without his permission, but Earl Algar had the jurisdiction.

26 [28]   LAND OF HUGH OF PORT

In STAPLOE Hundred
1 Hugh of Port holds 1½ hides and 20 acres in ISLEHAM. Land for 3 ploughs. In lordship 1;
   2 villagers with 3 smallholders have 2 ploughs.
   2 slaves; meadow for 1 plough; pasture for the village livestock.
The value is and was 40s; before 1066, 60s.
   Ordgar, King Edward's Sheriff, held this manor; he could withdraw without his lord's permission.

2 Hugh holds SNAILWELL himself from the Bishop of Bayeux's Holding. It has always answered for 5 hides. Land for 10 ploughs. In lordship 2; a third possible.
   6 Freemen; 8 villagers; 3 smallholders; 3 slaves.

Ibi . iiii . molini . de xiiii . foł 7 iiii . den . Ptū . ii . cař.

Silua ad claufurā . cū duobz currib̄ de filua regis de

chauelai . In totis ualent uał . xiiii . lib̄ . Q̃do recep̄ : xii.

lib̄ . T.R.E. xv . lib̄ . Hoc m̄ tenuit Stigand Archiep̄s

die q̃ rex . E . fuit uiuus 7 mortuus . 7 ibi fuer̄ . vi . fochi

hōes ejdē Archiep̄i . qui fine ej lictia poterax̄ recedere.

7 trā fuā dare ł uende . fed Soca Archiep̄o remanfit.

Hoc m̄ jacuit in ł æcclæ de Elȳ T.R.E . in dñica firma.

fed Abb̄ qui tc̄ erat præftitit eū Archiep̄o . ut hund̄ tef

tatur . Nc̄ abb̄ Sȳmeon reclamat p̄ anteceffores fuos.

TERRA ALBERICI DE VER. *IN CHAVELAI HVND.*

m̄ ALBERICVS de VER ten̄ *ESSELIE* . de rege . Eurard

ten de eo . p̄ . iii . hid̄ 7 dim̄ fe defd̄ . T.R.E . 7 m̄ p̄ . ii . hid̄.

Tra . e . iiii . cař . In dñio . ii . 7 uiłłi hn̄t . ii . cař . p̄ti una ać.

Silua . xii . porc̄ . Pafta ad pecun̄ . Int̄ tot̄ uał . c . foł.

Q̃do recep̄ : xl . foł . 7 tn̄td̄ T.R.E . Hoc m̄ tenuit Wluin

teign̄ regis . E.

★ m̄ Ipfe Alberic̄ ten̄ Sextone . 7 Eurard̄ de eo . p̄ v . hid̄ fe

defd̄ T.R.E . 7 m̄ p̄ . iii . hid̄ . Tra . e . vii . cař . In dñio funt

iii . cař . 7 x . uiłłi cū . iiii . bord̄ hn̄t . iiii . cař . Ptū . i . cař.

Pafta ad pecun̄ uillæ . Silua . xl . porc̄ . Int̄ tot̄ uał

viii . lib̄ . Q̃do recep̄ : vii . lib̄ . 7 tn̄td̄ T.R.E . Hoc m̄ te

nuit Wluuin teign̄ . R.E.

m̄ Ipfe Alberic̄ ten̄ *SEVERLAI* . p̄ . vi . hid̄ 7 dim̄ fe defd̄.

.T . regis . E . 7 m̄ p̄ . iiii . hid̄ . Tra . e . viii . cař . In dñio . ii . hide.

7 ibi funt . iiii . cař . 7 xii . uiłłi cū . ii . bord̄ hn̄t . iiii . cař.

Ibi . viii . ferui . 7 una ać p̄ti . Silua . xx . porc̄ . Pafta ad

pecun̄ uillæ . In totis ualent uał xvi . lib̄ . Q̃do recep̄ :

xx . lib̄ . 7 tn̄td̄ T.R.E . Hoc m̄ tenuit Wluuin teign̄ . R.E.

4 mills at 14s 4d; meadow for 2 ploughs; woodland for   199 c
   fencing, with two carts from the King's woodland at
   Cheveley.
Total value £14; when acquired £12; before 1066 £15.
   Archbishop Stigand held this manor in 1066. 6 Freemen
were there, the same Archbishop's men, who could withdraw
without his permission and grant or sell their land; but the
jurisdiction remained with the Archbishop.
   This manor lay in the lordship of the Church of Ely before
1066, in the lordship revenue, but the then Abbot leased it
to the Archbishop, as the Hundred testifies. Now Abbot
Simeon claims it back through his predecessors.

27 [29]   LAND OF AUBREY DE VERE

In CHEVELEY Hundred

1 M. Aubrey de Vere holds ASHLEY from the King. Evrard holds
   from him. It answered for 3½ hides before 1066; now for
   2 hides. Land for 4 ploughs. In lordship 2;
      the villagers have 2 ploughs.
      Meadow, 1 acre; woodland, 12 pigs; pasture for the livestock.
   Total value 100s; when acquired 40s; before 1066 as much.
   Wulfwin, King Edward's thane, held this manor.

2 M. Aubrey holds SAXON (Street) himself, and Evrard from him. It
   answered for 5 hides before 1066; now for 3 hides. Land for
   7 ploughs. In lordship 3 ploughs;
      10 villagers with 4 smallholders have 4 ploughs.
      Meadow for 1 plough; pasture for the village livestock;
        woodland, 40 pigs.
   Total value £8; when acquired £7; before 1066 as much.
   Wulfwin, King Edward's thane, held this manor.

3 M. Aubrey holds SILVERLEY himself. It answered for 6½ hides before
   1066; now for 4 hides. Land for 8 ploughs. In lordship 2 hides;
   4 ploughs there;
      12 villagers with 2 smallholders have 4 ploughs.
      8 slaves; meadow, 1 acre; woodland, 20 pigs; pasture for
        the village livestock.
   Total value £16; when acquired £20; before 1066 as much.
   Wulfwin, King Edward's thane, held this manor.

In Suafhā ten Albicus dim̄ hid̄.7 xx.ac̄s de rege.

Tra.ē ad.I.car̄ 7 ibi.ē cū.I.uitto.7 I.molin̄.VII.solidoꝛ.

Val̄ 7 ualuit sēp.x.sot.Hanc trā tenuit.I.soch̄s regis.E.

n̄ potuit recede̅ sine lictia.7 inuen̄ Auerā uicecomiti regis.

Hanc trā n̄ habuit Antecessor Alberici.ut hōes de hund̄

testant̄.f̧ ipse Albic̄ sup̣ regē occupauit.

M̄ Ipse Alberic ten̄ *WIBORGHA* de rege.´

Tra.ē.VIII.car̄.In dn̄io.II.hide.7 ibi.IIII.car̄.7 VIII.uitti

cū.v.bord̄ hn̄t.VII.car̄.Ibi.VII.serui.p̄tū.III.car̄.

7 I.molin̄.XXII.sot.In totis ualent̄ ual̄ XII.lib̄.Q̇do

recep̄.´x.lib̄.7 tn̄td̄ T.R.E.Hoc M̄ tenuit Wluuin̄ teign̄

In ead̄ uilla ten̄ Reinald̄ dim̄ hid̄ de Albico ⌐regis.E.

7 xxx.ac̄s.Tra.ē.I.car̄.7 ibi est cū.I.bord̄.Val̄ 7 ualuit

sēp.x.sot.Hanc trā tenuit Godric hō regis.E.n̄ tenuit

de Antecessore Albici.Hoc hōes de Hund̄ testant̄.sed

sup̄ regē Alberic occupauit. *IN CILDEFORD HVND̄*

M̄ In Canpas ten̄ Albicus de uer.II.hid̄ 7 dim̄.Tra.ē XI.

car̄.In dn̄io.I.hida 7 I.uirḡ.7 ibi.IIII.car̄.Ibi XVII.uitti

cū.IIII.bord̄ hn̄t.VII.car̄.Ibi.VI.serui.P̄tū.III.car̄.

Silua ad q̇ngent̄ porc̄.De herbagia uillæ.VIII.solid̄.

In totis ualent̄ ual̄ xv.lib̄.Q̇do recep̄.´XII.lib̄.7 tn̄td̄

T.R.E.Hoc M̄ tenuit Wluuin̄ teign̄ regis.E.

De hac trā ten̄ Norman̄ dim̄ hid̄ de Albico.Tra.ē.I.

car̄.7 ibi est.Val̄ 7 ualuit sēp.XL.sot.

199 d

In Horsei.ten̄ Normann̄ de Albico.I.hid̄ 7 dim̄.Tra

ē.III.car̄.In dn̄io.ē una.7 II.uitti 7 dim̄ cū.III.bord̄

hn̄t.II.car̄.Ibi.III.serui.7 IIII.ac̄ p̄ti.Silua.XL.porc̄.

Val̄ 7 ualuit sēp.LX.sot.Hanc trā tenuit Wluuin̄

teign̄.R.E.7 habuit sacā 7 socā.7 reddeb̄ Auerā 7 Jnew.

In STAINE Hundred
4   In SWAFFHAM Aubrey holds ½ hide and 20 acres from the King.
Land for 1 plough; it is there, with
1 villager;
1 mill, 7s.
The value is and always was 10s.
A Freeman of King Edward's held this land; he could not
withdraw without permission, and found cartage for the King's
Sheriff.
Aubrey's predecessor did not have this land, as the men of
the Hundred testify; but Aubrey appropriated it himself in the
King's despite.

5 M. Aubrey holds WILBRAHAM himself from the King. Land for 8
ploughs. In lordship 2 hides; 4 ploughs there;
8 villagers with 5 smallholders have 7 ploughs.
7 slaves; meadow for 3 ploughs; 1 mill, 22s.
Total value £12; when acquired £10; before 1066 as much.
Wulfwin, King Edward's thane, held this manor.

6   In the same village Reginald holds ½ hide and 30 acres from
Aubrey. Land for 1 plough; it is there, with
1 smallholder.
The value is and always was 10s.
Godric, King Edward's man, held this land; he did not hold
from Aubrey's predecessor. The men of the Hundred testify
to this; but Aubrey appropriated it in the King's despite.

In CHILFORD Hundred
7 M. In CAMPS Aubrey de Vere holds 2½ hides. Land for 11 ploughs.
In lordship 1 hide and 1 virgate; 4 ploughs there.
17 villagers with 4 smallholders have 7 ploughs.
6 slaves; meadow for 3 ploughs; woodland for 500 pigs;
from village grazing 8s.
Total value £15; when acquired £12; before 1066 as much.
Wulfwin, King Edward's thane, held this manor.
Norman holds ½ hide of this land from Aubrey. Land for
1 plough; it is there. The value is and always was 40s.

8   In HORSEHEATH Norman holds 1½ hides from Aubrey. Land   199 d
for 3 ploughs. In lordship 1;
2½ villagers with 3 smallholders have 2 ploughs.
3 slaves; meadow, 4 acres; woodland, 40 pigs.
The value is and always was 60s.
Wulfwin, King Edward's thane, held this land; he had full
jurisdiction, and paid cartage and escort.

Ↄ Ipſe Alberic̄ ten HILDRICESHÁ .p . v . hiđ ſe defđ.
Tra . e͞ . xɪ . car̄ . In dn͞io . ɪɪ . hiđ 7 dim̄ . 7 ibi ſuꝫˉ . ɪɪɪɪ . car̄.
Ibi . xvɪ . uiłłi hn͞t . vɪɪ . car̄ . Ibi . ɪɪɪɪ . ſerui . 7 ɪ . molin̄
de . x . ſoł . p͞tu . ɪɪɪ . car̄ . Silua xx . porc̄ . Int totū
uał . x . liƀ . Q̄do receᵽ . vɪɪɪ . liƀ . T.R.E. vɪɪɪ . liƀ.
Hanc tra͞ tenuit Wluuin̄ teign̄ . R.E.

Ↄ Ipſe Alberic̄ ten Abintone . 7 Firmat de eo . p vɪ . hiđ
ſe defđ . Tra . e͞ . vɪɪɪ . car̄ . In dn͞io . ɪɪ . car̄ . 7 ɪɪɪ . pot
fieri . Ibi . ɪx . uiłłi cū . v . borđ hn͞t . ɪɪɪɪ . car̄ . 7 v̄ᵗᵃ . pot
fieri . p͞tu . ɪɪ . car̄ . Silua . x . porc̄ . 7 ɪ . molin̄ de . ɪx.
ſoł . De paſta . vɪ . ſoc̄ . Vał 7 ualuit . vɪɪɪ . liƀ . T.R.E.
vɪ . liƀ . Hoc Ↄ tenuit Wluuin̄ p͞dict teign̄ . R E.
De hac tra͞ tenuit q̄da͞ pƀr . ɪ . hiđ de Eddeua pulchra.
n͞ potuit recede͞ ſine lictia ej . 7 m̄ reclam̄ Alan̄ com̄
ſuᵽ ho͞es Alberici . ſicut Hunđ teſtatur.

In Badburgha͞ ten Firmat de Alƀico dim̄ uirḡ.
Vał . xx . den̄ . Hanc tra͞ tenuit Goduin̄ ſub Wluuino
Anteceſſore Alƀici . n͞ potuit recedere.

In Abintone hт̄ . ɪ . ſoch̄s de rege dim̄ hida͞ . quæ . e͞
in cuſtodia   picot uicecom̄ . 7 uał . xɪɪ . den̄ ᵽ annū.
Hanc tenuit Elmær ſoch̄s regis . E . 7 potuit dare uel
uende͞ cui uoluit . T.R.E. 7 Albericus de ver inuaſit
hanc tra͞ de ſoca regis . ꝼꝫ Picot uicecom̄ deratioci
nauit aduſus eū . 7 adhuc retin̄ . ɪ . car̄ . 7 ccc . 7 q̄t xx.
oues . q̄s hт̄ Alƀic̄ ex illa tra͞ . ut ho͞es de Hunđ teſtant̄.

.XXVIII. TERRA EVSTACHIJ DE HVNTEĐ. *IN PÁPESWORD HĐ.*

Eᴠꜱᴛᴀᴄʜɪᴠꜱ de Huntindunej ᵗᵉⁿ in Papeuuorde . ɪ . hiđ
7 ɪɪɪ . uirḡ . Tra . e͞ . ɪɪɪ . car̄ . In dn͞io . e͞ una . 7 ɪɪɪɪ . uiłłi
hn͞t . ɪɪ . car̄ . Ibi . ɪ . ſeruus . 7 p͞tu . ɪ . car̄ . Vał . xʟ . ſoł.
Q̄do receᵽ . ɪɪɪɪ . liƀ . T . R . E . ʟ . ſoł . Hanc tra͞ tenuit

9 M. Aubrey holds HILDERSHAM himself. It answers for 5 hides.
Land for 11 ploughs. In lordship 2½ hides; 4 ploughs there.
16 villagers have 7 ploughs.
4 slaves; 1 mill at 10s; meadow for 3 ploughs; woodland,
20 pigs.
In total, value £10; when acquired £8; before 1066 £8.
Wulfwin, King Edward's thane, held this land.

10 M. Aubrey holds ABINGTON himself, and Firmatus from him. It
answers for 6 hides. Land for 8 ploughs. In lordship 2 ploughs;
a third possible.
9 villagers with 5 smallholders have 4 ploughs; a fifth possible.
Meadow for 2 ploughs; woodland, 10 pigs; 1 mill at 9s;
from the pasture 6 ploughshares.
The value is and was £8; before 1066 £6.
The said Wulfwin, King Edward's thane, held this manor. A
priest held 1 hide of this land from Edeva the Fair; he could not
withdraw without her permission. Now Count Alan claims it
back in despite of Aubrey's men, as the Hundred testifies.

11 In BABRAHAM Firmatus holds ½ virgate from Aubrey.
Value 20d.
Godwin held this land under Wulfwin, Aubrey's predecessor;
he could not withdraw.

12 In ABINGTON 1 Freeman has ½ hide from the King which is in
the charge of Picot the Sheriff.
Value 12d a year.
Aelmer, a Freeman of King Edward's, held it; he could grant
or sell to whom he would before 1066. Aubrey de Vere
annexed this land from the King's jurisdiction, but Picot the
Sheriff adjudged it against him and still keeps 1 plough and
380 sheep which Aubrey has from that land, as the men of the
Hundred testify.

28 [30]   LAND OF EUSTACE OF HUNTINGDON

In PAPWORTH Hundred
1 Eustace of Huntingdon holds 1 hide and 3 virgates in PAPWORTH.
Land for 3 ploughs. In lordship 1;
4 villagers have 2 ploughs.
1 slave; meadow for 1 plough.
Value 40s; when acquired £4; before 1066, 50s.

Ornod hō Roƀti filij Wimarch . potuit dare cui uoł.

Modo ten̄ Walter de Euſtachio.

In eađ uilla ten̄ Ornođ de Euſtachio juſſu regis

.i . hidā .7 iii . uirg̅ . Tra . ē . ii . car̅ . Ibi . ē . i . car̅ 7 dim̄.

7 dim̄ pot fieri . p̄tū . i . car̅ . Val 7 ualuit . xx . ſol.

T.R.E. L . ſol . Iſtemet tenuit de Roƀto . f . Wimarch.

7 uende̅ potuit.

In eađ uilla ten̄ Walter de Euſtachio . i . uirg̅ 7 dim̄.

Tra . ē . iiii . boƀ . 7 p̄tū totiđ boƀ . Val 7 ual v . ſol.

T.R.E. x . ſol . Hanc trā tenuit Goduin hō aƀƀis

de Elẏ . 7 uende̅ non potuit.

.XXIX. **WⱤTERRA WIDONIS DE RAINBVEDCVRT.**

W IDO de Rainbuedcurt ten̄ In Melrede . iii . hiđ

7 i . uirg̅ de rege . Tra . ē . v . car̅ . 7 ibi ſunt . In dn̄io

dim̄ hida . 7 ibi . ē . i . car̅ . 7 xv . borđ cū . iii . cot hn̄t

iiii . car̅ . Ibi un̄ ſeruus . 7 ii . molini de . x . ſol 7 viii . den̄.

p̄tū . v . car̅ . Paſta ad pecun̄ . Int tot ual lxx . ſol.

7 tntđ qdo recep̄ . T.R.E. c . ſol . Hanc trā tenuerun̄

200 a

xvi . ſochi . De his . x . habuer̅ , ii . hiđ 7 dim̄ uirg̅ de ſoca

S̄ Edeldride de Elẏ . quoᷠᷱ un̄ trā ſuā nec dare nec

uende̅ potuit . alij ū noue̅ potuer̅ cui uoluer̅ . ſᷟᷠ ſoca

om̄iū remanebat æcclæ . 7 v . alij ſochi tenuer̅ . i . hiđ

7 dim̄ uirg̅ . de comite Algaro . potuer̅ dare ł uende̅.

In eađ uilla ten̄ Wido . v . hiđ . 7 i . uirg̅ 7 dim̄ . 7 iiii.

part uni uirg̅ . Tra . ē . xi . car̅ . In dn̄io . ii . hiđ 7 dim̄.

7 ibi ſun̄ . ii . car̅ . 7 adhuc . ii . poſſ fieri . Ibi . vi . uiłłi cū

xviii . borđ 7 x . cot hn̄t . vii . car̅ . Ibi dim̄ moliñ

de . ii . ſol 7 viii . den̄ . p̄tū . vi . car̅ . Paſta ad pecun̄

Ordnoth, Robert son of Wymarc's man, held this land; he could grant to whom he would.

Now Walter holds (it) from Eustace.

2   In the same village Ordnoth holds 1 hide and 3 virgates from Eustace by the King's order. Land for 2 ploughs; 1½ ploughs there; [another] ½ possible.

Meadow for 1 plough.

The value is and was 20s; before 1066, 50s.

He held it himself from Robert son of Wymarc and could sell.

3   In the same village Walter holds 1½ virgates from Eustace. Land for 4 oxen;

meadow for as many oxen.

The value is and was 5s; before 1066, 10s.

Godwin, the Abbot of Ely's man, held this land and could not sell.

29 [31]   LAND OF GUY OF RAIMBEAUCOURT

[In ARMINGFORD Hundred]

1   Guy of Raimbeaucourt holds 3 hides and 1 virgate in MELDRETH from the King. Land for 5 ploughs; they are there. In lordship ½ hide; 1 plough there;

15 smallholders with 3 cottagers have 4 ploughs.

1 slave; 2 mills at 10s 8d; meadow for 5 ploughs; pasture for the livestock.

In total, value 70s; when acquired, as much, before 1066, 100s.

16 Freemen held this land. 10 of them had 2 hides and ½   200 a
virgate of St. Etheldrida of Ely's jurisdiction; of whom one could neither grant nor sell his land; the other 9 could (grant and sell) to whom they would, but the jurisdiction of all remained with the Church. 5 other Freemen held 1 hide and ½ virgate from Earl Algar; they could grant or sell.

2   In the same village Guy holds 5 hides and 1¾ virgates. Land for 11 ploughs. In lordship 2½ hides; 2 ploughs there; a further 2 possible.

6 villagers with 18 smallholders and 10 cottagers have 7 ploughs.

½ mill at 2s 8d; meadow for 6 ploughs; pasture for the village livestock.

uillæ. Int tot ual. **x**. lib 7 x. sol. Q̆do recep̄: vi. lib.

T.R.E. xiiii. lib. De hac t̄ra tenuit Edric spur. ii.

hiđ 7 dim̄. teign R.E. potuit dare t̃ uenđe.

7 vịii. sochi hōes abbis de Elẏ tenuer̄. ii. hiđ 7 dim̄ uirg̃.

7 alij. ii. sochi hōes regis. E. tenuer̄. ii. part. i. uirg̃.

7 ii. jnew inuenieb̄. Hi ōms t̄ras suas uenđe potuer̄.

Soca de. viii. sochis remansit abbi de Elẏ. ŕ HVND.

İn Bertone ten̄ Hunfrid de Widone *IN WEDERLAI*

iii. hiđ 7 dim̄. T̄ra. ē. vi. car̄. In dn̄io. iii. car̄. 7 iii.

uilti cū. xiii. borđ hn̄t. iii. car̄. Ibi un̄ seru. P̄t̄u

iiii. car̄. Int totū ual. vi. lib. Q̆do recep̄: x. lib.

7 tn̄td T.R.E. In hac t̄ra sunt. iii. milit francig̃.

Hanc t̄ra tenuer̄ xx. iiii. sochi. Hoᵹ un̄ dimiđ

hiđ tenuit sub Eddeua pulchra. 7 uenđe potuit.

7 ōms alij sochi regis. E. fuer̄. iii. hiđ tenuer̄. 7 dare

7 uenđe potuer̄. 7 vi. Aueras 7 xvii. jnewarđ

uicecomiti inuener̄.

İn Grantesete ten. ii. milites de Widone. iii. uirg̃.

T̄ra. ē. i. car̄. f̧ n̄ est ibi. P̄t̄u. iiii. bob̃. 7 iii. borđ.

Val. lv. sol. Q̆do recep̄: xl. sol. T.R.E. iiii. lib.

Hanc t̄ra tenuer̄. v. sochi hōes regis. E. 7 uenđe

potuer̄. 7 iiii. jnew inuenieb̄ uicecomiti regis.

İn Orduuelle ten̄ Radulf de Widone. iii. part. i. uirg̃

7 ibi. ē bos. Val 7 ualuit. ii. sol. 7 uenđe potuit. 7 iiii.

part̄e unị Aucre uicecom̄ inuenit.

İn Warateuuorde ten̄ Radulf de Widone dim̄ hiđ

T̄ra. ē dim̄ car̄. 7 ibi. ē. cū. ii. uilt̄is 7 ii. borđ. p̄t̄u dim̄

car̄. Nem̄ ad sepes reficienđ. Val xx. sol. Q̆do recep̄:

x. sol. T.R.E. xx. sol. Hanç t̄ra. ii. sochi regis. E. te

nuer̄. 7 ii. Aueras inuener̄. 7 uenđe potuer̄. *IN STOV*

İn Euresdone ten̄ Wido. vi. hiđ 7 x. ac̄s t̄ræ HVND.

In total, value £10 10s; when acquired £6; before 1066 £14.

Edric Snipe, King Edward's thane, held 2½ hides of this land; he could grant or sell. 8 Freemen, the Abbot of Ely's men, held 2 hides and ½ virgate. 2 other Freemen, King Edward's men, held 2 parts of 1 virgate, and found 2 escorts. All these men could sell their lands. The jurisdiction of the 8 Freemen remained with the Abbot of Ely.

In WETHERLEY Hundred

3 In BARTON Humphrey holds 3½ hides from Guy. Land for 6 ploughs. In lordship 3 ploughs;
3 villagers with 13 smallholders have 3 ploughs.
1 slave; meadow for 4 ploughs.
In total, value £6; when acquired £10; before 1066 as much.
There are 3 French men-at-arms on this land.
24 Freemen held this land. One of them held ½ hide under Edeva the Fair, and could sell. All the others were Freemen of King Edward's; they held 3 hides, and could grant and sell; they found 6 cartages and 17 escorts for the Sheriff.

4 In GRANTCHESTER 2 men-at-arms hold 3 virgates from Guy. Land for 1 plough, but it is not there.
Meadow for 4 oxen;
3 smallholders.
Value 55s; when acquired 40s; before 1066 £4.
5 Freemen, King Edward's men, held this land and could sell; they found 4 escorts for the King's Sheriff.

5 In ORWELL Ralph holds one-third virgate from Guy. An ox there. The value is and was 2s.
He could sell; he found ¼ cartage for the Sheriff.

6 In WRATWORTH Ralph holds ½ hide from Guy. Land for ½ plough; it is there, with
2 villagers; 2 smallholders.
Meadow for ½ plough; wood for repairing fences.
Value 20s; when acquired 10s; before 1066, 20s.
2 Freemen of King Edward's held this land; they found 2 cartages and could sell.

In LONGSTOW Hundred

7 In EVERSDEN Guy holds 6 hides and 10 acres of land. Land for

Tra.ē.x.car̄.In dn̄io sunt.iiii.7 v.pot fieri.Ibi.v.uilłi

cū.ii.bord 7 ix.cot hn̄t.v.car̄.Ibi.i.seruus.p̄tū

ii.car̄.7 ii.bob.Nem ad sepes.Int tot ual.ix.lib̄.Q̇do

recep̄.vi.lib̄ 7 v.sol.T.R.xvi.lib̄.De hac tra tenet

Picot dim̄ hid.7 totā alia trā ten Hunfrid de Widone.

Hanc trā tenuer̄.xxiii.sochi.Duo hoᷡ hoēs Stig

archiēpi.i.hid 7 iii.uirg tenuer̄.7 vii.hoēs Algari

iii.uirg habuer̄.7 un̄ hō Eddeue.i.hid habuit.

7 alij xiiii.hoēs.R.E.unā hid 7 dim 7 x.ac̄s tenuer̄.

7 ix.Aueras 7 v.jnew uicecomiti inueneruᷡ.

Om̄s ů terras suas dare ł uendere potueruᷡ.

.XXX. ☧ TERRA PICOT DE GRENTEBR̄ *IN STANES HVND*

m̄ ☧ ICOT de Grentebrige ten̄ In *COEIA* iiii.hid

7 dim.7 x.ac̄s.Tra.ē.v.car̄.In dn̄io.ē una.7 viii.

uilłi.hn̄t.iiii.car̄.Ibi.ii.molini 7 dim de.xxii.sol.

P̄tū car̄.Int tot ual 7 ualuit.viii.lib̄.

De hac tra tenuer̄ Alricus 7 Godric.iii.hid 7 dim.

hoēs abbis de Ramesy.n̄ potuer̄ recede absq̇ lictia ej.

7 iiii.sochi hoēs.R.E.tenuer̄.i.hid 7 x.ac̄s.n̄ potuer̄ ※

dare nec uende sine lictia regis. *IN CILDEFORD HVND.*

In P̄apesuuorde ten̄ Rad de picot.iii.uirg.Tra.ē

.i.car̄.7 ibi.ē.7 ii.ac̄ p̄ti.Val 7 ualuit sēp x.sol.Hanc

tenuit Ederic hō Alurici cilt.7 recede potuit eū tra.

I̧pse Picot ten̄ *HESTITONE.* *IN WITELESFORD HD.*

p xv.hid 7 dim se defd.Tra.ē xiii.car̄.In dn̄io.vii.

hide 7 iii.uirg.7 ibi.ē.i.car̄.7 iii.adhuc poss fieri.

10 ploughs. In lordship 4; a fifth possible.
 5 villagers with 2 smallholders and 9 cottagers have 5 ploughs.
 1 slave; meadow for 2 ploughs and 2 oxen; wood for fences.
In total, value £9; when acquired £6 5s; before 1066 £16.
 Picot holds ½ hide of this land, and Humphrey holds all the other land from Guy.
 23 Freemen held this land. 2 of them, Archbishop Stigand's men, held 1 hide and 3 virgates; 7, Earl Algar's men, had 3 virgates; 1, Edeva's man, had 1 hide; the other 14, King Edward's men, held 1½ hides and 10 acres, and found 9 cartages and 5 escorts for the Sheriff. All these men could grant or sell their lands.

30 [32]   LAND OF PICOT OF CAMBRIDGE   200 b

In STAINE Hundred
1 M. Picot of Cambridge holds 4½ hides and 10 acres in QUY.
 Land for 5 ploughs. In lordship 1;
  8 villagers have 4 ploughs.
  2½ mills at 22s; meadow for the ploughs.
 In total, the value is and was £8.
 Alric the monk and Godric, the Abbot of Ramsey's men, held 3½ hides of this land; they could not withdraw without his permission.
 4 Freemen, King Edward's men, held 1 hide and 10 acres; they could neither grant nor sell without the King's permission.

†32,2, *written at the foot of col. 200b and directed to its proper place by transposition signs, is entered within 32,8 below.*

In CHILFORD Hundred
3 In PAMPISFORD Ralph holds 3 virgates from Picot. Land for 1 plough; it is there;
  meadow, 2 acres.
 The value is and always was 10s.
 Edric, Young Aelfric's man, held it and could withdraw with the land.

In WHITTLESFORD Hundred
4 Picot holds HINXTON himself. It answers for 15½ hides. Land for 13 ploughs. In lordship 7 hides and 3 virgates; 1 plough there; a further 3 possible.

Ibi.xx.uilli cū.xii.borđ hīt.ix.cař.Ibi.ii.molini

de xxi.fot 7 iiii.den.p̃tū.iii.cař.In totis ualent uał

x.liƀ.Q̃do recep̃.xvi.liƀ.7 tn̄tđ T.R.E.Hanc t̃ra

recep̃ picot p.ii.manerijs ut dicit.Viginti foc̃hi tenuer̃.

★ Hoꝛ un̄ hō Algari dim̄ hiđ habuit.n̄ potuer̃ recede

Alij û hões R.E.fuer̃.7 recede potuer̃.7 viii.aueras

7 viii.jnew.7 iii.Heueward uicecomiti inuener̃.

In Herleſtone ten̄ Picot vii.hiđ *IN ŘEPESLAV HĐ.*

7 dim̄.Tra.ē.ix.cař.In dn̄io.iii.hidæ.7 ibi fuꝗ.ii.cař.

7 iii.pot fieri.Ibi.vi.uilli 7 xv.cot hn̄t.iiii.cař.

7 v.pot fieri.Ibi.i.molin̄ de.xxx.fot.P̃tū.v.cař.

Paſta ad pecun̄.In totis ualent uał.viii.liƀ.Q̃do

recep̃.iiii.liƀ 7 x.fot.T.R.E.x.liƀ.De hac t̃ra tenuit

Orgar.iiii.hiđ de Heraldo comite.7 recede potuit.

Ipſe Picot ten̄.i.hiđ 7 dim̄ de rege.7 in hac uilla ap̃pcia Q̃đā foc̃hs tenuit fub abbe de Ely.7 uende potuit. fed foca Abbi remānfit.

7 vi.foc̃hi hões.R.E.tenuer̃.ii.hiđ.7 i.Auerā 7 v.jneuuard

inuener̃.7 cū tra fua recede potuer̃.

Frideƀtus tenuit de abƀe de Ely.i.hiđ 7 dim̄.7 recede

cū tra fua potuit.f; foca remanfit æcc̃læ.De hac

hida 7 dim̄ feruit Picot abƀi.7 ten̄ eā juffu regis.

In Tru̅pintone ten̄ Herueus de Picot.ii.hiđ.7 i.uirg

7 dim̄.Tra.ē.ii.cař 7 dim̄.In dn̄io.i.cař 7 dim̄.7 iiii.

uilli cū.i.borđ hn̄t.i.cař.Ibi.iii.cot.7.i.feruus.

p̃tū cař.7 cccc.l.Anguill de gurg.Vał.iiii.liƀ.

Q̃do recep̃.xxx.fot.T.R.E.c.fot.Hanc t̃ra tenuit Orulf

fub rege.E.7 pot uende 7 recede ad q̃m̄ uoluit.

In Tadelai.ten̄ Picot.ii.hiđ *IN ERNINGFORD HVNĐ.*

7 i.uirg 7 dim̄.Tra.ē.vi.cař.In dn̄io.i.hiđ 7 dim̄ uirg.

7 ibi.ē.i.cař.7 alia pot fieri.7 ii.uirg 7 dim̄ q̃s ten̄   rq̃ q̃t uilł

uilli 7 xiii.borđ hn̄t.iii.cař.7 iiii.pot fieri.Ibi

.i.molin̄ de.x.fot.P̃tū.vi.cař.Paſta ad pec̃ uillæ.

20 villagers with 12 smallholders have 9 ploughs.
2 mills at 21s 4d; meadow for 3 ploughs.
Total value £10; when acquired £16; before 1066 as much.
Picot acquired this land as two manors, as he states.
20 Freemen held it. One of them, Earl Algar's man, had
½ hide; he could not withdraw. The others were King Edward's
men, and could withdraw; they found 8 cartages and 8 escorts
and 3 bodyguards for the Sheriff.

In THRIPLOW Hundred

5   In HARSTON Picot holds 7½ hides. Land for 9 ploughs. In
lordship 3 hides; 2 ploughs there; a third possible.
6 villagers and 15 cottagers have 4 ploughs; a fifth possible.
1 mill at 30s; meadow for 5 ploughs; pasture for the livestock.
Total value £8; when acquired £4 10s; before 1066 £10.
‡Picot holds 1½ hides himself from the King; it is assessed in
this village. A Freeman held it under the Abbot of Ely, and
could sell; but the jurisdiction remained with the Abbot.‡
Ordgar held 4 hides of this land from Earl Harold and could
withdraw. 6 Freemen, King Edward's men, held 2 hides; they
found 1 cartage and 5 escorts, and could withdraw with their
land. Fridebert held 1½ hides from the Abbot of Ely, and
could withdraw with his land; but the jurisdiction remained
with the Church. Picot owes service from this 1½ hides to
the Abbot; he holds it by order of the King.

6   In TRUMPINGTON Hervey holds 2 hides and 1½ virgates from
Picot. Land for 2½ ploughs. In lordship 1½ ploughs;
3 villagers with 1 smallholder have 1 plough.
   3 cottagers; 1 slave.
Meadow for the ploughs; from the weir 450 eels.
Value £4; when acquired 30s; before 1066, 100s.
Horwulf held this land under King Edward; he could sell and
withdraw to whom he would.

In ARMINGFORD Hundred

7   In TADLOW Picot holds 2 hides and 1½ virgates. Land for 6
ploughs. In lordship 1 hide and ½ virgate; 1 plough there;
another possible;
   2½ virgates which the villagers hold; 13 smallholders have
     3 ploughs; a fourth possible.
   1 mill at 10s; meadow for 6 ploughs; pasture for the village
     livestock.

Val LXX.fol.Q̃do recep̃:´IIII.lib̃.T.R.E.´VI.lib̃.

Hanc trã tenuer̃´.III.ẜfochi.7 inuenieb̃.I.Auerã 7 I.Heuow´.

7 trã ſuã potuer̃ dare & uendere.

In Mordune ten Picot.III.hiđ 7 dim.Trã.ẽ.VII.car̃.

In dñio.ẽ.I.hida.7 ibi.I.car̃.7 alia pot̃´ fieri.Ibi.VIII.

uilli cũ.XI.borđ 7 XVIII.cot̃ hñt.III.car̃ 7 dim.7 I.7 dim

pot̃ fieri.Ibi.I.moliñ de.IIII.fol.p̃tũ.VII.car̃.Paſtura

※ Ibiđ ten Picot.III.hiđ 7 III.uirg̃.Trã.ẽ.IIII.car̃.   ƒ ad pecuñ uillæ.

In dñio funt.II.7 v.uilli hñt.II.car̃.Ibi.I.feruus.7 p̃tũ.IIII.car̃.Val.VI.lib̃.Q̃do recep̃:´

ualeb̃.IIII.lib̃.7 tñtđ.T.R.E.Hanc trã tenuer̃.II.fochi abbis de Ely.ñ potuer̃ uendere

abſq̃ ej licentia.In hac uilla   dimiđ moliñ de.XL.deñ.

200 c

Int̃ tot̃´ ual.VI.lib̃.7 x.fol.Q̃do recep̃:´VIII.lib̃.

T.R.E.´x lib̃.Hanc trã tenuer̃.VIII.fochi.Hoᷔ.III.hõẽs

Stig̃ Archiep̃i.I.hiđ 7 III.uirg̃ habuer̃.7 dare 7 uendé

potuer̃.fᷤ Soca remanſit in Mordune.7 alij.II.hõẽs

Algari.III.uirg̃ habuer̃.7 uendé potuer̃.Soca comiti

remanſit.7 alij.II.hõẽs regis.E.III.uirg̃ tenuer̃.7 II.

jneuuarđ inuenieb̃.7 dare 7 uendé poteraᷘ.7 uñ hõ

Eddeue dim uirg̃ habuit.7 uendé potuit.

In Cloptune ten Picot uñũ hortũ de foca regis.E.qui

reddeb̃.I.jneuuarđ uicecomiti regis.

In Hatelai ten Picot.II.hiđ.Trã.ẽ.III.car̃.Ibi eſt

una car̃ 7 dim.7 totiđ poſſ fieri.p̃tũ.II.car̃.7 II.borđ.

Silua ad fepes reficiend.Val 7 ualuit.XL.fol.T.R.E.´

LX.fol.Hanc trã tenuer̃.VIII.fochi.7 dare 7 uendé

potuer̃.Hoᷔ.II.hõẽs..R.E.fuer̃.7 II.jnew inuener̃.

7 III.hõẽs.S.Archiep̃i fuer̃.foca eoᷔ jacuit in Mordune.

7 I.hõ Guerd comitis.7 I.hõ Robti.f.Wimarc.7 I.hõ

Vlmæri de Ettone.Vnã hidã de hac trã đc̃ Picot

fe habe ᷔp excãbio de Einuluefberie.7 aliã ᷔp excãbio

de Rifedene.q̃a Ilbt̃ de Hertford ei liberauit.

Value 70s; when acquired £4; before 1066 £6.

3 Freemen held this land; they found 1 cartage and 1 bodyguard; they could grant and sell their land.

8   In (Guilden) MORDEN Picot holds 3½ hides. Land for 7 ploughs.

In lordship 1 hide; 1 plough there; another possible.

    8 villagers with 11 smallholders and 18 cottagers have 3½ ploughs; [another] 1½ possible.

    1 mill at 4s; meadow for 7 ploughs; pasture for the village livestock.

†*Misplaced entry, directed to its proper place by transposition signs.*

2   There Picot also holds 3 hides and 3 virgates. Land for 4 ploughs.

In lordship 2;

    5 villagers have 2 ploughs.

    1 slave; meadow for 4 ploughs.

Value £6; when acquired the value was £4; before 1066 as much.

    2 Freemen of the Abbot of Ely's held this land; they could not sell without his permission.

    In this village (there is) ½ mill at 40d.

8   In total, value £6 10s; when acquired £8; before 1066 £10.   200 c
(*cont.*)   8 Freemen held this land. 3 of them, Archbishop Stigand's men, had 1 hide and 3 virgates; they could grant and sell, but the jurisdiction remained in (Guilden) Morden. 2 others, Earl Algar's men, had 3 virgates and could sell; the jurisdiction remained with the Earl. 2 others, King Edward's men, held 3 virgates and found 2 escorts; they could grant and sell. A man of Edeva's had ½ virgate and could sell.

9   In CLOPTON Picot holds a garden from King Edward's jurisdiction which paid 1 escort for the King's Sheriff.

10   In (East) HATLEY Picot holds 2 hides. Land for 3 ploughs; 1½ ploughs there; as many [more] possible.

    Meadow for 2 ploughs; 2 smallholders; woodland for repairing fences.

The value is and was 40s; before 1066, 60s.

    8 Freemen held this land; they could grant and sell. 2 of them were King Edward's men, and found 2 escorts. 3 were Archbishop Stigand's men; their jurisdiction lay in (Guilden) Morden. 1 was Earl Gyrth's man. 1 was Robert son of Wymarc's man. 1 was Wulfmer of Eaton's man.

    Picot states he had 1 hide of this land in exchange for Eynesbury; and (he had) the other in exchange for Rushden, because Ilbert of Hertford delivered (it) to him.

In Crauuedene. teñ Anſchil de picot. ii. hiđ dim
uirg̃ miñ.Tra. ē. ii. caŕ. ſ; ñ ſunt ibi niſi boues. cũ. i.
uilło 7 ii. borđ. Val. xxx. ſol. Qdo recep̃. xl. ſol. 7 tñtđ
T.R.E. Hanc tŕā tenuit. i. hõ Aſgari ſtalr. potuit dare 7 uendẽ.
In eađ uilla teñ Aluered de Picot. i. hiđ 7 i. uirg̃.
Tra. ē. ii. caŕ. 7 ibi ſuᷠ. In dñio. i. 7 v. borđ cũ alia. c̃.
7 ii. cot. p̃tũ. ii. caŕ. Nẹm ad ſepes reficienđ tantũ.
Val. iiii. lib̃. Qdo recep̃. xl. ſol. 7 tñtđ T.R.E. Hanc
tŕā tenuit. i. hõ Robti. f. Wimarc. dare 7 uendẽ
potuit. Soca ũ Robto remanſit.
In Abintone teñ Picot dim uirg̃. Tra. ē. ii. bob᷎.
Val 7 ualuit ſẽp. ii. ſol. Hanc tŕā tenuit Anſgot
hõ. S. Archiẽpi. jacet 7 jacuit in Mordune. Ṭ HVND.
In Cũbertone teñ. ii. hões de Picot IN WEDERLAI
ii. hiđ 7 ii. ac̃s. Tra. ē. iiii. caŕ. In dñio. ii. 7 vii. uilłi
cũ xi. borđ hñt. ii. caŕ. p̃tũ. i. caŕ. Val 7 ualuit. lx.
ſol. T.R.E. iiii. lib̃. De hac tra. tenueŕ vii. ſochi
regis. E. i. hiđ 7 i. uirg̃. 7 v. Aueras 7 iii. jnew inueniẹb̃.
7 alij. ii. ſochi. iii. uirg̃ habueŕ. 7 recedẽ potueŕ.
Hoᷤ un hõ. S. archiẽpi. 7 alt hõ Wallef com fuit.
In Granteſete teñ Robt de Picot dim uirg̃. Tra. ē
iii. bob. 7 ibi. ē. i. uilłs. Val 7 ualuit. v. ſol. Hanc tŕā
tenuit Wluric de ſoca regis.
In Haſlingefeld teñ Sæifriđ de Picot. iiii. hiđ 7 iii. uirg̃.
Tra. ē. iiii. caŕ. In dñio. ii. caŕ. 7 iiii. uilłi cũ xx.ii. borđ
hñt. ii. caŕ. 7 i. moliñ de. ii. ſol. p̃tũ. ii. caŕ. Val. iiii. lib̃.
Qdo recep̃. xl. ſol. T.R.E. iiii. lib̃. Hanc tŕā tenueŕ. vi.
ſochi. Hoᷤ un hõ Aſgari tenuit. i. hiđ 7 iii. uirg̃. 7 po
tuit uendere. 7 alij. v. hões. R.E. tenueŕ. iii. hiđ 7 ii. ãs
Aueras 7 iii. jnew inueneŕ. tŕā ſuã dare 7 uendẽ potueŕ.

11   In CROYDON Ansketel holds 2 hides less ½ virgate from Picot.
Land for 2 ploughs; but they are not there except for the oxen,
with
     1 villager and 2 smallholders.
Value 30s; when acquired 40s; before 1066 as much.
     A man of Asgar the Constable's held this land; he could grant
and sell.

12   In the same village Alfred holds 1 hide and 1 virgate from Picot.
Land for 2 ploughs; they are there. In lordship 1;
     5 smallholders with the other plough;
          2 cottagers.
Meadow for 2 ploughs; wood for fence repair only.
Value £4; when acquired 40s; before 1066 as much.
     A man of Robert son of Wymarc's held this land; he could grant
and sell, but the jurisdiction remained with Robert.

13   In ABINGTON (Pigotts) Picot holds ½ virgate. Land for 2 oxen.
The value is and always was 2s.
     Ansgot, Archbishop Stigand's man, held this land; it lies and
lay in (the lands of) (Guilden) Morden.

     In WETHERLEY Hundred
14   In COMBERTON 2 men hold 2 hides and 2 acres from Picot. Land
for 4 ploughs. In lordship 2;
     7 villagers with 11 smallholders have 2 ploughs.
     Meadow for 1 plough.
The value is and was 60s; before 1066 £4.
     7 Freemen of King Edward's held 1 hide and 1 virgate of this
land; they found 5 cartages and 3 escorts. 2 other Freemen had
3 virgates and could withdraw; one of them was Archbishop
Stigand's man, the other Earl Waltheof's man.

15   In GRANTCHESTER Robert holds ½ virgate from Picot. Land for 3
oxen.
     1 villager there.
The value is and was 5s.
     Wulfric held this land from the King's jurisdiction.

16   In HASLINGFIELD Sifrid holds 4 hides and 3 virgates from Picot.
Land for 4 ploughs. In lordship 2 ploughs;
     4 villagers with 22 smallholders have 2 ploughs;
     1 mill at 2s; meadow for 2 ploughs.
Value £4; when acquired 40s; before 1066 £4.
     6 Freemen held this land. One of them, Asgar's man, held 1
hide and 3 virgates, and could sell. The other 5, King Edward's
men, held 3 hides; they found 2 cartages and 3 escorts; they
could grant and sell their land.

In Herletone teñ Seifrid de Picot . ɪ . hid . Tra . ē . ɪ.

car . fed ñ eft . p̃tu . ɪɪɪɪ . bob . 7 ɪɪ . bord . Val 7 ualuit

sẽp xx . fol . Hanc trã tenuit Godman fub Afgaro

ftalre . 7 potuit recede.

In Barentone teñ Radulf de Picot xx . acs . Tra . ē

ɪɪɪ . bob . 7 ibi funt . cũ . ɪ . focho 7 ɪ . bord . p̃tu . ɪɪɪ . bob.

Val 7 ualuit sẽp . v . fol . Hanc trã tenuit Ezi fub

Robto . f . Wimarch . 7 potuit dare.

In Warateuuorde teñ Radulf de Picot . ɪɪɪ . uirg.

Ibi . ē . ɪɪɪ . bob tra . 7 ibi funt . cũ . ɪɪ . cot . p̃tu . ɪɪɪ . bob.

Val 7 ualuit . ɪɪɪ . fol . T.R.E . v . fol . Hanc trã tenuit

uñ fochs . R.E . 7 ɪ . jnew inueñ uicec . 7 trã fuã uende pot.

In Witeuuella teñ Radulf de Picot . ɪ . hid 7 ɪɪ.

part . ɪ . uirg . Tra . ē . ɪ . car 7 dim . In dñio . ē . ɪ . car.

7 uñ uilts cũ . ɪɪ . cot hñt dim car . p̃tu . ɪɪ . car . Nem

ad fepes claudend . Val . xxx . fol . Q̃do recep . xx . fol.

T.R.E . ɪɪɪɪ . lib . Hanc trã tenuer . ɪɪɪ . fochi . Hoʒ

uñ hõ Algari . 7 alter hõ Robti . F . Wimarch.

7 tcius hõ . R.E . Ifte Auerã inueñ . 7 pot uende.

In Chingeftone teñ Radulfus   *IN STOV HVND.*

de Picot . v . hid 7 dim . 7 xvɪ . acs . Tra . ē . vɪɪ . car

7 dim . In dñio . ɪɪ . car . 7 vɪɪɪɪ . uilti cũ . ɪɪ . bord

7 . v . cot hñt . v . car 7 dim . p̃tu . ɪɪɪ . car . Nem

ad fepes . Ibi . ɪɪɪɪ . serui . Int tot ual . vɪ . lib . Q̃do

recep . vɪɪɪ . lib . T.R.E . xɪɪ . lib . Hanc trã tenuer

xɪɪɪɪ . fochi . Hoʒ . x . habuer . ɪɪ . hid 7 ɪ . uirg 7 dim

de foca regis . 7 vɪɪ . Aueras 7 ɪɪɪ . jneward inuener.

7 ɪɪ . alij hões Algari . ɪ . uirg habuer . 7 uñ hõ Stig

archiepi . ɪɪɪ . uirg tenuit . 7 q̃dã iftoʒ hõ abbis

de Ely . ɪ . uirg habuit de foca abbis . 7 alij . ɪɪ . hões

Algari . ɪɪ . hid habuer . õs potuer recede.

17   In HARLTON Sifrid holds 1 hide from Picot. Land for 1 plough;   200 d
     but it is not (there).
        Meadow for 4 oxen; 2 smallholders.
     The value is and always was 20s.
        Godman held this land under Asgar the Constable and could
     withdraw.

18   In BARRINGTON Ralph holds 20 acres from Picot. Land for 3 oxen;
     they are there, with
        1 Freeman; 1 smallholder.
        Meadow for 3 oxen.
     The value is and always was 5s.
        Edsi held this land under Robert son of Wymarc and could grant.

19   In WRATWORTH Ralph holds 3 virgates from Picot. Land for 3 oxen;
     they are there, with
        2 cottagers.
        Meadow for 3 oxen.
     The value is and was 3s; before 1066, 5s.
        A Freeman of King Edward's held this land; he found 1 escort
     for the Sheriff, and could sell his land.

20   In WHITWELL Ralph holds 1 hide and 2 parts of 1 virgate from Picot.
     Land for 1½ ploughs. In lordship 1 plough;
        1 villager with 2 cottagers have ½ plough.
        Meadow for 2 ploughs; wood for making fences.
     Value 30s; when acquired 20s; before 1066 £4.
        3 Freemen held this land. One of them was Algar's man; the
     second was Robert son of Wymarc's man. The third was King
     Edward's man; he found cartage and could sell.

In LONGSTOW Hundred
21   In KINGSTON Ralph holds 5½ hides and 16 acres from Picot.
     Land for 7½ ploughs. In lordship 2 ploughs;
        9 villagers with 2 smallholders and 5 cottagers have 5½ ploughs.
        Meadow for 3 ploughs; wood for fences. 4 slaves.
     In total, value £6; when acquired £8; before 1066 £12.
        14 Freemen held this land. 10 of them had 2 hides and 1½
     virgates of the King's jurisdiction; they found 7 cartages and 3
     escorts. 2 others, Earl Algar's men, had 1 virgate. 1, Archbishop
     Stigand's man, held 3 virgates. One of them, the Abbot of Ely's
     man, had 1 virgate of the Abbot's jurisdiction. 2 others, Earl
     Algar's men, had 2 hides. They could all withdraw.

In Tofth . ten . ii . milites de Picot . i . hid 7 dim . 7 x̃ .
ac̃s . Tra . ẽ . iiii . car̃ . In dñio funt . ii . 7 iii . poteſt . ee.
7 ii . uilti cũ . vi . cot hñt . i . car̃ . P̃tũ . i . car̃ 7 dim.
Nem ad ſepes . Val . iiii . lib . Q̃do recep̃ . xx . fol.
T . R . E . vi . lib . De hac tra tenuit . i . hõ regis . E.
. i . hid 7 iiii . ac̃s . 7 . dare potuit . 7 un̄ hõ abbis de
Elŷ tenuit dim hid 7 vi . ac̃s . 7 cũ tra recede po
tuit . ſ; ſoca abbi remanſit.

Ipſe Picot . ten BRVNE . p̃ xiii . hid ſe defd̃ . Tra . ẽ
xv . car̃ . In dñio . v . hide . 7 ibi funt . ii . car̃ . 7 alie . ii.
poſſ . ee . Ibi . viii . uilti cũ . iiii . bord 7 vii . fochis
qui teneñ . iiii . hid̃ . hñt . iiii . car̃ . 7 adhuc vii . poſſ
fieri . Ibi . xiii . cot 7 vi . ſerui . p̃tũ xv . car̃ . Paſta
ad pecun̄ uillæ . Nem ad ſepes 7 domos reficiendas.
In totis ualent ual xiii . lib . Q̃do recep̃ . xviii . lib.
T . R . E . xxii . lib . De hac tra ten . ii . milites ſub
Picot . ii . hid . Tra . ẽ . ii . car̃ . 7 ibi funt . cũ . iiii . cot.
p̃tũ . ii . car̃ . Nem ad ſepes 7 domos . paſta ad pec̃ uillæ.
Valuit ſẽp 7 ual . xl . fol . De tra huj M T . R . E.
tenuit un̄ teignus ſub rege . E . iii . hidas . 7 ii . pbri

Iſti n̄ potuer̃ ſeparare ext̃ eccłam.
hões huj teigni . i . hid habuer̃ . 7 iii . fochi . S . ar
chiep̃i . iiii . hid . 7 un̄ hõ Aſgari ſtalre . i . hid habuit.
7 ii . hões abbis de Rameſŷ . i . hid 7 dim habuer̃.
7 un̄ hõ Algari dim hid habuit . 7 xiii . hões
regis . E . ii . hidas habuer̃ . 7 ipſi . vi . aueras 7 vii.
jneuuard uicecomiti inuener̃ . Õms itaq; xxii.
tras ſuas dare 7 uende potuer̃ . Hanc tra dic̃
Picot ſe recepiſſe p̃ duobȝ manerijs.

22 In TOFT 2 men-at-arms hold 1½ hides and 10 acres from Picot.
Land for 4 ploughs. In lordship 1; a third possible;
  2 villagers with 6 cottagers have 1 plough.
Meadow for 1½ ploughs; wood for fences.
Value £4; when acquired 20s; before 1066 £6.
  A man of King Edward's held 1 hide and 4 acres of this land,
and could grant. A man of the Abbot of Ely's held ½ hide and
6 acres, and could withdraw with the land; but the jurisdiction
remained with the Abbot.

23 M. Picot holds BOURN himself. It answers for 13 hides. Land for 15
ploughs. In lordship 5 hides; 2 ploughs there; 2 others possible.
  8 villagers with 4 smallholders and 7 Freemen who hold 4
    hides have 4 ploughs; a further 7 possible.
    13 cottagers; 6 slaves.
Meadow for 15 ploughs; pasture for the village livestock;
    wood for repairing fences and houses.
Total value £13; when acquired £18; before 1066 £22.
  2 men-at-arms hold 2 hides of this land under Picot. Land
for 2 ploughs; they are there, with
    4 cottagers.
Meadow for 2 ploughs; wood for fences and houses; pasture
    for the village livestock.
The value always was and is 40s.
  Before 1066 a thane held 3 hides of the land of this manor
under King Edward. 2 priests, this thane's men, had 1 hide;   201 a
‡they could not separate (it) outside of the Church.‡ 3 Freemen
of Archbishop Stigand's had 4 hides. A man of Asgar the
Constable's had 1 hide. 2 men of the Abbot of Ramsey's had 1½
hides. A man of Earl Algar's had ½ hide. 13 men of King Edward's
had 2 hides, and themselves found 6 cartages and 7 escorts for the
Sheriff. Accordingly, all 22 could grant and sell their lands.
  Picot states he acquired this land as two manors.

In Hatelai ten Roger de Picot . ii . hid . Tra . ē
ii . car . In dnio . ē una . 7 iiii . bord cū . vi . cot 7 uno
uitto hūt dim car . 7 dim pot fieri . Nem ad fepes
7 domos . Val xx . fol . Qdo recep̄ꞏ lx . fol . T . R . E ꞏ
c . fol . Hanc tra tenuit Aluuard hō Robti . F . Wim .
7 uende potuit.

In ead uilla ten Picot . i . hid . Tra . ē . i . car . Dim car
ibi . ē ꞏ 7 dim pot fieri . Nem ad fepes 7 domos . Ibi
. iii . uitti . Val . x . fol . Qdo recep̄ꞏ xx . fol . T . R . E ꞏ xl .
fol . Hanc tra tenuer̄ . iii . fochi regis . E . 7 i . Auerā
7 ii . jnew inuener̄ uicecomiti . Hanc dic Picot
fe habe ꝓ Excabio de Rifedene . Q ten Sigard
In Papeuuorde ten Picot *In Papeword hd.*
dim uirg . Tra . ē . ii . bob . Val 7 ualuit . ii . fol .
Hanc tra tenuit un fochs . R . E . 7 inuen . i . jneward
uicecomiti.

In Draitone ten Roger de Picot . i . hid . Tra . ē dim
car . 7 ibi funt . ii . boues . Ptū . iiii . bob . Val 7 ualuit
iii . fol . T . R . E ꞏ v . fol . Hanc tra tenuer̄ . ii . fochi . Hoꝝ
un hō abbis de Ely . tra fua uende pot fine foca.
Alt hō regis E . inuen . i . jnew uicecom . 7 tra|dare
In Oure ten Sauuin de Picot dim hidā. ⌠ potuit.
Tra . ē dim car . 7 ibi . ē . Ptū dim car . Pafta ad pec .
Val 7 ualuit . v . fol . T . R . E ꞏ x . fol . Hanc tra tenuit
un hō abbis de Ramefy . 7 uende potuit fine foca.
In Wiuelinghā ten Roger de Picot . i . uirg . Tra . ē
ii . bob . cū ꝓto . Pafta ad pecun . Val 7 ualuit . iii . fol .
Hanc tra tenuit Gold fub abbe de Ely . ñ potuit
dare ɫ uendere.   *In Norestov hd.*
In Stantone ten Wido de Picot . iii . hid . Tra . ē

24   In HATLEY (St. George) Roger holds 2 hides from Picot. Land for
2 ploughs. In lordship 1;
    4 smallholders with 6 cottagers and 1 villager have ½ plough;
      [another] ½ possible.
    Wood for fences and houses.
    Value 20s; when acquired 60s; before 1066, 100s.
    Alfward, Robert son of Wymarc's man, held this land and could
sell.

25   In the same village Picot holds 1 hide. Land for 1 plough; ½ plough
there; [another] ½ possible.
    Wood for fences and houses.
    3 villagers.
    Value 10s; when acquired 20s; before 1066, 40s.
    3 Freemen of King Edward's held this land; they found 1 cartage
and 2 escorts for the Sheriff.
    Picot states he had this in exchange for Rushden, which Sigar holds.

In PAPWORTH Hundred
26   In PAPWORTH Picot holds ½ virgate. Land for 2 oxen.
The value is and was 2s.
    A Freeman of King Edward's held this land, and found 1 escort
for the Sheriff.

27   In (Fen) DRAYTON Roger holds 1 hide from Picot. Land for ½ plough;
2 oxen there.
    Meadow for 4 oxen.
The value is and was 3s; before 1066, 5s.
    2 Freemen held this land. One of them, the Abbot of Ely's man,
could sell his land without the jurisdiction. The other, King
Edward's man, found 1 escort for the Sheriff and could grant his land.

28   In OVER Sawin holds ½ hide from Picot. Land for ½ plough; it is there.
    Meadow for ½ plough; pasture for the livestock.
The value is and was 5s; before 1066, 10s.
    A man of the Abbot of Ramsey's held this land, and could sell
without the jurisdiction.

29   In WILLINGHAM Roger holds 1 virgate from Picot. Land for 2 oxen, with
meadow.
    Pasture for the livestock.
The value is and was 3s.
    Gold held this land under the Abbot of Ely; he could not grant
or sell.

In NORTHSTOW Hundred
30   In LONGSTANTON Guy holds 3 hides from Picot. Land for 4 ploughs.

IIII . car . In dnio suɴ . II . 7 vi . bord cu v . cot poſſ
habe . II . car . ptu . II . car . Val . IIII . lib . Qdo recep.
VIII . lib . T.R.E. x . lib . Hanc tra tenuer . xv . sochi .
Hoʒ XI . hoes regis . E . I . hid 7 dim habuer . 7 II . aueras
7 v . jnew uicecom inuener . 7 tra sua dare 7 uende
potuer . 7 alij . III . sub abbe de Elẏ . I . hid habuer .
7 uende potuer . soca ū remansit abbi . 7 un hō
Sexi dim hid habuit . nec dare potuit .

Roger ten de Picot RANTONE . p vi . hid se
defd . T . R . E . 7 m̄ p IIII . hid 7 dim . Tra . ē . vi . car .

201 b

In dnio . ē una car . 7 ii . adhuc poſſ fieri . Ibi . XII .
uilli cū . VII . cot hnt . III . car . Ibi . I . seruus . 7 ptu
VI . car . Pasta ad pecun . In totis ualent ual . c . sol .
Qdo recep . VIII . lib . 7 tntd T.R.E . Hoc m̄ tenuer
VI . sochi . Hoʒ un hō Eddeue . I . uirg 7 dim habuit
7 recede potuit . 7 alij hoes abbis de Elẏ fuer . 7 IIII.
tra sua uende potuer . soca ū remansit abbi . 7 qntus
. I . uirg 7 dim habuit . 7 recede n̄ potuit .

In Lolesuuorde ten Robt de Picot . IX . hid . p . I . m̄ .
Modo p . v . hid . Tra . ē . v . car . In dnio suɴ . II . 7 IIII.
uilli cū . IX . bord 7 III . cot hnt . III . car . Ibi . I . francig
ht . I . hid 7 dim . 7 un seru . Ptu . I . car . 7 I . mol nil redd .
Nem ad sepes . In totis ualent ual . c . sol . Qdo recep .
XL . sol . T.R.E . vi . lib . Hoc m̄ tenuit una pbendaria
. R . E . Ipsa . III . hid 7 dim habuit . 7 x . sochi ibi fuer .
Ex his . VII . hoes . R . E . . I . hid 7 dim 7 IIII . tenuer . 7 II .
Aueras 7 IIII . Jnew inuener . 7 alij . II . hoes Eddeue . I . hid
habuer . Decim aut hō abbis de Elẏ . I . hid tenuit .
Hi om̄s tras suas uende potuer . Soca tantū hois
abbis de Elẏ remansit æcclæ

In lordship 2;
    6 smallholders with 5 cottagers could have 2 ploughs.
    Meadow for 2 ploughs.
Value £4; when acquired £8; before 1066 £10.
    15 Freemen held this land. 11 of them, King Edward's men, had 1½ hides and found 2 cartages and 5 escorts for the Sheriff; they could grant and sell their land. 3 others had 1 hide under the Abbot of Ely and could sell; but the jurisdiction remained with the Abbot. One, Saxi's man, had ½ hide; he could not grant.

31   Roger holds RAMPTON from Picot. It answered for 6 hides before 1066; now for 4½ hides. Land for 6 ploughs. In lordship 1   201 b plough; a further 2 possible.
    12 villagers with 7 cottagers have 3 ploughs.
    1 slave; meadow for 6 ploughs; pasture for the livestock.
Total value 100s; when acquired £8; before 1066 as much.
    6 Freemen held this manor. One of them, Edeva's man, had 1½ virgates and could withdraw. The others were the Abbot of Ely's men; 4 could sell their land, but the jurisdiction remained with the Abbot; the fifth had 1½ virgates and could not withdraw.

32   In LOLWORTH Robert holds 9 hides from Picot as one manor; now for 5 hides. Land for 5 ploughs. In lordship 2;
    4 villagers with 9 smallholders and 3 cottagers have 3 ploughs.
    1 Frenchman has 1½ hides; 1 slave.
    Meadow for 1 plough; 1 mill which pays nothing; wood for fences.
Total value 100s; when acquired 40s; before 1066 £6.
    An almswoman of King Edward's held this manor. She had 3½ hides. 10 Freemen were there. 7 of them, King Edward's men, held 1½ hides and 4 gardens; they found 2 cartages and 4 escorts. 2 others, Edeva's men, had 1 hide. The tenth, however, the Abbot of Ely's man, held 1½ hides. All these men could sell their lands; the jurisdiction of the Abbot of Ely's man alone remained with the Church.

In Madingelei teñ Picot. xi . hid 7 ii . uirg 7 dim.

Tra . e̅ . viii . car̅ . In d̅n̅io . iiii . hide 7 iii . uir̅g . 7 ibi
su̅ɲ . ii . car̅ . 7 iii . pot̅ fieri . Ibi . vii . uilli cu̅ . iiii . bord̅
7 vi . cot hn̅t . iiii . car̅ . 7 v . pot̅ fieri . Ibi . iii . serui .
P̊tu̅ . iiii . car̅ . Nem ad sepes . De hac t̅ra teñ . ii . milit̅
iii . hid 7 iii . uirg . In totis ualent ual . vi . lib̅ 7 v . sol̅ .
Q̇do recep̅ . ix . lib̅ . 7 x . sol̅ . 7 t̅n̅t̅d̅ T.R.E. Hoc m̅ te
nuer̅ . xii . sochi . Hoᵶ vii . ho̅es regis . E . viii . hid 7 i . uirg̅
tenuer̅ . 7 v . aueras 7 v . jnew inuener̅ . 7 alij . v . ho̅es
abbis de Elỹ iii . hid 7 i . uirg 7 dim habuer̅ . 7 iiii . ex eis
recede potuer̅ . quint u̅ dim hid teñ . s; recede n̅ potuit.

In Gretone teñ Wills de picot . iii . hid 7 iii . uirg . Tra . e̅
iii . car̅ . In d̅n̅io . i . car̅ . 7 dim pot̅ fieri . 7 ii . uilli cu̅ . viii .
bord̅ . hn̅t . i . car̅ 7 dim . p̊tu̅ dim car̅ . Val̅ . iii . lib̅ . Q̇do
recep̅ . iiii . lib̅ . T.R.E. v . lib̅ . Hanc t̅ra tenuit Blacuin
uicecom̅ . R.E. 7 recede potuit.

In Hochintone teñ . ii . milit̅ de Picot . iii . hid 7 i . uirg̅
7 x . ac̅s . 7 iii . miles ibid̅ teñ dim hid . 7 ix . ac̅s . 7 iii . ortcs .
Tra . e̅ . iii . car̅ 7 dim . Ibi su̅ɲ . ii . 7 i . 7 dim pot̅ fieri . Ibi
xii . uilli cu̅ . iii . bord̅ 7 viii . cot . Int tot ual . iiii . lib̅
7 x . sol̅ . Q̇do recep̅ . c . sol̅ . T.R.E. viii . lib̅ . De hac t̅ra
tenuit Blacuin de rege dim hid 7 ix . ac̅s . 7 alij . ii . ho̅es
regis . i . hid 7 iii . uirg tenuer̅ . 7 i . Auera 7 i . jnew inuener̅ .
7 un ho̅ abbis de Elỹ . i . hid 7 dim 7 x . ac̅s habuit . uende
potuit . s; soca abbi remansit.

In Epintone teñ Walt de Picot . iii . hid 7 dim . Tra . e̅
iii . car̅ . 7 ibi sunt cu̅ . iiii . bord̅ 7 iiii . cot . P̊tu̅ . i . car̅ .
Int tot ual lx . sol̅ . Q̇do recep̅ . l . sol̅ . T.R.E. iiii . lib̅ .
Hanc t̅ra tenuer̅ . iii . sochi abbis de Elỹ . Hoᵶ . ii . habuer̅
. i . hid 7 i . uirg . uende potuer̅ . s; soca abbi remansit.
Tere̅i u̅ . ii . hid 7 i . uirg habuit . s; uende n̅ potuit.

33 In MADINGLEY Picot holds 11 hides and 2½ virgates. Land for 8
    ploughs. In lordship 4 hides and 3 virgates; 2 ploughs there; a
    third possible.
        7 villagers with 4 smallholders and 6 cottagers have 4 ploughs;
        a fifth possible.
        3 slaves; meadow for 4 ploughs; wood for fences.
        2 men-at-arms hold 3 hides and 3 virgates of this land.
    Total value £6 5s; when acquired £9 10s; before 1066 as much.
        12 Freemen held this manor. 7 of them, King Edward's men,
    held 8 hides and 1 virgate; they found 5 cartages and 5 escorts.
    The other 5, the Abbot of Ely's men, had 3 hides and 1½ virgates;
    4 of them could withdraw; the fifth held ½ hide but could not
    withdraw.

34 In GIRTON William holds 3 hides and 3 virgates from Picot. Land
    for 3 ploughs. In lordship 1 plough; [another] ½ possible.
        2 villagers with 8 smallholders have 1½ ploughs.
        Meadow for ½ plough.
    Value £3; when acquired £4; before 1066 £5.
        Blackwin, King Edward's Sheriff, held this land and could
    withdraw.

35 In OAKINGTON 2 men-at-arms hold 3 hides and 1 virgate and 10 acres
    from Picot; also a third man-at-arms holds ½ hide and 9 acres and
    3 gardens there. Land for 3½ ploughs. 2 there; [another] 1½
    possible.
        12 villagers with 3 smallholders and 8 cottagers.
    In total, value £4 10s; when acquired 100s; before 1066 £8.
        Blackwin the Sheriff held ½ hide and 9 acres of this land from
    the King. 2 other men of the King's held 1 hide and 3 virgates;
    they found 1 cartage and 1 escort. A man of the Abbot of Ely's
    had 1½ hides and 10 acres; he could sell, but the jurisdiction
    remained with the Abbot.

36 In IMPINGTON Walter holds 3½ hides from Picot. Land for 3 ploughs;
    they are there, with
        4 smallholders; 4 cottagers.
        Meadow for 1 plough.
    In total, value 60s; when acquired 50s; before 1066 £4.
        3 Freemen of the Abbot of Ely's held this land. 2 of them had
    1 hide and 1 virgate; they could sell, but the jurisdiction remained
    with the Abbot. The third had 2 hides and 1 virgate, but he could
    not sell.

In Middeltone ten Radulf de Picot.xii.hiđ.Tra.e
vii.car.In đnio suу.ii.7 aliæ.ii.poſſ.ee.Ibi x.uiłłi
cu xii.borđ 7 ix.cot hnt.iii.car.Ibi.v.ſerui.ptu
iiii.car.Paſta ad pecun.De mareſch.ſexcent 7 l.
anguiłł.7 xii.den.In totis ualent uał.vii.liƀ.Qdo
receƿ.viii.liƀ.T.R.E.xii.liƀ.De hoc ꬉ tenuit
Ailƀtus dapifer abƀis.vi.hiđ 7 iii.uirg.ita qđ non
poterat uende nec ab æccła ſeparare.ſed poſt morte
ſua reſtitueret æcclæ de Ely.7 iiii.ſochi ſub abƀe
tenuer.iiii.hiđ.7 ii.uirg 7 dim.7 uende potuer
ſine ſoca.7 un hõ.R.E.ii.uirg 7 dim habuit.7 quo
uoluit uende potuit.

In Bech ten Oſmund de Picot.i.hiđ 7 dim.7 x.aĉs.
Tra.e.i.car 7 dim.In đnio.e una.car.7 dim pot
fieri.Ibi.viii.borđ 7 vi.cot.ptu.i.car 7 dim.Paſta
ad pecun.De mareſch miłł anguiłł 7 xii.den de
pſentat.Vał.xx.ſoł.Qdo receƿ.xxx.ſoł.7 tntđ.T.R.E.
De hac tra tenuit Blacuin.iii.uirg 7 xii.aĉs.7 po
tuit dare quo uoluit.7 iiii.ſochi.R.E.tenuer.iii.uirg.
una Auera 7 i.jneuuarđ inuenieƀ uicecomiti.

In Vtbech ten Muceullus de picot.vi.hiđ.Tra.e
iii.car.In đnio.e una.7 vi.uiłłi cu.iiii.borđ 7.ix.cot
hnt.ii.car.ptu.iii.car.Paſta ad pecun uillæ.Valet
.iiii.liƀ 7 vi.ſoł.Qdo receƿ.iii.liƀ.T.R.E.iiii.liƀ 7 x.ſoł.
De hac tra tenuit Blacuin de rege.ii.hiđ 7 iii.uirg.
7 iiii.hões.R.E.habuer.ii.hiđ.7 iii.Aueras 7 i.jnew
uicecomiti inuenieƀ.7 Alƀt hõ abƀis de Ely.i.hiđ ha
buit.qua nec uende nec ab æccła ſeparare potuit.
7 alt hõ abƀis.i.uirg habuit.7 uende potuit.ſoca u
remanſit abƀi.

37 In MILTON Ralph holds 12 hides from Picot. Land for 7 ploughs. 201 c
In lordship 2; 2 others possible.
  10 villagers with 12 smallholders and 9 cottagers have 3 ploughs.
   5 slaves; meadow for 4 ploughs; pasture for the livestock; from
    the marsh 650 eels and 12d.
Total value £7; when acquired £8; before 1066 £12.
  Albert, the Abbot's steward, held 6 hides and 3 virgates of this
manor on condition that he could not sell nor separate (it) from
the Church, but after his death it should be restored to the Church
of Ely. 4 Freemen held 4 hides and 2½ virgates under the Abbot,
and could sell without the jurisdiction. A man of King Edward's
had 2½ virgates and could sell whither he would.

38 In LANDBEACH Osmund holds 1½ hides and 10 acres from Picot.
Land for 1½ ploughs. In lordship 1 plough; [another] ½ possible.
  8 smallholders; 6 cottagers.
  Meadow for 1½ ploughs; pasture for the livestock; from the
    marsh 1,000 eels and 12d from presentations.
Value 20s; when acquired 30s; before 1066 as much.
  Blackwin the Sheriff held 3 virgates and 12 acres of this land,
and could grant whither he would. 4 Freemen of King Edward's
held 3 virgates; they found 1 cartage and 1 escort for the Sheriff.

39 In WATERBEACH Mucel holds 6 hides from Picot. Land for 3 ploughs.
In lordship 1;
  6 villagers with 4 smallholders and 9 cottagers have 2 ploughs.
  Meadow for 3 ploughs; pasture for the village livestock.
Value £4 6s; when acquired £3; before 1066 £4 10s.
  Blackwin held 2 hides and 3 virgates of this land from the King.
4 men of King Edward's had 2 hides; they found 3 cartages and
1 escort for the Sheriff. Albert, the Abbot of Ely's man, had
1 hide which he could neither sell nor separate from the Church.
Another man of the Abbot's had 1 virgate and could sell; but the
jurisdiction remained with the Abbot.

In Coteħā. teñ Roger de Picot. v. hiđ. Tra. ē. iii. car.

In dñio. ē una. 7 alia poť fieri. Ibi. vi. uiłłi cū. viii. cot

hñt. i. car. Ptū. iii. car. Pafťa ad pecuñ uillæ. De marefc:

cl. anguiłł. Vał. xl. fol. Qdo recep: l. fol. T.R.E. lx. sł.

Hanc trā tenueř. iii. fochi. Hoᴣ un hõ S Edeld tenuit

iii. hiđ 7 dim. xiiii. acs min. ñ potuit dare ợa erat de

dñio æcclæ. 7 ałť hõ abbis. . i. hiđ 7 dim habuit. 7 dare

potuit fine foca. 7 tcius hõ Wallef cõm. xiiii. acs habuit.

7 dare 7 uende potuit.

In Coteħā teñ Picot. xl acs 7 i. ortū de dñio æcclæ de Elŷ.

In ead Coteħā teñ ipfe Picot. xl. acs træ 7 v. acs pti. de

dñio æcclæ S Guthlaci.

In Weftuuiche teñ Odo de Picot. iii. hiđ. Tra. ē. ii. car.

In dñio. ē una 7 dim. 7 ii. uiłłi cū. i. borđ hñt dim car.

ptū. ii. car. Vał lx. fol. Qdo recep: lxx. fol. T.R.E:

c. foliđ. Hanc trā tenuit Blacuin hõ. R.E. 7 uende pot.

7 de hac tra. xl. acs habuit un fochs abbis de Elŷ. 7 re

cedere potuit. f; foca abbi remanfit.

In Cildelai teñ Rođt de Picot. ii. hiđ. Tra. ē. i. car.

Ħ eft aþpciata in Lolefuuorde. f; defđ fe in Cilderłai.

Hanc trā tenueř. iiii. fochi. hoᴣ. iii. hões. R.E. fueř.

7 iiii. hõ Eddeuæ pulchræ. 7 uende potuerunt.

201 d

.XXXI. TERRA PETRI DE VALONGIES *In Stov Hvnđ.*

Petrvs de Valonies teñ in Brone. i. hiđ 7 iii.

uirg. Tra. ē. ii. car. fed ibi non funt. Ibi funt

ii. borđ 7 iii. cot. Nem ad fepes. Vał xxx. fol. Qdo

recep . . . . fol. T.R.E: l. fol. Hanc trā tenuit

Almar teign. R.E. 7 uende potuit. Modo tenet

Picot de Petro uicecõm de Exeffe.

In CHESTERTON Hundred

40   In COTTENHAM Roger holds 5 hides from Picot. Land for 3 ploughs.
In lordship 1; another possible.
 6 villagers with 8 cottagers have 1 plough.
 Meadow for 3 ploughs; pasture for the village livestock;
  from the marsh 150 eels.
Value 40s; when acquired 50s; before 1066, 60s.
 3 Freemen held this land. One of them, St. Etheldreda's man,
held 3½ hides less 14 acres; he could not grant because it was of
the Church's lordship. Another man of the Abbot's had 1½ hides
and could grant without the jurisdiction. The third, Earl Waltheof's
man, had 14 acres; he could grant and sell.

41   In COTTENHAM Picot holds 40 acres and 1 garden of the lordship
of the Church of Ely.

42   In the same COTTENHAM Picot himself holds 40 acres of land and
5 acres of meadow of the lordship of the Church of St. Guthlac.

43   In WESTWICK Odo holds 3 hides from Picot. Land for 2 ploughs.
In lordship 1½;
 2 villagers with 1 smallholder have ½ plough.
 Meadow for 2 ploughs.
Value 60s; when acquired 70s; before 1066, 100s.
 Blackwin the Sheriff, King Edward's man, held this land and
could sell. A Freeman of the Abbot of Ely's had 40 acres of
this land; he could withdraw, but the jurisdiction remained with
the Abbot.

44   In CHILDERLEY Robert holds 2 hides from Picot. Land for 1 plough.
This (land) is assessed in Lolworth but it answers in Childerley.
 4 Freemen held this land. 3 of them were King Edward's men,
the fourth was Edeva the Fair's man; they could sell.

31 [33]   **LAND OF PETER OF VALOGNES**   201 d

In LONGSTOW Hundred

1 Peter of Valognes holds 1 hide and 3 virgates in BOURN.
Land for 2 ploughs; but they are not there.
 2 smallholders; 3 cottagers.
 Wood for fences.
Value 30s; when acquired ... s; before 1066, 50s.
 Aelmer, King Edward's thane, held this land and could sell.
Now Picot holds from Peter, the Sheriff of Essex.

.XXXII. Rannvlfvs fr̄ Ilgerij ten̄ In Gamelingei . 1 . hid̄ de
rege . Tra . ē . 1 . car̄ . Val 7 ualuit sēp . x . sol . Hanc
tram tenuit Inguare teign . R.E. 7 uend̄e potuit.

.XXXIII Terra Johis Filij Waleran. *In Flamiding h̄d*

Johs filius Waleranni . ten̄ . vi . hid̄ In Fuleberne
Tra . ē . vii . car̄ . In dn̄io . iii . hidæ . 7 ibi sunt . iii . car̄ . Ibi
viii . uilli cū . x . bord̄ . 7 iiii . cot h̄nt . iiii . car̄ . P̄tū . vii . car̄ .
Pasta ad pecun̄ uillæ . Val 7 ualuit sēp . xii . lib̄ . De hac
tra tenuit Sigar de . R.E. iii ꝼhid̄ . 7 uend̄e potuit . 7 un̄ h̄o
Algari . ii . hid̄ tenuit . 7 dare 7 uend̄e potuit . 7 iii . h̄oēs
Eddeue habuer̄ . i . hid̄ . de qua . ii . Aueras inueniebaɴ .
7 ab ea recede n̄ poteraɴ . Comes Alan reclam̄ hanc hid̄a .
h̄oēs de hund̄ ei attestant.

In Teuersh̄a ten̄ Johs . iii . hid̄ 7 dim̄ . Tra . ē . iiii . car̄
7 dim̄ . In dn̄io . ii . hide . 7 ibi sunt . ii . car̄ . Ibi . v . uilli cū . xvii .
bord̄ h̄nt . ii . car̄ 7 dim̄ . Ibi . i . seruus . P̄tū . ii . car̄ . Valet
7 ualuit . iii . lib̄ . T.R.E. iiii . lib̄ . De hac tra tenuer̄ . ii .
sochi de comite Algaro . i . hid̄ 7 dim̄ 7 xx . acs . n̄ potuer̄
recede ab eo . Tciā hid̄a huj uillæ emit Antecessor abbis
Symeonis de Ely ab Algaro . 7 tc inuenieb̄ h̄ tra auerā .
Postq̄ jacuit in æccla . n̄ inuenit . Cū hac hid̄a jacet una
æccla illi uillæ ut h̄oēs de hund̄ testant . 7 ii . h̄oēs Goduini
unā auerā 7 . ii . jneward inuener̄.

.XXXII. Terra Willi Filij Anscvlfi. *In Norestov hvnd.*

Willelm filius Ansculfi ten̄ jn Stantone dim̄
uirg de rege . Tra . ē . ii . boꝣ . p̄tū . ii . bob̄ . Val 7 ualuit
ii . sol . T.R.E. v . sol . Hanc trā tenuit Hoch sub comite
Wallef . n̄ potuit dare . Nc ten̄ Picot de Willelmo.

32 [34]   [LAND OF RANULF BROTHER OF ILGER]

In LONGSTOW Hundred
1   Ranulf brother of Ilger holds 1 hide in GAMLINGAY from the King.
Land for 1 plough.
The value is and always was 10s.
Ingvar, King Edward's thane, held this land and could sell.

33 [35]   LAND OF JOHN SON OF WALERAN

In FLENDISH Hundred
1   John son of Waleran holds 6 hides in FULBOURN. Land for 7 ploughs.
In lordship 3 hides; 3 ploughs there.
   8 villagers with 10 smallholders and 4 cottagers have 3 ploughs.
   Meadow for 7 ploughs; pasture for the village livestock.
The value is and always was £12.
   Sigar held 3 hides of this land from King Edward and could sell.
A man of Earl Algar's held 2 hides; he could grant and sell. 3 men
of Edeva's had 1 hide from which they found 2 cartages; they
could not withdraw from her. Count Alan claims this hide; the
men of the Hundred confirm him.

2   In TEVERSHAM John holds 3½ hides. Land for 4½ ploughs.
In lordship 2 hides; 2 ploughs there.
   5 villagers with 17 smallholders have 2½ ploughs.
   1 slave; meadow for 2 ploughs.
The value is and was £3; before 1066 £4.
   2 Freemen held 1½ hides and 20 acres of this land from Earl
Algar; they could not withdraw from him. Abbot Simeon of
Ely's predecessor bought the third hide of this village from Earl
Algar; then this land found cartage; after it lay in (the lands of)
the Church it did not find it. A church of that village lies with
this hide, as the men of the Hundred testify. 2 men of Young
Godwin's found 1 cartage and 2 escorts.

34 [36]   LAND OF WILLIAM SON OF ANSCULF

In NORTHSTOW Hundred
1   William son of Ansculf holds ½ virgate in LONGSTANTON from the
King. Land for 2 oxen.
   Meadow for 2 oxen.
The value is and was 2s; before 1066, 5s.
   Hoch held this land under Earl Waltheof; he could not grant.
Now Picot holds from William.

Willelm de Cahainges teñ in Bertone . i . uirg 7 dim.

Tra . e̅ . i . car̄ . f̧ n̄ eſt ibi car̄ . P̊tu̅ . i . car̄ . 7 un̅ uiłłs.

Val 7 ualuit ſe̅p . x . ſot . Hanc tra̅ tenuit . i . ho̅ Wallef

comitis . 7 dare 7 uende potuit . Hanc liḃauit Wiłło

eṗs baiocenſis . f̧ ho̅e̅s de Hund neſciuɲ qua ratione.

In Bertone teñ ipſe Wiłłs ad eund̅ modu̅ . ii . hid

7 dim . Tra . e̅ . v . car̄ . In dn̄io ſunt . iiii . 7 un̅ uiłłs

cu̅ . viii . bord hn̄t . ii . car̄ . Ibi . ii . ſerui . P̊tu̅ . ii . car̄.

Val . viii . liḃ . Q̧do recep̧ . x . liḃ . 7 tn̄td T . R . E.

Hanc tra̅ tenuer̄ . iiii . ſochi ho̅e̅s Wallef comitis.

Ho̧ . ii . tenuer̄ . i . hid 7 ii . uirg 7 dim . f̧ recede̅ ſine

lictia ej n̄ potuer̄ . Alij u̅ duo dare 7 uende̅ potuer̄.

Rotbert Fafiton in Badburgha̅ teñ . i . hid 7 i . uirg

de rcge . Tra . e̅ . ii . car̄ 7 dim . In dn̄io ſuɲ . iii . uirg.

7 ibi . e̅ una car̄ . 7 alia pot̄ fieri . 7 iiii . uiłłi hn̄t dim car̄.

Val xxi . ſot . Q̧do recep̧ . x . ſot . T . R . E . xxvi . ſot . 7 viii.

ꞇ den.

202 a

Hanc tra̅ tenuit Godeua ſub Algaro . jneward inueñ.

7 tam̄ recede̅ 7 dare tra̅ ſua̅ potuit . *In Kepeslav hd.*

In Trumpintone teñ Roḃt . ii . hid . Tra . e̅ . iii . car̄.

jn dn̄io . i . hid . 7 i . car̄ . 7 iiii . uiłłi cu̅ . i . bord . . v . cot

cu̅ . ii . car̄ . P̊tu̅ . i . car̄ . Paſta ad pecuñ . . . . Valet

7 ualuit . c . ſot . T . R . E . vi . liḃ . De hac tra tenuit Nor

mann de com̄ Toſti . i . hid 7 iii . uirg . 7 potuit uende̅.

7 recede̅ quo uoluit . 7 un̅ ho̅ regis . E . una̅ uirg tenuit.

7 Aura̅ inuenieḃ uicecomiti . 7 tam̄ cu̅ tra recede̅ pot̄.

Hanc uirg occupauit Roḃt ſup rege̅ . ut hund teſtat̄.

35 [37]   LAND OF WILLIAM OF KEYNES

In WETHERLEY Hundred

1 William of Keynes holds 1½ virgates in COMBERTON. Land for
1 plough; but the plough is not there.
Meadow for 1 plough;
1 villager.
The value is and always was 10s.
A man of Earl Waltheof's held this land; he could grant and
sell. The Bishop of Bayeux delivered this land to William, but
the men of the Hundred do not know for what reason.

2 In BARTON William holds 2½ hides himself in the same manner.
Land for 5 ploughs. In lordship 4;
1 villager with 8 smallholders have 2 ploughs.
2 slaves; meadow for 2 ploughs.
Value £8; when acquired £10; before 1066 as much.
4 Freemen, Earl Waltheof's men, held this land. 2 of them
held 1 hide and 2½ virgates but could not withdraw without
his permission. The other 2 could grant and sell their land.

36 [38]   LAND OF ROBERT FAFITON

In CHILFORD Hundred

1 Robert Fafiton holds 1 hide and 1 virgate in BABRAHAM from
the King. Land for 2½ ploughs. In lordship 3 virgates; 1 plough
there; another possible;
4 villagers have ½ plough.
Value 21s; when acquired 10s; before 1066, 26s 8d.
Godiva held this land under Earl Algar; she found escort;   202 a
however, she could withdraw and grant her land.

In THRIPLOW Hundred

2 In TRUMPINGTON Robert holds 2 hides. Land for 3 ploughs.
In lordship 1 hide and 1 plough;
4 villagers with 1 smallholder ... 5 cottagers with 2 ploughs.
Meadow for 1 plough; pasture for the livestock ...
The value is and was 100s; before 1066 £6.
Norman held 1 hide and 3 virgates of this land from Earl Tosti;
he could sell and withdraw whither he would. A man of King
Edward's held 1 virgate and found cartage for the Sheriff;
however, he could withdraw with the land. Robert appropriated
this virgate in the King's despite, as the Hundred testifies.

In Grantefete teñ Robt̃ . II . hiđ. *IN WEDERLAI HĎ.*

7 III . uirg . Tra . ē . IIII . car̃ . In dñio . I . hida . 7 ibi funt

II . car̃ . Ibi . IIII . uiłłi cū . VII . borđ . hñt . II . car̃ . Ibi XXII .

cot . 7 I . moliñ de XL . foł . De dim̃ Gorth . dim̃ miłł

Anguiłł . Int tot uał 7 ualuit . VII . liƀ . T.R.E. x . liƀ.

Hanc trā tenuer̃ . IIII . fochi . Ho₂ uñ hõ Algari com.

tenuit . III . uirg . 7 alij hões Wałłef com . tenuer̃ . II . hiđ .

7 dare 7 uende tras fuas potuer̃ . *IN STOV HVNĎ.*

In Gamelingei . teñ . II . hões . I . hiđ de Robto.

Tra . ē . I . car̃ . 7 ibi eft . cū . III . cot . p̃tū . I . car̃ . Nem

ad fepes . Vał 7 ualuit . XX . foł . T.R.E. XL . foł . Hanc

trā tenuit . I . hõ Algari . 7 uende potuit . *IN CESKET*

In Draitone teñ Auefgot de Robto . III . hiđ *HVNĎ.*

Tra . ē . III . car̃ . In dñio eft una . 7 IIII . uiłłi cū . I . borđ

hñt . II . car̃ . P̃tū . III . car̃ . Vał . XL . foł . Q̃do recep̃ . XIII .

foł 7 IIII . deñ . T.R.E. LX . foł . Hanc trā tenuit Sagar

hõ Wałłef . 7 potuit recede quo uoluit cū faca .

.XXXVII. TERRA DAVID DE ARGENTOMAGO. *IN STOV HVNĎ.*

DAVID de Argentomago jn Caldecote teñ . I . uirg

7 XX . aĉs . Tra . ē . I . car̃ . 7 ibi eft cū . III . borđ . 7 I . cot .

p̃tū . I . car̃ . Vał 7 ualuit . XX . foł . T.R.E. XXX . foliđ.

Hanc trā tenuit Sigar hõ Wałłef . 7 recede potuit.

In Crocheftone teñ Dauid . VI . hiđ . Tra . ē . IX . car̃

7 dim̃ . In dñio . III . hidæ . 7 ibi funt . II . car . 7 III . pot

fieri . Ibi . VII . uiłłi cū . VII . borđ 7 II . cot hñt . III . car̃ .

7 adhuc . III . 7 dim̃ poff fieri . P̃tū . IX . car̃ 7 dim̃ . Pafta

ad pecuñ . 7 de herbagio . XVI . deñ . De Marefch . qngent

In WETHERLEY Hundred

3 In GRANTCHESTER Robert holds 2 hides and 3 virgates. Land for 4 ploughs. In lordship 1 hide; 2 ploughs there.
  4 villagers with 7 smallholders have 2 ploughs.
    22 cottagers;
  1 mill at 40s; from ½ weir 500 eels.
In total, the value is and was £7; before 1066 £10.
  4 Freemen held this land. One of them, Earl Algar's man, held 3 virgates. The others, Earl Waltheof's men, held 2 hides; they could grant and sell their lands.

In LONGSTOW Hundred

4 In GAMLINGAY 2 men hold 1 hide from Robert. Land for 1 plough; it is there, with
    3 cottagers.
  Meadow for 1 plough; wood for fences.
The value is and was 20s; before 1066, 40s.
  A man of Earl Algar's held this land and could sell.

In CHESTERTON Hundred

5 In (Dry) DRAYTON Asgot holds 3 hides from Robert. Land for 3 ploughs. In lordship 1;
    4 villagers with 1 smallholder have 2 ploughs.
  Meadow for 3 ploughs.
Value 40s; when acquired 13s 4d; before 1066, 60s.
  Sigar, Earl Waltheof's man, held this land and could withdraw whither he would with the jurisdiction.

37 [39]   LAND OF DAVID OF ARGENTON

In LONGSTOW Hundred

1 David of Argenton holds 1 virgate and 20 acres in CALDECOTE.
  Land for 1 plough; it is there, with
    3 smallholders; 1 cottager.
  Meadow for 1 plough.
The value is and was 20s; before 1066, 30s.
  Sigar, Earl Waltheof's man, held this land and could withdraw.

2 In CROXTON David holds 6 hides. Land for 9½ ploughs.
  In lordship 3 hides; 2 ploughs there; a third possible.
    7 villagers with 7 smallholders and 2 cottagers have 3 ploughs; a further 3½ possible.
  Meadow for 9½ ploughs; pasture for the livestock; from grazing 16d; from the marsh 500 eels a year.

Anguill p annū . Quā occupauit Euſtachi de hunted
ſup Dauid . ut tot hund teſtat . In totis ualent ual
7 ualuit . VIII . lib . T.R.E. x . lib . Hoc ꝰ tenuer . III.
hões Algari . 7 IIII . hō Wallef com . 7 uende potuer.

In Weſtuuiche ten Robt de Dauid *IN CESKETON HD*
I . hid . Tra . ē . I . car . 7 ibi eſt . P̃tu . I . car . Val ; xx . ſol.
Q̃do recep: x . ſol . T.R.E. xx . ſol . Hanc trā tenuit
Godmund hō Wallef com . ſoca remanſit abbi de Elẏ.

.XXXVI. TERRA DVOꝵ CARPENTAR REGIS. *IN, OR ESTOV HD*

In Vtbech . teneN . II . carpentarij de rege . v . hid . Tra . ē
II . car 7 dim . In dñio . IIII . hidæ 7 I . uirg . 7 ibi ſunt . II . car.
Ibi . III . uilli cū . x . cot h̄nt dim car . Val . cx . ſol . Q̃do
recep: IIII . lib 7 x . ſol . T.R.E. VII . lib 7 x . ſol . De hac tra
tenuit . I . hō Wallef . I . hid 7 dim . 7 I . Auerā inuen . 7 uende pot.
7 Oſwi hō abbis de Elẏ . III . hid 7 dim tenuit . n̄ potuit
uende nec ab æccła ſeparare . ut hões de hund teſtant.

202 b

.XXXIX J TERRA JVDITÆ COMITISSE. *IN CAVELAI HVND*

ꝰ Jvdita comitiſſa ten *CHERTELINGE* . p x . hid ſe
defd . T.R.E. 7 m̃ p . VI . hid . Tra . ē ad . xx . I . car . In
dñio ſunt . IIII . hide . 7 ibi . IIII . car . Ibi . xxvIII . uilli
cū xvII . bord h̄nt . xvI . car . Ibi . vII . ſerui . p̃tu . xxI.
car . Silua . Lx . porc . Paſta ad pecun uille . Parc
beſtiarū ſiluaticarū . De piſcar . v . mill 7 dim Anguill.
In totis ualent 7 ual 7 ualuit | xvIII . lib . Hoc ꝰ
tenuit Herald comes.   *IN RADEFELLE HVND.*
In Dullingehā ten comitiſſa . x . acs . cū . I . bord.

Which (land) Eustace of Huntingdon appropriated in David's despite, as the whole Hundred testifies.

The total value is and was £8; before 1066 £10.

3 men of Earl Algar's and a fourth, Earl Waltheof's man, held this manor and could sell.

In CHESTERTON Hundred
3 In WESTWICK Robert holds 1 hide from David. Land for 1 plough; it is there.

Meadow for 1 plough.

Value 20s; when acquired 10s; before 1066, 20s.

Godmund, Earl Waltheof's man, held this land; the jurisdiction remained with the Abbot of Ely.

38 [40] LAND OF TWO OF THE KING'S CARPENTERS

In NORTHSTOW Hundred
1 In WATERBEACH 2 carpenters hold 5 hides from the King. Land for 2½ ploughs. In lordship 4 hides and 1 virgate; 2 ploughs there.

3 villagers with 10 cottagers have ½ plough.

Value 110s; when acquired £4 10s; before 1066 £7 10s.

A man of Waltheof's held 1½ hides of this land; he found 1 cartage and could sell. Oswy, the Abbot of Ely's man, held 3½ hides; he could not sell or separate (them) from the Church, as the men of the Hundred testify.

39 [41] LAND OF COUNTESS JUDITH 202 b

In CHEVELEY Hundred
1 M. Countess Judith holds KIRTLING. It answered for 10 hides before 1066; now for 6 hides. Land for 21 ploughs. In lordship 4 hides; 4 ploughs there.

28 villagers with 17 smallholders have 16 ploughs.

7 slaves; meadow for 21 ploughs; woodland, 60 pigs; pasture for the village livestock; a park for woodland beasts; from the fishery 5,500 eels.

The total value is and always was £18.

Earl Harold held this manor.

In RADFIELD Hundred
2 In DULLINGHAM the Countess holds 10 acres, with 1 smallholder.

In Weſlai ten̅ comitiſſa . III . uirg̅. ʃ Val̅ XII . den̅.
7 x . aĉs . Tra . e̅ . II . car̅ . Ibi . e̅ una . 7 alia pot̅ fieri.
Ibi . i̇ . uilłs cū . I . bord̅ . 7 II . aĉ p̅ti . Val̅ 7 ualuit se̅p
xx . ſoł . Hanc t̅ra tenuer̅ . II . ho̅es heraldi comitiṣ.
recede̅ n̅ potuer̅ . 7 Auera̅ in ſeruitio regis inuener̅.
In Carletone ten̅ comit̅ . III . hid̅ . Tra . e̅ . VIII . car̅.
In dn̅io . I . hida 7 dim̅ . 7 ibi ſunt . II . car̅ . 7 XII . uilłi
cū . II . bord̅ hnt . VI . car̅ . Ibi . II . ſerui . 7 II . aĉ p̅ti.
Silua . XII . porc̅ . Val̅ 7 ualuit ſe̅p . VI . lib̅ . Hanc
t̅ra tenuit Herald̅ com̅ . De ead̅ t̅ra ten̅ . III . ſocħi
de comit̅ . IIII . Aĉs . 7 dim̅ . 7 ipſi tenuer̅ T.R.E . 7 inew
inuener̅ . 7 un̅ ho̅ Algari . II . aĉs tenuit . 7 inew inuen̅.
In Badburgħa̅ ten̅ comitiſſa IN CILDEFORD HVND.
.I . uirg̅ 7 dim̅ . Tra . e̅ . IIII . bobʒ . Val̅ 7 ualuit . IIII . ſoł.
Hanc t̅ra tenuit un̅ ho̅ Guert comitis . 7 recede̅ n̅ pot̅.
In Pampeſuuorde ten̅ un̅ p̅br de comitiſſa dimid̅
uirg̅ . Val̅ 7 ualuit . LXIIIꝓ . den̅ . Hanc tenuit
q̅da̅ ſocħs Guert comitis . n̅ potuit recede̅ nec uende̅.
In Witelesforde ten̅ comitiſſa IN WITELESFORD HVND
XI . hid̅ . 7 I . uirg̅ . Tra . e̅ . XI . car̅ . In dn̅io . V . hide . 7 ibi ſuꝓ
II . car̅ . 7 XIII . uilłi cū xv . bord̅ hnt . IX . car̅ . Ibi . V . ſerui.
7 III . molin̅ de . LX . ſoł . p̅tu car̅ . In totis ualent̅ ual̅ . XVI.
lib̅ . Q̅do recep̅ . xv . lib̅ . 7 t̅ntd̅ T.R.E . Hoc m̅ tenuit Guert.
In Tru̅pintone ten̅ Gollam de comit̅ IN REPESLAV HVND.
dim̅ hid̅ . Tra . e̅ dim̅ car̅ . 7 ibi . e̅ . Val̅ 7 ualuit ſe̅p . x . ſoł.
Hanc t̅ra tenuit q̅da̅ ſocħs de Wallef . n̅ potuit recede̅.

Value 12d.

3   In WESTLEY (Waterless) the Countess holds 3 virgates and 10 acres. Land for 2 ploughs. 1 there; a second possible.
> 1 villager with 1 smallholder;
> meadow, 2 acres.

The value is and always was 20s.
> 2 men of Earl Harold's held this land; they could not withdraw; they found cartage in the King's service.

4   In CARLTON the Countess holds 3 hides. Land for 8 ploughs. In lordship 1½ hides; 2 ploughs there;
> 12 villagers with 2 smallholders have 6 ploughs.
> 2 slaves; meadow, 2 acres; woodland, 12 pigs.

The value is and always was £6.
> Earl Harold held this land.
> 3 Freemen hold 4½ acres of the same land from the Countess; they held it themselves before 1066 and found escort. A man of Earl Algar's held 2 acres and found escort.

In CHILFORD Hundred

5   In BABRAHAM the Countess holds 1½ virgates. Land for 4 oxen. The value is and was 4s.
> A man of Earl Gyrth's held this land and could not withdraw.

6   In PAMPISFORD a priest holds ½ virgate from the Countess. The value is and was 64d.
> A Freeman of Earl Gyrth's held it; he could not withdraw or sell.

In WHITTLESFORD Hundred

7 M. In WHITTLESFORD the Countess holds 11 hides and 1 virgate. Land for 11 ploughs. In lordship 5 hides; 2 ploughs there;
> 13 villagers with 15 smallholders have 9 ploughs.
> 5 slaves; 3 mills at 60s; meadow for the ploughs.

Total value £16; when acquired £15; before 1066 as much.
> Earl Gyrth held this manor.

In THRIPLOW Hundred

8   In TRUMPINGTON Godlamb holds ½ hide from the Countess. Land for ½ plough; it is there.

The value is and always was 10s.
> A Freeman of Earl Waltheof's held this land; he could not withdraw.

In Tadelai ten Picot de comitiſſa   IN ERNINGFORD HD̄
.ɪ.hiđ ⁊ ɪ.uirg ⁊ dim̄.Tra.ē.ɪɪ.caɼ ⁊ dim̄.In dñio poteſt
fieri.ɪ.caɼ.Ibi dim̄ uiłts cū.vɪɪ.borđ hn̄t.ɪ.caɼ ⁊ dim̄.
Silua ad ſep reficiend.Val ⁊ ualuit.xxx.ſot.T.R.E.́ xʟ.ſot.
Hanc trā tenuit Torchil p̄br Toſti com̄.⁊ uende potuit.
Iſđ Picot ten de comitiſſa.ɪɪɪ.uirg.   IN STOV HVND.
Tra.ē.ɪ.caɼ.ſed n̄ eſt ibi.niſi.ɪ.borđ.Nem̄ ad ſepes.Valet.
v.ſot.Qđo recep.́ x.ſot.T.R.E.́ xx.ſot.Hanc trā tenueɼ
ɪɪ.ſochi.R.E.⁊ uende potueɼ.   IN PAPEWORD HVND.
Iſdē Picot ten de comitiſſa.ɪ.hiđ.Tra.ē.ɪ.caɼ.ſʒ n̄ eſt ibi.
p̄tū.ɪ.caɼ.Val ⁊ ualuit.vɪɪ.ſot.T.R.E.́ xx.ſot.Hanc trā
tenuit.ɪ.Huſcarle Wallef com̄.⁊ uende potuit.
Iſđ Picot ten de comitiſſa.ɪɪɪ.hiđ   IN NORESTOV HVND.
Tra.ē.ɪɪ.caɼ.Ibi.ē una.⁊ altera pot fieri.Ibi.ɪɪɪɪ.uiłti
⁊ ɪɪɪɪ.borđ.Val.xxx.ſot.Qđo recep.́ xʟ.ſot.⁊ tn̄td T.R.E.
Hanc trā tenueɼ.ɪɪɪɪ.hões Wallef com̄.⁊ uende potueɼ.
202 c
In Ḟochintone ten Rog de comitiſſa.ɪ.hiđ ⁊ dim̄
⁊ x.acs.Tra.ē.ɪ.caɼ ⁊ dim̄.Ibi.ē dimiđ.⁊ caɼ poteſt
fieri.Ibi.ɪ.uiłts.⁊ vɪ.cot.Val.xxx.ſot.Qđo recep.́
xx.ſot.T.R.E.́ ɪɪɪɪ.lib.Hanc trā tenuit Goduinus
hō Wallef.⁊ uende potuit.   IN PAPEWORD HD̄.
In Oure ten Roger de comit dim̄ hiđ.Tra.ē.ɪɪɪɪ.
bob.⁊ ibi ſunt.⁊ p̄tū ipſis bob.⁊ ɪɪɪ.cot.Paſta ad
pecun uillæ.Val ⁊ ualuit ſēp xx.ſot.Hanc trā
tenuit Goduin hō Wallef com̄.⁊ dare potuit.ſed
ſoca remanſit ab̄b̄i de Rameſy.

In ARMINGFORD Hundred

9 In TADLOW Picot holds 1 hide and 1½ virgates from the Countess.
Land for 2½ ploughs. In lordship 1 plough possible.
½ villager with 7 smallholders have 1½ ploughs.
Woodland for repairing fences.
The value is and was 30s; before 1066, 40s.
Thorkil, Earl Tosti's priest, held this land and could sell.

In LONGSTOW Hundred

10 Picot also holds 3 virgates from the Countess. Land for 1 plough;
but it is not there, except for
1 smallholder.
Wood for fences.
Value 5s; when acquired 10s; before 1066, 20s.
2 Freemen of King Edward's held this land and could sell.

In PAPWORTH Hundred

11 Picot also holds 1 hide from the Countess. Land for 1 plough;
but it is not there.
Meadow for 1 plough.
The value is and was 7s; before 1066, 20s.
A guard of Earl Waltheof's held this land and could sell.

In NORTHSTOW Hundred

12 Picot also holds 3 hides from the Countess. Land for 2 ploughs.
1 there; a second possible.
4 villagers; 4 smallholders.
Value 30s; when acquired 40s; before 1066 as much.
4 men of Earl Waltheof's held this land and could sell.

13 In OAKINGTON Roger holds 1½ hides and 10 acres from the   202 c
Countess. Land for 1½ ploughs. ½ there; [another] plough
possible.
1 villager; 6 cottagers.
Value 30s; when acquired 20s; before 1066 £4.
Godwin, Earl Waltheof's man, held this land and could sell.

In PAPWORTH Hundred

14 In OVER Roger holds ½ hide from the Countess. Land for
4 oxen; they are there;
meadow for the oxen themselves; 3 cottagers; pasture for
the village livestock.
The value is and always was 20s.
Godwin, Earl Waltheof's man, held this land and could grant,
but the jurisdiction remained with the Abbot of Ramsey.

In Draitone ten̄ Rogeri de comitiſſa . III . uirḡ

Tra . ē . IIII . boƀ . 7 ibi ſunt 7 p̃tū ipſis . ƀƀ . Ibi . I . uilłs.

Val xvr . ſol . Q̇do recep̃ xxx . ſol . T.R.E. xx . ſol.

Hanc tr̄a tenuit . I . hō Wallef com̄ . 7 uendē potuit.

In Cilderlai ten̄ Picot de comit . v . hid . Tra . ē . v .

car̄ . In dn̄io . ē una . 7 v . uilłi cū . vi . bord 7 III . cot̄

hn̄t . IIII . car̄ . Ibi un̄ ſeruus . Nem ad ſepes . Valet

IIII . liƀ . Q̇do recep̃ LXX . ſol . T.R.E. VIII . liƀ . Hanc

tr̄a tenuit. I . hō Wallef com̄ . 7 uendē potuit.

TERRA VXORIS RADVLFI. *IN ERNINGFORD HD.*

XL. **A**ZELINA uxor Radulſi tallgeboſc In Tadelai ten̄

de rege . I . hid 7 I . uirḡ Tra . ē . II . car̄ . 7 ibi ſunt

cū . v . bord . p̃tū . II . car̄ . Paſta ad pecun̄ uillæ.

Val xL . ſol . Q̇do recep̃ x . ſol . T.R.E. xL . ſol.

Hanc tr̄a tenuit Vlmar de Ettone . teign̄ regis . E.

N̄c ten̄ Walter monach de p̄dicta Azelina.

VXORIS BOSELINI DE DIVE. *IN ORNESTON HVND.*

.XLI. **I**n Hochintone ten̄ uxor Boſelini de Dive . I . hid

7 dim̄ . quā ei libauit eps baiocenſis . ſ; hoes de hund

neſciunt quā ratione . Tra . ē . I . car̄ 7 dim̄ . Ibi ſuɴ

★ vi . boues . 7 I . car̄ pot fieri . Ibi . III . uilłi 7 III . cot̄.

Val 7 ualuit xxx . ſol . T.R.E. Lx . ſol . Hanc tr̄a tenuit

Siuuard hō Wallef com̄ . 7 uendē potuit . ſ̧ ſoca re

manſit abƀi de Ely.

In CHESTERTON Hundred

15 In (Dry) DRAYTON Roger holds 3 virgates from the Countess.
Land for 4 oxen; they are there;
meadow for the oxen themselves.
1 villager.
Value 16s; when acquired 30s; before 1066, 20s.
A man of Earl Waltheof's held this land and could sell.

16 In CHILDERLEY Picot holds 5 hides from the Countess.
Land for 5 ploughs. In lordship 1;
5 villagers with 6 smallholders and 3 cottagers have
4 ploughs.
1 slave; wood for fences.
Value £4; when acquired 70s; before 1066 £8.
A man of Earl Waltheof's held this land and could sell.

40 [42]   LAND OF THE WIFE OF RALPH TALLBOYS

In ARMINGFORD Hundred

1 Azelina wife of Ralph Tallboys holds 1 hide and 1 virgate in
TADLOW from the King. Land for 2 ploughs; they are there, with
5 smallholders.
Meadow for 2 ploughs; pasture for the village livestock.
Value 40s; when acquired 10s; before 1066, 40s.
Wulfmer of Eaton, King Edward's thane, held this land.
Now Walter the monk holds from the said Azelina.

41 [43]   [LAND] OF THE WIFE OF BOSELIN OF DIVES

In NORTHSTOW Hundred

1 In OAKINGTON the wife of Boselin of Dives holds 1½ hides which
the Bishop of Bayeux delivered to her, but the men of the Hundred
do not know for what reason. Land for 1½ ploughs. 6 oxen there;
[another] 1 plough possible.
3 villagers; 2 cottagers.
The value is and was 30s; before 1066, 60s.
Siward, Earl Waltheof's man, held this land and could sell;
but the jurisdiction remained with the Abbot of Ely.

ETERRA·ERCHENGERIJ. *IN WEDERLAI HD.*

ERCHENGER Piftor ten de rege In Cubertone
.I.hidā.xx.acs min.Tra.e.ii.car.In dnio|dim
hida.xx.acs min.Ibi.IIII.uilli cū.vIII.bord hūt
.I.car.Ibi.I.feru.7 ptu.IIII.bob.Val.xxx.fol.Qdo
recep:xx.fol.T.R.E.xl.fol.Hanc trā tenuer.III.
focħi.Hoz un ħo regis.I.uirg habuit.7 dim auerā
inuen.7 alt ħo.S.Archiepi.I.uirg 7 dim.7 tcius ħo
Wallef.I.uirg 7 dim.7 uende 7 recede potuer.

In Tofth ten|de rege.I.hidā.Tra.e.II.car. *IN STOV HD*
In dnio pot fieri.I.car.7 I.uilts cū.v.cot hūt.I.car.
Ptu.IIII.bob.Nem ad fepes 7 ad focū.Val xl.fol.
Qdo recep:x.fol.T.R.E.lx.fol.Hanc trā tenuer
v.focħi abbis de Ely.Non potuer dare nec uende
ext æcclam S Æld.T.R.E.7 in morte ipfius regis.

42 [44]   LAND OF ERCHENGER

1   Erchenger the baker holds 1 hide less 20 acres in COMBERTON from the King. Land for 2 ploughs. In lordship 1 plough; ½ hide less 20 acres.

4 villagers with 8 smallholders have 1 plough.
1 slave; meadow for 4 oxen.
Value 30s; when acquired 20s; before 1066, 40s.

3 Freemen held this land. One of them, the King's man, had 1 virgate and found ½ cartage; the second, Archbishop Stigand's man, (had) 1½ virgates; the third, Waltheof's man, (had) 1½ virgates; they could sell and withdraw.

In LONGSTOW Hundred

2   In TOFT Erchenger holds 1 hide from the King. Land for 2 ploughs. In lordship 1 plough possible;

1 villager with 5 cottagers have 1 plough.
Meadow for 4 oxen; wood for fences and for fuel.
Value 40s; when acquired 10s; before 1066, 60s.

5 Freemen of the Abbot of Ely's held this land; before and in 1066, they could not grant or sell outside St. Etheldreda's Church.

CAMBRIDGESHIRE HOLDINGS
ENTERED ELSEWHERE IN THE SURVEY

The Latin text of these entries is given in the county volume concerned

In ESSEX

1   **LAND OF THE KING**   1 b

EE1   Hundred of UTTLESFORD   3 b

   9   Earl Edgar held CHESTERFORD before 1066 as 1 manor, for 10 hides. Now Picot the Sheriff (holds it), in the King's hand ... (In the lands of) this manor lie 1½ hides which are in Cambridgeshire. [*HINXTON: 1,10; 22*]

      Always 7 villagers; 3 smallholders; 1 mill; 3 men's ploughs ... Attached to this manor before 1066 were 1½ hides which Hardwin of Scales holds, but the Hundred does not know how; ½ hide was of lordship (land) in which 1 man dwelt [*? HINXTON: 26,14*]; another hide 1 Freeman held who paid suit in the King's manor [cf. *BABRAHAM: 26,11*]. Also Picot holds ½ hide which 1 Freeman held before 1066 [*BABRAHAM: 1,15*]. In these 2 hides, 2 ploughs. Value 40s.

EE2   Hundred of UTTLESFORD   7 a

  28   Harold held NEWPORT before 1066 as a manor, for 8½ hides. Now King William (holds it) ...
Then it paid (a revenue of) 2 nights' provisions.
There is besides 1 outlier which lies in Cambridgeshire and is called SHELFORD, with 3 hides and 46 acres.

      Always 8 villagers; 5 smallholders; 1 plough in lordship; 2 men's ploughs.

      Meadow, 15 acres. Then 1 cob, now none; always 10 cattle. Then 80 pigs, now 50; then 80 sheep, now 87; then 13 goats, now 24.

This outlier was in the above-mentioned revenue before 1066, but now it pays £25 16s.

CHISHILL, HEYDON.   See Notes to the Translation, below.

In HERTFORDSHIRE

?STETCHWORTH.   See Notes to the Translation, below.

In HUNTINGDONSHIRE
19   **LAND OF EUSTACE THE SHERIFF**   206 a

EHu   TOSELAND Hundred   206 c
24 M. In PAPWORTH 1 hide taxable. Land for 1 plough. Eustace
has 1 plough in lordship.
Meadow, 10 acres.
Value before 1066, 60s; now 20s.

In SUFFOLK
3   **LAND OF COUNT ALAN**   292 b

ESf   RISBRIDGE Hundred ...
1   ... In this same Hundred, 9 acres.
1 [plough] with the villagers. It is in the assessment of
WESTON (Colville) in Cambridge[shire] [*14,80*].

NOTES

ABBREVIATIONS used in the Notes: Appx...Appendix. arr...*arrondissement*. DB...Domesday Book. DG...H.C. Darby and G.R. Versey, *Domesday gazetteer* (Cambridge 1975). EHR...*English Historical Review*. Ellis...Sir H. Ellis, *A general introduction to Domesday Book* (2 vols. 1833; reprinted 1971). EPNS...*The place-names of Cambridgeshire and the Isle of Ely*, ed. P.H. Reaney (*English Place-Name Society* xix, Cambridge 1943). .Forssner...T. Forssner, *Continental-Germanic personal names in England in Old and Middle English times* (Uppsala 1916). Harmer, *ASWrits*...F.E. Harmer, *Anglo-Saxon writs* (Manchester 1952). HRH...*The heads of religious houses, England and Wales 940–1216*, ed. D. Knowles, C.N.L. Brooke, V.C.M. London (Cambridge 1972). ICC, IE, IEBrev, IENV...for these texts see above, The Cambridgeshire Inquiry and The Ely Inquiry, references are to pages in *Inquisitio Comitatus Cantabrigiensis*, ed. N.E.S.A. Hamilton (1876); in the notes, page numbers are not repeated when they are the same as for the preceding note within each DB section. LibEl...*Liber Eliensis*, ed. E.O. Blake (*Camden Society*, 3rd series, xcii). ME...Middle English. MLat...Medieval Latin. MS... Manuscript. ODan...Old Danish. OE...Old English. OEB...G. Tengvik, *Old English bynames* (*Nomina Germanica* iv, Uppsala 1938). OFr...Old French. OG...Old German. ON...Old Norse. O.S....Ordnance Survey. OWScand...Old West Scandinavian. PNDB...O. von Feilitzen, *The pre-conquest personal names of Domesday Book* (*Nomina Germanica* iii, Uppsala 1937). Reaney... P.H. Reaney, *A dictionary of British surnames* (2nd. ed. by R.M. Wilson, 1977). VCH...*The Victoria History of the county of Cambridgeshire and the Isle of Ely*, i, ed. L.F. Salzman (1938), with Domesday and ICC translations by J. Otway-Ruthven. VCH Essex...*The Victoria History of the county of Essex*, i, ed. H.A. Doubleday, W. Page (1903).

The manuscript is written on either side of leaves, or folios, of parchment (sheep-skin) measuring about 15 by 11 inches (38 by 28 cms). On each side, or page, are two columns, making four to each folio. The folios were numbered in the 17th century, and the four columns of each are here lettered a, b, c, d. Red ink was used to emphasise words and to distinguish most chapters and sections. Underlining was used to indicate deletion.

CAMBRIDGESHIRE. In red, across the top of the page, spread above both columns, *GRENTEBR(IGE)SCIRE.*

References to other DB counties are to the Chapter and Sections of the editions in this series.

B   ICC(51) contains a reference, omitted in DB, to 1 virgate of land in Cambridge, held by a burgess in 1086, whose defence obligations (*wara*) lay in Trumpington.

B1-10   TEN WARDS. For purposes of defence and administration, the Borough of Cambridge was divided into ten districts, or wards, before 1066. After 1068 the land making up one of these wards was appropriated for the site of the Norman castle (see *Royal Commission on Historical Monuments, City of Cambridge*, ii (1959), 304). Presumably for this reason, only nine wards (the first to the fifth and the seventh to the tenth) render account in DB. IE(21) informs us that the second ward was called Bridge Ward and that, before 1066, the Abbot of Ely had 10 dwellings within the Borough (of which 2 are now unoccupied), as well as 2 houses (both now unoccupied), 4 gardens (1 now unoccupied) and 1 church; the Abbot also claimed the fourth penny of the shire, that is, a quarter of its revenue; cf. B12 note.

B1-2   COUNT ALAN. See 14,12.

B1   JUDICAEL. See 12,2-4.
          5s 8½d. DB uses the old English currency system, which lasted for a thousand years until 1971. The pound contained 20 shillings, each of 12 pence, abbreviated respectively as £(ibrae), s(olidi), d(enarii). Note however that, in common with other medieval records, DB frequently omits to convert quantities of pence into shillings and of shillings into pounds.
          RALPH BANKS. DB *de bans*; the founder of the Cambridgeshire family of Banks (VCH 340, n.1). Reaney(22) suggests that the name is from ME *banke,* 'a bank, ridge'. Ralph was also called *de scamnis, de scannis* (see 14,17 note; 32,2 note; Appx K), from MLat *scannum,* 'bench' (perhaps referring to the same topographical feature as the *banke*), while in Appx H he is called Ralph of Barrington from his holding at 32,18. OEB 70 suggests a possible

connection between the name *de bans* and Baons-le-Comte (Seine Inf.). An alternative to the topographical significance of *banke* and *scannum* might be the more literal meaning of 'bench', perhaps in relation to a court of law with which Ralph was associated.

ROGER, BISHOP REMIGIUS'S MAN. Probably Roger of Childerley (3,6. Appx O). For Remigius, see 3,2 note.

B2-5,10 DUES. *Consuetudo*, normally translated 'customary dues'; in the Borough chapter, 'customary' is here omitted to avoid repetition.

B2 REMAINING 32. Apparently a DB error, of *xxxii* for *xxxiii*.

LANDS OF THE ENGLISH. The significance of this phrase is not clear.

B6 HAVE. Farley does not show a gap in the text after *h(abu)nt*, caused by a hole (repaired) in the MS.

B10 LAND-TRIBUTE. A burghal rent owed to the King.

ORA. Literally an ounce, in Scandinavia a monetary unit and coin still in use; in DB valued at 16 (assayed) or 20 (unassayed) pence, see S. Harvey, 'Royal revenue and Domesday terminology', *Economic History Review*, 2nd series, xx (1967), 221-228.

B11 CARTAGE NOR CARTS. The distinction between *avera* and *currus* is that between the provision of a draught-beast and of the cart itself.

THROUGH HIM AND BY HIM. A phrase perhaps intended to include both the pasture lost through Picot's building of 3 mills for his own profit (B12) and that lost through his actions in the official capacity of Sheriff.

B12 3 MILLS. IE(123) states that Picot has 2 mills in the Borough, at £8.

MILL OF THE ABBOT. Not mentioned in IE (see B1-10 note).

B13-14 HERIOT. A payment due at the time of his death from a warrior to his lord, representing the return of his military equipment.

LAWMEN. 24 Burgesses who propounded the law in the Cambridge Borough-court. They are mentioned in connection with pre-Conquest lawsuits recorded in LibEl(xiv,88,97).

B14 AELFRIC GODRICSON. Sheriff of Cambridge before 1066.

L Chapters 32 and 33 were originally entered in reverse order in the List but the order was later corrected by the use of suprascript letters (*a,b*), in reversed alphabetical order, above the respective landowners' names and preceding the letter (*c*) above the entry for Chapter 34. Chapters 15-18 are misnumbered 25-28 in the text, where also Chapter 19 is misnumbered 25, Chapters 20-21 are not numbered, and Chapters 22-44 are misnumbered 20-42. In the translation, the actual sequence of the misnumbered Chapters is shown by Chapter-numbers in square-brackets; all references to the content of these Chapters in the notes and indices are to the numbers in square-brackets.

1,1 9½ HIDES. ICC(6), '9½ hides less 6 acres'.

16 VILLAGERS...12 PLOUGHS. Placed, unusually, before the lordship ploughs.

3,500 EELS. The roman numeral *D* (for 500) is explained by an interlineal gloss (*quingenti*).

MEADOW...14 PLOUGHS. Enough meadow to maintain 14 plough-teams (each of 8 oxen).

ACCORDING...CAN. That is, in proportion to their catch.

ASSAYED AND WEIGHED. The coins being melted down and assessed for their bullion content and any deficiency made good up to the decreed official weight of £25 of silver pence.

AT FACE VALUE IN WHITE PENCE. This phrase is a reference to the nominal assaying of coins; not actually melting them down but requiring an extra number of pence to be paid in compensation for any loss of value from worn coins. The extra coins paid seem to have represented an additional ¼ of face value, and the 'assay' was effected by using the *ora* of 20d instead of 16d (see B10 note and article cited). The £13 8s 4d referred to here represents the final amount to be paid (3,220d or 161 *ora* at 20d).

1,2 2 MILLS...FEED 2 PIGS. Cf. 5,25 note.

1,2-3 MADE GOOD...FINE...SHERIFF. The Sheriff, as the King's agent, had the right to profits of jurisdiction over these Freemen. Cf. 22,6.

1,4 WOODLAND. See also 28,2.

1,5 8 PLOUGHS. 9 are listed.

ORA. See B10 note.

1,6 WHICH...HOLDS. Farley and MS *quãtten'*, facsimile *quãcten'*; probably an error for *qua(m) ten(et)*.

EARL WALTHEOF. Of Huntingdon and Northumbria, executed for treason in 1076 (having joined two of his fellow Earls in rebellion, see 19,4 note). Countess Judith (*41*) was his widow.

1,7;9   IN PROPORTION TO THIS. Translating *contra hoc*. The amount paid in kind varied from year to year but was not to exceed a particular proportion of the money paid per year.

1,10   IN WHITTLESFORD HUNDRED. Not rubricated in MS.

HINXTON. The present section is repeated in error at 1,22.

DEFENCE OBLIGATION. Cf. Hertfordshire 1,5 (where translated simply as 'obligations').

CHESTERFORD. Essex, see EE1. Cf. 1,15.

IN ESSEX. As B6 note, with reference to a gap in the MS after *in*.

EARL ALGAR. Of Mercia (d.?1062).

1,11   13 PLOUGHS POSSIBLE. DB error of *xiii* for *xi;* land for 16 ploughs of which 5 are present, thus a further 11 are possible. ICC(10) has the correct figure.

WILLIAM OF NOYERS. Probably named from Noyers (Calvados) rather than Noyers (Eure), OEB 103.

ARCHBISHOP STIGAND. See 2,3 note. Stigand had appropriated Woodditton during a vacancy in the abbacy of Ely, see LibEl 168,425.

1,12   EXNING. Now in Suffolk.

TOTAL VALUE £53. ICC(4), £52.

GODRIC. ICC states 'Godric now holds it from the King at a revenue'.

EDEVA THE FAIR. She held extensive lands in Cambridgeshire, Hertfordshire, Norfolk and Suffolk before 1066, most of which were acquired by Count Alan (*14*). Her identification by Ellis(ii 79-80) as Ealdgyth, King Harold's wife, is rejected by VCH 354-355.

A CARTAGE. ICC, 'one horse for cartage'.

A PLEDGE. ICC has 'an escort for the King's service', *Inuuardum ministerio Regis*. However, as VCH 337 observes, the duty of providing an escort does not alternate with that of providing cartage elsewhere in DB. *Inuuardum* in ICC may represent a misreading of an abbreviated form of *mancipium*.

1,13   This section is not separately noted in ICC(6-7) but appears to be a part of the King's manor at Soham (1,1) which has been entered twice in DB.

IN HIS WRIT. 'Writ' here has the general OE meaning of 'writing, something written' and probably refers to a list of the King's estates.

1,14-16   PICOT. Sheriff of Cambs., see *32*.

1,14   UNDER THE KING'S HAND. That is, Picot held it on the King's behalf.

HORSES. For cartage, see foll.

ONLY...CARTAGES AND ESCORTS OR 12s. 8d. ICC(26) 'only 12s 7d'.

1,15   CHESTERFORD. In Essex, see EE1. Cf. 1,10.

1,16   Cf. 29,12 referring to the same holding.

ABINGTON. DG(25) erroneously identifies this as Abington Pigotts (in Armingford Hundred), but see ICC(32).

UNDER THE KING'S HAND. As 1,14 note.

SIGAR. DB *Sagar*; perhaps Old Scandinavian *Sigar* (PNDB 359) but possibly OE *Sǽgār* or *Sigegār*, or Continental Germanic *Sigger, Siger*. The name recurs at 38,5.

1,17   NEWPORT. In Essex, see EE2.

CAMBRIDGE. ICC(49), 'Cambridgeshire'.

EARL HAROLD. Earl of Wessex (1053-), King 1066.

1,18   GUARD-PENNY. Payment in lieu of guard-service.

1,20   ALWIN COCK THE BEADLE. ICC(61). 'Alwin Maimcock (*Hamelecoc*), the King's beadle'.

ICKLETON. ICC, Litlington. Ickleton is a DB error, a misreading of *Ichelintone* for *Lidlintone*. Cf. 26,23 note.

1,21   LAND FOR 4 OXEN. ICC(90) adds, 'and they are there'.

1,22   This section repeats 1,10 in error and is deleted in DB. It has *Cestres'* in error for *Cestref'*.

1,23   UNDER THE KING'S HAND. As 1,14 note.

2,1   BISHOP WALKELIN. Of Winchester, 1070-98. For his brother Simeon, see 28,2 note.

2,1-4   ST. PETER'S CHURCH. The Old Minster, Winchester; later called St. Swithin's Priory.

2,3   ABINGTON (PIGOTTS). DG(25) erroneously identifies this as Abington (in Chilford Hundred), but see ICC(60).

HUGH. ICC, 'Hugh Butler' (*pincerna*). Possibly the landholder of that name in Beds. (*35*).

	9 SMALLHOLDERS. ICC, '9 smallholders, 3 cottagers'.
	BEFORE 1066 £8. *viii* has been altered in the MS, perhaps from *iiii*.
	ARCHBISHOP STIGAND. Bishop of Elmham 1043-7, of Winchester 1047-. He retained the see of Winchester in plurality upon becoming Archbishop of Canterbury in 1052, until his deposition in 1070. See also 1,11 note.
2,4	1 HIDE AND 2½ VIRGATES. ICC(61-62), '1½ hides and ½ virgate'.
	4 SMALLHOLDERS. ICC(62), '3 smallholders, each with 5 acres'.
	SELL. ICC, 'withdraw whither he would'.
3,1	GRANT. ICC(40), 'grant and sell'.
3,2;5-6	BISHOP R(EMIGIUS). Of Dorchester-on-Thames, 1067-; he transferred his see to Lincoln in 1072 and died in 1092.
3,2	BISHOP WULFWY. Remigius's predecessor at Dorchester (1053-67).
	BLACKWIN. Probably Blackwin the Sheriff; cf. 32,34-35; 38-39; 43 which were also later held by Picot the Sheriff.
3,5	WULFWIN. ICC(115), 'Wulfwin the mead-keeper of Ely Abbey'; he was the official (*medarius*) in charge of Ely Abbey's mead supplies, which presumably explains his ability to pay a rent of honey.
	SESTER OF HONEY. Usually 4, but sometimes 5 to 6 gallons, see R.E. Zupko, *A dictionary of English weights and measures from Anglo-Saxon times to the nineteenth century* (Univ. of Wisconsin Press, 1968), 155.
3,6	ROGER. A juror in Chesterton Hundred (Appx O). Cf. also B1 note.
4,1	1½ HIDES. MS thus, but the facsimile omits *i* before *hid(am)*.
	ARCHBISHOP LANFRANC. Of Canterbury, 1070-89. In 1086, he was holding Isleham following a dispute over its ownership between Picot the Sheriff (*32*) and the see of Rochester. It was confirmed by Lanfranc to Rochester in 1087, see VCH 353.
	GRANT AND SELL. ICC(8), 'withdraw from their land without their lord's permission'.
5	ABBOT OF ELY. The Ely Inquiry (IE, see above) also describes the holding of Ely Abbey in 1086.
5,1	3½ HIDES. IE(104), '3½ hides and ½ virgate'.
	5 SMALLHOLDERS. ICC(18), '5 smallholders with 5 acres'.
5,2	HARDWIN OF SCALES. See 26,50.
	GODWIN. ICC(18) adds 'the Abbot's man'; below 26,50, 'the Abbot of Ely's man'.
	SELL. ICC, 'withdraw'.
	SAERIC OF AUBERVILLE. ICC, 'Siric of Auberville'. Perhaps named from Auberville-la-Renaut (Seine-Inf.), OEB 104-105.
	1½ VIRGATES. IE(104) adds 'value 10s'.
	ST. WANDRILLE'S. See *10*, but the present holding is not mentioned there.
5,3	ICC(19) adds '1 hide and 3 virgates and 5 acres in lordship', shows that the 2 ploughs belonged to the villagers, and describes the smallholders as 'with 5 acres' and the meadow as '2 acres'. IE(104), '1 hide and 3 virgates in lordship'. IEBrev(168) lists 2 ploughs in lordship and 2 with the villagers.
5,4	2 PLOUGHS THERE. IEBrev(169) lists 3 ploughs in lordship.
	3 SMALLHOLDERS. ICC(23), '3 smallholders with 3 acres'.
5,5	HARDWIN. Of Scales, see 26,51.
	FROM THE ABBOT. ICC(23), 'from the King'. IE(105), 'under the Abbot'.
	IN LORDSHIP 2. See 26,51 note.
	6 OF THEM. ICC, '7 of them'.
	THEY PAID. ICC, 'they each gave'.
5,6	12 VILLAGERS. IEBrev(169), 18.
	12 SMALLHOLDERS. ICC(24), '12 smallholders with 10 acres'.
	PASTURE 32d. ICC, 'Pasture at 2 *orae*', see B10 note.
5,7	HARDWIN. ICC(24), 'Hardwin of Scales'. See 26,52.
	FROM THE ABBOT. ICC, 'from the King'. IE(105) 'under the Abbot'.
	CARTAGE AND ESCORT. ICC adds 'for the Sheriff'.
5,8	10 SMALLHOLDERS. IE(101), '10 cottagers'.
	1 BOAT...RIGHT. ICC(6), 'The mere of Soham Mere (*mara de saham lacus*) where 1 boat fishes by the customary right of 3 ports'. See also 6,3 and 14,73-74.

5,9	FROM THE FISH-NET TOLL. ICC(13), 'from the landing (*de appulatione*) of the boats'. FROM THE MARSH 6d. ICC, '3 ploughshares from the marsh or 6d'.
5,10	HARDWIN. Of Scales (ICC 14); see 26,53.
5,11	QUY. ICC(15). 'Quy and Stow'.
	PICOT. The Sheriff, see 32,2.
	LORDSHIP. ICC(16) adds '3½ hides in lordship' and '10 acres in lordship'.
	2 FREEMEN. IE(102) names them as Brictwin and Aelfric.
	WITHDRAW. IE, 'withdraw or sell'.
5,12	NONE...THERE. IEBrev(168) lists 2 ploughs in lordship.
	MEADOW...PLOUGHS. Cf. ICC(26), *pratum carrucis*.
5,13	1 HIDE. ICC(28), '1 hide and 8 acres'. This hide is not that mentioned at 35,2, see IE(103).
	2 VILLAGERS; 2 SMALLHOLDERS. IEBrev(168) lists only 2 villagers and credits them with 1 plough (as does IENV 174).
5,14	17 PLOUGHS. IE(103), 17½. An error in DB and ICC.
	8½ PLOUGHS. ICC(28), 8.
	22 VILLAGERS. ICC, 25.
	14 SMALLHOLDERS. ICC, '14 smallholders with their gardens alone'.
	MEADOW...PLOUGHS. Preferring here IE(103), 'meadow for all the village ploughs', to ICC, *pratum carruce*.
	TOTAL VALUE £18...AS MUCH. ICC, 'Total value £16'.
5,15	(WEST) WICKHAM. IE(103), '(West) Wickham and Streetly'.
	4 PLOUGHS. 4½ are listed.
	VALUE 65s. IE, £5.
5,16	BARHAM. In Linton parish (EPNS 109).
	ESCORT FOR THE SHERIFF. ICC(34), 'bodyguard in the Sheriff's service'.
5,17	HARDWIN. Of Scales, see 26,54.
	½ VIRGATE. ICC(36), 1 virgate, held by Durand from Hardwin. Durand was he of 26,11.
5,19	HARDWIN. Of Scales, see 26,55.
	SNELLING...LAND. ICC(38), 'Snelling holds this land and held it before 1066'.
5,20	6½ hides. ICC(43), 5½.
	PASTURE...LIVESTOCK. ICC has, in addition, 'pasture at 2 ploughshares'.
5,21	HARDWIN. Of Scales, see 26,56.
	UNDER THE ABBOT. ICC(43), 'under the King'; below 26,56, 'from the King'.
	DEFERMENT...ABBOT. The Abbot's claim had been deferred pending a judgement by the King.
	1 PLOUGH. IE(106) adds 'the plough is there'.
5,22	HARDWIN. Of Scales, see 26,57.
	HELD. Note the past tense, presumably showing that the 2 acres had been returned to Ely Abbey.
	PATRON NOR A DELIVERER. Hardwin held the 2 acres neither as a legitimate under-tenant nor as a legitimate landholder, having been given neither limited nor full tenure by any recognized process. See also 13,8 note.
5,23	4 SMALLHOLDERS. ICC(47),2.
5,24	The information in this section is described twice more in 32,5.
	ASSESSED IN HARSTON. IE(106) adds 'value 30s'.
	A FREEMAN. Named as Fridebert in 32,5 and ICC(46).
	REMAINED WITH THE ABBOT. ICC, 'remained (in) Harston'. Cf. 32,5 'remained with the Church'.
5,25	24 ACRES. ICC(47),29.
	PAY 2 PIGS. ICC(48), '2 pigs are fattened from the mills' (cf. 1,2 note); pasture for the village livestock'.
	TOTAL VALUE...£12. ICC, 'Total value £7; when acquired £12'.
5,26	HARDWIN. Of Scales, see 26,18.
	IE(107) adds 'value £3'.
5,27	Cf. 26,18 where this land is held by Hardwin of Scales; it may also be the same as that at 14,22.
	7 FREEMEN HOLD. *ten(unt)* is a DB error for *teneb(ant)*, cf. IE(107), '6 Freemen held', and below 26,18.

NOT WITHDRAW...WITH THE CHURCH OF ELY. IE, 'not grant or withdraw, except for 3 virgates, without his permission; and if they sold the other 3 virgates before 1066, the Abbot still had the jurisdiction'. IE adds 'value 40s'.

5,28 FENCES. IE(107), 'village fences'.

5,29 [IN ARMINGFORD HUNDRED]. Hundred rubric omitted in DB, but see ICC(63).
HARDWIN. Of Scales, see 26,27.

5,30 HARDWIN. Of Scales, see 26,29.

5,31 ...10 SMALLHOLDERS. Farley reproduces a gap in the MS before x, caused by an erasure. ICC(66), '10 smallholders, 3 cottagers'.
3 PLOUGHS. ICC,5. The DB figure is in error.

5,32 HARDWIN. Of Scales, see 26,30.

5,33 This section was added in the top margin of fo. 191 verso and its correct position indicated by an insertion mark.
GUY OF RAIMBEAUCOURT, 10 FREEMEN. See 31,1.

5,34 1 HIDE AND 1 VIRGATE. IE(109), '1½ hides'.
1½ PLOUGHS...POSSIBLE. IEBrev(169) lists 2 ploughs in lordship.
9 SMALLHOLDERS. IEBrev,12. This includes the 3 cottagers of DB.
1 MILL AT 2s 8d. ICC(66), '½ mill at 3s 8d'.

5,35 [IN WETHERLEY HUNDRED]. Hundred rubric omitted in DB, but see ICC(77).
HARDWIN. Of Scales, see 26,33.

5,36-37 HARDWICK. Described as part of Toft in ICC(87-88).

5,36 1½ HIDES. IE(110),1.

5,37 RALPH. ICC(88), Ralph Latimer.
LAND...OX. ICC adds 'wood for fences'.
CABE. ICC, Algar *Cappe*.

5,38 1 PLOUGH...2 POSSIBLE. IEBrev(169) lists 3 ploughs in lordship.
3 SMALLHOLDERS. ICC(88), '3 smallholders each with 10 acres'; IE(111), '3 smallholders with 15 acres'.
ON THE WOODLAND 2s. ICC, 2s a year.

5,39 ANSWERS FOR 7 HIDES. ICC(92), 'answered for 7½ hides before 1066; now for 5. The Abbot of Ely holds 7 of these 7½ hides'.

5,40 15 ACRES. IE(113) and IENV(177), '1 virgate'.

5,41 ANSWERS FOR 6½ HIDES. IE(113), 'answered for 10 hides before 1066; now for 5. Of these, the Abbot of Ely has 6½ hides'.
[ANOTHER] 1½ PLOUGHS POSSIBLE. IE, '2 ploughs possible'. IEBrev(169) lists 2 ploughs in lordship.
8 SMALLHOLDERS. IE, '2 smallholders each with 7 acres'. IEBrev lists 15 smallholders, representing the 8 smallholders and the 7 cottagers of DB.
2 POSSIBLE. Farley does not show a gap in the MS before *poss(unt)*, caused by an erasure.
7 COTTAGERS. IE, '3 cottagers with gardens, and 4 each with 5 acres'.

5,42 1 PLOUGH. IE(114) adds 'another possible'. IEBrev(169) lists 2 ploughs in lordship.

5,44 TWO HUNDREDS OF ELY. Distinguished here as E1 and E2 by reference to their order of appearance in DB. See further, below, note on the Hundreds.
ELY CHURCH...2 HIDES. IE(115), 'Whittlesey answered for 6 hides before 1066, and now [for the same]. St. Etheldreda holds 2 of these 6 hides'. For the other 4 hides, see 8,1.
1½ PLOUGHS. IEBrev(170) lists 2 ploughs in lordship.
8 VILLAGERS. IE adds 'each with 12 acres'.
FROM THE WEIR 2s. IE, 2s a year.

5,45 24 VILLAGERS. IE(116) adds 'each with 7½ acres'.
PRESENTATIONS. IE adds 'of fish'.

5,46 6 OXEN. IEBrev(170) lists 2 ploughs in lordship.
2 SMALLHOLDERS. IE(116) adds 'each with 8 acres'. IEBrev lists the 2 smallholders and the 2 cottagers as 4 smallholders.
MEADOW FOR 3 PLOUGHS. Farley prints *ii* in error for the *iii* of MS. IE and IEBrev add '2 slaves'.

5,47 15 VILLAGERS. IE(116), '13 villagers each with 9 acres, and 2 villagers each with 12 acres'.
8 COTTAGERS. IE adds 'each with 1 acre'.

5,48 1 PLOUGH. IEBrev(170) lists 2 ploughs in lordship.

	6 VILLAGERS. IE(117) adds 'each with 10 acres'.
	5 COTTAGERS. IEBrev describes them as 'smallholders'.
	3 SLAVES. Probably transposed in error (in the MS) before the ploughs.
	VALUE...£10 14s. IE, 'value £10 14s; when acquired £10'.
5,49	IT...LORDSHIP. IE(117), '1 plough and 1 hide less 6 acres in lordship'.
	1 VILLAGER. IENV(174) credits the village with 1 plough.
	4 COTTAGERS. IEBrev(170) describes them as 'smallholders'.
5,50	4 PLOUGHS. IEBrev(170) lists only 3 ploughs in lordship.
	VILLAGERS. IEBrev lists only 12.
	10 COTTAGERS. IE(117) adds 'each with 1 acre'.
5,51	3 PLOUGHS. IE(117),4; IEBrev(170),3.
	4 FREEMEN...9 VILLAGERS. IE, '9 villagers each with 10 acres and 4 other villagers with 1 virgate'.
	9 COTTAGERS. IE,10; IEBrev, '10 smallholders'.
5,52	LINDEN (END). In Haddenham parish (EPNS 234).
	2 FREEMEN. IE(117) adds 'who have 1½ virgates'.
	WITHDRAW. IE 'grant or sell without the Abbot's permission'.
	14 VILLAGERS. IE adds 'each with 8 acres'.
	2 PLOUGHS. IEBrev(170),5; IENV(175),2.
	9 COTTAGERS. IEBrev describes them as 'smallholders'.
	1 SMALLHOLDER. IE(117-118) adds 'with 4 acres'.
5,53	HILL (ROW). In Haddenham parish (EPNS 233).
	10 VILLAGERS. IE(118) adds 'each with 8 acres'.
	2 PLOUGHS. IEBrev(170),4.
5,54-55	WITHDRAW. IE(118), 'grant or sell without the Abbot's permission'.
5,55-63	In Hundred E2, see 5,44 note.
5,55	8 PLOUGHS. IEBrev(171) and IENV(175),4.
	17 COTTAGERS. IE(118),18; IEBrev describes them as '18 smallholders'.
	FISHERIES...EELS. IE adds '12d from the presentations of the fishery'.
5,56-57	PRESENTATIONS. IE(119) adds 'of fish'.
5,57	5 PLOUGHS...POSSIBLE. IEBrev(170) lists 8 ploughs in lordship.
	28 COTTAGERS. IE(119),18; IEBrev,28.
	ARPENTS. A French measure of extent, especially of vineyards; of uncertain and possibly variable size.
5,58	HAINEY...LAND. IE(119) adds 'which a servant held on a lease from the Abbot'.
5,59-63	COTTAGERS. Described by IEBrev(170) as 'smallholders'.
5,60	2 PLOUGHS...POSSIBLE. IEBrev(170) lists 3 ploughs in lordship.
	WITHDRAW. IE(119), as 5,54-55 note.
5,61	1 PLOUGH...POSSIBLE. IEBrev(170) lists 3 ploughs in lordship.
	SELL. IE(120), 'grant or sell'.
	UNDER THESE FREEMEN. IE puts the 9 villagers under the first 2 Freemen only.
5,62	GRANT. IE(120), 'grant or sell'.
	2 VILLAGERS...ACRES. IE, '2 villagers each with 15 acres and a third with 10 acres'; IEBrev(170), '3 villagers'.
5,63	IN LORDSHIP 2 HIDES. IE(120),2½.
	3 PLOUGHS...POSSIBLE. IEBrev(170) lists 4 ploughs in lordship.
	WITHDRAW. IE, 'sell'.
	6 PLOUGHS. IEBrev and IENV(174), 5.
6	LAND OF SAINT EDMUND. That is, of Bury St. Edmunds Abbey, Suffolk, founded in honour of King Edmund of East Anglia who was killed by the Vikings in 869.
6,1	TWO HUNDREDS OF ELY. See 5,44 note.
	16 ACRES. IE(116) states that the Abbot of Ely had their jurisdiction.
	OR OXEN. Added overline. Meadow for 4 oxen (half a plough-team) would tally with the arable land available (½ plough). The overline addition was perhaps meant as a tentative correction by the scribe of DB.
6,2	1 FISHERMAN. IE(119) states that the Abbot of Ely had his jurisdiction.
6,3	[IN STAPLOE HUNDRED]. Hundred rubric omitted in DB, but see ICC(7).
	MERE. See also 5,8 and 14,73-74.
7,2	LONGSTOWE. See also 26,41 where it is recorded that 3 Freemen of the Abbot of Ramsey

	held part of Longstowe in 1066.

	held part of Longstowe in 1066.
	GUY. A juror in Longstow Hundred (Appx L).
7,4	SLAVES. Placed, unusually, after the meadow; they may perhaps have been interlineated in the return, cf. 7,11 note. Cf. 7,7.
	WOOD FOR THE COURT'S HOUSES. Referring to the provision of wood for the repair of houses built within an enclosure or 'court' (presumably that belonging to the Abbot of Ramsey), cf. Huntingdonshire 7,8.
7,5	8 PLOUGHS. Only 2 listed.
7,7	MEADOW FOR 4 OXEN. Expressed by ICC(90) as 'Meadow for ½ plough'.
	SLAVES. As 7,4 note.
	ICC adds '3 smallholders' and 'Pasture for the village livestock'.
7,8	10 HIDES AND 3 VIRGATES. ICC(91) expresses this as '11 hides less 1 virgate'.
7,9	42½ VILLAGERS. Thus, in ICC(4). The ½ villager either held only half what each of the villagers held, or held land which was divided between two manors, see VCH 347.
7,11	TWO HUNDREDS OF ELY. See 5,44 note.
	LAND FOR 4 PLOUGHS. IE(116), 3.
	2 SLAVES. Written above the line and presumably intended to follow the ploughs, although this is not indicated. They may have been interlineated in the Abbot of Ramsey's return; cf. 7,4 and 7,7 where the slaves are placed, unusually, after the meadow.
	MEADOW FOR 4 PLOUGHS. IE, 3.
	PRESENTATIONS. IE adds 'of fish'.
	THIS LAND...CHURCH. IE adds 'and the Abbot of Ely has the jurisdiction'.
7,12	FISHERMEN. IE(118) states that the Abbot of Ely had their jurisdiction. Cf. 9,4.
8,1	TWO HUNDREDS OF ELY; 4 HIDES. See 5,44 notes.
	WHITTLESEY. Its Mere, on which the Abbot of Thorney had 2 boats (for fishing), is entered in Huntingdonshire 7,8.
	ABBOT OF ELY. Rather than 'Abbey', see IE(116). Cf. 5,44.
9,4	ELY HUNDRED [E1]. See 5,44 note.
	FISHERMEN. As 7,12 note.
10	ST. WANDRILLE'S. Near Caudebec (Normandy). See also 5,2.
10,1	LIVESTOCK. ICC(17), 'village livestock'.
	TOTAL VALUE £12. ICC, £10.
	EARL ALGAR. Of East Anglia 1051-52, 1053-57; of Mercia 1057-62. He was probably dead by 1066, see Harmer, ASWrits, 546-547.
11	CHATTERIS CHURCH. The Benedictine nunnery of the B.V.M., founded between 1007 and 1016 by Ednoth, successively Abbot of Ramsey and Bishop of Dorchester, see LibEl, 141. See also Hertfordshire 12.
11,2	CHATTERIS CHURCH. MS has cietriz with cecelie interlineated; cecelie is probably a copying error for æccl(es)ie. All the other references to the Church of Chatteris in this chapter contain the word æcclesia.
	THIS LAND...LORDSHIP. ICC(5-6), 'The nuns of Chatteris held this land before 1066 and hold (it) now'.
11,3	CHATTERIS CHURCH. ICC(75), 'St. Mary's, Chatteris'.
	5 COTTAGERS. ICC, '5 cottagers each with 5 acres'.
	IN THE LORDSHIP...CHURCH. ICC, 'in (the lands of) St. Mary's, Chatteris'.
11,4	4 COTTAGERS. ICC(76), '4 cottagers each with 9 acres'.
	VALUE IS AND WAS 30s. ICC, 'Total value 30s; when acquired 40s'.
	IN THE LORDSHIP...CHURCH. ICC, 'in (the lands of) St. Mary's Church, Chatteris'.
11,5	ICC(79, and MS) omits some text and erroneously conflates this section and 31,5 into a single holding.
	IT ALWAYS BELONGED...CHURCH. ICC, 'This land lies and lay in (the lands of) St. Mary's Church, Chatteris'.
11,6	[IN PAPWORTH HUNDRED]. Hundred rubric omitted in DB, but see ICC(91-92).
	LIVESTOCK. ICC(92), 'village livestock'.
	IN THE LORDSHIP...CHURCH. ICC, as 11,4 note.
12	COUNT OF MORTAIN. Robert, the half-brother of King William.
12,1	GRESTAIN. The Norman Abbey, founded by Count Robert's father, Duke Robert I.
	1 MILL, 26s 2d. ICC(39), '1 mill at 16s 2d'.

12,2-3   ROBERT. ICC(70,72), Robert Fafiton; for him, see *38*.

12,2-4   JUDICAEL. See also B1.

12,2   GRANT. ICC(70), 'grant and sell'.

12,4-5   MORIN. The name is OG in origin (OEB 190). His son Roger was a juror in Northstow Hundred (Appx N).

13   EARL ROGER. Of Montgomery, Earl of Arundel and Shrewsbury (d.1094).

13,1-2;   GODA. The name Goda was applied to both men and women (PNDB 263). The
   4-7   description 'Earl Algar's man' in ICC(54) does not necessarily show that the present Goda was masculine, since 'man' (*homo*), when used in connection with commendation, could be applied to both male and female. However, the present Goda has been taken to be the same as the female one at 26,22, as both held under Earl Algar.

13,1   IN LORDSHIP ½ HIDE...VIRGATE. This statement does not occur in ICC(52). ICC adds '2 slaves'.

13,2   LAND FOR 1 PLOUGH AND 2 OXEN. That is, for 1¼ ploughs.
          SHINGAY. See 13,4.
          HARDWIN OF SCALES. ICC(54), 'Alfred, Hardwin's man'; probably he of 26,20; 22 and 32,12 all in Armingford Hundred.

13,3   SELL. ICC(58), 'withdraw when he would'. ICC adds '1 smallholder'.

13,4   ANSWERS FOR 5 HIDES. ICC(59), 'answered for 5 hides before 1066; now for 4'.
          PAYMENTS OF THE MEADOW. ICC, 'payments'.

13,5   SHINGAY. See 13,4.

13,6   ST. EVROUL. The Norman Abbey, refounded in the late 11th century.
          BEFORE 1066 £8. ICC(65), £6.
          COULD SELL. ICC, 'could grant to whom she would and could withdraw'.

13,7   LESS. ICC(68) has a misreading of *unius* for *minus*, and consequently omits *minus* itself.
          SELL. ICC, 'grant or sell to whom she would before 1066'.

13,8   [IN WETHERLEY HUNDRED]. Hundred rubric omitted in DB, but see ICC(77).
          3 SMALLHOLDERS. ICC, '3 smallholders each with 5 acres'.
          WOOD. ICC, 'woodland' (*silva*).
          6 FREEMEN. Besides King Edward's man, ICC distinguishes 2 of the others as men of Edeva, 1 as a man of Archbishop Stigand, 1 as a man of Robert son of Wymarc, and 1 as a man of Earl Algar; all of them could withdraw (78).
          PICOT LENT...LANDS. Thus in ICC(77-78). Picot was the Sheriff, see *32*. The three men were presumably needed by the Earl's court to provide information on local custom; their temporary presence was however converted by the Earl's men into a more permanent obligation to attend, carrying with it some rights over their lands.
          WITHOUT A DELIVERER. Without any lawful transfer of tenure by a representative of the King. Cf. 5,22 note.

13,9   WRATWORTH. A lost village whose site is within the parishes of Orwell and Wimpole (EPNS 80).
          2 COTTAGERS. Not present in ICC(79).
          BEFORE 1066, 60s. ICC, 40s (but probably in error, reading *xl* for *lx*).
          6 FREEMEN. ICC(79-80), 5 Freemen, of whom 1 was Edeva the Fair's man, 1 was Archbishop Stigand's, 1 was Earl Algar's, 1 was King Edward's, and 1 was Robert son of Wymarc's.
          SELL...WOULD. ICC(80), 'withdraw or grant to whom they would'.

13,10   WHITWELL. In Barton parish (EPNS 73).
          3 FREEMEN. ICC(81), one of them was Archbishop Stigand's man, another was Edeva the Fair's.
          SELL...WOULD. ICC, 'withdraw'.

13,11   WOOD. ICC(83), as 13,8 note.
          WHEN ACQUIRED...£11. Not in ICC.
          AELFRIC...HELD THIS MANOR. ICC adds 'and Aelfric himself held 1 hide, 1 virgate and the third part of 1 virgate in this manor'.
          EARL WALTHEOF'S MAN. ICC describes Waltheof as *consul* rather than *comes*; it also states that his man held 1 hide.
          ABBOT OF ELY'S MAN. IE(110) names him as Edward and states that he held 1 hide; ICC, incorrectly, credits him with 2 hides.

	MAN OF ROBERT SON OF WYMARC. ICC states that he held 2 parts of 1 virgate.

MAN OF ROBERT SON OF WYMARC. ICC states that he held 2 parts of 1 virgate. Robert was Sheriff of Essex in 1066.

13,12   2 PARTS OF 1 VIRGATE. ICC(86) expresses this as '20 acres'.
       AELMER. ICC, Aelmer, son of Goding (*filius Godinci*).

14   COUNT ALAN. Of Brittany, son-in-law of King William. Most of his land in Cambridgeshire had previously been held by Edeva the Fair (see, 1,12 note).

14,1   FULBOURN. Count Alan also claimed another hide there, see 35,1.
       MEADOW FOR THE PLOUGHS. Cf. ICC(25), *pratum carrucis*.
       COULD NOT WITHDRAW. ICC adds 'without her permission'.

14,2   22 SMALLHOLDERS. ICC(27), '21 smallholders with 20 acres'. ICC adds '2 cottagers'.
       4 PLOUGHSHARES...CARTS 6d. DB appears to be in error here. ICC has '4 ploughshares from the marsh; 25s 6d from carts'.
       TOTAL VALUE...£18. ICC, 'Total value £19; when acquired £18'.
       4 ESCORTS. ICC, 'escorts'.

14,3   (CHERRY) HINTON. See 14,2.

14,3-4   WITHDRAW FROM HER. Rather than 'from it'.

14,4   ROBERT. Very probably Robert of Cherry Hinton, a juror in Flendish Hundred (Appx E).

14,5   2 HIDES AND 2½ VIRGATES. ICC(29), '2½ hides and ½ virgate'.
       8 VILLAGERS...SMALLHOLDERS. ICC(30) adds '5 villagers hold under him'.
       2 FREEMEN...THERE. ICC, '2 Freemen with 1 virgate were there'.

14,6   2 SMALLHOLDERS. ICC(30), '2 smallholders with 2 ploughs'.
       GODWIN. Young Godwin (ICC).

14,7   2 PLOUGHS. Farley prints *i* in error for *ii*.
       BEFORE 1066 £8. ICC(32), £7.
       EDEVA. The Fair (ICC).
       2 FREEMEN. ICC, '3 Freemen of hers had one virgate under her'; cf. following.
       1 FREEMAN. Not separately mentioned in ICC; cf. preceding.

14,8   ANSKETEL. ICC(33), Ansketel of Fourneaux (Calv.: arr. Caen; or La Manche: arr. St.-Lô; OEB 89).
       3 HIDES LESS ½ VIRGATE. ICC, '2½ hides less 1 virgate'.

14,9   EDEVA. The Fair (ICC 34).
       TWO LANDS. Referring to 14,8-9.

14,11   EDEVA. The Fair (ICC 34).
       1 FREEMAN WAS THERE. ICC states 'he was Alfsi Squtrebil's man; he could grant and sell to whom he would before 1066'. See also 15,1 note.

14,12   See B1,2.

14,13   TOTAL VALUE £7. ICC(34), £2.

14,14-16 EDEVA. The Fair (ICC 35).

14,15   BRIAN. Very probably Brian of Scales, a juror in Chilford Hundred (Appx F).

14,16   LESS ½ VIRGATE. ICC(35), 'less 1 virgate'.
       MEADOW...PLOUGH. Placed, unusually, before the population details.

14,17   2 MEN-AT-ARMS. ICC(37) names them as Ralph *de scamnis* (the same as Ralph Banks, see B1 note) and Ralph the Breton (*Brito*).
       5 SMALLHOLDERS. ICC, 2.
       WITHDRAW. ICC, 'grant and sell to whom he would'.

14,18   GERARD. Probably Gerard of Lorraine, see 14,19 note.
       FULL JURISDICTION. ICC(39), 'jurisdiction' (*sochum*).
       A MAN...EDEVA HELD THEM. Not in ICC.
       ICC adds (concerning the ½ virgate), 'A man (held it) from Earl Gyrth; he could not withdraw'. For Earl Gyrth's tenure of Whittlesford, see 41,7.

14,19   GERARD. Of Lorraine (ICC 42); he was a juror in Whittlesford Hundred (Appx G).
       FROM THE COUNT. Repeated by the scribe of DB, but underlined for omission.
       4 PLOUGHS. ICC, 3.
       EDEVA. The Fair (ICC).

14,20   BEFORE 1066, 25s. ICC(45), 20s.
       EDEVA. The Fair (ICC).

14,21   ODO. The Chamberlain (ICC 46).
       15s; 30s. *sol(idi)* was at first omitted in the MS after both *xv* and *xxx* but was subsequently

added after *xxx* (which stood at the end of the line).
4 FREEMEN. ICC(47), 3.

14,22   HARDWIN. Of Scales (ICC 49). The land described here may be the same as the 1½ hides and 6 acres at Shelford described at 5,27 and 26,18.
2 SMALLHOLDERS. ICC, '2 smallholders with 2 acres'.
EDEVA. The Fair (ICC). Her Freemen may have held this land from Ely Abbey (cf. 5,27 and 26,18); this would account for Hardwin of Scales's tenure of it from Count Alan.

14,23-24 AELMER. Of Bourn (ICC 56-57). Probably the same as Aelmer, son of Colswein (?14,28), a juror in Armingford Hundred (Appx J). See also 14,47; 49-52 notes.

14,23   1 HIDE AND 3 VIRGATES. Expressed by ICC(56) as '1½ hides and 1 virgate'.
LAND FOR 3 PLOUGHS. 4 listed.
5 SMALLHOLDERS. ICC, 6.
FOR FENCES. ICC, 'for repairing fences'.
UNDER EDEVA. Not in ICC.
WITHDRAW. ICC, 'withdraw and sell to whom he would'.

14,24   2½ VIRGATES. Expressed by ICC(57) as '½ hide and ½ virgate'.
GODIVA. ICC adds 'Edeva the Fair's man'; *homo* being used in its technical sense (see 13,1-2; 4-7 note).

14,25   FULKWY. DB *Fulcheius*. ICC(57), *Fulcheus*. Probably he of 14,45, since both 14,25 and 45 had previously been held by Leofeva under Edeva.
LEOFEVA. ICC, '*Lefhese* (with -*s*- in error for *f*), Edeva's man'. Cf. preceding, and 14,45 note.

14,26   ODO. The Chamberlain (ICC 58).
FOR FENCES. ICC, 'for repairing fences'.

14,27   10 COTTAGERS. ICC(61), '10 cottagers with their gardens'.
EDEVA. The Fair (ICC).
COULD SELL THEIR LAND. ICC, 'could withdraw and grant their land without her permission'.
THE OTHER 2...MEN. ICC adds 'held 1 virgate'.
THEY COULD SELL THEIR LAND. ICC, 'they could withdraw and grant their land without his permission'.

14,28   COLSWEIN. Probably the juror of this name in Armingford Hundred (Appx J) and father of Aelmer (14,23-24 etc.). Also at 14,30;32-33.
SELL. ICC(64), 'withdraw and grant to whom he would'.

14,29   RALPH. The priest (ICC 64).
1 VIRGATE. ICC, 1½.
ASGAR THE CONSTABLE. On him, see Harmer,*ASWrits* 560-561 (s.n. Esgar, the staller); Ellis ii 43.
GRANT AND SELL. ICC, 'withdraw and grant'.

14,30   BEFORE 1066, 6s. ICC(64), 5s.
ONE...MAN. ICC adds 'he held ½ virgate'.
ST. ETHELDREDA'S. Ely Abbey, see IE(108, 184). IE(108) values the Abbey's ½ virgate (? in error) at 40s.
SELL. ICC, 'grant and withdraw'.

14,31   ODO. The Chamberlain (ICC 64).
2½ VILLAGERS. Thus in ICC. Cf. 7,9 note.
EDEVA. The Fair (ICC).
WAS AND IS 1 FREEMAN. ICC, 'was a Freeman'.
EDEVA'S MAN HELD IT. ICC, 'The Freeman himself was Edeva's man'.

14,33   EDEVA. The Fair (ICC 67).
WITHDRAW FROM HER. ICC, 'grant and sell to whom he would without her permission'.

14,34   GODLAMB. DB *Gollan*, ICC(71) *Godlamb*. The name recurs at 41,8. It is quite often recorded in ME, see B. Selten in *English Studies* xlvi (2),4.
GODMAN. DB *Gogan*; ICC *gomanus*. OE *Godmann* (PNDB 265).
EDEVA. The Fair (ICC).

14,35   2 MILLS. It is not possible to locate them precisely, within Wetherley Hundred.
FOR £8. The meaning is probably 'when they answered for £8'.
EDEVA. ICC(72), 'Edeva the Fair, Count Alan's predecessor'.

14,36	ROBERT. The priest (ICC 72).
	IN LORDSHIP 1 PLOUGH. ICC(72–73), 1½.
	WHEN ACQUIRED 22s. ICC(73), 12s.
	EDEVA. The Fair (ICC).
14,37	SWAVESEY. See 14,55.
14,38	EDEVA. The Fair (ICC 73).
	HE COULD GRANT. Not in ICC.
14,39	PICOT. The Sheriff (ICC 75); see 32.
	2 SMALLHOLDERS. ICC, '2 cottagers'.
	32d. ICC expresses this as 2s 8d.
	MAN. ICC, 'Freeman'.
	HE FOUND...WOULD. ICC(75–76), 'he found one bodyguard; he could withdraw when he would before 1066'.
14,40	WHEN ACQUIRED...8s. Not in ICC(77).
	SELL HIS LAND. ICC, 'grant to whom he would'.
14,41	PICOT. The Sheriff (ICC 78); see 32.
	FROM THE COUNT. ICC, *de consule alano*.
	1½ PLOUGHS. ICC, '1 plough in lordship and ½ with the villagers'.
	THORBERN. DB *Turbernus*; ICC *Turbertus*. A juror in Wetherley Hundred (Appx K). Confusion between the names Thorbern and Thorbert (see PNDB 391) is common in the Norman period, as between Osbern and Osbert.
	EDEVA. The Fair (ICC).
14,42	WRATWORTH. See 13,19 note.
	LAND FOR ½ PLOUGH. ICC(80) adds 'it is there'.
	MEADOW FOR 4 OXEN. Expressed in ICC as 'for ½ plough'.
	GRANT AND SELL. ICC, 'withdraw when he would'.
14,43	WHITWELL. See 13,10 note.
	FULKWY. DB *Fulcheius*; ICC(82) *fulcuinus*. OG *Fulcwig*, (Forssner 98). The ICC form is probably for *Fulcuuius*.
	WOOD FOR FENCES. ICC, 'woodland (*silva*) for repairing fences'.
	GODWY. ICC, Godwin (*goduuinus*).
	FROM HER. ICC, 'without her permission'.
14,44	COUNT. ICC(82), *consul alanus*.
	2 HIDES AND 2½ VIRGATES. Expressed by ICC as '2½ hides and ½ virgate'.
	1 SMALLHOLDER. ICC, '1 smallholder with 15 acres'.
14,45	FULKWY. DB *Fulcuius*; ICC(83) *fulco*. Probably he of 14,25.
	FENCES. ICC, 'repairing fences'.
	LEOFEVA. ICC *Leshusa*, 'Edith the Fair's man'. Cf. 14,25 note.
	EDEVA. The Fair (ICC).
	FROM HER. ICC, 'whither she would'.
14,46	3 SMALLHOLDERS. ICC(84), '3 smallholders with 5 acres'.
	EDEVA. The Fair (ICC).
	GRANT AND SELL. ICC, 'withdraw'.
14,47	AELMER. Of Bourn (ICC 86). See 14,23–24 note.
	2s. ICC, 2s 8d.
	ALFGEAT. ICC, Alfgeat Ghost (*gaest*); see OEB 346.
	SELL. ICC, 'withdraw'.
14,48	Farley indicates the gap in the MS caused by a hole (later repaired).
	TOFT. The DB spelling *Tosth* (here and at 32,22 and 44,2) shares with the ICC form (87; *Tosta*), a misreading of insular long *s* for insular *f*.
	LAND FOR 4 PLOUGHS. ICC(in error) 53, with *LIII* for *IIII*.
	HAVE 4 PLOUGHS. Probably a DB error; ICC, '3 ploughs with the villagers'.
	WHEN ACQUIRED £3. Expressed by ICC as 60s.
	SWAVESEY. See 14,55.
	EDEVA. The Fair (ICC).
14,49	AELMER. Of Bourn (ICC 89); see 14,23–24 note.
14,53	GODA. See 13,1–2 note. There is no reason to suppose that the present Goda is feminine however.

14,55	SWAVESEY. See also 14,37; 48.
14,56	5 SMALLHOLDERS. ICC(90), 2.

14,55   SWAVESEY. See also 14,37; 48.

14,56   5 SMALLHOLDERS. ICC(90), 2.
BEFORE 1066, 27s. ICC, 17s.
EDEVA. The Fair (ICC).
SELL TO WHOM THEY WOULD. ICC, 'sell or grant'.

14,57   MEADOW...OXEN. ICC(92) adds 'pasture for 2 oxen'.
EDEVA. The Fair (ICC 93).
SELL. ICC, 'withdraw'.
ELY ABBEY. Cf. 5,39.

14,58   PICOT. The Sheriff (ICC 93); see 32.
5 PLOUGHS. 8 listed.
12 SMALLHOLDERS. ICC, '12 smallholders each with 5 acres'.
100s. ICC expresses this as £5.
BISHOP WULFWY'S MAN. ICC(94) adds 'he held ½ virgate'. For Bishop Wulfwy, see
3,2 note.
THE REST. ICC, '10'.
GRANT AND SELL THEIR LAND. ICC, 'withdraw'.

14,59   LANDBEACH. Not (as VCH 377) Waterbeach. The latter is distinguished by the OE prefix
ut- 'outlying' in DB, see 32,39 and 40,1; also EPNS (179,185).
FULL JURISDICTION. Both *soca* (see Technical Terms) and *saca* (from OE *sacu*, 'dispute,
crime', implying the right to determine lawsuits in a private court).
ELY ABBEY. Rather than 'Abbot of Ely'; cf. IE(114), 'of the jurisdiction of St.
Etheldreda, Ely'.
VIRGATE. IE gives its value as 5s.

14,60   [IN CHESTERTON HUNDRED]. Hundred rubric omitted in DB, but cf. 9,3. 26,49.
38,5. 41,15.
MONKS OF SWAVESEY. Belonging to the priory established by the Church of Saints
Sergius and Bachus, Angers, on land given by Count Alan, see VCH 355.

14,61   WIGHEN. ICC(10), Wighen Delamere (*de mara*). *Wighen* is the OFr form of the Old Breton
personal name *Wicon, Guegon*, see Reaney, s.n. Wigan. Wighen was perhaps related to
William Delamere, a juror in Cheveley Hundred (Appx B), where Wighen's man Wulfmer
was also a juror.
3 HIDES. ICC, 4.
EDEVA. The Fair (ICC).

14,62   ENISANT. Enisant Musard (*Enisam musardus*), ICC(11). *Enisant* is a Breton personal
name (Forssner 75); for *musardus*, 'stupid', see OEB 352.
HORWULF. DB and ICC, *Herulfus*; see 15,2 note.
EDEVA. The Fair (ICC).

14,63   GEOFFREY. ICC(13), *Gaufridus*; see 14,72 note.

14,64   HUSCARL. A juror in Staine Hundred (Appx C). *Huscarl* is here used as a personal
name (OEB 255-256; PNDB 296-297). See 41,11 for the appellative use.
WULFWY...VIRGATE. Not in ICC(14).

14,65   This section concerns land at Wilbraham, see ICC(15).

14,66   This section concerns land at Quy and Stow, see ICC(15).
2 PLOUGHS; IT IS THERE. DB has *ii* in error for *i*; ICC has 1.
VALUE...40s. Not in ICC.
GRIMBALD. ICC, Grimbald the Goldsmith (*aurifaber*).

14,67   ORDMER. A juror in Staploe Hundred (Appx A).
BADLINGHAM. In Chippenham parish (EPNS 190).
MILLING. *Molitura*, multure, payment for grinding corn.

14,68   EXNING. Now in Suffolk.
WYMARC. ICC(4), Wymarc, Count Alan's steward (*dapifer*); cf. 14,71.
1 PLOUGH. ICC, 3.
A FISHERY. Not in ICC.
WITHDRAW...PERMISSION. ICC, 'grant to whom he would'.

14,69   ALAN. A juror in Staploe Hundred (Appx A).
WHEN ACQUIRED £3. ICC(5), 70s.
WITHDRAW...PERMISSION. ICC, 'grant their land to whom they would'.

ESCORT OR 4d. ICC adds 'a year'.
14,70   VILLAGE LIVESTOCK. ICC(5), 'their livestock'.
1 FREEMAN. ICC names him as Edwin.
WITHDRAW...PERMISSION. ICC, 'grant to whom he would'. ICC adds 'He also paid 8d or cartage if the King came into the Sheriffdom'.
14,71   WYMARC. The Steward (ICC 7); see 14,68.
FREEMEN...PLOUGHS. The number of these Freemen is specified neither in DB nor in ICC; in the latter they are said to 'hold 2½ hides from (Wymarc) the steward himself'.
VALUE...70s. ICC(8) gives the value of the Freemen's land separately from that of the 1 hide held by Wymarc in lordship. The combined total however tallies with that given in DB.
3 FREEMEN. Edeva's men are named in ICC(7) as Dot and Wulfmer and are said to have held 1 hide; Anselm (*Anfelm'*), Earl Algar's man, held 1½ hides.
WITHDRAW...PERMISSION. ICC, 'withdraw with their land to what lord they would'.
FOUND ESCORT...SHERIFF. ICC(8), 'paid cartage or 8d a year to the King'.
14,72   GEOFFREY. In the present translation, both *Goisfridus* (OG *Gosfrid*) and *Galfridus* (OG *Galfrid*) are given as 'Geoffrey', the modern form of both names (Forssner 101–102, 125–126).
4 OXEN. Expressed in ICC(8) as '½ plough'.
MEADOW...OXEN. ICC adds 'pasture for their livestock'.
WITHDRAW. ICC(8–9), 'withdraw with their land to what lord they would'.
CARTAGE...SHERIFF. ICC(9), 'cartage or 8d a year'.
14,73-74 SOHAM MERE. O.S. TL 57 73. See also 5,8 and 6,3.
14,73   ADESTAN. ICC(7), *Alstanus*. Probably OE *Æðelstan*.
8 SMALLHOLDERS. ICC states that they 'hold nothing but gardens'.
HAVE 2 PLOUGHS...POSSIBLE. ICC credits the villagers with 3 ploughs and says that a fourth is possible.
EELS. ICC adds 'from the fish pond (*piscina*)'.
[FOR]...DUES. DB has omitted *per*, cf. 14,74. MS has a gap caused by erasure here, not shown by Farley.
14,74   3 HIDES. Not in ICC(9).
28s. ICC, 38s.
4,250. ICC has the misreading *animal'* for *mill'*.
BEFORE 1066 £6. So in MS. ICC, £16. DB is probably in error here.
14,75   9 SMALLHOLDERS. ICC(18), '9 smallholders with 9 acres'.
3 FREEMEN. ICC names them as Horwulf (*Horulfus*; see 15,2 note; cf. also 14,62 note), Edeva's man, who held ½ hide; Alstan, Ordgar's man, who held ½ hide less 10 acres; and Viking, Earl Harold's man, who held 1 hide.
14,76   GRIM. Possibly Grim of West Wratting, a juror in Radfield Hundred (Appx D).
14,77   2 MEN-AT-ARMS. ICC(19) gives the tenant of this holding as Geoffrey (*Gaufridus*).
14,78   HAVE 4 PLOUGHS. ICC(20), 4½.
MEADOW, 4 ACRES. ICC, 'meadow for 4 oxen'.
PARK...BEASTS. A hunting reserve; cf. 41,1.
14,79-80 WYMARC. ICC(21), Wymarc, Count Alan's steward.
14,80   This holding was at Weston Colville, see ICC(22). See also ESf.
HAVE 1 PLOUGH. ICC, 2.
£3. ICC expresses this as 60s.
COULD NOT WITHDRAW. ICC, 'could not grant without permission'.
14,81   60s. ICC(24) expresses this as £3.
ONE OF THEM. ICC names him as Guthlif (*gothlif*); the name is ODan, see PNDB 279. The other 'Freeman' is not named in ICC, but was perhaps Leofled of 14,82, see note.
14,82   AELMER. ICC(25), 'Aelmer, Count Alan's man'.
40 ACRES. ICC(in error), 43 ploughs (with *car'* for *acr'*).
THE OTHER LAND. The meaning of this is unclear, but if Leofled is the other 'Freeman' of 14,81, then it refers to her land in West Wratting.
[15]   Misnumbered in DB as 25, see L note.
COUNT EUSTACE. Of Boulogne, brother-in-law of King Edward.
15,1   30 VILLAGERS. ICC(41) adds 'and 11 of these 30 villagers each hold ½ hide, 1 holds 1 virgate and 1 holds 1 hide'.

	ALFSI. ICC, Alfsi Squtrebil. The byname is OWScand *Skítr-Bíldr*, 'dirty Bíldr', OEB 225. Cf. 14,11 note.
15,2	2 VILLAGERS WITH 6 SMALLHOLDERS. ICC(41), '2½ villagers; 5 smallholders and 3 virgates. 1 slave'.
	ARNULF. Probably Arnulf of Ardres, who succeeded Horwulf in 15,3.
	HORWULF. DB *Herulfus*; ICC *Horulfus*. The name is OE *Heoruwulf* (PNDB 289).
	GUY. Of Anjou (*andegauensis*), ICC(42).
	½ HIDE. ICC, 1.
	INGVAR. See 34,1 note.
	SELL. ICC, 'grant and sell to whom he would'.
15,3	ARNULF OF ARDRES. He also held from Count Eustace in Bedfordshire (15,1–2;4–6) and probably came from Ardres (Pas-de-Calais: arr. Saint-Omer), see OEB 69. Cf. 15,2 note.
	1½ VIRGATES. ICC(50), ½.
	MEADOW...PLOUGHS. ICC, *pratum carrucis*.
	HORWULF. DB *Herulfus*; ICC(51) *Horulfus*. See 15,2 note; and 32,6.
15,4	2 OF WHOM ... MEN. ICC(71) adds 'held 2 hides and 1 virgate'.
	COULD SELL. ICC, 'they could grant their land to whom they would'.
	HE...LAND. ICC, 'he could grant his land to whom he would'.
[16]	Misnumbered in the text as 26, see L note.
	CANONS OF BAYEUX. This is their only holding in DB.
[17]	Misnumbered in the text as 27, see L note.
	WALTER GIFFARD. Earl of Buckingham, he held extensive lands in Buckinghamshire (*14*).
17,1	3 PLOUGHSHARES. ICC(12), 4.
	WHOSE MAN HE WAS. ICC, 'whose Holding (*honor*) it was'; the scribe of ICC has probably misread *homo* as *honor* here.
17,2–3	SWAFFHAM (Bulbeck). See following note, and 17,3 note.
17,2	HUGH. Of Bolbec (ICC 12). Named from Bolbeck (Seine-Inf.: arr. Le Havre), OEB 73. He also held lands from Walter Giffard in Buckinghamshire (14,1–2;16) and Bedfordshire (16,1;3–4).
	30s LESS 4d. ICC, 30s less 3d.
	ELY. The Ely Abbey holding here is valued at £8 in IE(102).
	3 FREEMEN. Named in ICC as Huscarl, Brictwin and Alfsi.
	THESE MEN...2 HIDES. Not in ICC.
17,3	HUGH. Of Bolbec (ICC 14). See 17,2 note.
	4 SMALLHOLDERS. ICC, 4 oxen (with *bob(us)* for *bord(ariis)*). Cf. 25,5 note;41,10 note.
	VALUE...10s. ICC, 'Value 10s; when acquired 5s'.
17,4	HARLTON. See also 17,6.
	MEADOW...PLOUGHS. ICC(74) adds 'woodland for repairing fences'.
	5 FREEMEN. ICC adds '4 of them were Aki's men and held 1½ virgates. The fifth was Arnulf's man; he held ½ virgate'.
	SELL...LAND. ICC, 'withdraw whither they would'.
17,5	AKI. ICC(75), Aki the Dane (*achillus danau'*). Perhaps not he of 17,4. Cf. 17,6.
	GRANT...SELL. ICC, 'withdraw when he would'.
17,6	WALTER. Son of Aubrey (ICC 79).
	VALUE...2s. ICC, 'Value 2s; when acquired as much; before 1066, 2s 8d'.
	AKI. ICC adds 'he could grant to whom he would'. Probably he of 17,5.
	BELONGS TO. ICC, 'lies in (the lands of)'.
	HARLTON. See 17,4.
[18]	Misnumbered in the text as 28, see L note.
	WILLIAM OF WARENNE. Later created Earl of Surrey by William II.
18,1	WALTER OF GRAND-COURT. Named from Grand-Court (Seine-Inf.: arr. Neufchatel), OEB 90. His man William was a juror in Radfield Hundred (Appx D).
18,2	ABBOT OF CLUNY. In Burgundy. Ralph of Cluny was a juror in Radfield Hundred (Appx D).
	2 ACRES. ICC(21), 22.
	14 SMALLHOLDERS. ICC, 13.
	3 PLOUGHS. ICC, 4. Probably a DB error.
18,3	2 PLOUGHS...POSSIBLE. IE(104) lists 4 ploughs in lordship.

TOKI. ICC(22) adds 'William's predecessor'.

SEPARATE...CHURCH. ICC, 'grant without the Abbot's permission or separate (it) from the Church'.

IT BEING. Translating *q(ua)m...erat*, although this is a grammatical error in DB for *quae...erat*. Cf. ICC, *Hec terra iacuit in dominica firma sancte Æðeldrede de ely. t.r.e.*

WITHDRAW FROM HIM. IE(105), 'withdraw without permission'.

18,4   WALTER. Of Grand-court (ICC 23); see 18,1 note.

18,5   IT FOUND 1 CARTAGE. ICC(24), 'this land found cartage'.

18,6   TOKI. ICC(32–33) adds 'William of Warenne's predecessor'.

18,7   WILLIAM HOLDS. ICC(50), 'William of Cailly holds from William of Warenne'. This William was named from Cailly (Seine Inf.: arr. Rouen) and was a juror in Thriplow Hundred (Appx H).

      5 PLOUGHS. ICC, 6.

      9 VILLAGERS...PLOUGHS. ICC adds '2 slaves'.

      4 PLOUGHSHARES. IE (107, in error), 4 Freemen (*sochem'*).

      SEPARATE...CHURCH. ICC adds 'without the monks' permission'.

      FREDERICK, WILLIAM'S BROTHER. ICC, 'Frederick, William of Warenne's brother'. He was apparently William's brother-in-law, see VCH 355.

18,8   NICHOLAS. He was a juror in Staploe Hundred (Appx A).

      7 VILLAGERS. ICC(1), 6.

      5 SMALLHOLDERS. ICC, '1 priest'.

      TOKI. ICC, *Thobillus* (probably for *Thokillus*).

      1 FREEMAN. ICC names him as Godric.

      OR 8d. ICC(2), 'oats, 57 pennies (*nummi*)', with *auena(m)LVII* in error for *auera(m) f.viii.*

      GRANT AND SELL. ICC, 'grant without his lord's permission'.

18,9   [E2]. See 5,44 note.

      6 FISHERMEN. IE(119) states that the Abbot of Ely had their jurisdiction.

[19]   Misnumbered in the text as 25. See L note.

      RICHARD SON OF COUNT GILBERT. Richard of Tonbridge. His wife Rohais occurs in Hertfordshire (*42a*) and Huntingdonshire (*28*).

19,1   WILLIAM. The Breton (*brito*; IE 111). He held part of Eynesbury (Huntingdonshire 28,1) from Richard's wife.

      WITHDRAW FROM HIM. IE, 'grant or sell his land without his permission'.

      RECEIVED. IE, 'took' (*sumpsit*).

19,4   HARDWIN. Of Scales (ICC 62); see *26*.

      4 OXEN. ICC expresses this as '½ plough'.

      GRANT. ICC(63), 'withdraw and grant'.

      RALPH WADER. ICC, 'Earl Ralph'. Earl of East Anglia; with Earl Waltheof (see 1,6 note) and Earl Roger of Hereford, he rebelled against King William in 1075 and ended his life in exile. The name 'Wader', DB *Waders*, may be a place-name, see OEB 119.

[20]   Not numbered in the text, but see L note.

      ROBERT OF TOSNY. Named from Tosny (Eure), see OEB 116.

20,1   GILBERT. ICC(42) adds 'with the beard' (*cum barbo*).

      ULF. ICC adds 'Robert's predecessor'.

[21]   Not numbered in the text, but see L note.

      ROBERT GERNON. The byname is from OFr *grenon* 'moustache', OEB 314–315.

21,1   THURSTAN. ICC(29) adds 'son of Richard'.

      6 SLAVES. ICC, 7.

      12 PIGS. So MS; the facsimile has *xi*.

      BEFORE 1066, 40s. Not in ICC.

21,2   [IN WHITTLESFORD HUNDRED]. Hundred rubric omitted in DB, but see ICC(43).

      BEFORE 1066, 6s. ICC, 6s 8d.

      AELFRIC...WITHDRAW. ICC, 'Aelfric Kemp held this land'. See 21,3 note.

21,3   MEADOW...PLOUGHS. ICC(44), 'meadow for 11 ploughs'.

      AELFRIC KEMP. The byname is either OE *cempa* 'warrior' or a derivative of OWScand *kampr* 'moustache', see OEB 243. See also 21,1 note and 25,2.

21,4   1 COTTAGER. ICC(46) adds 'with his garden'.

      SELL. ICC, 'grant to whom he would'.

	KING EDWARD. Farley shows the gap in the MS, caused by an erasure, after *rege*.
21,5	2½ VIRGATES. ICC(74), 1½.
	3 COTTAGERS. ICC adds 'with 1 acre'.
	15 FREEMEN...SHERIFF. ICC, '15 Freemen, King Edward's men, held 4 hides and 1½ virgates and 12½ acres and found 4 escorts for the King's Sheriff'. The scribe of ICC has probably misread 'acres' (*acras*) for 'cartages' (*aueras*).
	2 HIDES AND ½ VIRGATE. ICC(75), '2 hides less ½ virgate'.
	EDRIC SNIPE. DB *pur*, see OEB 364. He is described by ICC(74) as 'King Edward's thane'; see also 31,2.
	COULD SELL. ICC, 'could withdraw'.
	CHURCH OF CHATTERIS. See *11*. Cf. 11,3.
21,6	SELL...LAND. ICC(79), 'withdraw'.
21,7-8	PICOT. The Sheriff, see 21,9.
21,7	LONGSTANTON. Cf. 36,1.
21,9	PICOT THE SHERIFF. See *32*.
	MARRIAGE PORTION. DB distinguishes *maritagium*, provided by the bride's father, from *dos*, the dowry provided by the husband. Cf. 25,1-2 note.
[22]	Misnumbered in the text as 20. See L note.
	GEOFFREY DE MANDEVILLE. Ancestor of the Earls of Essex. The place from which he was named has not been positively identified, see OEB 96.
22,1	WILLIAM. ICC(26) adds 'Geoffrey de Mandeville's nephew'.
	ASGAR. The Constable (ICC).
	GRANT. ICC, 'grant and sell'.
22,2	ROGER. ICC(39), Roger of Sommery (Seine-Inf.: arr. Neufchatel; see OEB 115). Also at 22,8 note.
	26s 8d. ICC, 26s 2d.
	SIGAR. ICC adds 'Asgar's steward (*dapifer*)'. A juror in Thriplow Hundred (Appx H); cf. 22,3-4.
	WITHOUT...PERMISSION. ICC, 'to whom he would'.
22,3-4	SIGAR. Probably he of 22,2, see note.
22,3	LIVESTOCK. ICC(44), 'village livestock'.
22,4	VALUE...£4. ICC(45), 'In total, value £4; when acquired £4; before 1066 £4 10s'.
	JURISDICTION...LORD. ICC, 'Asgar had his jurisdiction'.
22,5	TESTIFY. Inserted two lines too early in the MS.
22,6	A SHERIFF. ICC(2), 'a Sheriff of this Sheriffdom'; probably Ordgar, see below.
	19 VILLAGERS. ICC, 29.
	PASTURE...LIVESTOCK. ICC adds '1 mill'.
	FISH POND. ICC, *piscina*.
	ORDGAR. See also 28,1.
	FORDHAM. Cf. 1,2-3 where fines are also mentioned in connection with Fordham.
	WRIT. The meaning of *breue* here may still be the general sense of OE *(ge)writ*, 'written evidence, writing, letter' rather than more specifically 'sealed writ'.
	COMMISSIONER. ICC(3), 'messenger' (*nuntius*).
22,7	RICHARD. A juror in Armingford Hundred (Appx J).
	3 VIRGATES. Expressed in ICC(54) as '½ hide and 1 virgate'.
	5 COTTAGERS. ICC adds 'with 5 acres'.
	3 OTHER COTTAGERS. ICC, '3 cottagers with 3 acres'.
	LIVESTOCK. ICC, 'village livestock'.
	GODWIN. ICC, Godwin Wombstring (*Wabestrang*); see OEB 357.
	SELL. ICC(55), 'grant and sell to whom he would'.
22,8	ROGER. Of Sommery (ICC 73); see 22,2 note.
	GRANT OR SELL. ICC, 'withdraw whither he would'.
	JURISDICTION...LORD. ICC, 'Asgar had the jurisdiction'.
22,9	VALUE IS AND WAS 20s. ICC(76), 'In total, value 20s; when acquired 23s'.
	GRANT OR SELL. ICC, 'grant to whom he would'.
22,10	SELL. ICC(78), 'withdraw'.
[23]	Misnumbered in the text as 21, see L note.
	GILBERT OF GHENT. Named from Gent (Flanders), see OEB 89.

23,1;4	(FEN) STANTON. See Huntingdonshire 21,1: held by Gilbert of Ghent in 1086, but by Ulf in 1066.
23,1-6	ULF. He is named in ICC(91) as Ulf Fenman (*fenesce*). See also Huntingdonshire (B1;21,1).
23,6	GRANT AND SELL. ICC(91), 'withdraw whither he would'.
[24]	Misnumbered in the text as 22, see L note.
24,1	HUGH. ICC(93), Hugh Hubald (*hubolt*). He held lands in Bedfordshire (44,1-4). GRANT OR SELL. ICC, 'withdraw'.
[25]	Misnumbered in the text as 23, see L note. EUDO SON OF HUBERT. The King's Steward.
25,1-2	PIROT. DB *Pirot'*, ICC(36,38) *Picot'*. Almost certainly a DB error, a misreading of (horned) *c* as insular *r*. For Picot, see *32*; other land held by him at Babraham and Pampisford is described at 1,15 and 32,3. The same misreading occurs in Bedfordshire (21,14-15 (also in Eudo son of Hubert's holding); 24,18;24). The entry at Bedfordshire 24,18 refers to Picot's wife's marriage-portion, as does 21,9 above.
25,1	ORA. See B10 note. AELFRIC. ICC(37), Aelfric Kemp; see 25,2. GRANT AND SELL. ICC, 'grant'.
25,2	AELFRIC KEMP. On the name, see 21,3 note. See also 25,1 note; 25,3 note.
25,3	PIROT. DB *Pirot'*, also ICC(39); but see 25,1 note. AELFRIC. ICC, Aelfric Kemp; see 25,2 note. WITHDRAW. ICC, 'withdraw without his permission'.
25,4-6	HUMPHREY. See 25,7 note.
25,4;6-7	EARL GYRTH. Of East Anglia, brother of King Harold; killed at Hastings in 1066.
25,5	2 SMALLHOLDERS. ICC(56), '2 oxen'; probably a misreading of *boues* for *bord'*. Cf. 17,3 note.
25,7	HUMPHREY. Of Anneville (ICC 82); see also 25,4-6;8 and 31,3 note. He was a juror in Armingford Hundred (Appx J). FENCES. ICC, 'repairing fences'. VALUE...100s. ICC(82-83), 'In total, value 100s; when acquired 100s; before 1066, 110s'.
25,8	HUMPHREY. See 25,7 note. AELMER. ICC(86) adds 'son of Goding'. WITHDRAW. ICC 'grant to whom he would'.
25,9	WULFMER OF EATON. A thane of King Edward's; see Bedfordshire (21,1;5-6; 9-10; 14-15; 17) where Eudo also took over several of Wulfmer's manors. See also 32,10. 42,1. (LITTLE) GRANSDEN. See 5,38. The Abbot of Ely's 1 virgate at Gamlingay is valued at 3s in IE(111). LISOIS OF MOUTIERS. Also mentioned in connection with one of Eudo's manors in Bedfordshire (21,13). He probably took his name from Moutiers-Hubert (Calvados), see OEB 102.
[26]	Misnumbered in the text as 24; see L note. HARDWIN OF SCALES. The place from which he took his name has not been identified, see OEB 87. Summaries of his lands in Cambridgeshire and Hertfordshire are given in IE(121, 123-124), and a list of Cambridgeshire lands taken by him from the Church of Ely is given in IEBrev(176-177).
26,2	ICC(6) shows that this section refers to land at Burwell. THORK. The name is probably a reduced form of ON *Thorkell*, see PNDB 389. WITHDRAW. ICC, 'grant his land'. ESCORT OR 4d. ICC adds 'a year'.
26,3	7 VILLAGERS. ICC(17), 6. 16 FREEMEN. ICC, 8. HELD. *inuenerunt* (cf. following line) corrected to *tenuerunt*. GRANT AND SELL. ICC, 'grant to whom they would'.
26,4	ICC(19) adds '1 smallholder'.
26,5	HAROLD. ICC(21), Earl Harold. 1 ESCORT. ICC, 'escorts'. Perhaps each of the Freemen supplied an escort.
26,7	THIS LAND...ESCORT. ICC(22), 'One (of the 2 Freemen) found cartage, the other (found) escort'. WITHDRAW. ICC adds 'without his permission'.

26,8   2 SMALLHOLDERS THERE; TOKI AND WITHGAR HELD IT. ICC(23) has '2 men there', and goes on to identify them as Toki and Withgar. They perhaps represent Englishmen who remained after 1066 in a depressed status in the village of which they were formerly lords.

26,9   5 VILLAGERS HOLD ½ HIDE. ICC(30) has Hardwin holding the ½ hide himself and the 5 villagers holding meadow for ½ plough.
24 PIGS. ICC, 29.
4 MEN...ESCORTS. ICC names one of these men as Godwin of Linacre (in Horseheath parish; EPNS 108), who held ½ virgate and found (1) escort. The other three are described as Freemen, who held 1 virgate and found 1 cartage and 1 escort.
AUBREY DE VERE'S PREDECESSOR. Wulfwin, King Edward's thane, see 29,8 and 29,1 note.

26,10   BEFORE 1066, 5s 4d. ICC(33), 5s.
1 CARTAGE. ICC, '1 cartage and 1 escort'.

26,11   DURAND. See 5,17 note.
½ HIDE. ICC(36) expresses this as '2 virgates'.
18s 8d. ICC, 18s (*xviii.f*).
OF THE KING'S HOLDING. According to ICC, the 4 Freemen held from King Edward. Cf. EE1.

26,12   1 VIRGATE. ICC(38), ½. ICC adds 'Land for 2 oxen'.
65d. ICC, 4 *ora* (64 or 80 pence; see B10 note).
COULD NOT WITHDRAW. ICC reads 'could withdraw' and adds 'they found escorts'.

26,14   HINXTON. Cf. EE1.
GRANT...WOULD. ICC(41), 'withdraw without his permission'.

26,15   ICKLETON. DB *Inchelintone* is in error for *Hichelintone*.
32d. ICC(41), 2 *ora*; see B10 note.
SELL. ICC, 'grant his land to whom he would'.

26,16   PAYNE. Very probably Hardwin of Scales's steward, a juror in Whittlesford Hundred (Appx G).
4 SMALLHOLDERS. ICC(43), 3.
COULD SELL...LANDS. ICC, 'could withdraw when (*qn̄* for *quando*) they would'.
EARL ALGAR'S MAN. Not mentioned in ICC.
EDEVA'S MAN. ICC has 'Edeva the Fair's man' and says that he held 3 virgates.
SELL... LAND. ICC, 'withdraw'.

26,17   ABBOT OF ELY. Cf. 5,23. The Abbot's 3 virgates are valued at 40s in IE(106).
COULD SELL...ABBOT. ICC(47), 'could withdraw when he would and sell his land without the jurisdiction'.
WITHDRAW...LAND. ICC, 'grant and sell to whom he would'.

26,18   8 PLOUGHS. The 1 plough in lordship plus the 7 belonging to the villagers. Given here as a total to draw attention to the excess of ploughs over capacity (6 ploughs and 2 oxen).
4 SMALLHOLDERS. ICC(48) adds 'with 4 acres'.
LIVESTOCK. ICC, 'village livestock'.
VALUE £6. ICC, 'In total, value £6; when acquired £7'.
2½ HIDES...TESTIFIES. See 5,26.
7 FREEMEN...ELY. See 5,27 and cf. 14,22.
WHITTLESFORD. See 41,7.

26,19   2 *ORA*. ICC(52), '2s 8d' (that is, 32d). See B10 note.
7 FREEMEN. ICC, 6.
GRANT...LAND. ICC, 'withdraw'.

26,20   (GUILDEN) MORDEN. For this identification, cf. ICC(55).
ALFRED. See 13,2 note.
1 COTTAGER. ICC adds 'with 3 acres'.
SELL. ICC, 'grant or sell his land'.
LITLINGTON. See 26,23.

26,21   ALFLED. ICC(58), *lefleda*, 'Archbishop Stigand's man' (*homo*; cf. 13,1-2;4-7 note).
PATRONAGE. Farley prints the first abbreviation-mark above *c* of *co(m)m(en)data*; MS has it above *o*. See 26,22 also.
A MAN. ICC names him as Aelfric.
HE...SELL. ICC, 'he could grant to whom he would'.

26,22	LAND...OXEN. ICC(59) adds '3 oxen there. 2 smallholders'.
	GODA. See 13,1–2 note. Although ICC has 'Goda, Earl Algar's man (*homo*), the feminine sex is at least implied here by the adjective *commendata* in DB.
26,23	2½ VIRGATES. ICC(59) expresses this as '½ hide and ½ virgate'.
	1 SMALLHOLDER. ICC adds '1 cottager. Meadow for 4 oxen'.
	ALGAR...½HIDE. ICC(60) adds 'he could withdraw'.
	HE...ICKLETON. ICC, 'he (Alfwy) could not grant or sell (it) outside Litlington Manor'. Ickleton is a DB error, as in 1,20.
26,24	2 MEN-AT-ARMS. ICC(60) names them as Ralph and Robert.
	2 OTHER FREEMEN. According to ICC, these held the land (apart from 1 virgate) before 1066.
26,25	2 SMALLHOLDERS. ICC(62), '1 smallholder; 2 cottagers'.
	GRANT...WOULD. ICC, 'they could (?withdraw) whither they would (*potuerunt qua parte uoluerunt*), without his permission'.
26,26	1 HIDE AND 3 VIRGATES. ICC(62) expresses this as '1½ hides and 1 virgate'.
	3 VILLAGERS. ICC, 2.
	5 COTTAGERS. ICC adds 'with their gardens'.
	ARCHBISHOP STIGAND'S MAN. Named by ICC as 'Thorbert the priest'. Hardwin of Scales also took over a holding of Thorbert's at Clothall in Hertfordshire (37,3).
26,27	Cf. 5,29 which describes the same holding.
	15 COTTAGERS. ICC(63) adds 'with their gardens'.
	THORBERN. Thorbern White, see 5,29. ICC, Thorbert. See 14,41 note.
26,29	Cf. 5,30 referring to the same holding.
	VALUE...2s. IE(108) gives the value as 3s.
	AELMER. ICC(66),'Aelmer the priest'.
	SELL. ICC, 'withdraw'.
26,30	Cf. 5,32 referring to the same holding.
	HUGH. ICC(66), Hugh *pedeuolt* (see OEB 325–326); a juror in Armingford Hundred, see Appx J. Cf. 26,33 note.
	MONASTERY. ICC, 'church' (*ecclesia*).
26,31	1 VIRGATE. ICC(67–68), ½.
	LIVESTOCK. ICC(68), 'village livestock'.
	GRANT AND SELL. ICC, 'withdraw when he would'.
26,32	[IN WETHERLEY HUNDRED]. Hundred rubric omitted in DB, but see ICC(76).
	THEY ARE THERE. ICC, 'the ploughs are there'.
	EARL ALGAR'S MAN. ICC states that he held ½ hide and ½ virgate.
	KING EDWARD'S MEN...ESCORTS. ICC states that they held 1½ hides and that it was they who provided the cartages and escorts.
	THEY...LAND. ICC, 'all of them could grant'.
26,33	Cf. 5,35 referring to the same holding.
	HUGH. ICC(77), Hugh *pedeuolt*; see 26,30 note.
26,34	4 COTTAGERS. ICC(78) adds 'each with 5 acres'.
	MEADOW FOR 6 OXEN. ICC, 'meadow for 1 plough'.
	WOOD...FENCES. ICC, 'woodland (*silva*) for repairing fences'.
	WALTHEOF. ICC, Earl Waltheof.
	THEY...ESCORTS. According to ICC, only King Edward's man found the 2 escorts.
26,35	WRATWORTH. See 13,9 note.
	WALTHEOF'S MAN. ICC(80), 'Earl Waltheof's man'; he held ½ hide and 2 parts of 1 virgate.
	ROBERT SON OF WYMARC'S MAN. He held the third part of 1 virgate (ICC).
	GRANT AND SELL. ICC, 'withdraw whither they would'.
26,36	WHITWELL. See 13,10 note.
	R(OBERT). See 26,39.
	WOOD...FENCES. ICC(81) as 26,34 note.
	5 VIRGATES. ICC(82) expresses this as '1 hide and 1 virgate'.
26,37	WITHDRAW. ICC(85), 'grant or sell to whom he would without his permission'.
26,38	MEADOW. ICC(86), 'meadow for 3 oxen'.
26,39	GRANT. ICC(86), 'withdraw'.

26,41	ABBOT OF RAMSEY. Cf. 7,2.
26,42	THESE MEN. Farley prints *Iste* in error for *Isti* of MS.
26,48	RALPH. Perhaps Ralph of Feugères, a juror in Papworth Hundred (Appx M).

26,48 continues:
LIVESTOCK. ICC(91), 'village livestock'.
BEFORE 1066, 50s. ICC, 60s.
[10 FREEMEN]. Omitted in DB, but see ICC.
1 FREEMAN. Named in IE(112) as Stanhard (*standard*'). His land is valued there at 20s.
2 OTHER FREEMEN. Their land is valued in IE at 15s.
ABBOT OF RAMSEY. Cf. 7,8.
SELL WITHOUT THE JURISDICTION. ICC(91), 'sell or grant without the jurisdiction'.

26,49   ABBOT OF ELY'S MEN. IE(115) values their land at 20s.
1 HIDE. Farley shows a gap in the MS, caused by an erasure, after *hid*'.
ST. GUTHLAC'S MEN. That is, of the Abbot of Crowland; cf. 9,3.

26,50   Cf. 5,2 referring to the same holding.

26,51   Cf. 5,5 referring to the same holding.
IN WESTLEY HUNDRED. This is a DB error, since West Wratting was in Radfield Hundred, cf. ICC(23). Westley Waterless (5,3) preceded West Wratting in the record of Ely Abbey's holding (5) and its name there seems to have been misread as a Hundred rubric standing before both Ely Abbey's (5,4) and Hardwin's (5,5) holdings at West Wratting and to have been transferred as such to 26,51, perhaps during a cross-check to the reference to Hardwin in 5,5. In the MS, the error is indicated by a pointing hand (not contemporary and hence not shown by Farley).
IN LORDSHIP 2. ICC adds 'and 1½ hides less 10 acres'.
VALUE £6. ICC, £4.
10 FREEMEN...SELL. ICC adds 'or grant their land. 7 of them found cartages and 4 escorts if the King came into the Sheriffdom; if not, each gave 8d for cartage and 4d for escort'.

26,52   Cf. 5,7 referring to the same holding.
HARDWIN. Farley shows a gap in the MS after *Hard*', caused by an erasure.

26,53   Cf. 5,10 referring to the same holding.

26,54   Cf. 5,17 referring to the same holding.
IN FLENDISH HUNDRED. Not rubricated in MS. This is in any case a DB error as Babraham was in Chilford Hundred, see ICC(35-37).
½ VIRGATE. ICC(36), 1.

26,55   Cf. 5,19 referring to the same holding.

26,56   Cf. 5,21 referring to the same holding.

26,57   ABBOT. Of Ely, cf. 5,22 referring to the same holding.

[27]   Misnumbered in the text as 25, see L note.
HUGH OF BERNIÈRES. Named from one of the places called Bernières (-d'Ailly; -le Patry; - sur la Mer) in Calvados, see OEB 72.

27,1   GRANT OR SELL. ICC(85), 'grant'.

[28]   Misnumbered in the text as 26, see L note.
HUGH OF PORT. Named from Port-en-Bessin (Calv.: arr. Bayeux), see OEB 108.

28,1   60s. ICC(8; ? in error), 40s.
ORDGAR. See also 22,6.
MANOR. ICC, 'land'.
WITHDRAW...PERMISSION. ICC, 'grant to whom he would'.

28,2   BISHOP OF BAYEUX'S HOLDING. Odo of Bayeux, King William's half-brother. This is the only place in Cambridgeshire associated with his Holding, but (in spite of his imprisonment in 1082) DB records him as an extensive landholder in the neighbouring counties of Bedfordshire (2), Buckinghamshire (4) and Hertfordshire (5). Cf. 37,1-2.
PLOUGHS. ICC(3) adds '8 with the villagers'.
6 FREEMEN. ICC, 7.
3 SMALLHOLDERS. IE(101), '3 cottagers'.
3 SLAVES. Not in ICC.
TWO CARTS. That is, cart-loads of wood.
KING'S WOODLAND. ICC, 'King's lordship woodland'.
CHEVELEY. See 1,4.

ARCHBISHOP'S MEN. IE states that they were the Abbot of Ely's men.

WITH THE ARCHBISHOP. IE, 'with the Abbot'.

THEN ABBOT. ICC, 'Abbot Leofsi'. 1029-?1044, see HRH 44. If Leofsi's terminal date is 1044, Stigand must have acquired this lease before becoming Archbishop (1047). See also 35,2 note.

ABBOT SIMEON. 1082-93, the brother of Bishop Walkelin of Winchester (2), see HRH 45.

[29] Misnumbered in the text as 27, see L note.

AUBREY DE VERE. Named from Ver (La Manche: arr. Coutances) or Ver (Calvados), see OEB 118.

29,1 EVRARD. ICC(9), 'Evrard son of Brian'. A juror in Cheveley Hundred (Appx B).

LIVESTOCK. ICC(10), 'village livestock'.

40s. ICC, 60s.

WULFWIN. ICC, 'Wulfwin, his predecessor'. Aubrey de Vere took over his land *en bloc*, see 29,2-3; 5,7-11; and 26,9.

29,2 In the MS there is a marginal *T* (for *tempore*) added before *def(en)d(it)*. This was not shown by Farley as it was subsequently cancelled, having been placed one entry too soon, see 29,3 note.

SAXON (STREET). In Woodditton parish (EPNS 127-128).

LAND FOR 7 PLOUGHS. ICC(10), 10.

VILLAGERS...4 PLOUGHS. ICC, 7.

TOTAL VALUE £8. ICC, £10.

29,3 MARGINAL *T*. This is a later addition standing for *tempore*, cf. 29,2 note.

VILLAGERS...4 PLOUGHS. ICC(9) does not credit them with any ploughs.

8 SLAVES. ICC, 9.

29,4 IT IS THERE...VILLAGER. ICC(13), '1 is there with the villagers'.

1 MILL, 7s. ICC, 5s 8d.

FOUND CARTAGE. ICC, 'always found cartage through the year'.

AUBREY'S PREDECESSOR. Wulfwin, see 29,1 note.

29,5 8 PLOUGHS. 11 listed.

29,6 This holding was at Quy and Stow, see ICC(15-16).

30 ACRES. ICC(15), 20.

GODRIC. ICC(16), Godric the deacon.

AUBREY'S PREDECESSOR. As 29,4 note.

29,7 LAND FOR 11 PLOUGHS. ICC(29; ? in error), 12.

NORMAN...OF THIS LAND. DB erroneously places this ½ hide in the same paragraph as Aubrey de Vere's 2½ hides, although ICC shows them to be separate estates. Norman was probably Norman of Nosterfield (End), a juror in Chilford Hundred (Appx F).

29,8 HORSEHEATH. See also 26,9.

60s. ICC(30), 40s.

FULL JURISDICTION. See 14,59 note. Not mentioned in ICC(30).

29,10-11 FIRMATUS. Possibly the same person as Firmin, a juror in Chilford Hundred (Appx F).

29,10 6 PLOUGHSHARES. ICC(31), 5.

29,11 ICC(36) adds 'land for 1 ox'.

GODWIN. ICC, Godric.

29,12 Cf. 1,16 referring to the same holding.

CHARGE. Farley indicates the small gap in the MS after *custodia*.

1 FREEMAN. Named in 1,16 as Sigar.

[30] Misnumbered in the text as 28, see L note.

EUSTACE OF HUNTINGDON. Sheriff of Huntingdonshire in 1086.

30,1 PAPWORTH HUNDRED. The name-form shows confusion with that of Pampisford.

30,3 WALTER. IE(111), Walter of *Helmes* (unidentified, OEB 44).

LAND FOR 4 OXEN. IE(111) adds 'they are there'.

GODWIN. IE, 'Godwin the priest'. A juror in Papworth Hundred (Appx M).

SELL. IE, 'withdraw because the land and the jurisdiction always remained with the Abbot of Ely before and in 1066'.

[31] Misnumbered in the text as 29, see L note.

GUY OF RAIMBEAUCOURT. Possibly named from Ribeaucort (Somme: arr.Doullens) but no early spellings of the place-name have been found, see OEB 109. Summaries of his

	lands in Cambridgeshire are given in IE(121,124) and a list of Cambridgeshire lands taken by him from Ely Abbey is given in IEBrev (176).
31,1	[IN ARMINGFORD HUNDRED]. Hundred rubric omitted in DB, but see ICC(65–66).

31,1 [IN ARMINGFORD HUNDRED]. Hundred rubric omitted in DB, but see ICC(65–66).
3 HIDES. ICC(65; in error), 4.
LIVESTOCK. ICC, 'village livestock'.
70s. ICC expresses this as £3 10s.
16 FREEMEN. ICC, 15. DB is in error here, as is shown by the details which it itself gives.
10 OF THEM...CHURCH. See 5,33 referring to the same men. IE(108) names them as follows: Grim; Young Alfsi; Wynsi; Alfsi; Leofwin the priest; Edric the priest; Godwin the priest; Aelmer the priest; Aelfric, brother of Godwin the priest; and Edric Snipe.
OF WHOM ONE...LAND. ICC, 'One of them held 1½ virgates of these 2 hides and ½ virgate; he could neither grant nor sell without the Abbot's permission'. IE, 'Two of them...'.
THEY...SELL. ICC(65–66), 'they could withdraw whither they would before 1066 but the jurisdiction remained with Earl Algar'.

31,2 IN THE SAME VILLAGE. DB is in error here. This holding is shown by ICC(67) to be in Melbourn.
IN LORDSHIP 2½ HIDES. ICC, '2 hides and ½ virgate'.
18 SMALLHOLDERS AND 10 COTTAGERS. ICC(? in error), '18 cottagers'.
EDRIC SNIPE. DB *spur*, ICC *pur*; see 21,5 note.
FREEMEN. IE(109) names them as follows: Alfsi Beard; Alric Godingson; Aelfric Mouse; Ordmer; Goding Bolt; Aelsi Bereson; Wynstan; Alwin Blond; Alwin the Abbot's reeve; Alfred.
2 HIDES AND ½ VIRGATE. ICC, '2½ hides and ½ virgate.

31,3 HUMPHREY. Of Anneville (ICC 70). See 25,7 note. He may also be the Humphrey who held 1 hide, 1 virgate and 3 acres from Guy of Raimbeaucourt at Haslingfield (ICC 73), an entry omitted from DB.

31,5–6 RALPH. Ralph Banks (*de bans*; ICC 79–80); see B1 note.

31,5 ICC(79) erroneously conflates this section with 11,5.

31,6 WRATWORTH. See 13,9 note.
2 SMALLHOLDERS. ICC(80), '2 cottagers'.
WOOD. ICC, 'woodland'.
SELL. ICC(81), 'withdraw whither they would'.

31,7 2 SMALLHOLDERS. ICC(84) adds 'each with 5 acres'.
WOOD FOR FENCES. ICC, 'woodland for repairing fences'.
PICOT. The Sheriff (ICC). See 32.
HUMPHREY. Probably Humphrey of Anneville, cf. 31,3.
7. ICC, 6. The DB figure is in error.
EDEVA. The Fair (ICC).

[32] Misnumbered in the text as 30, see L note.
PICOT OF CAMBRIDGE. Sheriff of Cambridgeshire in 1086. For Ely Abbey's opinion of him ('a hungry lion, a roving wolf, a crafty fox, a filthy pig, a shameless dog'), see LibEl 211. Summaries of his lands in the county are given in IE(121, 123), and a list of Cambridgeshire lands taken by him from Ely Abbey is given in IEBrev (175–176). See also 25,1–2 note.

32,1 QUY. This section includes Stow, see ICC(16–17).
8 VILLAGERS. ICC(16), 7.
2½ MILLS AT 22s. ICC, '½ mill at 40d, 1 mill at 7s, and another at 10s 8d'; this totals 21s.
ALRIC...3½ HIDES. ICC states that Alric held 1½ hides and Godric held 2 hides.

32,3 RALPH. Banks (*de scannis*; ICC 37); see B1 note.
MEADOW, 2 ACRES. ICC, 2½.
WITHDRAW...LAND. ICC, 'grant his land to whom he would'.

32,4 12 SMALLHOLDERS. ICC(40) adds 'with 12 acres'.
20 FREEMEN...COULD WITHDRAW. ICC, '19 Freemen held these two manors; they were King Edward's men. A twentieth held ½ hide of the jurisdiction of Earl Algar and could not withdraw without his permission. The others could (withdraw)'.
HE COULD NOT WITHDRAW. Farley prints *potuer(unt)* in error for *potuit*, anticipating the following line.

32,5 9 PLOUGHS. 8 listed.
VILLAGERS...4 PLOUGHS. ICC(45), 3½.
15 COTTAGERS. ICC(45–46) adds 'with their gardens'.

LIVESTOCK. ICC(46), 'village livestock'.

WHEN ACQUIRED £4 10s. ICC, £4.

‡PICOT...ABBOT‡. This paragraph is entered in the margin, without any indication of its intended location. In fact it refers to the same 1½ hides as at 5,24 and as were held by Fridebert, below; see ICC.

FRIDEBERT...KING'S ORDER. See previous note.

REMAINED...CHURCH. ICC, 'remained (in) Harston'. Cf. 5,24 'remained with the Abbot'.

32,6   MEADOW...PLOUGHS. ICC(50), *pratum carrucis*.

HORWULF. DB *Orulfus*, ICC(50) *Horulfus*. Probably he of 15,3.

32,7   2½ VIRGATES WHICH THE VILLAGERS HOLD. This appears to represent an error in DB's exemplar. ICC(52) reads simply '2½ villagers'. The DB scribe realised that his text was faulty and added the marginal note *r(e)q(uire) q(uo)t uill(ani)*, 'inquire how many villagers'.

13 SMALLHOLDERS. ICC adds '4 slaves'.

PASTURE...LIVESTOCK. ICC adds 'woodland for repairing fences'.

3 FREEMEN...THIS LAND. ICC(53), '7 (? in error for 3) Freemen held this land. Ordric, King Edward's man, held 1 hide and 1½ virgates and Ansketel, this Ordric's man, held ½ hide and the fourth part of 1 virgate; Godric, Algar's man, held ½ hide less the fourth part of 1 virgate'.

32,2   This section is written in four lines at the foot of col. 200b, with a sign indicating its correct position in the text after 32,1.

THERE. In Quy and Stow, see ICC(16). This section repeats the information given at 5,11.

32,8   3 OF THEM...VIRGATES. ICC(54) names these men of Archbishop Stigand as Osgot (cf. 32,13 note) with 1½ hides, and Godwin and William with 1 virgate between them.

2 OTHERS, EARL ALGAR'S MEN. ICC names them as Godman and Alwin.

2 OTHERS, KING EDWARD'S MEN. ICC names them as Alnoth and Alfward.

A MAN OF EDEVA'S. ICC, 'Aelmer...Edeva the Fair's man'.

32,10   MEADOW...PLOUGHS. ICC(56) adds 'pasture for the village livestock'.

2 SMALLHOLDERS. Placed here, unusually, after, instead of before, the meadow. Cf. 32,17 note.

8 FREEMEN...LAND. ICC, '8 Freemen held this land before 1066 and now hold (it) under Picot'. ICC adds 'all of them could grant and sell to whom they would before 1066'.

(GUILDEN) MORDEN. Cf. 32,8.

WULFMER OF EATON. See 25,9 note.

EYNESBURY. In Huntingdonshire, but this exchange is not mentioned there.

RUSHDEN. In Hertfordshire; see 32,25 note.

ILBERT OF HERTFORD. Sheriff of Hertfordshire at some time between 1066 and 1086 (see Hertfordshire, 1,9).

32,11   EXCEPT FOR THE OXEN. ICC(57), 'except for 6 oxen'.

A MAN. ICC names him as Godmer.

32,12   ALFRED. See 13,2 note.

A MAN. ICC(57) names him as Alward.

GRANT AND SELL. ICC, 'withdraw when he would'.

32,13   ABINGTON (PIGOTTS). The place-name commemorates Picot's tenure.

ANSGOT. ICC(61), Osgot; cf. 32,8 note.

(GUILDEN)MORDEN. Cf. 32,8.

32,14   2 MEN. ICC(68), '2 men-at-arms' (*milites*).

WITHDRAW. ICC(69), 'grant or sell to whom they would'.

32,15   ROBERT. ICC(72), Robert Fafiton; cf. 38,3.

3 OXEN. ICC, 4.

WULFRIC...JURISDICTION. ICC adds 'he could grant to whom he would'.

32,16-17 SIFRID. Probably the same as Sifrid the reeve of Wetherley Hundred (Appx K).

32,16   4 HIDES AND 3 VIRGATES. ICC(72) expresses this as '4½ hides and 1 virgate'.

ASGAR. The Constable (ICC).

32,17   4 OXEN. ICC(74), 3.

2 SMALLHOLDERS. As 32,10 note.

32,18-21 RALPH. Banks (*de bans*; ICC 75); see B1 note.

32,18   1 FREEMAN. Not in ICC(75).

5s. ICC(74), 4s.

EDSI. DB *Ezi*; OE *Ēadsige* (PNDB 236).

32,19   WRATWORTH. See 13,9 note.

3 VIRGATES. ICC(80), 1 virgate. The DB figure is probably wrong here, having added the ½ hide at Wratworth which Ralph held from Guy of Raimbeaucourt (31,6).

3s. ICC, 4s.

32,20   WHITWELL. See 13,10 note.

MEADOW FOR 2 PLOUGHS. ICC(81), 1½.

MAKING FENCES. ICC, 'repairing fences'.

ALGAR'S MAN. ICC states that he was Earl Algar's man and held ½ hide less the third part of 1 virgate.

ROBERT SON OF WYMARC'S MAN. He held 1 virgate (ICC).

KING EDWARD'S MAN. He held ½ hide (ICC).

COULD SELL. ICC, 'they (all three) could withdraw'.

32,21   9 VILLAGERS. ICC(85), 3.

VALUE £6. ICC, £5.

14 FREEMEN. In the following paragraph and in ICC(85-86), 16 are mentioned.

EARL ALGAR'S MEN...1 VIRGATE. ICC(86), '1 hide'.

ABBOT OF ELY'S MAN. IE(110) values his 1 virgate at 2s.

ALL WITHDRAW. The Abbot of Ely however retained jurisdiction over the 1 virgate, according to IE.

32,22   A MAN (x2).. ICC(87), 'A Freeman' (*sochemannus*).

A MAN OF THE ABBOT OF ELY'S. Named by IE(11) as Siward, but misplaced there under Hardwick; it is also stated that Siward's land is now held by Erchenger the Baker and is worth 10s, but see 44,2 note.

32,23   4 SMALLHOLDERS. ICC(88) adds 'each with 5 acres'.

WOOD...HOUSES. ICC(88-89), 'woodland for fences and for repairing houses'.

PASTURE...LIVESTOCK (2nd occurrence). Not in ICC(89).

‡THEY...THE CHURCH‡. This sentence is added at the top of col. 201a.

OUTSIDE OF. ICC, 'from'.

MAN (x2), MEN (x2). ICC, 'Freeman', 'Freeman'.

ACCORDINGLY. Translating *itaq(ue)*, which is probably however a mistake for *isti* which occurs here in ICC.

ALL 22. Referring to the men in this paragraph other than the thane. 22 is in error for 20 however, if the 2 priests could not separate their land from the Church. The number is not given in ICC.

32,25   RUSHDEN...SIGAR HOLDS. Sigar of Chocques, see Hertfordshire 41,1 but this exchange is not mentioned there. Cf. 32,10.

32,27   2 OXEN. IE(111), 3.

ABBOT OF ELY'S MAN. IE(111-112) names him as Gold (cf. 32,29) and states that he held 3 virgates.

32,28   A MAN. ICC(92) names him as Godric the Falconer (*ancipitrarius*).

32,29   WITH MEADOW. ICC(93), 'Meadow for 2 oxen'.

PASTURE...LIVESTOCK. ICC, 'Pasture for 2 oxen'.

GOLD. See 32,27 note.

GRANT OR SELL. ICC, 'withdraw without his permission'; IE(112), 'sell'.

32,30   GUY. Of Raimbeaucourt (ICC 94); see *31*.

VALUE £4. ICC expresses this as '60s and 20s'.

15 FREEMEN. ICC, 14. DB has counted Saxi's man twice, see below, note on ONE.

GRANT AND SELL...LAND. ICC, 'withdraw'.

3 OTHERS. IE(112) gives the value of this hide at 20s.

ONE. ICC 'One of them'. ICC shows that he was included in the total of 14 Freemen. DB however counts him again and gives the total as 15.

32,31   LIVESTOCK. ICC(94), 'village livestock'.

MANOR. ICC(95), 'land'.

EDEVA. The Fair (ICC 95).

COULD WITHDRAW. ICC 'could withdraw or sell his land to whom he would'.

4...LAND. ICC, '4 had 5 hides and 1 virgate; they could withdraw without the jurisdiction'. IE(112) values their land at £3.

THE FIFTH. IE names him as Sugga and gives the value of his 1½ virgates at 10s.

32,32   IN LOLWORTH...5 HIDES. The sentence is confused in DB but ICC(95) shows that Robert held from Picot the whole of Lolworth, which had answered for 9 hides before 1066 and now for 5 hides. See also 32,44.
9 SMALLHOLDERS. ICC adds 'each with 5 acres'.
AN ALMSWOMAN. ICC names her as *Saloua* (OE *Sǣlufu*; PNDB 353).
THE TENTH. IE(113) values his 1½ hides at 10s.
ALL THESE MEN...CHURCH. ICC, 'All these men could withdraw and sell their land to whom they would'. ICC does not make an exception of the Abbot of Ely's man.

32,33   11 HIDES AND 2½ VIRGATES. ICC(96) expresses this as '11½ hides and ½ virgate'.
4 SMALLHOLDERS. ICC adds 'each with 5 acres'.
4 OF THEM. IE(113) values their land at 40s.
THE FIFTH. IE values his ½ hide at 10s.

32,34–35;43   BLACKWIN. Sheriff of Cambridgeshire in 1066. See also 3,2 note.
38–39;43

32,35   MAN OF THE ABBOT. Cf. IE(113), 'Roger, brother of Picot the Sheriff, holds 1½ hides which Siward holds (? *recte* held) from the Abbot of Ely; he could grant but the jurisdiction remained with the Abbot of Ely. Value 20s'. For Siward, see also 43,1 note.

32,36   4 SMALLHOLDERS. IE(113; in error), '2 smallholders, 1 slave, each with 10 acres'.
2 OF THEM. IE values their land at 20s.
THE THIRD. IE names him as Albert; cf. 32,39.

32,37   3 PLOUGHS. IE(114), 4.

32,38   LANDBEACH. See 14,59 note.

32,39   WATERBEACH. See 14,59 note.
MUCEL. DB *Muceullus*, IE(114) *Mucellus*; *Mucel* is a variant of OE *Mocca*, 'the thick, heavy one', OEB 394.
ALBERT. Probably he of 32,36 note. IE values his 1 hide at 10s.
ANOTHER MAN. IE values his 1 virgate at 3s.

32,40   ST. ETHELDREDA'S MAN. That is, a man of the Abbot of Ely, see 5.
14 ACRES. The suprascript letters above *xiiii* are *ci(m)*, the ending of *quattuordecim*, see facsimile.

32,41   IE(115) values this land at 10s.

32,42   CHURCH OF ST. GUTHLAC. Crowland Abbey (9).

32,43   A FREEMAN. IE(115) names him as Leofwin and values his 40 acres at 3s.

32,44   ROBERT. Probably he of 32,32.
LOLWORTH. See 32,32.

[33]   Misnumbered in the text as 31, see L note.
PETER OF VALOGNES. Named from Valognes (La Manche), OEB 117. He was Sheriff of both Essex and Hertfordshire in 1086; on him, see VCH Essex 349.
WHEN ACQUIRED... The MS is obscured by an ink-blot here.

[34]   Misnumbered in the text as 32, see L note.
[LAND...ILGER]. Omitted in the text, but see L.

34,1   INGVAR. Ranulf brother of Ilger also took possession of Everton (Huntingdonshire 24,1) which had previously been held by Ingvar. The name *Ingvar* is ON (PNDB 298) and hence the spelling 'Ingward' used in the Hunts. translation is incorrect and should be altered to 'Ingvar'. The name recurs at 15,2 above.

[35]   Misnumbered in the text as 33, see L note.

35,1   3 PLOUGHS THERE. ICC(25) adds 'a fourth possible'.
4 COTTAGERS. ICC, 3.
COULD SELL. ICC(26), 'could withdraw without his permission'.
A MAN OF EARL ALGAR'S. Named in ICC as Leofric.
GRANT AND SELL. ICC 'grant his land to whom he would'.
3 MEN OF EDEVA'S. Described as 'Freemen' in ICC.
COUNT ALAN CLAIMS. ICC, 'Count Alan claims through his predecessor'. For Count Alan, see 14. His predecessor was Edeva the Fair.

35,2   5 VILLAGERS WITH 17 SMALLHOLDERS. ICC(27), '5 villagers and 17 smallholders with ½ hide'.
£3. ICC(28) expresses this as '60 shillings'.

2 FREEMEN. Named by ICC as Edsi (with 1 hide and 20 acres) and Suneman (with ½ hide).

ABBOT SIMEON OF ELY'S PREDECESSOR. As Earl Algar appears to have died before 1066 (see 1,10 note), this refers to either Abbot Leofsi (1029–?1044, HRH 44; cf. 28,2 note) or Abbot Wulfric (?1044–66; see HRH 45).

THIRD HIDE. That is, the third full hide of the 3½ hides apart from the 2 hides in lordship and the ½ hide held by the villagers (see note, above). This hide is not that at 5,13, see IE(103) which values the present hide at 20s.

2 MEN OF YOUNG GODWIN'S. ICC describes them as 'Freemen' and states that they held ½ hide.

[36]   Misnumbered in the text as 34, see L note.

36,1   LONGSTANTON. See also 21,7.

MEADOW...OXEN. ICC(94) adds '1 smallholder'.

GRANT. ICC, 'grant or sell without his permission'.

PICOT. The Sheriff (ICC); see 32. Cf. 21,7.

[37]   Misnumbered in the text as 35, see L note.

WILLIAM OF KEYNES. Probably named from Cahagnes (Calvados) rather than Cahaignes (Eure), see OEB 79.

37,1   COMBERTON. For this identification, cf. ICC(69). The DB form has *Bertone* in error for *Cubertone* (see 1,6 etc.); *Cū-* was probably misread as *In*.

MEADOW FOR 1 PLOUGH. ICC, 'meadow for ½ plough'.

1 VILLAGER. Placed, unusually, after, rather than before, the meadow.

A MAN OF EARL WALTHEOF'S. Named in ICC as *Areli* but this is an error in Hamilton's edition for the MS form *Akeli*, see PNDB 142, n.2.

BISHOP OF BAYEUX. See 28,2 note. See also 37,2 note. Odo appears to have been acting here in an official capacity as the King's representative (cf. F.M. Stenton, *Anglo-Saxon England*, 3rd ed., Oxford 1971, 610).

37,2   IN THE SAME MANNER. ICC(69), 'This land was of Countess Judith's revenue when William of Keynes acquired it, as the men of the Hundred testify, in the same manner as above'. William apparently received it from the Bishop of Bayeux, as Comberton (see 37,1).

5 PLOUGHS. 6 listed.

WITHDRAW. ICC(70), 'grant or withdraw'.

OTHER 2. According to ICC, one held 1½ hides and ½ virgate and the other held 1 virgate. There is some confusion in the text of ICC here however and, if the DB combined figure (1 hide and 2½ virgates) is correct, then the first of these two Freemen probably held 1 hide and 1½ virgates.

[38]   Misnumbered in the text as 36, see L note.

ROBERT FAFITON. Called 'Robert, son of Fafiton' in Huntingdonshire (25,1) and ICC 51,70–72, but simply 'Robert Fafiton' here and elsewhere (Bedfordshire 30; Middlesex 15; ICC 35,51). Fafiton is here used as a patronymic byname; it is OFr in origin (OEB 182,217).

38,1   2½ PLOUGHS. ICC(35), 1½.

1 PLOUGH THERE. ICC(36), 'the plough is not there'.

26s 8d. ICC, 26s 4d.

ESCORT. ICC, '1 escort'.

38,2   3 PLOUGHS. Farley is probably correct in printing *iii* (see ICC 51) although the MS is obscured by an ink-blot here and only the first minim is visible.

1 SMALLHOLDER... The MS is obscured by an ink-blot. ICC adds 'with 1½ acres'.

5 COTTAGERS. ICC adds 'with their gardens'.

LIVESTOCK... The MS is obscured by an ink-blot. ICC, 'village livestock; from the weir 500 eels'.

SELL...WOULD. ICC, 'sell without his lord's permission'.

MAN. ICC, 'Freeman'.

38,3   ROBERT. Cf. 32,15 note.

1 HIDE. ICC(71), 1½.

GRANT...LANDS. ICC, 'withdraw and grant to whom they would'.

38,5   ASGOT. DB *Auesgot*; ON *Ásgautr* (PNDB 165).

JURISDICTION. *saca*, see 14,59 note.

SIGAR. As 1,16 note.

[39]   Misnumbered in the text as 37, see L note.

DAVID OF ARGENTON. Probably named from Argenton or Argenton Château (Deux-Sèvres), OEB 69.

39,2	EUSTACE OF HUNTINGDON. See *30*.
39,3	ROBERT. The Usher (*ostiarius*; IE 115).
[40]	Misnumbered in the text as 38, see L note.

KING'S CARPENTERS. According to a writ of King William copied into LibEl (204–205), they had also appropriated 1 hide and 3 virgates of the lordship lands of Ely Abbey before 1087.

40,1   NORTHSTOW HUNDRED. MS has *INOR ESTON* corrected to *IN'N'OR ESTOV*; the exemplar may have had *ĪNOR ESTOU*. Cf. 43,1 note.

WATERBEACH. See 14,59 note.

OSWY. IE(114) values his land at £3.

[41]   Misnumbered in the text as 39, see L note.

41,1   COUNTESS JUDITH. Niece of King William and widow of Earl Waltheof (see 1,6 note).

4 PLOUGHS THERE. ICC(11) adds 'a fifth possible'.

PARK...BEASTS. As 14,78 note.

41,3   MEADOW, 2 ACRES. ICC(19), 'meadow for 2 oxen'.

2 MEN. ICC describes them as 'Freemen'.

41,4   2 SMALLHOLDERS. ICC(20) adds 'with 2 acres'.

MEADOW, 2 ACRES. ICC, 'meadow for 1 plough'.

£6. ICC, £16.

4½ ACRES. According to ICC(21), 'value is and was 12d'.

2 ACRES. According to ICC, 'value 3[s]'.

41,5   LAND...4 OXEN. Expressed by ICC(37) as 'land for ½ plough'. ICC adds 'Meadow, 2 acres'.

MAN OF EARL GYRTH'S. Named by ICC as Leofmer.

41,6   ½ VIRGATE...COUNTESS. ICC(38) adds 'land for 2 oxen'.

64d. ICC expresses this as '4 *ora*'; see B10 note.

41,7   60s. Expressed by ICC (38) as '£3'.

MEADOW...PLOUGHS. ICC, 'meadow for 12 ploughs'.

£16. ICC(39), £17.

EARL GYRTH. Cf. 14,18 note.

41,8   GODLAMB. DB *Gollam*; ICC(51) *godlamb*. See 14,34 note.

WITHDRAW. ICC, 'withdraw without his permission'.

41,9-12   PICOT. The Sheriff (ICC 53); see *32*.

41,9   ½ VILLAGER. ICC(53), 1½. See 7,9 note.

7 SMALLHOLDERS. ICC, 6.

SELL. ICC, 'grant or sell to whom he would'.

41,10   1 SMALLHOLDER. *bord*' may however be in error for *bos*, 'ox'. Cf. 17,3 note.

41,11   GUARD. *Huscarl* is here used as a descriptive term, probably denoting a trained soldier. For *Huscarl* used as a name, see 14,64.

41,14   MEADOW...THEMSELVES. ICC(92), 'meadow for 4 oxen'.

3 Cottagers. Placed, unusually, among the resources.

GODWIN. ICC, Godwin Shield (*scild*).

GRANT. ICC, 'grant or sell'.

41,15   1 VILLAGER. Placed, unusually, after the resources.

41,16   PICOT. Probably Picot the Sheriff, cf. 32,44.

[42]   Misnumbered in the text as 40, see L note.

42,1   AZELINA WIFE OF RALPH TALLBOYS. A widow who also held land in Bedfordshire (*55*), some of which was of her marriage-portion and of her dowry. Ralph Tallboys's daughter occurs as a landholder in Hertfordshire (*44*), where his niece (or granddaughter) is also mentioned in connection with a marriage-portion (25,2).

THEY ARE THERE. ICC(53), '1 plough in lordship; a second with the villagers'. In this context in ICC, 'villagers' can refer to *villani*, *bordarii*, or *cotarii*; here to the 5 *bordarii*, 'smallholders'.

WULFMER OF EATON. See 25,9 note. Azelina also held part of Chicksands and Stondon in Bedfordshire (55,12-13) after Wulfmer's men.

WALTER THE MONK. A juror in Armingford Hundred (Appx J). He also held Old Warden (Bedfordshire 55,8) from Azelina.

[43]	Misnumbered in the text as 41, see L note.

[43]   Misnumbered in the text as 41, see L note.

[LAND]. Omitted in the text.

43,1   NORTHSTOW HUNDRED. DB has *ORNESTON*, a corrupt spelling of *NORESTOV*. The scribe probably first wrote *OR ESTON* (for *OR ESTOV*), realised he had omitted a letter *N* and then inserted it in the wrong place. Cf. 40,1 note.

BISHOP OF BAYEUX. See 28,2 note.

[ANOTHER] 1 PLOUGH POSSIBLE. In fact, only another 6 oxen possible.

2 COTTAGERS. Farley prints *iii* in error for *ii*. The MS appears to have been corrected from *iii* to *ii*.

VALUE IS AND WAS 30s. IE(113) gives the value as 20s.

SIWARD. See 32,35 note. DB seems to have wrongly named Siward as the man in the present entry rather than he of 32,35, cf. IE.

[44]   Misnumbered in the text as 42, see L note.

44,1   ERCHENGER THE BAKER. ICC(69), 'the King's baker'.

½ HIDE LESS 20 ACRES. ICC expresses this as '1 virgate and 10 acres'.

½ CARTAGE. ICC, '½ cartage and 4d'.

WALTHEOF. ICC, Earl Waltheof.

SELL AND WITHDRAW. ICC, 'grant or sell to whom they would'.

44,2   TOFT. IE(110) states that Erchenger also held ½ hide and 6 acres in Hardwick (in error for Toft) which a Freeman named Siward had held under the Abbot of Ely, value 10s. ICC(87) shows however that Siward's land was that at Toft held in 1086 by 2 men-at-arms from Picot the Sheriff (32,22).

60s. ICC(88), £4

5 FREEMEN. IE(110) names them as follows: Alric Brownson; Alware; Hunuth; Hunwin; Brictstan. Their land is valued there at 20s.

OUTSIDE...CHURCH. ICC, 'without his (the Abbot's) permission'.

CAMBRIDGESHIRE HOLDINGS ... ELSEWHERE ...

ESSEX. Chishill and Heydon, now in Cambridgeshire, were in Essex until 1895 and are entered there in DB (see Essex 20,72-73. 22,21. 26,5. 30,46. 90,34; 86 and 10,5. 76,1).

HERTFORDSHIRE. The 1 hide at 'Stetchworth' (Hertfordshire 33,12) may possibly refer to the Cambridgeshire place of that name but this is on the whole unlikely.

THE HUNDREDS

The DB Hundreds were substantially the same as those in existence in the nineteenth century. The only major difference was the reorganization of the Two Hundreds of Ely into three Hundreds by 1298 (*Ely*; *Wisbech*; and *Witchford*: EPNS 213) and later into four (*Witchford* being divided into North and South Witchford). The Two Hundreds of Ely have been distinguished in the present volume as E2 (consisting of Ely itself and its immediate surrounds, together with Wisbech in the extreme north of the Isle of Ely: 5,55-63. 6,2. 7,12. 9,4. 18,9) and E1 (the remainder of the Isle of Ely: see 5,44-54. 6,1. 7,11. 8,1); according to the rubric before 5,44 both Hundreds met at Witchford in 1086. Hainey, which was in Hundred E2 in 1086, was later included (in Soham) in Staploe Hundred (EPNS 199, s.n. Henny).

The order of Hundreds within each Holding in DB is neither wholly self-consistent nor identical to that in ICC, which represents a topographical sequence (see above, The Cambridgeshire Inquiry); the ICC sequence is that followed in the Appendix, below. The sequence followed by IE is mostly similar, but not identical, to that of ICC.

THE COUNTY BOUNDARY

The Domesday county of Cambridge (with the Isle of Ely) was remarkably similar to that in existence before the reorganization of local government in 1974. Exning was however included in Suffolk from the twelfth century (VCH 340,n.3). Great and Little Chishill and Heydon were only transferred from Essex to Cambridgeshire in 1895 (EPNS 373–374) and will be included in the Essex volume.

APPENDIX

Both the Ely Inquiry (IE) and the Cambridgeshire Inquiry (ICC) (see above, after Introduction) give the names of the jurors who represented the Cambridgeshire Hundreds during the DB Survey. These were 'the men of the Hundred' who are sometimes mentioned (but anonymously) in the text of DB. Their function was both to ratify the commissioners' findings for each Hundred and to give evidence in the case of disputes over the title to land. Eight men swore in each Hundred, four of them French and four English. Some are identifiable as landholders in DB, usually holding land in the Hundred in which they swore, but occasionally in another Hundred. A few appear to have sworn in more than one Hundred. Picot the Sheriff seems to have sworn once for all in the first Hundred (Staine), but some of his men also swore in other Hundreds.

In order to maintain consistency with the Hertfordshire volume, the translations given here have been made from the lists of jurors in IE, apart from Chilford Hundred (omitted in IE) which has been translated from ICC. The order in which the Hundreds are given here is however that of ICC, since this represents a topographical sequence (see above, the Cambridgeshire Inquiry). Places and landholders named in Cambridgeshire DB, or in the notes to the translation above, are printed in capitals; DB references to the persons are given in round brackets. References to places in other Hundreds are marked by the appropriate abbreviation. In this Appendix, references to 'Hamilton' are to pages in N.E.S.A. Hamilton, *Inquisitio Comitatus Cantabrigiensis* (1876), an edition of both ICC and IE from British Library, Cotton MS Tib. A. vi, with the IE text of that MS collated to Trinity College Cambridge, MSS 0.2.41 (MS B) and 0.2.1 (MS C). For a facsimile of part of the lists in IE, from the Cotton MS, see DB 4, ed. Sir H. Ellis (*Record Commission*, 1816), after page 496.

A (IE, see DB 4,497 and Hamilton 97; ICC, see Hamilton 1)

In STAPLOE Hundred these men swore,
NICHOLAS of KENNETT (18,8)	Robert the Englishman of FORDHAM
William of CHIPPENHAM,	ORDMER of BADLINGHAM (14,67)
GEOFFREY (de MANDEVILLE)'S	ALAN of BURWELL (14,69)
man (22)	Aelfric of SNAILWELL
Hugh of EXNING*	
Warin of SOHAM	

(and all the other Frenchmen and Englishmen of this Hundred swore).†

>   * MS *Heselinge*; *Hexeninge* MS C; *Heselinges* ICC
>   † ICC, PICOT the SHERIFF (32) and all the Frenchmen
>   and Englishmen (of this Hundred swore)

B (IE, see DB 4,497 and Hamilton 97–98; ICC, see Hamilton 9)

In CHEVELEY Hundred (these men) swore, namely
Richard, the reeve of this Hundred	Stanhard§ of SILVERLEY
[EVRARD] *, AUBREY de VERE'S	Frawin‖ of KIRTLING
man (29,1–2)	Karl of CHEVELEY
Ralph of Hotot†	Wulfmer, WIGHEN'S man (14,61)
William Delamere‡	

(and all the other Frenchmen and Englishmen of this Hundred swore).

>   * IE Edward; ECC Evrard son of Brian
>   † *Hoitot* MS C. Probably Hottot-en-Auge (Calv.: arr.
>   Pont-l'Eveque) rather than Hottot-Les Bagues
>   (Calv.: arr. Bayeux), see OEB 93
>   ‡ *de Mara* MS and ICC; *de Marœ* MS C. Possibly the
>   William Delamere who held from William of Eu in
>   Herts. (28,3;8) and Wilts. (32,4). Cf. Wighen Delamere
>   in 14,61 note.

§ MS *Standard*; *Stanhardus* MS C and ICC;
Stanhard̃ MS B
‖ *Frawis* MS C

C   (IE, see DB 4,497 and Hamilton 98; ICC, see Hamilton 11-12)

In STAINE Hundred (these) men swore, namely

Aleran*	HUSCARL of SWAFFHAM (14,64)
Roger, WALTER GIFFARD'S man(*17*)	Leofwin†
Richard, the reeve of this Hundred	Harold, HARDWIN of SCALES'S
Farman	man (*26*)
	Aelfric of WILBRAHAM

and all the other Frenchmen and Englishmen of this Hundred swore.

     * ICC Aleran the Frenchman
     † ICC Leofwin of BOTTISHAM

D   (IE, ibid.; ICC, see Hamilton 17)

In RADFIELD Hundred these (men) swore

Manfrid*	Adestan‡ of WESTON (COLVILLE)
David of BALSHAM	GRIM§ of (WEST) WRATTING
William, WALTER (of GRAND-	(? 14,76)
COURT)'S man (18,1;4)	Algar of DULLINGHAM
Ralph of CLUNY† (18,2)	Pinna‖ of BALSHAM

and all the other Frenchmen and Englishmen of this Hundred swore.

     * ICC *Mathfrid'*
     † ICC *Cliue*
     ‡ ICC *Alestan'*
     § ICC *Grip'*
     ‖ ICC *Win'*

E   (IE, ibid.; ICC, see Hamilton 25)

In FLENDISH Hundred (these men) swore

ROBERT of (CHERRY) HINTON*	Edwin the priest
(14,4)	Wulfric of TEVERSHAM
Osmund Little†	Silac‖
Fulk‡, the ABBOT of ELY'S man (5)	Godwin of FULBOURN¶
Baldwin Cook§	

(and all the other Frenchmen and Englishmen of this Hundred swore).

     * MS *de Histona*; *de Histonona* MS C;
       de Hintona ICC
     † *Paruus* MSS; *Paruulus* ICC
     ‡ MS *Fulcold*; *Fulchold* MSS B,C; *Fulcard'* ICC
     § ICC Baldwin with the beard
     ‖ MS *Syla*; *Silac* MS B; *Silacus* MS C; *Silac'* of
       TEVERSHAM ICC
     ¶ ICC Godwin Nabson

F   (ICC, see Hamilton 28-29; not in IE)

In CHILFORD Hundred (these) men swore, namely

NORMAN of NOSTERFIELD (END)*	Leofgeat§, COUNT (ALAN)'S
(29,7-8)	man (*14*)
Walter of Clais†	Wulfric
BRIAN of SCALES (14,15)	Hag of LINTON
Firmin‡	Aelfric of HORSEHEATH

and all the other Frenchmen and Englishmen (of this Hundred swore).

* In SHUDY CAMPS (EPNS 105)
† MS *de claí*. He also swore in Northstow
    Hundred (Appx N)
‡ Possibly identical with Firmatus (29,10–11).
    Firmin is the OFr form of *Firminus* a
    derivative of Latin *Firmus* 'firm, strong',
    see Reaney s.n.
§ MS *lifg&*

G   (IE, see DB 4,497 and Hamilton 99; ICC, see Hamilton 38)

In WHITTLESFORD Hundred (these men) swore

Ansketel of Hérouville*	Ledmer (of) WHITTLESFORD
PAYNE, HARDWIN OF SCALES'S	Leofwy‡ of DUXFORD
steward (26,16)	Leofric son of Grim
GERARD of LORRAINE (14,18–19)	Leofmer§ of HINXTON ‖
Hervey† of SAWSTON	

(and all the other Frenchmen and Englishmen of this Hundred swore).

* *de Herolfuilla* MSS; *de Herouilla* ICC
† ICC omits this personal-name
‡ MS *Lefo*; *Lefue* MS C; *Liefhun'* ICC
§ MS *Lemarais*; *Lemma* MS C; *Lemar'* ICC
‖ MS *de Haustitona*; *de Hincstitona* MS C;
    de Hestitona ICC

H   (IE, See DB 4,497 and Hamilton 98; ICC, see Hamilton 43)

In THRIPLOW Hundred (these men) swore, namely

Ralph, the reeve of this Hundred	Stanhard§ of HAUXTON
WILLIAM of CAILLY* (18,7)	Godric of FOWLMERE
RALPH of BARRINGTON† (32,18 W)	Aelfric of THRIPLOW
Theodbald‡, HARDWIN of SCALES'S	SIGAR the STEWARD (22,3–4)‖
man (26)	

and all the other Frenchmen and Englishmen of the Hundred swore.

* MS *de Caleio*; *de Cheleia* MS C; *de Caillei* ICC
† The same as Ralph Banks, see 32,18 note. He
  held no land in this Hundred but was a tenant
  of PICOT the SHERIFF (32), who did. See
  also Appx K.
‡ Probably the same as Theodbald who held from
  Hardwin in Herts. (37,2–3;5;9–11;15–19)
§MS *Standard*; *Stanhard* MS B; *Stanhardus* MS C;
  Stanhard' ICC
‖ He was Steward of Asgar the Constable, see
  22,2 note.

J   (IE, ibid.; ICC, see Hamilton 51)

In ARMINGFORD Hundred (these men) swore

WALTER* (42,1)	COLSWEIN (14,28;30;32–33)
HUMPHREY of ANNEVILLE (25,4-6)†	AELMER, his son (?14,23–24)§
HUGH PEDEFOLD‡ (26,30;33)	Thorulf
RICHARD of (GUILDEN) MORDEN	Aelfwin Odson
(22,7)	

and all the other Frenchmen and Englishmen in this Hundred swore.

* Walter the monk MS B and ICC; see 42,1
† See also Herts. (31,1;8. B5)
‡ *Pedenfot* MS C; *Petuuolt* ICC

§ If this identification is correct, he is Aelmer
of Bourn who also held at 14,47;49-52, in
Longstow Hundred.

K   (IE, see DB 4,498 and Hamilton 99; ICC, see Hamilton 68)

In WETHERLEY Hundred (these men) swore
SIFRID*, the reeve of the Hundred   Saeward of HARLTON ‖
    (32,16-17)   THORBERN¶ of ORWELL (14,41)
RALPH BANKS† (32,18)   Brictgeat** of BARTON
Fulk‡, [PICOT] the SHERIFF'S   Aelmer Blackson
    man (32)
Rumold§, COUNT EUSTACE'S
    man (15)
and all the other Frenchmen and Englishmen of this Hundred swore.

          * MS Siurid'; Sifridus MSS B,C: Sefrid' ICC
          † MS de bans; de bancs MS B, desbans MS C;
              ICC de scannis. Ralph Banks (or of Barrington)
              also swore in Thriplow Hundred (Appx H).
          ‡ ICC Fulk Waruhel
          §ICC Rumold of COTON
          ‖ MS Harlestona; Harlestone MS C; Harletona ICC
          ¶MS Turbert; Turbern MS C; Turbert' ICC
          ** MS Brixcet; Brixcecus MS C; Bricter ICC

L   (IE, ibid.; ICC, see Hamilton 83)

In LONGSTOW Hundred (these men) swore
William, PICOT the SHERIFF'S   Godric of CROXTON
    man (32)   Aelfric, EUDO (SON of HUBERT)'S
Tihel*, the ABBOT of ELY'S reeve (5)   reeve (25)
Warin the priest   Wulfwy of HATLEY (ST. GEORGE)†
GUY, the ABBOT of RAMSEY'S   Young Aelmer
    man (7,2)
and all the other Frenchmen and Englishmen of this Hundred swore.

          * Tehel MSS; Thielus ICC. The name is either
              Breton Tihellus or ContGerm Ticheld.
          † ICC Wulfwy of Doesse

M   (IE, ibid.; not in ICC)

In PAPWORTH Hundred (these men swore)
Richard, HARDWIN of SCALES'S   Leofwin Gric'
    man (26)   Osmund, GILBERT of GHENT'S
Ralph of Feugères*   man (23)
Albert, the ABBOT of RAMSEY'S   Brictstan, GILBERT of GHENT'S
    man (7)   man (23)
Theodard†, the ABBOT of ELY'S   GODWIN the PRIEST (30,3)
    man (5)
and all the other Frenchmen and Englishmen of this Hundred swore.

          * Possibly identical with Ralph at 26,48
          † MS Thehard; Tehard MSS B,C

N   (IE, see DB 4,498 and Hamilton 99; ICC, see Hamilton 93)

In NORTHSTOW Hundred (these men) swore
Walter of Clais*   Godlive§
Roger son of MORIN† (12,4-5)   Azor
Hugh Farsit‡   Godmer of GIRTON
Robert son of Warin   Wulfric ‖ of GIRTON
and all the other Frenchmen and Englishmen of this Hundred swore.

* *Cleris* MS C. Perhaps from Clais (Seine Inf.: arr.
Dieppe), OEB 82. He also swore in Chilford
Hundred (Appx F).
† *Maurini* (genitive) MSS; *Morini* ICC
‡ ICC *Farsi*
§ ICC *Godlid* of LONGSTANTON
‖ MS *Waluric'*; *Wluicus* MS C; *Vluric'* ICC

O   (IE, ibid.; not in ICC)

In CHESTERTON Hundred (these men) swore

ROGER of CHILDERLEY (3,6)	Bruning of CHESTERTON
Giffard of (DRY) DRAYTON	Aelmer of COTTENHAM
Gilbert of HISTON	Ledmer of (DRY) DRAYTON
Sturmid* of COTTENHAM	Ernwy of CHILDERLEY

and all the other Frenchmen and Englishmen of this Hundred swore.

* *Surmi* MS C

P   (IE, DB 4,498 and Hamilton 100; not in ICC)

In the TWO HUNDREDS of ELY which meet at Witchford (these) men swore, namely

Reginald of DOWNHAM	Huna of ELY
Geoffrey*, the reeve of these Hundreds	Alric Worship-pound‡
Tancred of SUTTON	Alric the Saddler§
Osmund of STRETHAM	Osmund of WITCHAM
Gilbert of LINDEN (END)	Alnoth of SUTTON
Geoffrey, the ABBOT of ELY'S	Ledmer of WITCHFORD
constable (5)	Ledman the priest
Robert the Chamberlain	Aelfwin of HINTON (HALL)‖
Bernard of HILL (ROW)†	

(and all the other Frenchmen and Englishmen of these Hundreds swore).

* MS *Gostrid'*; *Goisfridus* MS C. See 14,72 note.
† *de Monte* MSS
‡ *Wordepund* MSS. See OEB 389.
§ MS *Serdere*; *Sellere* MS C. See OEB 269.
‖ In HADDENHAM (EPNS 231)

INDEX OF PERSONS

Familiar modern spellings are given where they exist. Unfamiliar names are usually given in an approximate late 11th century form, avoiding variants that were already obsolescent or pedantic. Spellings that mislead the modern eye are avoided where possible. Two, however, cannot be avoided; they are combined in the name 'Leofgeat', pronounced 'Leffyet', or 'Levyet'. The definite article is used before bynames where there is a probability that they described the individual, rather than one of his ancestors. While an attempt has been made, with the aid of additional information supplied by IE and ICC, to differentiate individuals with the same name, there remain several individuals who cannot be so differentiated. Readers are therefore advised that a group of references given under a single name (e.g. Aelmer) do not necessarily refer to the same individual. *References are to persons named in the text of DB, to those identified in the notes from information supplied by IE or ICC, and to jurors named in the Appendix. All names or name-forms which are not contained in DB itself are printed in italics, as are the chapter-numbers of listed landholders.*

Chatteris		11. 21,5
	Abbess	11,1. 21,5
	Nuns	11,2
Cluny	Abbot	18,2. Cf. also Ralph
Crowland (St. Guthlac's)		9. 26,49. 32,42
	Abbot	9
[Dorchester-on-Thames], Bishop ...		see Wulfwy
Ely (St. Etheldreda's)		5. 1,11. 14,30; 57; 59. 18,3; 7. 26,18; 30; 33; 56. 28,2. 31,1. 32,37; 40-41. 44,2
	Abbot	5. B12. 3,5. 6,1-2. 7,11-12. 8,1. 9,4. 13,11. 17,2-3. 18,3; 9. 19,1. 25,9. 26,17-18; 27; 29; 48-55; 57. 27,1. 28,2. 30,3. 31,2. 32,2; 5; 21-22; 27; 29-33; 35-37; 39-40; 43. 39,3. 40,1. 43,1. 44,2. Appx E; L; M; P. See also Leofsi, Simeon, Wulfric.
	Monks	5,26. 17,2. 26,30; 56
Grestain	Abbot	12,1
Lincoln	Bishop	3. See also Remigius
Ramsey (St. Benedict's)		7
	Abbot	7. 17,1. 26,2; 41; 48. 32,1; 23; 28. 41,14. Appx L; M
Rochester	Bishop	4
St. Evroul	Abbot	13,6-7
St. Wandrille's		10. 5,2
	Abbot	10
Swavesey	Monks	14,60
Thorney		8
	Abbot	8
Winchester (St. Peter's) [the Old Minster]		2
	Bishop	2. See also Walkelin

Deacon, see Godric. **Monks,** see Alric, Walter. **Priests,** see Aelfric, Aelmer, Alfgeat, Alric, Edric, Edwin, Godwin, Ledman, Leofwin, Ralph, Robert, Thorbert, Thorkil, Warin.

Secular Titles and Occupational Names

Chamberlain (*camerarius*) ... Odo, Robert, William. Constable (*cunestabulius*) ... Geoffrey. Constable (*stalre*) ... Asgar. Cook (*cocus*) ... Baldwin. Count (*comes*) ... Alan, Eustace, Gilbert, Mortain. Countess (*comitissa*) ... Judith. Earl (*comes*) ... Algar, Edgar, Gyrth, Harold, Roger, Tosti, Waltheof. Falconer (*ancipitrarius*) ... Godric. Goldsmith (*aurifaber*) ... Grimbald, Otto. Guard (*huscarl*) ... Huscarl, and see 41,11. Harper (*harparius*) ... Alwy. Hundred-reeve (*prepositus hundredi*) ... Goeffrey, Ralph, Richard (2), Sifrid. King's Baker (*pistor regis*) ... Erchenger. King's Beadle (*bedellus regis*) ... Alwin Maimcock. King's Carpenters (*carpentarii regis*) ... 40. King Edward's Huntsman (*venator regis Edwardi*) ... Judicael, Wulfwin. Mead-keeper of Ely Abbey (*medarius de Eli*) ... Wulfwin. Reeve (*prepositus*) ... Aelfric, Alwin, Tihel. Sheriff (*vicecomes*) ... Aelfric Godricson, Blackwin, Eustace, Ordgar, Peter of Valognes, Picot. Steward (*dapifer*) ... Albert, Eudo, Payne, Sigar, Wymarc. Usher (*ostiarius*) ... Robert. Young (*cilt*) ... Aelfric, Aelmer, Alfsi, Godwin.

INDEX OF PLACES

The name of each place is followed by (i) the abbreviated name of its Hundred and its location on the Map in this volume; (ii) its National Grid reference; (iii) chapter and section references in DB, or a reference to a note on a particular DB section which identifies the place, or a reference to the Appendix. Bracketed chapter and section references denote mention in sections dealing with a different place. Unless otherwise stated, the identifications of EPNS and the spellings of the Ordnance Survey are followed for places in England; of OEB for places abroad. The National Grid reference system is explained on all Ordnance Survey maps, and in the Automobile Association Handbooks; the figures reading from left to right are given before those reading from bottom to top of the map. All places in the index are in the 100 km grid square lettered TL, except for Wisbech which is in square TF. Places with bracketed Grid references do not appear on 1 inch or 1 : 50,000 maps. Where DB does not differentiate between what are now two distinct settlements (e.g. Castle Camps and Shudy Camps), both sets of Grid references are given. The Cambridgeshire Hundreds are Armingford (A), Chesterton (Ct), Cheveley (Cv), Chilford (C), Flendish (F), Longstow (L), Northstow (N), Papworth (P), Radfield (R), Staine (Sn), Staploe (Sp), Thriplow (T), Wetherley (W), Whittlesford (Wf) and the Two Hundreds of Ely (E1 and E2); they are listed after the index, immediately before the Map. *Places or information mentioned only in the notes or the Appendix are printed in italics.* Chishill, Heydon, *Linacre*, Newport and Rushden are not shown on the Map.

	Map	Grid	Text
[Great and Little] Abington	C 2	52 49	1,16. 14,14. 29,10;12
Abington Pigotts	A 10	30 44	1,19-20. 2,3. 13,5. 26,24. 32,13
Armingford Hundred	A	- -	Appx J
Arrington	W 8	32 50	13,11. 14,45
Ashley	Cv 2	69 61	29,1
Babraham	C 1	50 50	1,15. 5,17. 14,15-16. 25,1. 26,11; 54. 29,11. 38,1. 41,5. EE1
Badlingham	Sp 5	67 70	14,67. Appx A
Balsham	R 8	58 50	5,6-7. 14,82. 26,52. Appx D
Barham	C 10	57 46	5,16. 14,8-10
Barrington	W 11	39 49	11,3. 14,39. 17,5. 21,5. 32,18. Appx H
Barton	W 4	40 55	12,2. 31,3. 37,2. Appx K
Bassingbourn	A 11	33 44	2,4. 14,27. 26,25
Bottisham	Sn 4	54 60	17,1. Appx C
Bourn	L 5	32 56	7,1. 14,49. 32,23. 33,1. See Aelmer
Boxworth	P 8	34 64	7,6. 14,54. 21,8. 23,4. 26,47

	Map	Map	Text
Burrough Green	R 4	63 55	14,78
Burwell	Sp 9	58 66	7,9. 11,2. 14, 69-70. 26,2. Appx A
Caldecote	L 6	34 56	14,50. 26,40. 39,1.
Cambridge		44 58	B. 14,12. (1,17) 21,1. 29,7
[Castle and Shudy] Camps, see also Nosterfield End	C 11	63 43) 62 44)	
Carlton	R 6	64 53	14,79. 18,1-2. 26,5. 41,4
Caxton	L 3	30 58	26,42
Chatteris	E1 5	39 85	5,46. 7,11. See also Churches and Clergy (1,10;15;22). EE1
Chesterford (Essex)	1	50 42	1,9. Appx O
Chesterton	Ct 6	46 59	Appx O
Chesterton Hundred	Ct	- -	
Cheveley	Cv 3	68 60	1,4. 14,62. (28,2). Appx B
Cheveley Hundred	Cv	- -	Appx B
Childerley	Ct 5	35 61	3,6. 32,44. 41,16. Appx O
Chilford Hundred	C	- -	Appx F
Chippenham	Sp 6	66 69	22,6. Appx A Holdings Elsewhere, note
Chishill (Essex)	- -	- -	
Clopton	A 3	30 48	2,2. 25,4. 32,9

	Map	Grid	Text		Map	Grid	Text
Comberton	W 3	38 55	1,6. 32,14. 37,1. 44,1	Graveley	P 6	24 64	7,3
Conington	P 5	32 66	21,7. 23,3. 26,46	Haddenham, see also Hinton Hall	E1 9	46 75	5,54
Coton	W 1	40 58	Appx K	Hainey	E2 8	55 75	5,58
Cottenham	Ct 1	45 67	5,42. 9,2. 30,40-42. Appx O	Hardwick	L 4	37 58	5,36-37
Croxton	L 1	25 59	26,43. 39,2. Appx L	Harlton	W 6	38 52	17,4. 32,17. (17,6). Appx K
Croydon	A 2	31 49	13,3. 14, 24-25. 25,6. 26,21. 32, 11-12	Harston	T 5	41 50	5,24. 14,21. 21,4. 32,5
				Haslingfield	W 7	40 52	1,7. 14,36-38. 22,8. 32,16. (31,3)
Doddington	E1 3	40 90	5,45	East Hatley	A 1	28 50	14,23. 25,5. 32,10
Downham	E2 2	52 84	5,59. Appx P	Hatley St. George	L 13	27 51	14,52. 25,10. 32,24-25. Appx L
Dry Drayton	Ct 4	37 62	9,3. 14,60. 26,49. 38,5. 41,15. Appx O	Hauxton	T 2	43 52	5,23. 26,17. Appx H
Fen Drayton	P 4	33 68	1,21. 7,7. 14,56. 23,6. 32,27	Heydon (Essex)	- -	- -	Holdings Elsewhere, note 29,9
Dullingham	R 2	63 57	10,1. 14,75. 26,3. 41,2. Appx D	Hildersham	C 5	54 48	
				Hill Row	E1 8	44 75	5,53. Appx P
Duxford	Wf 3	47 46	14,19. 15,2. 20,1. 21,2. 26,16. Appx E	Cherry Hinton	F 3	48 56	14,2. (14,3). Appx E
Elsworth	P 9	31 63	7,4. 23,2. 26,45	Hinton Hall (in Haddenham)	E1 10	46 75	Appx P
Eltisley	L 2	27 59	16,1	Hinxton	Wf 4	49 45	1,10;22. 3,1. 26,14. 32,4. EE1. Appx G
Ely	E2 4	54 80	5,57. (5,49-50). See also Churches and Clergy Appx P	Histon	Ct 3	43 63	3,3-5. 5,43. 12,5. Appx O
Ely Hundreds	E1,2	- -		Horningsea	F 1	49 62	5,14
[Great and Little] Eversden	L 11	36 53) 37 53)	14,46. 26,37. 27,1. 31,7	Horseheath see also Linacre	C 8	61 47	14,5-6. 19,2. 26,9. 29,8. Appx F
Exning (Suffolk)	Sp 10	62 65	1,12. 14,68. Appx A	Ickleton	Wf 5	49 43	15,1. 26,15. (1,20. 26,23)
Eynesbury (Hunts.)	1	18 59	(32,10)	Impington	N 7	44 63	5,41. 32,36. (5,43)
Flendish Hundred	F	- -	Appx E	Isleham	Sp 1	64 74	1,3. 4,1. 14,72. 28,1
Fordham	Sp 4	63 70	1,2. 14,71. (22,6). Appx A	Kennett	Sp 7	69 68	18,8. Appx A
Fowlmere	T 8	42 45	14,20. 21,3. Appx H	Kingston	L 9	34 55	1,8. 13,12. 14,47. 25,8. 26,38-39. 32,21
Foxton	T 6	41 48	11,1. 22,4-5	Kirtling	Cv 6	68 57	41,1. Appx B
Fulbourn	F 4	52 56	1,14. 5,12. 14,1. 22,1. 35,1. Appx E	Knapwell	P 10	33 62	7,5
				Landbeach	N 3	47 65	14,59. 32,38
Gamlingay	L 12	24 52	25,9. 34,1. 38,4	Linacre (in Horseheath)	- -	- -	See Godwin
Girton	N 8	42 62	12,4. 7,10. 32,34. (12,5). Appx N	Linden End	E1 11	46 74	5,52. (5,53). Appx P
				Linton	C 9	56 46	14,11. Appx P
				Little Linton	C 7	55 47	14,13
Little Gransden	L 7	27 55	5,38. (25,9) 12,3. 14,34. 15,4. 31,4. 32,15. 38,3	Litlington	A 14	31 42	1,18. 26,23. (1,19-20. 26, 20;23)
Grantchester	W 5	43 55		Littleport	E1 4	56 86	5,47
				Longstanton [All Saints and St. Michael]	N 2	39 66	14,58. 24,1. 32,30. 36,1. (21,7). Appx
				Longstow Hundred	L	- -	Appx L

	Map	Grid	Text		Map	Grid	Text
Whittlesford	Wf 2	47 48	14,18. 26,13. 41,7. (26,18). Appx G	Willingham	P 2	40 70	5,39. 14,57 32,29
				Wimpole	W 9	33 50	14,44. 25,7
Whittlesford Hundred	Wf	- -	Appx G	Wisbech	E2 1	46 09	5,55-56. 6,2. 7,12. 9,4. 18,9
Whitwell	W 2	40 58	13,10. 14,43. 26,36. 32,20	Witcham	E2 3	46 80	5,62. Appx P
Wicken	Sp 3	57 70	14,74	Witchford	E2 7	50 78	5,60. (5,44). Appx P
West Wickham	C 3	61 49	5,15. 14,7. 18,6. 19,3. 26,10	West Wratting	R 7	60 52	5,4-5. 14,81. 18,5. 26,8;51. Appx D
[Great and Little] Wilbraham	Sn 5	54 57) 54 58)	1,5. 14,65. 29,5. Appx C	Woodditton	Cv 4	65 59	1,11. 14,61
Wilburton	E1 12	47 74	5,51	Wratworth	W12	(34 48)	13,9. 14,42. 26,35. 31,6. 32,19

Places not named, at present unlocated

1,23. 14,35. 41,10. 41,11. 41,12.
Places not named in DB but which have been located are included in the Index of Places.

Places not in Cambridgeshire

References are to entries in the Indices of Persons and Places.

Elsewhere in Britain

BEDFORDSHIRE ... Eaton [Socon], see Wulfmer. ESSEX ... Chesterford, Newport. See also Chishill, Heydon. HAMPSHIRE ... Winchester, see Churches. HERTFORDSHIRE ... Hertford, see Ilbert. Rushden. HUNTINGDONSHIRE ... Eynesbury. Huntingdon, see Eustace. Ramsey, see Churches. KENT ... Canterbury, Rochester; see Churches. LINCOLNSHIRE ... Crowland, Lincoln; see Churches. OXFORDSHIRE ... Dorchester-on-Thames, see Churches. SUFFOLK ... Bury St. Edmunds, see Churches. Exning. UNIDENTIFIED ... Doesse, see Wulfwy.

Outside Britain

Anjou ... Guy. Anneville ... Humphrey. Ardres ... Arnulf. Argenton ... David. Auberville ... Saeric. Bayeux ... Bishop, Canons. Bernières ... Hugh. Bolbec ... Hugh. Brittany ... see Ralph, William the Breton. Cahagnes ... William of Keynes. Cailly ... William. Chocques ... Sigar. Clais ... Walter. Cluny ... Abbot, Ralph. (?)Delamere ... Wighen, William. Denmark ... see Aki the Dane. Dives ... Boselin. Feugères ... Ralph. Fourneaux ... Ansketel. France ... see Aleran the Frenchman. Ghent ... Gilbert. Grand-court ... Walter. Grestain ... Abbot. (?)Helmes ... Walter. Hérouville ... Ansketel. Hotot ... Ralph. Lorraine ... Gerard. Mandeville ... Geoffrey, William. Moutiers ... Lisois. Noyers ... William. Port ... Hugh. Raimbeaucourt ... Guy. Scales ... Brian, Hardwin. Sommery ... Roger. St. Evroul ... see Churches. St. Wandrille ... see Churches. Tosny ... Robert. Valognes ... Peter. Vere ... Aubrey. (?)Wader ... Ralph. Warenne ... Frederick, William.

MAP AND MAP KEYS

The County Boundary is marked by thick lines, Hundred boundaries by thin lines, dotted where uncertain. The southern boundary of the Isle of Ely is shown by a thick broken line.

An open circle denotes a place identified in footnotes but not named in DB itself; such places are printed in italics in the Map Key. An open square denotes a place in an adjoining county but referred to in this text.

The letters of National Grid 10-kilometre squares are shown on the map border. Each four-figure square covers one square kilometre (5/8 of a square mile).

Armingford Hundred (A)

Abington Pigotts	10
Bassingbourn	11
Clopton	3
Croydon	2
East Hatley	1
Litlington	14
Melbourn	12
Meldreth	8
Guilden Morden	9
Steeple Morden	13
Shingay	5
Tadlow	4
Wendy	6
Whaddon	7

Chesterton Hundred (Ct)

Chesterton	6
Childerley	5
Cottenham	1
Dry Drayton	4
Histon	3
Westwick	2

Cheveley Hundred (Cv)

Ashley	2
Cheveley	3
Kirtling	6
Saxon Street	5
Silverley	1
Woodditton	4

Chilford Hundred (C)

Abington	2
Babraham	1
Barham	10
Camps	11
Hildersham	5
Horseheath	8
Linton	9
Little Linton	7
Nosterfield End	12
Pampisford	4
Streetly	6
West Wickham	3

Flendish Hundred (F)

Fulbourn	4
Cherry Hinton	3
Horningsea	1
Teversham	2

Longstow Hundred (L)

Bourn	5
Caldecote	6
Caxton	3
Croxton	1
Eltisley	2
Eversden	11
Gamlingay	12
Little Gransden	7
Hardwick	4
Hatley St. George	13
Kingston	9
Longstowe	8
Toft	10

Northstow Hundred (N)

Girton	8
Impington	7
Landbeach	3
Lolworth	5
Longstanton	2
Madingley	10
Milton	9
Oakington	6
Rampton	1
Waterbeach	4

Papworth Hundred (P)

Boxworth	8
Conington	5
Fen Drayton	4
Elsworth	9
Graveley	6
Knapwell	10
Over	1
Papworth	7
Swavesey	3
Willingham	2

Radfield Hundred (R)

Balsham	8
Burrough Green	4
Carlton	6
Dullingham	2
Stetchworth	1
Westley Waterless	3
Weston Colville	5
West Wratting	7

Staine Hundred (Sn)

Bottisham	4
Quy	2
Stow	3
Swaffham	1
Wilbraham	5

Staploe Hundred (Sp)

Badlingham	5
Burwell	9
Chippenham	6
Exning (now Suffolk)	10
Fordham	4
Isleham	1
Kennett	7
Snailwell	8
Soham	2
Wicken	3

Thriplow Hundred (T)

Fowlmere	8
Foxton	6
Harston	5
Hauxton	2
Shelford	3
Stapleford	4
Thriplow	7
Trumpington	1

Wetherley Hundred (W)

Arrington	8
Barrington	11
Barton	4
Comberton	3
Coton	1
Grantchester	5
Harlton	6
Haslingfield	7
Orwell	10
Shepreth	13
Whitwell	2
Wimpole	9
Wratworth	12

Whittlesford Hundred (Wf)

Duxford	3
Hinxton	4
Ickleton	5
Sawston	1
Whittlesford	2

The Two Hundreds of (the Isle of) Ely

E 1

Chatteris	5
Doddington	3
Haddenham	9
Hill Row	8
Hinton Hall	10
Linden End	11
Littleport	4
March	2
Stretham	13
Stuntney	6
Little Thetford	7
Whittlesey	1
Wilburton	12

E 2

Downham	2
Ely	4
Hainey	8
Sutton	5
Wentworth	6
Wisbech	1
Witcham	3
Witchford	7

Other Counties

Essex

Chesterford	1

Huntingdonshire

Eynesbury	1
Fen Stanton	2

Not Mapped

Linacre
Chishill (Essex)
Heydon (Essex)
Newport (Essex)
Rushden (Herts.)

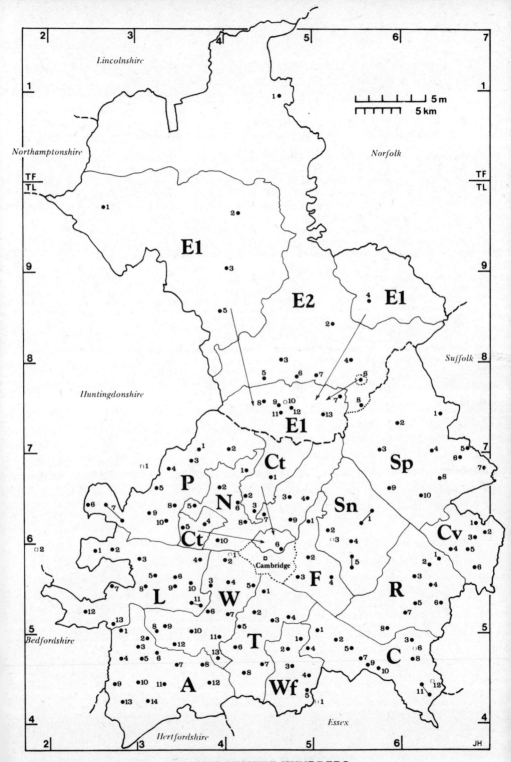

CAMBRIDGESHIRE HUNDREDS

SYSTEMS OF REFERENCE TO DOMESDAY BOOK

The manuscript is divided into numbered chapters, and the chapters into sections, usually marked by large initials and red ink. Farley did not number the sections and later historians, using his edition, have referred to the text of DB by folio numbers, which cannot be closer than an entire page or column. Moreover, several different ways of referring to the same column have been devised. In 1816 Ellis used three separate systems in his indices: (i) on pages i–cvii, 435–518, 537–570; (ii) on pages 1–144; (iii) on pages 145–433 and 519–535. Other systems have since come into use, notably that used by Vinogradoff, here followed. The present edition numbers the sections, the normal practicable form of close reference; but since all discussion of DB for two hundred years has been obliged to refer to folio or column, a comparative table will help to locate references given. The five columns below give Vinogradoff's notation, Ellis's three systems, and that used by Welldon Finn and others. Maitland, Stenton, Darby, and others have usually followed Ellis (i).

Vinogradoff	Ellis (i)	Ellis (ii)	Ellis (iii)	Finn
152 a	152	152 a	152	152 ai
152 b	152	152 a	152.2	152 a2
152 c	152 b	152 b	152 b	152 bi
152 d	152 b	152 b	152 b2	152 b2

In Cambridgeshire, the relation between the Vinogradoff column notation, here followed, and the chapters and sections is

189 a	B 1	-	B 14	194 a	14,9	-	14,19	199 a	26,42	-	26,49
b	Landholders and 1,1			b	14,19	-	14,27	b	26,49	-	28,2
c	1,1	-	1,6	c	14,28	-	14,38	c	28,2	-	29,7
d	1,6	-	1,13	d	14,39	-	14,48	d	29,8	-	31,1
190 a	1,14	-	1,23	195 a	14,49	-	14,57	200 a	31,1	-	31,7
b	2,1	-	3,3	b	14,57	-	14,64	b	32,1	-	32,8
c	3,3	-	5,2	c	14,64	-	14,72	c	32,8	-	32,16
d	5,3	-	5,11	d	14,72	-	14,82	d	32,17	-	32,23
191 a	5,11	-	5,22	196 a	15,1	-	17,1	201 a	32,23	-	32,31
b	5,22	-	5,32	b	17,2	-	18,3	b	32,31	-	32,36
c	5,32	-	5,42	c	18,3	-	19,3	c	32,37	-	32,44
d	5,43	-	5,50	d	19,4	-	21,5	d	33,1	-	38,1
192 a	5,50	-	5,58	197 a	21,5	-	22,5	202 a	38,1	-	40,1
b	5,58	-	6,3	b	22,6	-	23,2	b	41,1	-	41,12
c	7,1	-	7,8	c	23,2	-	25,5	c	41,13	-	44,2
d	7,8	-	9,2	d	25,5	-	26,5				
193 a	9,3	-	11,6	198 a	26,6	-	26,17				
b	12,1	-	13,5	b	26,17	-	26,24				
c	13,6	-	13,12	c	26,24	-	26,33				
d	14,1	-	14,9	d	26,34	-	26,42				

TECHNICAL TERMS

Most of the words expressing measurements have to be transliterated. Translation may not, however, dodge other problems by the use of obsolete or made-up words which do not exist in modern English. The translations here used are given below in italics. They cannot be exact; they aim at the nearest modern equivalent.

ANTECESSOR. Person whom a tenant had followed in the rightful possession of his holding; also the previous holder of an office. *predecessor*

AVERA. Provision of draught-horses or mules (cf. B11 note) for the King's use; sometimes commuted to a money payment. *cartage*

BORDARIUS. Cultivator of inferior status, usually with a little land. *smallholder*

CARUCA. A plough, with the oxen who pulled it, usually reckoned as 8. *plough*

COTARIUS. Inhabitant of a *cote*, cottage, often without land. *cottager*

DOMINICUS. Belonging to a lord, or lordship. *the lord's*, or *lordship* (adj.)

DOMINIUM. The mastery or dominion of a lord (*dominus*); including ploughs, land, men, villages, etc., reserved for the lord's use; often concentrated in a *home farm* or *demesne*. *lordship*

FEUDUM. Continental variant, not used in England before 1066, of *feuum* (the Latin form of Old English *feoh*, cattle, money, possessions in general); either a landholder's holding, or land held under the terms of a specific grant. *Holding*

FIRMA. Old English *feorm*, provisions due to the King or lord; a fixed sum paid in place of these and of other miscellaneous dues. *revenue*

GELDUM. The principal royal tax, originally levied during the Danish wars, normally at an equal number of pence on each *hide* of land. *tax*

HEUUARD. Old English *heafodweard*, the obligation to guard one's lord; the service of providing a bodyguard for the King when he visited the shire; sometimes commuted to a money payment. *bodyguard*

HIDA. A unit of land measurement, reckoned in DB at 120 fiscal acres, see Sussex, Appendix. *hide*

HUNDREDUM. An administrative district within a shire, whose assembly of notables and village representatives usually met once a month. *hundred*

INUUARD. Provision of a mounted man for the King's use, originally to escort the King when he visited the shire; sometimes commuted to a money payment. *escort*

M. Marginal abbreviation for *manerium* (see following).

MANERIUM. A territorial and jurisdictional holding. *manor*

PRESENTATIONES. A payment in return for the right to fish; probably in origin a proportion of the catch (cf. 1,1). *presentations*

SOCA. 'Soke', from Old English *socn*, seeking, comparable with Latin *quaestio*. Jurisdiction, with the right to receive fines and other dues; also the district in which such *soca* was exercised. *jurisdiction*

SOCHEMANNUS. 'Soke man', liable to attend the court of a *soca* and serve its lords; before 1066 often with more land and higher status than villagers; bracketed in the Commissioners' brief with the *liber homo* (free man); see Bedfordshire, Appendix. *Freeman*

TEIGNUS. Person of superior status; originally one of the King's military companions, later often in his service in an administrative capacity. *thane*

T.R.E. *tempore regis Edwardi*, in King Edward's time. *before 1066*

VILLA. Translating Old English *tun*, estate, town, village. The later distinction between a small *village* and a large *town* was not yet in use in 1066. *village* or *town*

VILLANUS. Member of a *villa*, usually with more land than a *bordarius*. *villager*

VIRGATA. A quarter of a hide (40 fiscal acres in DB). *virgate*

WARA. Literally 'defence' (cf. 1,10); liability for military service, or payment in lieu thereof. *defence obligations*